The Illicit and Illegal in Regional and Urban Governance and Development

Discussions of the illicit and the illegal have tended to be somewhat restricted in their disciplinary range to date, and have been largely confined to the literatures of anthropology, criminology, policing and, to an extent, political science. However, these debates have impinged little on cognate literatures, not least those of urban and regional studies which remain almost entirely undisturbed by such issues.

The Illicit and Illegal in Regional and Urban Governance and Development is a multidisciplinary volume that aims to open up these debates, extending them empirically and questioning the dominant discussions of governance and development that have been rooted largely or entirely in the realm of licit and legal actors. The book investigates these issues with reference to a variety of different geographical contexts, including, but not limited to, places traditionally considered to be associated with illegal activities and extensive illicit markets, such as some regions in the so-called Global South. The chapters consider the ways in which these questions deeply affect the daily lives of several cities and regions in some advanced countries. Their comparative perspectives will demonstrate that the illicit and the illegal are an underappreciated structural aspect of current urban and regional governance and development across the globe.

The book is an edited collection of research-informed essays, which will primarily be of interest to those taking advanced undergraduate and taught postgraduate courses in human geography, urban and regional planning and a range of social science disciplines that have an interest in urban and regional issues and issues related to crime and corruption.

Francesco Chiodelli is Senior Research Fellow at Gran Sasso Science Institute, Italy.

Tim Hall is Professor of Interdisciplinary Social Studies and Head of the Department of Applied Social Sciences at the University of Winchester, UK.

Ray Hudson is Professor of Geography at Durham University, UK.

Regional Studies Association
THE GLOBAL FORUM FOR CITY AND REGIONAL RESEARCH, DEVELOPMENT AND POLICY

Routledge
Taylor & Francis Group

Regions and Cities

Series Editor in Chief
Joan Fitzgerald, *Northeastern University, USA*

Editors

Maryann Feldman, *University of North Carolina, USA*
Gernot Grabher, *HafenCity University Hamburg, Germany*
Ron Martin, *University of Cambridge, UK*
Kieran P. Donaghy, *Cornell University, USA*

In today's globalised, knowledge-driven and networked world, regions and cities have assumed heightened significance as the interconnected nodes of economic, social and cultural production, and as sites of new modes of economic and territorial governance and policy experimentation. This book series brings together incisive and critically engaged international and interdisciplinary research on this resurgence of regions and cities, and should be of interest to geographers, economists, sociologists, political scientists and cultural scholars, as well as to policy-makers involved in regional and urban development.

For more information on the Regional Studies Association visit www.regionalstudies.org

There is a **30% discount** available to RSA members on books in the ***Regions and Cities*** series, and other subject related Taylor and Francis books and e-books including Routledge titles. To order just e-mail Joanna Swieczkowska, Joanna.Swieczkowska@tandf.co.uk, or phone on +44 (0)20 3377 3369 and declare your RSA membership. You can also visit the series page at www.routledge.com/Regions-and-Cities/book-series/RSA and use the discount code: **RSA0901**

124. The Rural and Peripheral in Regional Development
An alternative perspective
Peter de Souza

123. In the Post-Urban World
Emergent transformation of cities and regions in the innovative global economy
Edited by Tigran Haas and Hans Westlund

122. Contemporary Transitions in Regional Economic Development
Global reversal, regional revival?
Edited by Turok et al.

121. The Illicit and Illegal in Regional and Urban Governance and Development
Corrupt places
Edited by Francesco Chiodelli, Tim Hall and Ray Hudson

120. The Political Economy of Capital Cities
Heike Mayer, Fritz Sager, David Kaufmann and Martin Warland

119. Data and the City
Edited by Rob Kitchin, Tracey P. Lauriault and Gavin McArdle

118. The Unequal City
Urban Resurgence, Displacement and the Making of Inequality in Global Cities
John Rennie Short

117. Urban Transformations
Geographies of renewal and creative change
Edited by Nicholas Wise and Julie Clark

116. The Scottish Economy
A living book
Edited by Kenneth Gibb, Duncan Maclennan, Des McNulty and Michael Comerford

115. Reanimating Regions
Culture, Politics, and Performance
Edited by James Riding and Martin Jones

114. Territorial Policy and Governance
Alternative paths
Edited by Iain Deas and Stephen Hincks

113. Economics of Planning Policies in China
Infrastructure, location and cities
Wen-jie Wu

112. The Empirical and Institutional Dimensions of Smart Specialisation
Edited by Philip McCann, Frank van Oort and John Goddard

111. EU Cohesion Policy
Reassessing performance and direction
Edited by John Bachtler, Peter Berkowitz, Sally Hardy and Tatjana Muravska

110. Geography of Innovation
Edited by Nadine Massard and Corinne Autant-Bernard

109. Rethinking International Skilled Migration
Edited by Micheline van Riemsdijk and Qingfang Wang

108. The EU's New Borderland
Cross-border relations and regional development
Andrzej Jakubowski, Andrzej Miszczuk, Bogdan Kawałko, Tomasz Komornicki, and Roman Szul

107. Entrepreneurship in a Regional Context
Edited by Michael Fritsch and David J. Storey

106. Governing Smart Specialisation
Edited by Dimitrios Kyriakou, Manuel Palazuelos Martínez, Inmaculada Periáñez-Forte, and Alessandro Rainoldi

105. Innovation, Regional Development and the Life Sciences
Beyond clusters
Kean Birch

104. Unfolding Cluster Evolution
Edited by Fiorenza Belussi and Jose Luis Hervás-Olivier

103. Place-based Economic Development and the New EU Cohesion Policy
Edited by Philip McCann and Attila Varga

102. Transformation of Resource Towns and Peripheries
Political economy perspectives
Edited by Greg Halseth

101. Approaches to Economic Geography
Towards a geographical political economy
Ray Hudson

100. Secondary Cities and Development
Edited by Lochner Marais, Etienne Nel and Ronnie Donaldson

99. Technology and the City
Systems, applications and implications
Tan Yigitcanlar

98. Smaller Cities in a World of Competitiveness
Peter Karl Kresl and Daniele Ietri

97. Code and the City
Edited by Rob Kitchin and Sung-Yueh Perng

96. The UK Regional–National Economic Problem
Geography, globalisation and governance
Philip McCann

95. Skills and Cities
Edited by Sako Musterd, Marco Bontje and Jan Rouwendal

94. Higher Education and the Creative Economy
Beyond the campus
Edited by Roberta Comunian and Abigail Gilmore

93. Making Cultural Cities in Asia
Mobility, assemblage, and the politics of aspirational urbanism
Edited by Jun Wang, Tim Oakes and Yang Yang

92. Leadership and the City
Power, strategy and networks in the making of knowledge cities
Markku Sotarauta

91. Evolutionary Economic Geography
Theoretical and empirical progress
Edited by Dieter Kogler

90. Cities in Crisis
Socio-spatial impacts of the economic crisis in Southern European cities
Edited by Jörg Knieling and Frank Othengrafen

89. Socio-Economic Segregation in European Capital Cities
East meets West
Edited by Tiit Tammaru, Szymon Marcińczak, Maarten van Ham, Sako Musterd

88. People, Places and Policy
Knowing contemporary Wales through new localities
Edited by Martin Jones, Scott Orford and Victoria Macfarlane

87. The London Olympics and Urban Development
The mega-event city
Edited by Gavin Poynter, Valerie Viehoff and Yang Li

86. Making 21st Century Knowledge Complexes
Technopoles of the world revisited
Edited by Julie Tian Miao, Paul Benneworth and Nicholas A. Phelps

85. Soft Spaces in Europe
Re-negotiating governance, boundaries and borders
Edited by Philip Allmendinger, Graham Haughton, Jörg Knieling and Frank Othengrafen

84. Regional Worlds: Advancing the Geography of Regions
Edited by Martin Jones and Anssi Paasi

83. Place-making and Urban Development
New challenges for contemporary planning and design
Pier Carlo Palermo and Davide Ponzini

82. Knowledge, Networks and Policy
Regional studies in postwar Britain and beyond
James Hopkins

81. Dynamics of Economic Spaces in the Global Knowledge-based Economy
Theory and East Asian cases
Sam Ock Park

80. Urban Competitiveness
Theory and practice
Daniele Letri and Peter Kresl

79. Smart Specialisation
Opportunities and challenges for regional innovation policy
Dominique Foray

78. The Age of Intelligent Cities
Smart environments and innovation-for-all strategies
Nicos Komninos

77. Space and Place in Central and Eastern Europe
Historical trends and perspectives
Gyula Horváth

76. Territorial Cohesion in Rural Europe
The relational turn in rural development
Edited by Andrew Copus and Philomena de Lima

75. The Global Competitiveness of Regions
Robert Huggins, Hiro Izushi, Daniel Prokop and Piers Thompson

74. The Social Dynamics of Innovation Networks
Edited by Roel Rutten, Paul Benneworth, Dessy Irawati and Frans Boekema

73. The European Territory
From historical roots to global challenges
Jacques Robert

72. Urban Innovation Systems
What makes them tick?
Willem van Winden, Erik Braun, Alexander Otgaar and Jan-Jelle Witte

71. Shrinking Cities
A global perspective
Edited by Harry W. Richardson and Chang Woon Nam

70. Cities, State and Globalization
City–regional governance
Tassilo Herrschel

69. The Creative Class Goes Global
Edited by Charlotta Mellander, Richard Florida, Bjørn Asheim and Meric Gertler

68. Entrepreneurial Knowledge, Technology and the Transformation of Regions
Edited by Charlie Karlsson, Börje Johansson and Roger Stough

67. The Economic Geography of the IT Industry in the Asia Pacific Region
Edited by Philip Cooke, Glen Searle and Kevin O'Connor

66. Working Regions
Reconnecting innovation and production in the knowledge economy
Jennifer Clark

65. Europe's Changing Geography
The impact of inter-regional networks
Edited by Nicola Bellini and Ulrich Hilpert

64. The Value of Arts and Culture for Regional Development
A Scandinavian perspective
Edited by Lisbeth Lindeborg and Lars Lindkvist

63. The University and the City
John Goddard and Paul Vallance

62. Re-framing Regional Development
Evolution, innovation and transition
Edited by Philip Cooke

61. Networking Regionalised Innovative Labour Markets
Edited by Ulrich Hilpert and Helen Lawton Smith

60. Leadership and Change in Sustainable Regional Development
Edited by Markku Sotarauta, Ina Horlings and Joyce Liddle

59. Regional Development Agencies: The Next Generation?
Networking, knowledge and regional policies
Edited by Nicola Bellini, Mike Danson and Henrik Halkier

58. Community-based Entrepreneurship and Rural Development
Creating favourable conditions for small businesses in Central Europe
Matthias Fink, Stephan Loidl and Richard Lang

57. Creative Industries and Innovation in Europe
Concepts, measures and comparative case studies
Edited by Luciana Lazzeretti

56. Innovation Governance in an Open Economy
Shaping regional nodes in a globalized world
Edited by Annika Rickne, Staffan Laestadius and Henry Etzkowitz

55. Complex Adaptive Innovation Systems
Relatedness and transversality in the evolving region
Philip Cooke

54. Creating Knowledge Locations in Cities
Innovation and integration challenges
Willem van Winden, Luis de Carvalho, Erwin van Tujil, Jeroen van Haaren and Leo van den Berg

53. Regional Development in Northern Europe
Peripherality, marginality and border issues
Edited by Mike Danson and Peter De Souza

52. Promoting Silicon Valleys in Latin America
Luciano Ciravegna

51. Industrial Policy Beyond the Crisis
Regional, national and international perspectives
Edited by David Bailey, Helena Lenihan and Josep-Maria Arauzo-Carod

50. Just Growth
Inclusion and prosperity in America's metropolitan regions
Chris Benner and Manuel Pastor

49. Cultural Political Economy of Small Cities
Edited by Anne Lorentzen and Bas van Heur

48. The Recession and Beyond
Local and regional responses to the downturn
Edited by David Bailey and Caroline Chapain

47. Beyond Territory
Edited by Harald Bathelt, Maryann Feldman and Dieter F. Kogler

46. Leadership and Place
Edited by Chris Collinge, John Gibney and Chris Mabey

45. Migration in the 21st Century
Rights, outcomes, and policy
Kim Korinek and Thomas Maloney

44. The Futures of the City Region
Edited by Michael Neuman and Angela Hull

43. The Impacts of Automotive Plant Closures
A tale of two cities
Edited by Andrew Beer and Holli Evans

42. Manufacturing in the New Urban Economy
Willem van Winden, Leo van den Berg, Luis de Carvalho and Erwin van Tuijl

41. Globalizing Regional Development in East Asia
Production networks, clusters, and entrepreneurship
Edited by Henry Wai-chung Yeung

40. China and Europe
The implications of the rise of China as a global economic power for Europe
Edited by Klaus Kunzmann, Willy A Schmid and Martina Koll-Schretzenmayr

39. Business Networks in Clusters and Industrial Districts
The governance of the global value chain
Edited by Fiorenza Belussi and Alessia Sammarra

38. Whither Regional Studies?
Edited by Andy Pike

37. Intelligent Cities and Globalisation of Innovation Networks
Nicos Komninos

36. Devolution, Regionalism and Regional Development
The UK experience
Edited by Jonathan Bradbury

35. Creative Regions
Technology, culture and knowledge entrepreneurship
Edited by Philip Cooke and Dafna Schwartz

34. European Cohesion Policy
Willem Molle

33. Geographies of the New Economy
Critical reflections
Edited by Peter W. Daniels, Andrew Leyshon, Michael J. Bradshaw and Jonathan Beaverstock

32. The Rise of the English Regions?
Edited by Irene Hardill, Paul Benneworth, Mark Baker and Leslie Budd

31. Regional Development in the Knowledge Economy
Edited by Philip Cooke and Andrea Piccaluga

30. Regional Competitiveness
Edited by Ron Martin, Michael Kitson and Peter Tyler

29. Clusters and Regional Development
Critical reflections and explorations
Edited by Bjørn Asheim, Philip Cooke and Ron Martin

28. Regions, Spatial Strategies and Sustainable Development
David Counsell and Graham Haughton

27. Sustainable Cities
Graham Haughton and Colin Hunter

26. Geographies of Labour Market Inequality
Edited by Ron Martin and Philip S. Morrison

25. Regional Innovation Strategies
The challenge for less-favoured regions
Edited by Kevin Morgan and Claire Nauwelaers

24. Out of the Ashes?
The social impact of industrial contraction and regeneration on Britain's mining communities
Chas Critcher, Bella Dicks, David Parry and David Waddington

23. Restructuring Industry and Territory
The experience of Europe's regions
Edited by Anna Giunta, Arnoud Lagendijk and Andy Pike

22. Foreign Direct Investment and the Global Economy
Corporate and institutional dynamics of global-localisation
Edited by Jeremy Alden and Nicholas F. Phelps

21. Community Economic Development
Edited by Graham Haughton

20. Regional Development Agencies in Europe
Edited by Charlotte Damborg, Mike Danson and Henrik Halkier

19. Social Exclusion in European Cities
Processes, experiences and responses
Edited by Judith Allen, Goran Cars and Ali Madanipour

18. Metropolitan Planning in Britain
A comparative study
Edited by Peter Roberts, Kevin Thomas and Gwyndaf Williams

17. Unemployment and Social Exclusion
Landscapes of labour inequality and social exclusion
Edited by Sally Hardy, Paul Lawless and Ron Martin

16. Multinationals and European Integration
Trade, investment and regional development
Edited by Nicholas A. Phelps

15. The Coherence of EU Regional Policy
Contrasting perspectives on the structural funds
Edited by John Bachtler and Ivan Turok

14. New Institutional Spaces
TECs and the remaking of economic governance
Martin Jones, Foreword by Jamie Peck

13. Regional Policy in Europe
S. S. Artobolevskiy

12. Innovation Networks and Learning Regions?
James Simmie

11. British Regionalism and Devolution
The challenges of state reform and European integration
Edited by Jonathan Bradbury and John Mawson

10. Regional Development Strategies
A European perspective
Edited by Jeremy Alden and Philip Boland

9. Union Retreat and the Regions
The shrinking landscape of organised labour
Ron Martin, Peter Sunley and Jane Wills

8. The Regional Dimension of Transformation in Central Europe
Grzegorz Gorzelak

7. The Determinants of Small Firm Growth
An inter-regional study in the United Kingdom 1986–90
Richard Barkham, Graham Gudgin, Mark Hart and Eric Hanvey

6. The Regional Imperative
Regional planning and governance in Britain, Europe and the United States
Urlan A. Wannop

5. An Enlarged Europe
Regions in competition?
Edited by Louis Albrechts, Sally Hardy, Mark Hart and Anastasios Katos

4. Spatial Policy in a Divided Nation
Edited by Richard T. Harrison and Mark Hart

3. Regional Development in the 1990s
The British Isles in transition
Edited by Ron Martin and Peter Townroe

2. Retreat from the Regions
Corporate change and the closure of factories
Stephen Fothergill and Nigel Guy

1. Beyond Green Belts
Managing urban growth in the 21st century
Edited by John Herington

The Illicit and Illegal in Regional and Urban Governance and Development

Corrupt Places

Edited by Francesco Chiodelli, Tim Hall and Ray Hudson

Routledge
Taylor & Francis Group
LONDON AND NEW YORK

First published 2018
by Routledge

2 Park Square, Milton Park, Abingdon, Oxfordshire OX14 4RN
52 Vanderbilt Avenue, New York, NY 10017

Routledge is an imprint of the Taylor & Francis Group, an informa business

First issued in paperback 2019

British Library Cataloguing in Publication Data
A catalogue record for this book is available from the British Library

Library of Congress Cataloging in Publication Data
A catalog record for this book has been requested

ISBN: 978-1-138-23064-4 (hbk)
ISBN: 978-0-367-88420-8 (pbk)

Typeset in Times New Roman
by Deanta Global Publishing Services, Chennai, India

Contents

Illustrations

Figures

Tables

Contributors

Editors

Francesco Chiodelli, PhD in Urban Policies and Projects at the Polytechnic of Milan, is currently Senior Research Fellow at Gran Sasso Science Institute (L'Aquila, Italy), where he is a member of the committee of the international PhD Program in Urban Studies and Regional Sciences. His research deals with the social effects of the space regulation, with a focus on issues of transgression and informality. He also works on planning theory, urban conflicts and questions of pluralism and tolerance in public and private spaces. His papers have appeared in international journals such as: *Planning Theory*; *Town Planning Review*; *European Planning Studies*; *Land Use Policy*; *Cities; Geoforum*; *Journal of Urban Affairs*; *Planning Perspectives*; *Journal of International Development*; *Urban Research and Practice*; and *City, Culture and Society*. He is the author of *Shaping Jerusalem. Spatial Planning, Politics and the Conflict* (Routledge, 2017) and co-editor of *Cities to Be Tamed? The Space of Urbanism and Planning in the Urban South* (Cambridge Scholars Publishing, 2014).

Tim Hall is Professor of Interdisciplinary Social Studies and Head of the Department of Applied Social Sciences at the University of Winchester. He is a human geographer interested in economic geography and contemporary globalisation with a particular focus on the roles of organised criminal groups. He is the author/editor of a number of books, including *The Sage Companion to the City* (2008), *Urban Geography* (5th edition, Routledge, 2018) and *The Illicit Global Economy of Organized Crime: An Economic Geography* (Guilford, forthcoming). He has presented his work at a number of international conferences and meetings and was the winner of the *Journal of Geography in Higher Education* Award for Promoting Excellence in Teaching and Learning (2001/2002) and The Geographical Association Award for Excellence in Leading Geography (2010/2011), the latter for his article 'Where the money is: the geographies of organised crime'. His work on the geographies of organised crime has appeared in the journals *Geoforum*, *Geography* and *Progress in Human Geography* and in edited books.

Ray Hudson is Professor of Geography at Durham University. He was previously Deputy Vice Chancellor and then Acting Vice Chancellor. He holds the degrees of BA, PhD and DSc from Bristol University, DLitt from Durham, and an honorary DSc from Roskilde University. His main research interests are in political economy, economic geography and regional development. He has published widely on these topics, including *Wrecking a Region* (Pion, 1989), *Producing Places* (Guilford Press, 2001), *Economic Geographies: Circuits, Spaces and Flows* (Sage, 2005) and *Changing Approaches to Economic Geography: Towards a Geographical Political Economy* (Routledge, 2016). His research has been recognised by a number of awards, including the Victoria Medal from the Royal Geographical Society and the Sir Peter Hall Award from the Regional Studies Association and by election to the Fellowship of the Academy of Social Sciences, of the British Academy, the Royal Geographical Society and of Academia Europaea. He has chaired the Conference of Heads of Geography Departments in the UK and was elected as Vice-President and Chair of the Research Division of the Royal Geographical Society. As a result of his research, he has served as a Special Advisor to the House of Commons Select Committee on coalfields regeneration and as Expert Advisor to the Audit Commission in its evaluation of coalfield regeneration programmes.

Contributors

Edoardo Altavilla is a PhD candidate in Urban Studies at the Gran Sasso Science, L'Aquila. He studied Economics and Planning in Rome La Sapienza and Cardiff University. His current research interests are mainly within Political Science and particularly regard group theory, pressure group politics and collective action. He is employing these topics both to explore new practices of common property management (like urban commons, for instance), or to investigate the economic rationale of groups' political influence. His ongoing doctoral thesis makes use of such issues for exploring the meaning of the implementation of a main public work in the city of Rome, the new metro line, as a case study for giving account of public policy failures and metropolitan city governance, wondering whether the political-economic 'alliance' which emerged could be interpreted as a political coalition, or a form of corruption which involves public administration and rent-seeking groups (land owners and real-estate investors).

Margrete Bjone Engelien is an architect. She graduated from the Royal Danish Academy of Architecture, Design and Conservation, Copenhagen, within the department Political Architecture: Critical Sustainability in 2016, where she conducted research on the influence of grassroots movements on recovery in post-3.11 Japan, focusing on urban and architectural interventions. An article presenting her research, 'Producing States of Emergency', will feature in a forthcoming Political Architecture: Critical Sustainability publication. Margrete currently works at Transborder Studio in Oslo on a broad range of projects related to urban planning, architectural design and research. She is also involved in the organisation and management of Europan Norway.

John Edom is an M.Arch candidate at the Royal Danish Academy of Architecture, Design and Conservation, Copenhagen, within the department Political Architecture: Critical Sustainability. He has degrees in Anthropology from the University of Sussex and in Architecture from the École Nationale Supérieure d'Architecture Paris-Malaquais. He is currently carrying out research on the effects of newly introduced EU working time regulations for international road transport on the city of Tbilisi, Georgia. John is co-founder and vice-president of the association New South, a research platform that investigates how to design, build and represent metropolises of the Global South, and interrogates the role of the architect in these processes.

Monica García Quesada is Postdoctoral Researcher at Université Libre de Bruxelles (ULB) in Belgium. She is a political scientist (PhD in Government, London School of Economics) with a keen interest in policy compliance, public policy and natural resources management. Her publications include: 'The EU as an "enforcement patchwork". The impact of national enforcement for compliance with EU water law in Spain and Britain', *Journal of Public Policy* 34(2) (2014); 'Can't control/won't control: opportunities and deterrents for local urban corruption in Lanzarote' (with Fernando Jiménez Sánchez and Manuel Villoria), *Crime Law and Social Change* 62(4) 2014; 'Building local integrity systems in Southern Europe: the case of local corruption in Spain', (with Fernando Jiménez Sánchez and Manuel Villoria), *International Review of Administrative Sciences* 79(4) (2013); 'Integrity systems, values, and expectations: explaining differences in the extent of corruption in three Spanish local governments' (with Fernando Jiménez Sánchez and Manuel Villoria), *International Journal of Public Administration* 37(2) (2014).

Sasha Jesperson is Director of the Centre for the Study of Modern Slavery at St Mary's University Twickenham. Her research focuses on the role of organised crime in facilitating human trafficking, and the potential of development in preventing trafficking. Before coming to St Mary's, Sasha was leading research on organised crime at the Royal United Services Institute, working closely with government departments to ensure that research is useful for strengthening policymaking on organised crime. Her research background is on organised crime and particularly the role of development is preventing and responding to criminal activity. Sasha completed her PhD at the London School of Economics. Her research examined international initiatives to address organised crime through peace building missions under the framework of the security-development nexus, comparing examples from Sierra Leone and Bosnia. Sasha also completed an MSc in Human Rights at the London School of Economics and worked for Amnesty International for three years, primarily focusing on human rights in conflict and post-conflict contexts. Recent books include *Rethinking the Security-Development Nexus: Organised Crime in Post-Conflict States* (Routledge) and *Militarised Responses to Transnational Organised Crime: The War on Crime* (Palgrave).

Fernando Jiménez Sánchez is Associate Professor of Political Science at the University of Murcia (Spain). He is an evaluator for GRECO's (Council of Europe), Third round of evaluation on corruption risks in political financing. His main research fields are corruption and political financing. Among his last publications in English are: 'Can't control/won't control: opportunities and deterrents for local urban corruption in Lanzarote', *Crime, Law and Social Change*, 63 (1): 1–20 (with Mónica García Quesada and Manuel Villoria); 'Integrity systems, values and expectations. Explaining differences in the extent of corruption in three Spanish local governments', *International Journal of Public Administration*, 37 (2): 67–82 (with Mónica García Quesada and Manuel Villoria); 'Building Local Integrity Systems in Southern Europe: The case of urban local corruption in Spain', *International Review of Administrative Sciences*, 79(4): 618–637 (with Mónica García Quesada and Manuel Villoria); 'Political Finance, Urban Development and Political Corruption in Spain', in Jonathan Mendilow (ed.), *Money, Corruption and Competition in Established and Emerging Democracies*. Lexington Books (with Manuel Villoria); '(Un)sustainable territories: Causes of the speculative bubble in Spain (1996–2010) and its territorial, environmental and socio-political consequences', *Environment and Planning C. Government & Policy*, 30: 467–486 (with Joan Romero and Manuel Villoria).

Laure Leibler is a geographer and PhD candidate at the École des Hautes Études en Sciences Sociales. Her PhD research is on territorial control of illegal enterprises in Medellín, Colombia, the case of intra-urban forced displacement.

Stefano Moroni is Professor in Planning with Milan Polytechnic (Italy). He works on planning theory and ethics. He has published in international journals (*Planning Theory*; *Journal of Socio-Economic*; *Town Planning Review*; *Geoforum*; *City, Territory and Architecture*; *Journal of Urban Affairs*; *Cosmos & Taxis*: *Studies in Emergent Order and Organization*) and recently edited the following books: *Ethics, Design and Planning of the Built Environment* (with C. Basta), Berlin, Springer, 2013; *Cities and Private Planning: Property Rights, Entrepreneurship and Transaction Costs* (with D. E. Andersson), Cheltenham, Edward Elgar, 2014; *Space and Pluralism. Can Our Cities Today be Places of Toleration?* (with D. Weberman), Budapest, Central European University Press, 2016.

Md. Nadiruzzaman is a human geographer with an MA and PhD from Durham University, UK, where he problematised traditional knowledge framing of cyclones, and demonstrated how marginality in everyday life constrains peoples' resilience to withstand extreme events. Based on multi-year fieldwork in rural areas in Bangladesh, Dr. Nadiruzzaman has intimate knowledge about the interactions between disaster impacts and livelihood resilience. He is currently working as a Knowledge Management Director in a USAID-funded food security program of World Vision Bangladesh. Previous to this, he was a post-doctoral research fellow at the University of Exeter, working with Prof. Neil Adger (IPCC AR5 Coordinating Lead Author, Chapter 13: Human Security) on ESPA-Deltas project.

With Ecosystem Services for Poverty Alleviation in Deltas (ESPA-Deltas), he was looking at spatial and temporal dynamics of ecosystem services use for recovery and rebuilding from cyclone-induced loss and damage. Migration, climate change and development are three keys areas of his interest. He is collaborating with Flowminder in MDEEP (Mobile Data, Environmental Extremes and Population Movements), a 'big data' project to understand population movements. His papers appeared on international journals such as *Geoforum*, *Nature, Climate Change*, *Global Environmental Change*, and *Environmental Hazards*.

Martin O'Brien is a Reader in the Lancashire Law School at the University of Central Lancashire. He has published on social theory and social research, social policy, environmental sociology, criminological theory and crime and culture. He is the author of several books and articles, including 'The Deviance of the Zookeepers', *International Journal of Criminology and Sociological Theory*, 6 (4) (2013), 'Criminal Degradations of Consumer Culture', *Global Harms. Ecological Crime and Speciesism*, NOVA Publishers, Oslo (2011) and (with Professor Majid Yar) *Criminology. The Key Concepts*, Routledge, (2008).

Sue Penna retired as Senior Lecturer from the Sociology Department at Lancaster University in 2014. She has been researching the geo-political characteristics of organised crime for some time, and is the author (with Professor Stuart Kirby) of several articles, including 'Bridge over the river crime: mobility and the policing of organised crime', *Mobilities*, 8(4) (2013), 'Policing mobile criminality: implications for UK police forces', *Policing: An International Journal of Police Strategies and Management*, 34(2) (2011); 'Policing mobile criminality: towards a situational crime prevention approach to organised crime', in Bullock, K., Clarke, R.V. and Tilley, N. (eds) *Situational Prevention of Organised Crimes*, Willan, Cullompton (2010); and (with Martin O'Brien) 'Policing organised crime in the European Union: technological zones and contingent irregularities (2016), *European Review of Organised Crime*.

Barbara Pizzo, PhD, is Researcher and Senior Lecturer in Urban and Regional Planning at Sapienza Università di Roma. She works mainly in the field of planning theory, with a critical orientation. Her interests are in the processes of socio-spatial structuration, their link to socio-economic changes and to politics, the relationship between planning, conflict and power. She investigates the role of land and land rent in urban/metropolitan transformations, and the relationship between urban policies and planning. She has focused on the concept of landscape as an instrument to investigate the social construction of reality, the importance of time and scale and the political meaning of nature and related environmental issues. Her recent publications include, 'Problematizing resilience: implications for planning theory and practice', *Cities*; 'A muddled landscape of conflicts: what we can learn about planning/conflict relationship from the story of Tor Marancia, Rome, and its unexpected shift', in: *Planning/Conflict. Critical Perspectives on Contentious Urban Developments*, Routledge, (edited by E. Gualini); and 'Riding roughshod over people. Reading politics, economy and civil society in metropolization. A case study in Rome', in: *The Governance of Local Communities. Global Perspectives and Challenges*. New York: Nova Publ. (edited by T. Reilly).

Michael Polson is currently Ciriacy-Wantrup Postdoctoral Fellow in Natural Resource Economics and Political Economy at University of California, Berkeley. His primary research, based on 19 months of fieldwork in Northern California, concerns the contentious transformation of marijuana from an illegal to a legal-medical commodity. His work focuses on the role of producer-patient activism in Northern California's regional political economy. He has published in *PoLAR: Political and Legal Anthropology Review* on the production and capture of rent in the marijuana economy and *Territory, Politics, Governance* on the reterritorialisation of marijuana in the transition from criminal to civil governance. He is currently working on a contribution to an edited volume on neoliberalism and economic deviance and transforming his dissertation, entitled *Through the Gateway: Marijuana Production, Governance, and the Drug War Détente*, into a book manuscript for the University of Minnesota Press.

Luca Raineri is Research Fellow in International Relations and Security Studies at the Sant'Anna School of Advanced Studies of Pisa, Italy, where he also completed his PhD in Global Politics and Human Rights in 2016. He is also a member of the Research School on Peace and Conflict of Oslo. His areas of expertise include critical security studies, African politics, geopolitics and peace and conflict studies. His research focuses mainly on the impact of extralegal economies (narcotics, arms and people smuggling and trafficking) on security and development in Africa, where he has carried out several rounds of field-research since 2010. With a view to exploring the links between border practices, international security and organised crime, his work has appeared in edited volumes and international journals such as *African Security* and *Journal of Peacebuilding and Development*. Dr Raineri has been working as a consultant for several international NGOs, IOs and private research institutions dealing with development, security and human rights, with a particular focus on West Africa.

Vincenzo Scalia was born and bred in Palermo. He is Senior Lecturer in Criminology at The University of Winchester (UK). He has taught for several years in both undergraduate and graduate courses in several universities in Italy (Bologna, Macerata, Padua, Palermo, Pisa, Rome III), UK (Anglia Ruskin) and Argentina (Universidad del Museo Social). He is member of the editorial board of two Italian criminology journals: *Studi sulla questione criminale* and *Antigone*. He has written two books and more than 40 essays focused on his main research interests: organised crime, juvenile deviance, prisons, penology and criminological theory. His works have been published in Italian, English, Turkish, Spanish. He has translated several criminology articles and books from English, French and Spanish into Italian. Among his most recent work is: 'Cosa non solo loro. L'espansione delle mafie nella Riviera romagnola', *Polis*, 3/15; 'The rogue from within. The denial of torture in Italian prisons', *Critical Criminology*, 1/2016; and 'Una boda que tiene que hacerse. Criminologia critica y criminalidad organizada', in Tenorio Tgle, F. (ed.), *Ensayos en honor a Massimo Pavarini,* UNAM, 2015.

James Scambary is Visiting Fellow at the State, Society and Governance in Melanesia program at the Australian National University. In addition to academic research roles, James has performed research consultancies for a range of agencies including the New York Social Science Research Council, the World Bank and the Geneva Small Arms Survey. His research has focused on an ethnographic understanding of the intersections between informal security groups, conflict, corruption and organised crime in East Timor. Among his recent publications: 'The Road to nowhere: the rise of a neo-patrimonialist state in East Timor' in Del Rama, M. (ed.), *Corruption in the Asia Pacific*, Elsevier, Sydney (2017); 'In search of white elephants: the political economy of resource income expenditure in Timor-Leste', *Critical Asian Studies*, 47 (2) (2015); 'Conflict and resilience in an urban squatter settlement: Dili, East Timor', *Urban Studies*, 50 (10) (2013).

Jorge Ignacio Selfa Clemente obtained his degree in History and Geography at the University of Valencia, and the DEA degree (Diploma de Estudios Avanzados) in Human Geography at the Universitat Autònoma de Barcelona. Since 2013, he is a PhD researcher in the Department of Human Geography of the Universitat Autònoma de Barcelona. Currently, his main theme of research is focused on the urban and regional politics after the financial crisis in the regional space of the Comunitat Valenciana, East Spain. Other areas of interest have been the cultural urban policies in Post-Olympic Barcelona and the analysis of urban regional transport and logistic planning.

Hosna J. Shewly is Research Fellow in Social and Cultural Anthropology at Vrije Universiteit, Amsterdam. She holds the degrees of MA and PhD from the Department of Geography, University of Durham. Her research deals with migration, gender, law, rights and statelessness. She is also interested in actors (legal, illegal, extra-legal) constructing urban and borderland merginalities. Her recent publications include: '*De facto* statelessness in the enclaves in India and Bangladesh', *Singapore Journal of Tropical Geography* (2017); 'Survival mobilities: tactics, legality & mobility of undocumented borderland citizens in India & Bangladesh', *Mobilities* (2016); 'Citizenship, abandonment & resistance in the India–Bangladesh borderland', *Geoforum*, 67 (2015); and 'Abandoned spaces and bare life in the enclaves of the India–Bangladesh border', *Political Geography*, 32 (2013).

Svetlana Stephenson is Reader in Sociology at London Metropolitan University. She holds a PhD in Sociology from the Institute of Sociology, the Russian Academy of Sciences. She is the author of *Gangs of Russia, From the Streets to the Corridors of Power*, Cornell University Press, 2015, *Crossing the Line. Vagrancy, Homelessness and Social Displacement in Russia*, Ashgate, 2006 and the co-editor of *Youth and Social Change in Eastern Europe and the Former*

Soviet Union, Routledge, 2012 (with Charles Walker). Her research was published in *Radical Philosophy, Criminal Justice Matters, Journal of Youth Studies, The Sociological Review, Europe-Asia Studies, International Journal of Comparative Sociology, Slavic Review, Social Justice Research* and *Work, Employment and Society*, among others. Her research has involved studying informal and criminal social networks in Russia (street children and adult homeless people, youth street gangs and organised criminal groups, child labourers and sex workers), as well as perceptions of social justice and human rights in a comparative context.

Jayaraj Sundaresan is a comparative urbanist currently based at the Indian Institute for Human Settlements (IIHS) in Bangalore. His current research examines the interactive spaces and practices of urban activism, planning and governance in the management of urban commons. Theoretically his current research explores governance beyond the state, and planning power. He has written about urban commons; planning practice, violations and illegalities; ecological transformations; urban politics, planning and participation; urban activism and communal geographies. His primary research field sites are cities in India and London in the UK. Currently he is the Co-Director of Urban Fellows Program at the IIHS. Apart from his academic pursuits, he had worked with local governments in London as a consultant on planning, economic regeneration and urban design policy and was also a founder director of an Architecture and Planning consultancy in India between 2001 and 2004. He has taught at the UCL, LSE, IIHS and NIT-C (India). He holds Masters in Urban Design from CEPT (Ahmedabad-India), MSc in City Design from LSE (Sociology) and a PhD in Regional and Urban Planning Studies from LSE (Human Geography). His papers have appeared in international journals such as *Progress in Planning, Economic and Political Weekly* and in edited books.

Hannah Wood is an architect and writer based in Copenhagen, Denmark. Her master thesis focused on the post-disaster condition in urban Japan, and was completed at the Royal Danish Academy of Architecture, Design and Conservation, Copenhagen, within the department Political Architecture: Critical Sustainability in 2016. She has a background in architectural journalism, contributes to a number of publications, and is currently a feature writer for the online platform Archinect. Hannah is the co-founder of nomadic research and design studio Freiraum Kollektive, which aims to interrogate the boundaries of contemporary cultural theory by facilitating discussion between architects, educators and critical key voices which exist parallel to but excluded from architectural discourse. Their pan-Asian project, 'Mapping Architectural Resilience on the Silk Road' focused on the ability of communities to regain vitality in the face of adversity through a series of propositional workshops, discussions and events, a number of which were conducted in Japan during the research period for the chapter included in this volume.

Evgenia Zakharova is Researcher and PhD candidate in Social Anthropology at the Peter the Great Museum of Anthropology and Ethnography (Russian Academy of Sciences). Her main research interests lie in the fields of urban anthropology, legal anthropology, economic anthropology, friendship and kinship studies. In her PhD research on street-corner societies of Tbilisi ("*birzhas*") she deals with issues of honor, informal social regulation, masculine socialisation, behavioral codes and interactional patterns in Tbilisi neighborhoods, whose street culture is deeply influenced by prison norms. She has presented her work at international conferences (including Crisis and Imagination, the EASA 11th Biennial conference at Humboldt University in Berlin and the Ivane Javakhishvili Tbilisi State University workshop: Urban Spaces, Caucasian Places: Transformations in Capital Cities). Her papers have been published in journals, including *Antropologicheskiy Forum* [Forum for Anthropology and Culture], *Etnograficheskoe Obozrenie* [Ethnographic Review] and *Laboratorium*, as well as in edited books, including *State and Legal Practice in the Caucasus: Anthropological Perspectives on Law and Politics* (Ashgate, 2015). She has conducted fieldwork in urban and rural Georgia, the North Caucasus, Iran, Turkey and Central and Northern Russia.

Acknowledgements

This volume arises out of a series of workshops held in the UK and Italy in 2015 and 2016. These were three events from the Regional Studies Association funded research network 'Illicit actors, regional governance and development', which took place at the University of Winchester (September 2015); the British Academy, London (March 2016); and the Gran Sasso Science Institute, L'Aquila, Italy (September 2016). In addition, the volume draws on work presented at the seminar, 'Corrupt cities: corruption and organised crime in urban planning', Gran Sasso Science Institute (July 2015). Many thanks to all of the contributors to those events, the host institutions in each case and to the Regional Studies Association for providing the funding to support these events.

Acknowledgements

1 Grey governance and the development of cities and regions

The variable relationship between (il)legal and (il)licit

Francesco Chiodelli, Tim Hall, Ray Hudson and Stefano Moroni

Introduction: Key questions on the illicit and the illegal

It has long been recognised within political, legal, criminal justice, media and civic circles that a range of illicit actors and acts have been – and continue to be – part of the processes and institutions of urban and regional governance and development across a diverse, international terrain. There are numerous historical and contemporary examples that have caught the broader imagination and upon which this view is founded. They include: the deep embedding of criminal organisations within the societies, economies and cultures of countries such as Italy and Japan (Glenny, 2008; Hill, 2005; Paoli, 2005; Sergi and Lavorgna, 2016); the criminalisation of the Russian economy during the phase of its chaotic transition to a market economy during the 1990s (Castells, 2000; Dunn, 1997; Galeotti, 2005a and 2005b); the significant revenues derived from illegal markets such as those associated with drug and people trafficking in places such as Afghanistan, Colombia and China (Bagley, 2005; Castells, 2000; Goodhand, 2009; Goodhand and Mansfield, 2013; Goodhand and Sedra, 2015; Scott-Clark and Levy, 2008); internationally dispersed cases of corruption (Brown and Cloke, 2007); and the deep involvement of illicit actors in money laundering and the investment of illicit finance in real estate and urban development (Unger and Ferwerda, 2011). These illicit actors and activities have, for example, been cited as significant players in the development of cities as diverse as Las Vegas (McCracken, 1997) and Mumbai (Weinstein, 2008). It should be stressed, however, that the influence stretches far beyond this handful of examples – something that this collection will demonstrate.

The roles that illicit and illegal activities have played in urban and regional development and governance are also extremely diverse. They include the generation of economic revenues, in some instances within urban and regional contexts otherwise characterised by poverty and a lack of legitimate economic alternatives; social governance through fear; the threat of violence and normative influence over urban and regional cultural spheres; political governance through the development of symbiotic relations with the state at regional and urban scales; and corruption and the capture of the state and its associated development institutions and processes.

Despite the presence and significance of the illicit and the illegal in the governance and development of cities and regions, in its many forms, systematic attention by academics interested in these issues has been extremely limited. Those contributions that have emerged have tended to be very restricted in their disciplinary range, and they have been largely confined to the literatures of anthropology, criminology, sociology, policing and, to some extent, political science. However, these debates have impinged little on cognate literatures, not least those of economic and political geography, regional studies, planning and urban development, which remain almost entirely undisturbed by such issues. The editors of this volume have all independently been engaged in attempts to open up the space for the discussion of these issues within the aforementioned disciplines (Chiodelli and Moroni, 2015; Chiodelli, 2017; Hall, 2013; Hudson, 2014).

This volume aims to open up debates in urban and regional studies to the questions posed by the involvement of illicit and illegal actors and acts in urban and regional governance and development. In so doing, its intention is not only to extend empirically the scope of debates in urban and regional studies, but also to question conceptually the hitherto dominant discussions of governance and development that have been rooted largely or entirely in the realm of the licit and legal. It will seek to open up a multidisciplinary perspective, which critically interrogates both empirical and theoretical material.

The dialogues that this volume seeks to foster will be organised around four groups of key questions. These are obviously closely intertwined, but they can be separated at least from an analytical viewpoint. These key questions are as follows:

- First, *conceptual and definitional questions*, which refer, for instance, to the way in which we conceptualise and define what is licit and what is illicit, what is legal and what is illegal. Issues related to the variability of these definitions and to their shifting and blurred boundaries are very relevant here.
- Second, *empirical and explanatory questions*, which refer to the description of the phenomenon. These examine, for instance, the features and forms assumed by illicit and illegal acts in a specific context, and the reasons why a certain illicit or illegal act is performed (that is, its determining cultural, socio-economic and institutional factors).
- Third, *evaluative questions*, which refer, broadly speaking, to different aspects of societal judgement of an illicit or illegal act.
- Fourth, *policy questions*, which refer to what can be done and who has the power to act (for instance, in terms of public actions) in order to deal with illicit and illegal acts.

The spatial dimension in the study of illicitness and illegality

It should be stressed that, with reference to each of these key questions, the role of the spatial dimension is important. To mention just one example, consider the spatial variability of definitional questions, that is, the fact that the definition of what is (il)legal and (il)licit changes – sometimes profoundly – in different geographical contexts. The example of cybercrime neatly illustrates this spatial contingency. Cybercrime, in its now many guises, is universally prohibited in law. Despite this, there is compelling evidence that it, or rather practices that, empirically, do not differ from what is recognised in law as cybercrime, have been practised by governments, or their agents, from nations such as Russia, China, North Korea, the USA and the UK. In addition to this illegality, cybercrime tends to be regarded as a socially unacceptable illicit practice. However, this is not universal. In some contexts, such as in Nigeria, it is seen, even celebrated, as a socially licit, politically and economically motivated act. For example, the hugely popular song 'I Go Chop your Dollar' was a celebration of 419 (cyber) scams that targeted Western victims. This particular view of cybercrime arose out of combinations of a number of factors specific to Nigeria, including a history of early pioneering of fax and computer scams, a lack of opportunities within the legitimate economy, a history of predation by Western colonial powers and a more recent history of aggressive exploitation, and the associated environmental damage, by Western corporations (Glenny, 2008: 207–210). Cybercrime in Nigeria would appear to be viewed there through discourses of economic necessity, cultural legitimacy and political revenge. Such locational analyses of potentially criminal activities open up the often multiple discourses of licit and illicitness attached to them across international space.

When the disciplines of anthropology, criminology, economics, political science and sociology have engaged with issues concerning the presence of illicit and illegal activities within developmental and governance spheres and their impacts, they have framed them in distinctive ways and considered a number of the questions outlined above. However, the spatial dimensions of the illicit and the illegal are often neglected within the perspectives of these disciplines. This is a significant omission, since many illicit and illegal activities (such as corruption and organised crime) tend to have specific spatial aspects and contexts that are yet to be fully articulated within academic literatures. On the other hand, the disciplines that focus mainly on socio-spatial concerns, spatial forms and their generative social processes (such as geography, urban and regional studies and planning) rarely recognise and analyse the relevance of the illicit and the illegal in regard to those issues.

There are, however, a number of examples of human geographers who have explored various dimensions of criminal markets, examining, for example, the circulations, networks and local impacts associated with the international drugs trade (Allen, 2005; Rengert, 1996; Taylor *et al.*, 2013), and the spatialities of financial corruption (Brown and Cloke, 2007). Nevertheless, despite the pioneering nature of many of these studies, their focus on the influence of illicit and illegal actors and acts on urban and regional development remains exceptional within human geography and other spatially oriented disciplinary literatures. In short, the spatial disciplines such as geography, planning and urban and regional studies have done little to date to acknowledge that illicit/illegal actors and the realms that they influence constitute processes with both global reach and local significance.[1]

Given the only very limited engagement of these spatial disciplines with the illicit/illegal as a factor in urban and regional development, it should be of little surprise to find that scholars from other disciplines concerned with various aspects of the illicit/illegal have not turned to the literatures of geography, planning and urban and regional studies for inspiration (and vice versa). However, there are reasons to argue that more sustained dialogues between these disciplines and their varying treatments of the issues would do more than merely expand the empirical horizons of geography, planning and urban and regional studies. It would appear, then, that there is potential for the literatures of geography, planning and urban studies to engage with and make contributions to the wider articulations of the illicit/illegal that have traditionally emerged across its multidisciplinary terrain. This has the potential, as this volume hopes to demonstrate, to produce more nuanced understandings of the illicit and the illegal, and their varying significance spatially (and temporally).

Conceptual and definitional questions: What do we mean by (il)licit and by (il)legal, and what is the nexus between them?

It is widely recognised that it is difficult to draw a line among categories such as licit and illicit, legal and illegal, formal and informal within the processes of economies, urban and regional governance and development and their spaces (Aas, 2007; Bhattacharyya, 2005; Chiodelli and Moroni, 2014; Hall, 2013; Hudson, 2014; McFarlane, 2012; Nordstrom, 2007; Payne, 2002; Roy, 2005; Wilson, 2009). This refers both to the difficulty of tracing the *internal* boundary of each category (between, for instance, what is licit and what is illicit, or between what is formal and what is informal)[2] and to the difficulty of tracing the *external* boundaries among those categories, for instance, between what we mean by illicit and by illegal.

With reference to *internal boundaries*, the problem is mainly related to the limitations of reading the question as a strict dichotomy – however, we define the components of this dichotomy. The threshold between licit and illicit (or legal and illegal) is often not clearly definable. In fact, licit and illicit acts and practices can be most properly conceived as relationally defined, as the extremes of a complex continuum, of a single system composed of ‘different “bundles of lines”, representing the different flows and practices of the urban world’ (McFarlane, 2012: 101). Moreover, the threshold is not static. On the contrary, it is fluid, spatially and temporally determined:

> Because of inconsistent definitions of crime across different jurisdictions and the absence of a sovereign international authority, it may not always be possible to attribute a single category of ‘legal’ or ‘illegal’ to practices and flows that cross national boundaries … Legal restrictions often come up against socially sanctioned practices, and while this may have the effect of driving these practices into the sphere of formal criminality, it does not eliminate them nor does it necessarily force them into hiding. Likewise, the absence of the law does not imply that all is permissible. Prevailing social mores

> can work in the opposite direction as well, to sanction practices that are not legally prevented and indeed to cause the law to be adjusted in order to reflect dominant social values.
>
> (Abraham and van Schendel, 2005, pp. 18–19)

This emphasises that definitions of both the illicit and illegal are *spatially* contingent. They vary over space (as well as through time) and reflect qualitatively different features which characterise a specific place – such as the institutional, regulatory and legal frameworks, but also social perceptions, customs, cultures and practices (see Table 1.1). Spatial contingency means that context matters. The definitions of, and boundaries between, the licit and the illicit (the same point can be made with respect to the legal and the illegal) vary between places at any given point in time.

This variability, the shifting, permeable and blurred boundaries, complicates conceptualisation and definitional issues in a globalising economy. As the literatures of global commodity chains and global production networks emphasise (for example, see Yeung and Coe, 2015), the globalising economy is characterised by complex flows and high levels of mobility of capital, commodities and people. Over the course of their diverse journeys, they pass between different places and jurisdictions with differing definitions of what is legal and illegal, and what is licit and illicit – although this is rarely acknowledged in the mainstream globalisation literatures (on this issue see Windsor and Getz, 1999; Gregson and Crang, 2016). In this context of differing definitions and crossovers from illegal to legal, illicit to licit as money and people move from place to place, and material commodities move from their places of production to those of consumption, simple binaries can become difficult to maintain and, indeed, a barrier to understanding.

With reference to *external boundaries*, the difficulty is related to the identification of a clear and complete meaning for each word. However, despite the impossibility of having a perfect, comprehensive and shared definition of each term, we can be satisfied with a 'thick' definition which identifies (il)legal in terms of the political and the state regulatory system in a given time/space, and (il)licit in terms of moral judgement, customary practice and social acceptability in a given time/space. In other words, an illegal act is something which violates the letter of the law in a specific time/space context, while an illicit act is one that is considered as unacceptable in terms of the dominant social perception, custom and practice in a specific time/space context. Obviously, this implies that there can be licit and illicit legal acts, as well as licit and illicit illegal acts (and vice versa). For instance, a legal act like tax avoidance can be seen as illicit, that is, socially disapproved. Or a formally illegal act like smoking marijuana for medical purposes can be socially accepted and hence be seen as licit. It should be acknowledged, of course, that within any specific social context there will inevitably be considerable variation in the views of its members as to what is licit and illicit. Acts can be seen as both licit and illicit by different groups. Indeed, study of this internal contestation of the definitions and boundaries of the licit and illicit is a potentially revealing endeavour. The interplay between these categories determines different (ideal-typical) situations in terms of behaviours and domains of governance (see Table 1.1).[3]

Table 1.1 Ideal-typical situations of (il)licitness and (il)legality in terms of behaviours and domains of governance

		The domains of social perceptions, custom and practice	
		Licit	**Illicit**
The domain of formal and legal definitions	**Legal**	(A) The formal economy and society. Governance is via state and markets, formal regulatory systems and people behaving according to the law, etc.	(B) Behaviours that are legal and governed as such, but which are subject to social disapproval. These might include aspects of the arms trade and privatised security and military economies which may shade into other categories.
	Illegal	(C) A wide spectrum of activities. They include those of the 'informal' economy, and a range of illegal activities seen as acceptable in relation to custom and practice. These may be illegal activities per se or legal activities but performed by people who are not legally entitled or qualified to do so – however, their actions are seen as socially legitimate, as a way of 'getting by'. Furthermore, illegal business practices are routinely accepted as legitimate in the everyday conduct of the formal 'legal' economy. Governance is via social relations of tolerance, trust among citizens and colleagues outside formal regulatory structures or concealment of practices within them.	(D) Illegal behaviours that are seen as socially unacceptable, such as tax evasion, human trafficking, trafficking hard drugs, arms dealing, money laundering. Governance is via a combination of trust among criminals and others carrying out such activities and fear – and, if necessary, physical violence and murder by powerful social groups ('mafias').

Empirical and explanatory questions: What are the roles and impacts of the illicit and the illegal?

Developing reliable and valid empirical evidence on the extent of the impacts and influence of illicit and illegal behaviours within urban and regional development is beset with difficulties. This has long been a barrier to critical understanding of the illicit/illegal. These difficulties are not only conceptual, as we have stressed in the previous section with reference to definitional questions (how can we measure something which is inadequately conceptualised and defined, or not defined at all, or whose definition varies through space and time?) (Holmes, 2016). These difficulties are also methodological – and would endure even if we were able to reach a satisfactory conceptualisation and definition.

In fact, there are inherent difficulties in measuring phenomena that are clandestine in nature and are most successful when they are most able to avoid external scrutiny (the least successful illegal actors are likely to be those who are most visible and standing trial or already incarcerated). As a result, there are questions of access, and, at times, ethics and researcher safety (Brooks, 2014; Lunn, 2014). Given these issues, it is perhaps unsurprising that there has, so far, been little critical discussion of empirical approaches to exploring the scale of illicit/illegal activities and their impacts – with the exception of a small and emergent literature that has begun critically to discuss some of the political, conceptual and technical problems that have bedevilled empirical studies of the illicit/illegal produced by both academic researchers and government agencies (Hobbs and Antonopoulos, 2014; Holmes, 2016; Midgley *et al.*, 2014). Thus, it is safe to conclude that measuring the extent and scale of illicit/illegal activities is a very difficult endeavour (Holmes, 2016: 42). Therefore, official spatial data relating to the illicit and the illegal are frequently missing or too unreliable to be treated with any degree of confidence (Inkster and Comolli, 2012: 15–16; Levi, 2014: 8; Midgely *et al.*, 2014: 18).

Furthermore, all too frequently there is a paucity of reliable data produced through careful social scientific research. However, this challenge should not impede efforts to expand our empirical and broader understanding of the roles and impacts of the illicit/illegal (Hudson, 2014: 781). For instance, in this case more than any other, it seems that we are critically in need of 'thoroughly executed case studies' (Flyvberg, 2006: 242) in order to make our knowledge in the field more effective and grounded. If an overall quantitative account of these phenomena cannot be reached with an acceptable degree of accuracy, we should not stop at the formulation of general theories; we should at least build exemplary case studies, most probably using a multi-methods approach. In fact, the somewhat scant urban and geographical research available at present lacks in-depth explorations that would provide greater insights into the real function of illicit and illegal practices, for instance, revealing the inner mechanisms, channels and specific actors involved.[4] Empirical questions developed through case studies, and the methodologies with which they are approached, are central to the majority of chapters in this volume.

From this viewpoint, empirical and explanatory efforts should also focus on investigating the specific role of geographical variables. In fact, the illicit and the illegal are connected to place and space[5] in many and complex ways. This does not refer only to the simple fact that certain specific places are used for illicit and illegal activities, and that this determines a different geography of these activities. It refers also to other, less obvious spatial situations. Broadly speaking, the nexus between the illicit/illegal and the spatial materialises in four main forms: (i) distributions of the illicit and the illegal across space; (ii) the use of places and space for illicit and illegal activities; (iii) illicit and illegal acts on space; (iv) 'illicit spaces'.

First, there is a specific geographical distribution of illicit and illegal activities. Obviously, not all the places around the world are characterised by the same amount of illegal and illicit activities. For instance, this is well represented by the maps provided by Transparency International (2015) on the global spread of corruption: even if the phenomenon is global, there are some countries which are much more affected by corruption than others. At the same time, there is also a geographical variability of illegal and illicit activities within each country – and within each region and city. Description of these local differences is far less frequent, as is their explanation: for what reasons is a specific area (for instance, a region or a neighbourhood) characterised by a larger amount of these activities than another? Are any of these reasons related to the actual *geography* of that place, for instance in terms of localisation or physical conformation (Hall, 2010)?

Second, a space or particular place can simply be used for illicit/illegal activities, such as drug smuggling. However, even in this case, the relationship between space, place and the illicit/illegal is complex: in many instances, the features and structuring of the space impinge on illicit/illegal acts. For example, some places allow and favour illicit activities, because their spatial conformation makes control by the police difficult.

Third, illicit and illegal acts can change the social character and the physical features of place. For instance, this happens through the illegal distortion of public policies and decisions, such as decisions related to building and land transformation (e.g. via illegal pressure to obtain a specific change in a zoning plan, or the illegal building of a house on farmland) or to the location of public infrastructures (e.g. preferring location X for infrastructure W in order to favour A) (Chiodelli & Moroni, 2015). But this can happen also through illicit and illegal practices outside the public sphere, as in the case of the spread of illegal housing. Also, territorial control by illegal actors (such as gangs and organised crime) falls within this latter category. In all these cases, the use of a specific space or place for illicit activities impinges on its features, for instance, in terms of social practices and use by the inhabitants (and, in some cases, also in terms of physical conformation).

The fourth case is that of what we can label 'illicit spaces'. Offshore financial centres and tax havens (which are not only located in the Global South) are an important category of illicit space. By creating environments facilitating illicit activities, such as money laundering, they are central to the contemporary global economy and closely linked to, and even in some cases present within, major OECD economies (Hudson, 2014: 787; Roberts, 1999: 132; Unger and Rawlings,

2008: 332, 335, 349). They may also provide a place for the illegal as a result of the opacity of their regulatory environments. In diverse ways, they demonstrate the centrality of the illicit and the illegal to many processes and spaces which tend, conventionally, to be seen as legal and 'mainstream'.

It is worth noting that the kinds of spatialised illicitness and illegalness previously mentioned can occur at different scales (international, national, local); obviously, this both reflects and affects the features of the illicit and illegal activities that take place. Much of the literature that has explored the spatialities of the illicit/illegal has been characterised by the adoption of a single-scale approach, choosing to focus on either the global (Bhattacharyya, 2005; Glenny, 2008), national (Galeotti, 2005b) or local scale (Hobbs, 2013). However, there have recently been many calls in the social sciences generally, but specifically within economic geography, that have questioned the validity of these relatively narrowly conceived scalar approaches. They question, for instance, which single scale can adequately capture processes that operate and are constituted across multiple scales. For example, many recent empirical studies on organised criminal actors and markets have chosen to locate their analysis at either the national state or global scale. These have drawn criticism, however, for their supposed lack of local nuance and detail, and for their failure to articulate with the connected realities of a globalised world (Abraham and van Schendel, 2005; Aas, 2007).

It is possible to discern two primary responses to these criticisms (in particular with reference to economic geography). The first is recognition that analysis should reflect the multiple scales across which processes unfold over space (Coe *et al.*, 2007: 20). However, it is rare to find examples of such multi-scalar approaches within the multidisciplinary literatures of the illicit/illegal. The second response emerges from a set of approaches broadly labelled 'network ontologies'. Despite being influential in many fields of social research, and despite finding particular traction within the literatures of economic geography (Dicken *et al.*, 2001; Sheppard, 2002), network ontologies have made little impression to date on the study of the illicit and the illegal within disciplines such as anthropology, criminology, economics, political science and sociology. Network ontologies seek to transcend many of the enduring dualisms, such as local-global, that have dominated much social science theory and research in recent decades. Provided that they remain sensitive to power asymmetries within networks (Hadjimichalis and Hudson, 2006), they appear to offer alternatives to the scalar approaches which have prevailed within the research literatures on the illicit/illegal (see Hall, 2010).

Evaluative questions: Are illicit and illegal acts bad or good? And why?

Generally speaking, we can approach the evaluation of the illicit and the illegal from two ethical viewpoints: a *deontological* one and a *consequentialist* one.[6] According to deontological (i.e. non-consequentialist) arguments, illicit and illegal acts are *bad in themselves*: they are intrinsically, inherently wrong. They clash with the fundamental principles of fairness and respect for the rules of the game. For instance, a public role requires in itself a certain kind of transparent and accountable behaviour; telling the truth to the client is intrinsically required of any practitioner or technician; keeping promises and respecting contracts is what an honest entrepreneur must do. To sum up: it is the 'eidos' of role/situation X doing/being B.

If one assumes a deontological viewpoint, *all* illicit and illegal acts are bad. However, the situation changes if one adopts a consequentialist stance. According to *consequentialist* arguments, illicit and illegal acts are bad if *their (cumulative) effect is bad*. This is the case, for instance, with instances of corruption in land use transformations which do not favour the more 'performative' developers (hence, they reduce competition and experimentation) and alter the allocation of public funding. As is obvious, this viewpoint implies that illicit and illegal acts can also be good if their effects are good (regardless of the illicit/illegal nature of the action). Typically, illicit/illegal actors and activities are portrayed as predatory, although there is evidence that they can perform important and positive governance and development functions in some circumstances, where legitimate state institutions are either absent or where their reach is incomplete or contested (Bhattacharyya, 2005: 118; Glenny, 2008: 291; Goodhand, 2009; Van Dijk, 2007: 54). This raises the provocative question of those times, places and circumstances in which the illicit and the illegal may be developmentally progressive (Méon and Weill, 2010). For instance, several authors have discussed the potentially positive developmental outcomes of illicit and illegal activities – particularly in Global South contexts where there are few, if any legal alternatives (see for instance Bhattacharyya, 2005 and Goodhand, 2009).[7] This refers also to important material impacts on the places and spaces where illicit and illegal markets and activities take place, and upon the political governance and regulatory functions of those areas. This raises the question of whether it could be legitimate to govern with illicit and illegal actors who are able to extend governance and development into such difficult to reach spaces. In some senses this question is already answered by the many instances where collaborative forms of governance, either through direct collaboration or implicit co-operation through governmental tolerance and uneven policing of illegal activities which bring positive or desired economic, political or social outcomes which span aspects of the licit/illicit, legal/illegal spectrum, have been observed (Bhattacharyya, 2005; Goodhand, 2009; Nordstrom, 2007; Woodiwiss, 2001).

Consider for instance the fundamental role played by informal housing (that is, illegal housing) in many urban areas of the so-called Global South, where informality is the only way in which the poor can access a roof over their heads in the city, hence becoming 'a normal and stable mode of life in contemporary cities' (AlSayyad, 2004: 7). It is exactly in light of informality's positive outcomes that for several decades there has been international agreement that informality is part of the solution to housing problems, and that recognition and regularisation policies are needed, instead of a repressive approach based on demolition of such housing (Chiodelli, 2016).

However, such perspectives are not shared by other authors, who strongly argue that the illicit and illegal cannot and should not be used as a basis for development:

more than being *oil* which greases the wheels, illicit and illegal action seems to always be, in the end, *sand* in the (institutional and social) machine (Ades and Di Tella, 1997; David-Barrett, 2014; Kaufmann, 1997). There is then a clear lack of consensus around these questions. Advances beyond the polarised position that currently characterises the literature are likely to be sustained primarily through empirical research.

Policy questions: How to deal with illicit and illegal acts?

When addressing the question of how to deal with illicit and illegal acts, if we think that we must – and also think it is possible[8] – to fight them, we can consider three general strategies.[9]

The first is based on 'virtue ethics' (that is, Aristotelian-style arguments) (Everett *et al.*, 2006). This perspective is based more on the characteristics of actors than on behaviour according to principles. In this view, cultural and social actions – such as education and activism – are fundamental in order, for instance, to change bad habits, increase collective awareness, activate collective attention, consolidate social capital and increase the moral costs of illegal and illicit acts. The effectiveness of specific virtue ethics-based strategies is obviously closely related to the features of each social and geographical context.

The second strategy is based on 'rule ethics' (that is, Kantian-style arguments). This perspective is focused more on behaviour according to principles than on the characteristics of actors. If we want to fight the illicit/illegal, from this perspective we must reduce the institutional incentives to commit illicit and illegal acts, and increase the costs of acting in these ways. These actions may include the reform of (central and local) institutions in order to: increase transparency and accountability; reduce discretionality and *ad hoc* public powers; reduce bureaucracy; and increase the effectiveness of controls and sanctions (for public officials, practitioners and entrepreneurs). All these actions can also be applied to illicit and illegal acts in the specific sphere of urban and regional development. Take, for instance, the case of illegal and illicit activities in the domain of urban planning, such as corruption and infiltration by organised crime (Chiodelli, 2017). The incentives for these activities may be decreased through reform of the planning system aimed at reducing discretionality in land use decisions (which is the basis of traditional spot-zoning) and the economic returns associated with them, and a reform aimed at reducing bureaucracy and the number of agencies that can intervene in assessing and permitting land use transformation or building, (e.g. using a 'single window' to grant permits and introducing appropriate electronic systems) (Chiodelli and Moroni, 2015). This raises important questions as to the times and places in which these differing strategies to deal with illicit and illegal acts can be adopted. This would suggest the applied value of the spatial perspective explored by all the authors within this volume.

This second strategy (based on rule ethics) refers exclusively to institutional design and public policies; the first (based on virtue ethics) refers mainly to cultural and social action. Obviously, the two approaches are not mutually exclusive and can be combined.

A third strategy, collaborative governance, was briefly alluded to in the previous section, and it entails working in patterned formation with illicit or illegal actors and practices. Certainly, this has been widely observed across extensive historical and geographical terrains. Such collaborations tend to remain, where they involve direct collaboration between governments and illicit/illegal actors and practices, clandestine processes or where this collaboration is effected through tolerance of some illicit and illegal acts, beyond the formal policy arena. Where this collaboration is a formally acknowledged aspect of policy, as in the case of informal housing noted above, it would seem relatively rare and, further, relatively little acknowledged and commented upon within critical academic literatures. This third strategy, particularly if this collaborative governance is articulated through policy, potentially challenges both of the previous strategies outlined above and is perhaps a barrier to reform.

Overview of the volume: Multiple views on the interplay of the spatial and the illicit/illegal

The volume offers an innovative multidisciplinary collection of studies exploring the roles of illicit and illegal activities and actors of various kinds in processes of urban and regional governance and development. It also explores the effects of illicit/illegal networks on the spaces and places in which they are grounded and to which they are connected. In fact, the main purpose of the book is to analyse simultaneously two issues, the illicit/illegal and the spatial, issues that have not previously been engaged together in their multiple and varied connections (as we have already stressed, the spatial disciplines do not as a rule consider the role of illicit/illegal acts, and disciplines more properly interested in the illicit/illegal tend to omit the key role played by spatial variables).

The chapters investigate these issues with reference to a variety of geographical contexts, including, but not limited to, places traditionally considered to be associated with extensive illicit/illegal markets and activities such as some regions in the so-called Global South: case studies touch upon a number of regions and countries, such as the Sahara desert in Mali and Niger, the India–Bangladesh borders, East Timor, Spain, rural California and New Jersey, and cities like Bangalore, Ishinomaki (Japan), London, Medellín, Moscow, Palermo, Rome, Tbilisi and Valencia. The comparative perspective of the volume demonstrates that the illicit and the illegal are under-appreciated structural aspects of current urban and regional governance and development across the globe.

In selecting chapters to include in the collection, we favoured works which are grounded in empirical evidence, filling a significant gap in the existing literature. However, we have not been prescriptive as to the type of methodology or form of evidence (or theory) to be used in order to approach the research. The theoretical and methodological eclecticism of the chapters collected in this volume, while they remain united in their focus on the illicit and the illegal, maps out the variety of perspectives available to students of the illicit/illegal working within, and indeed across, a number of disciplines, but who are explicitly concerned with the *interplay between the spatial and the illicit/illegal.*

This collection is composed of 15 chapters (including this introduction). They are not grouped and enclosed into sub-sections so as not to break the continuity amongst the issues they deal with and their constant interplay. The book starts with two chapters on illicit/illegal flows in border regions. The first, by Luca Raineri, shows the transformative nature of illicit/illegal flows of various kinds of goods (such as illegal drugs). These flows are shaping the places (and, in particular, a border region in the Sahara Desert between Mali and Niger) through which they are organised, contributing especially to fuelling land grabbing and articulating a peculiar, hybrid form of territorial control, which includes both formal state actors and non-state informal/illicit/illegal actors. The second chapter, by Hosna J. Shewly and Md. Nadiruzzaman, in contrast, analyses how the geography of the India–Bangladesh border shapes illicit/illegal flows across it. The authors, in particular, focus on the circuits of illegal and provisional migration from one country's coastal zone to the other country's megacities, and on how the journeys and methods of these migrations adapt to the spatial features of this border region.

Then, the book moves to the analysis of the interplay between space/places and illicit/illegal organisations of various kinds. The chapter by James Scambary deals with the relations of an array of informal and illegal groups (such as gangs, martial arts groups and informal security groups) with formal institutions, and shows how these groups have been institutionalised, becoming part of the formal governance of East Timor, leading to the emergence of a clientelist, neo-patrimonial State. The following contribution, by Vincenzo Scalia, moves to the scale of the city and analyses, within an historical perspective, the relationship between criminal organisations and urban development. It demonstrates that the Mafia played a prominent role in the massive urban transformation of Palermo (Italy) between the 1950s and 1970s (the so-called 'Sack of Palermo'), moulding the spatial development of the city according to its own interests, thanks to its control of the territory, as well as its network of relations with politicians, professionals and entrepreneurs. This is followed by a chapter by Svetlana Stephenson and Evgenia Zakharova, which, in the same vein as the previous chapter, points to the scale of the city, but, in this case, the focus is on the micro-governance at the neighbourhood scale in Moscow (Russia) and Tbilisi (Georgia). Here, actors who are illegal but licit within these social contexts (such as peer groups of young people variously connected with members of criminal communities) form neighbourhood organisations, which have a fundamental role in the management of various aspect of the daily life of the local community. The chapter by Laure Leibler also centres on the governance role of illegal actors at the neighbourhood scale. However, in this case the focus is on Medellín (Colombia), and on the role of organised crime groups in shaping the daily practices of inhabitants and the space of the neighbourhoods they control. The pivotal role of controlling the space of these areas for building and keeping the power of these armed groups is highlighted.

The chapter by Sasha Jesperson offers a different perspective. After several case studies, Sasha Jesperson proposes a theoretical exploration of the governance and development roles of criminal groups in fragile and conflict-affected states. She shows that governance and development vacuums not only provide opportunities for criminal groups, but can also open new entry points to address organised crime.

The rest of the chapters address the interplay between the spatial and the illicit/illegal from different points of view: the focus is less on illegal/illicit flows and actors, such as gangs or organised crime, and more on illegal/illicit activities carried on by legal and formal actors.

The first three of these chapters analyse, in different contexts and from different viewpoints, the mobile and porous borders between what is conceived as legal and illegal, and what is conceived as licit and illicit. The chapter by Michael Polson centres on the impacts within the realm of both governance and development of the shift between legality and illegality. The author explores these links between development, governance and (il)legality through the rise and fall of marijuana regulations in the city of Eureka in Humboldt County (California, USA). The following chapter, by Barbara Pizzo and Edoardo Altavilla, questions the clear separation between illegality and illicitness focusing on three cases of informal/illegal/illicit housing in Rome, against the backdrop of the planning policies that shaped the transformation of the city in the last decades. Here, informal housing practices and markets materialise the constant interplay between what is defined and perceived as (il)legal and (il)licit. Subsequently, Margrete Bjone Engelein, John Edom and Hannah Wood apply architectural theory to the realm of the illicit. The authors investigate how understandings of the licit and illicit inscribed in the aesthetics of the urban space of Ishinomaki (Japan) changed after the reconstruction of the city that followed the Great Tōhoku Earthquake and Tsunami of 2011, and how the reconstruction process led to the emergence of new non-state groups as legitimate urban actors in Japan.

The remaining chapters move the analysis to questions more related to corruption and to its link with the spatial. The chapter by Sue Penna and Martin O'Brien reminds us of the presence of the illicit at the heart of the capitalist economy and show how lightly regulated global financial spaces set up environments where the illicit and illegal are potential activities that become actualised. They focus on two different places – New Jersey in the United States and London in the United Kingdom – where, due precisely to the regulatory features of these areas, various actors can move easily and at their own convenience from the sphere of the legal to the illegal and vice versa. In so doing, the authors highlight the artificial analytical distinction between legal and illegal actors and practices, and suggest that organised crime is a symptom of corruption, rather than its agent.

The following two chapters centre on corruption in the field of local urban development in Spain. The contribution by Monica Garcia Quesada and Fernando Jiménez Sánchez analyses potential explanations for the causes of corruption in this sector and it identifies the consequences for the functioning of subnational political systems. In the pursuit of this aim, it proposes a comparative analysis, based essentially on a quantitative approach, of different local councils affected by scandals from across Spain. In contrast, Jorge Ignacio Selfa Clemente focuses on a specific case, related to the creation of a free-trade zone in the municipality of Paterna, in the metropolitan area of Valencia. The project of the free-trade zone of Paterna was at the centre of a harsh public and political debate for alleged cases of corruption, lack of transparency and waste of public funds, which led to the cancellation of the project and which contributed to a replacement of the local government. This analysis is an opportunity for raising relevant questions relating to the rhetoric about corruption, and on its conceptualisations as central object of political debate in the midst of the economic crisis. Jayaraj Sundaresan concludes the volume with an investigation of land use planning violations in Bangalore, India. Through an ethnographic analysis of planning and violation networks, the author discovers that, in Bangalore, planning violations are driven in particular by a strong collective 'demand' by many sectors of the society (individual landowners as well as specific social groups like the urban poor, middle class or neighbourhood groups and political parties). This demand materialises through various forms of corruption and illicit pressures towards public officials, and gives rise to a specific form of 'vernacular urban governance', where public decisions and norms are constantly negotiated and reshaped in informal ways.

Notes

1 The literatures of economic geographies, for example, rest upon empirical foundations almost exclusively derived from analysis conducted within the licit/legal economy. Given the prevalence of illicit and illegal activities in many spheres of the economy, this is a major limitation. Accounts of regional and urban development are the stock in trade of many economic, political and development geographers. However, it is rare for these accounts to seek to describe the roles played by illicit/illegal actors, illicit/illegal governance and the development that stems therefrom, despite there being clear evidence from other accounts of their significance within fragile regional trajectories in the so-called Global South (Bhattacharyya, 2005; Kilcullen, 2013; Madsen, 2009; Nordstrom, 2007; Potter, 2001).

2 This problem is less significant in the case of the legal/illegal dichotomy: in fact, generally speaking, the legalistic definition of what is legal (or illegal) in a specific context can take as a (relatively) solid frame of reference. That said, the definition of such boundaries is typically socially contested, as different groups seek to draw the line in a way that favours their interests. The situation become far more controversial in contexts where the legal system is less defined (for instance, because a Western-liberal legal system coexists with a traditional-customary one) or if one wants to take transnational spaces which encompass differing legal systems and flows among these into consideration.

3 A similar matrix is proposed by Abraham and van Schendel (2005, p. 20) with reference to the political space emerging from the interaction between formal political authority and non-formal social authority.

4 For instance, this gap is particularly evident in the field of urban planning. Although there are several general accounts of the problem of illegal and illicit activities in the planning domain (such as problems of corruption; see for instance: Gardiner and Lyman, 1978; Cullingworth, 1993), and although some explanatory theories have been developed (Chiodelli and Moroni, 2015; Murray and Frijters, 2016), there is no research describing the specific everyday functioning of those illegal practices.

5 For further elaboration of this distinction, see Beynon and Hudson (1993).

6 For the distinction between deontological and consequentialistic approaches, see for instance Cooper (1993: 148–190). On consequentialism in general, see Mulgan (2001).

For the critical debate on consequentialism, see Scheffler (1998). For an empirical analysis of consequentialist and deontological approaches in urban planning, see Heller (1994).

7 It is worth stressing that, in many cases, their arguments tend to focus on economic and developmental benefits, paying less attention, for instance, to social and environmental harms.

8 In fact, we could also assume a sceptical or nihilistic stance: the illicit/illegal will be always with us, for instance, because it is intrinsic to human nature; therefore, nothing can be done to fight it.

9 For the distinction between *rule-based* and *virtue-based* ethical systems: see, for instance, Pojman (1990: 91–135). On virtue ethics, see for instance Crisp and Slot (1997), Oakley and Cocking (2001) and Swanton (2003). For a defence of virtue ethics, see MacIntyre (1981).

References

Aas, K. F. 2007. *Globalization and Crime*, London: Sage.

Abraham, I. and van Schendel, W. 2005. Introduction: the making of illicitness. In van Schendel, W. and Abraham, I. (eds.) *Illicit Flows and Criminal Things: States, Borders and the Other Side of Globalization*, Bloomington, IN: Indiana University Press, 1–37.

Ades, A. and Di Tella, R. 1997. The new economics of corruption, *Political Studies*, 45, 496–515.

Allen, C. M. 2005. *An Industrial Geography of Cocaine*, London: Routledge.

AlSayyad, N. 2004. Urban informality as a 'new' way of life. In Roy, A. and AlSayyad, N. (eds.) *Urban Informality: Transnational Perspectives from the Middle East, Latin America, and South Asia*, Oxford: Lexington Books, 7–29.

Bagley, B. 2005. Globalisation and Latin American and Caribbean organised crime. In Galeotti, M. (ed.) *Global Crime Today: The Changing Face of Organised Crime*, London: Routledge, 32–53.

Beynon, H. and Hudson R, 1993. Place and space in contemporary Europe: some lessons and reflections, *Antipode*, 25, 177–190.

Bhattacharyya, G. 2005. *Traffick: The Illicit Movement of People and Things*, London: Pluto.

Brooks, A. 2014. Controversial, corrupt and illegal: ethical implications of investigating difficult topics. Reflections on fieldwork in southern Africa'. In Lunn, J. (ed.) *Fieldwork in the Global South: Ethical Challenges and Dilemmas*, London: Routledge, 34–48.

Brown, E. and Cloke, J. 2007. Shadow Europe: alternative European financial geographies, *Growth and Change*, 38: 304–327.

Castells, M. 2000. *End of Millennium*, Oxford: Blackwell.

Chiodelli, F. 2016. International housing policy for the urban poor and the informal city in the Global South: a non-diachronic review, *Journal of International Development*, 28: 788–807.

Chiodelli, F. 2017. Urbanistica tra corruzione e 'Ndrangheta: il caso di Desio, *Archivio di studi urbani e regionali* (forthcoming).

Chiodelli, F. and Moroni, S. 2014. The complex nexus between informality and the law: reconsidering unauthorised settlements in light of the concept of nomotropism, *Geoforum*, 51: 161–169.

Chiodelli, F. and Moroni, S. 2015. Corruption in land-use issues: a crucial challenge for planning theory and practice, *Town Planning Review*, 86(4): 437–455.

Coe, N., Kelly, P. and Yeung, H. 2007. *Economic Geography: A Contemporary Introduction*, Oxford: Blackwell.

Cooper, D. 1993. *Value Pluralism and Ethical Choice*, New York: St. Martin's Press..
Crisp, R. and Slot, M. (eds.) 1997. *Virtue Ethics*, Oxford: Oxford University Press.
Cullingworth, J. B. 1993. *The Political Culture of Planning*, London: Routledge.
David-Barrett, E. 2014. Are some bribes more harmful than others? Exploring the ethics behind anti-bribery laws, *Journal of Interdisciplinary Economics*, 26(1/2): 119–144.
Dicken, P., Kelly, P. F., Olds, K. and Yeung, H. W-C. 2001. Chains and networks, territories and scales: towards a relational framework for analysing the global economy, *Global Networks*, 1(2): 89–112.
Dunn, G. 1997. Major mafia gangs in Russia. In Williams, P. (ed.) *Russian Organised Crime: The New Threat?* London: Frank Cass, pp. 65–87.
Everett, J., Neu, D., Shiraz Rahaman, A. 2006. The global fight against corruption: a Foucaultian, virtues-ethics framing, *Journal of Business Ethics*, 65: 1–12.
Flyvbjerg, B. 2006. Five misunderstandings about case-study research, *Qualitative Inquiry*, 12(2): 219–245.
Galeotti, M. 2005a. The Russian 'Mafiya': consolidation and globalisation. In Galeotti, M. (ed.) *Global Crime Today: The Changing Face of Organised Crime*, London: Routledge, 54–69.
Galeotti, M. (ed.) 2005b. *Global Crime Today: The Changing Face of Organised Crime*, London: Routledge.
Gardiner, J. A. and Lyman, T. R. 1978. *Decisions for Sale. Corruption and Reform in Land-Use and Building Regulation*, New York: Praeger.
Glenny, M. 2008. *McMafia: Crime without Frontiers*, London: Bodley Head.
Goodhand, J. 2009. *Bandits, borderlands and opium wars: Afghan state-building viewed from the margins. Markets for peace?* DIIS Working Paper, 26: 1–28. Copenhagen: DIIS. Retrieved from: www.econstor.eu/bitstream/10419/44703/1/615075703.
Goodhand, J. and Mansfield, D. 2013. Drugs and (dis)order: the opium economy, political settlements and statebuilding in Afghanistan. In Schetter, C. (ed.) *Local Politics in Afghanistan: A Century of Intervention in the Social Order*, London: Hurst, 211–243.
Goodhand, J. and Sedra, M. 2015. *The Afghan Conundrum: Intervention, Statebuilding and Resistance*, London: Routledge.
Gregson, N. and Crang, M. 2016. Illicit economies: customary illegality, moral economies and circulation, *Transactions of the Institute of British Geographers*, DOI: 10.1111/tran.12158.
Hadjimichalis C and Hudson R, 2006. Networks, Regional Development and Democratic Control, *International Journal of Urban and Regional Research*, 30(4), 858–872.
Hall, T. 2010. Where the money is: The geographies of organised crime, *Geography*, 95(1): 4–13.
Hall, T. 2013. Geographies of the illicit: globalisation and organised crime, *Progress in Human Geography*, 37(3): 366–385.
Heller, E. 1994. *Acting on Ethics in City Planning*, New Brunswick: CUPR.
Hill, P. 2005. The changing face of the Yakuza. In Galeotti, M. (ed.) *Global Crime Today: The Changing Face of Organised Crime*, London: Routledge, 97–116.
Hobbs, D. 2013. *Lush Life: Constructing Organized Crime in the UK*, Oxford: Oxford University Press.
Hobbs, D. and Antonopoulos, G.A. 2014. How to research organised crime. In Paoli, L. (ed.) *The Oxford Handbook of Organized Crime*, Oxford: Oxford University Press.
Holmes, L. 2016. *Advanced Introduction to Organised Crime*, Cheltenham: Edward Elgar.
Hudson, R. 2014. Thinking through the relationships between legal and illegal activities and economies: spaces, flows and pathways, *Journal of Economic Geography*, 14(4): 775–795.

Inkster, N. and Comolli, V. 2012. *Drugs, Insecurity and Failed States: The Problems of Prohibition*, London: Routeldge/IISS.

Kaufmann, D. 1997. Corruption: The facts, *Foreign Policy*, 107: 114–31.

Kilcullen, D. 2013. *Out of the Mountains: The Coming Age of the Urban Guerrilla*, Oxford: Oxford University Press.

Levi, M. 2014. Thinking about organised crime: structure and threat, *The RUSI Journal*, 159(1): 6–14.

Lunn, J. (ed.) 2014. *Fieldwork in the Global South: Ethical Challenges and Dilemmas*, London: Routledge.

McCracken, R.D. 1997. *Las Vegas: The Great American Playground* [Expanded edition], Reno, Las Vegas: University of Nevada Press.

McFarlane, C. 2012. Rethinking informality: politics, crisis, and the city, *Planning Theory & Practice*, 13(1): 89–108.

MacIntyre, A. 1981. *After Virtue*, Notre Dame, IN: University of Notre Dame Press.

Madsen, F. 2009. *Transnational Organized Crime*, London: Routledge.

Méon, P.-G. and Weill, L. 2010. Is corruption an efficient grease?. *World Development*, 38(3): 244–259.

Midgley, T., Briscoe, I. and Bertoli, D. 2014. *Identifying Approaches and Measuring Impacts of Programmes Focused on Transnational Organised Crime*, London: Department for International Development.

Mulgan, T. 2001. *The Demands of Consequentialism*, Oxford: Oxford University Press.

Murray C. K. and Frijters P. 2016. Clean money, dirty system: connected landowners capture beneficial land rezoning. *Journal of Urban Economics*, 93, 99–114.

Nordstrom, C. 2007. *Global Outlaws: Crime, Money, and Power in the Contemporary World*, Berkley: University of California Press.

Oakley, J. and Cocking, D. 2001. *Virtue Ethics and Professional Roles*, Cambridge: Cambridge University Press.

Paoli, L. 2005. Italian organised crime: mafia associations and criminal enterprises. In Galeotti, M. (ed.) *Global Crime Today: The Changing Face of Organised Crime*, London: Routledge, 19–31.

Payne, G. 2002. Lowering the ladder: regulatory frameworks for sustainable development. In Westendorff, D., Eade, D. (eds.) *Development and Cities. Essay from Development in Practice*, Oxford: Oxfam Professional, 248–262.

Pojman, L.P. 1990. *Ethics. Discovering Right and Wrong*, Belmont: Wadsworth.

Potter, M. 2001. *Outlaws Inc.: Under the Radar and On the Black Market with the World's Most Dangerous Smugglers*, New York: Bloomsbury.

Rengert, G.F. 1996. *The Geography of Illegal Drugs*, Boulder: Westview Press.

Roberts, S. 1999. Confidence men: offshore finance and citizenship. In Hampton, M.P. and Abbott, J.P. (eds.) *Offshore Finance Centres and Tax Havens: The Rise of Global Capital*, Basingstoke: Macmillan.

Roy, A. 2005. Urban informality: toward an epistemology of planning. *Journal of the American Planning Association*, 71(2): 147–158.

Scheffler, S. (ed.) 1998. *Consequentialism and its critics*, Oxford: Oxford University Press.

Scott-Clark, C. and Levy, A. 2008. It's down your street and in your lane. *The Guardian Weekend*, 11/10/08: 36–45.

Sergi, A. and Lavorgna, A. 2016. *'Ndrangheta. The Global Dimensions of the Most Powerful Italian Mafia*, London: Palgrave Macmillan, 117–139.

Sheppard, E. 2002. The spaces and times of globalization: place, scale, networks and positionality, *Economic Geography*, 78(3): 307–330.

Swanton, C. 2003. *Virtue Ethics. A Pluralistic View*, Oxford: Oxford University Press.

Taylor, J.S., Jasparro, C. and Mattson, K. 2013. Geographers and drugs: a survey of the literature, *The Geographical Review*, 103(3): 415–430.

Transparency International. 2015. Corruption Perceptions Index 2015. Retrieved from https://www.transparency.org/whatwedo/publications/#1.

Unger, B. and Ferwerda, J. 2011. *Money Laundering in the Real Estate Sector*, Cheltenham: Edward Elgar.

Unger, B. and Rawlings, G. 2008. Competing for criminal money, *Global Business and Economics Review*, 10(3): 331–352.

Van Dijk, J. 2007. Mafia markers: assessing organized crime and its impact upon societies, *Trends in Organized Crime*, 10(1): 39–56.

Weinstein, L. 2008. Mumbai's development mafias: globalization, organized crime and land development, *International Journal of Urban and Regional Research*, 32(1): 22–39.

Wilson, E. 2009. Deconstructing the shadows. In Wilson, E. (ed.) *Government of the Shadows: Parapolitics and Criminal Sovereignty*, London: Pluto Press, 13–55.

Windsor, D. and Getz, K. A. 1999. Regional market integration and the development of global norms for enterprise conduct: the case of international bribery, *Business & Society*, 38(4): 415–449.

Woodiwiss, M. 2001. *Organized Crime and American Power*, Toronto: University of Toronto Press.

Yeung, H. W.-C. and Coe, N., 2015. Toward a dynamic theory of global production networks, *Economic Geography*, 91(1): 29–58.

2 Drug trafficking in the Sahara Desert

Follow the money and find land grabbing

Luca Raineri

Is there a nexus between drug trafficking and land grabbing in the Sahara?

According to the World Bank, two major parallel phenomena have radically modified the patterns of land governance in Africa in the last decades. On the one hand, no region in the world exhibits the pace of urbanisation and urban growth of Africa (Rafei, 2014). Noteworthy, the remotest and poorest Saharan countries do not seem to diverge from this continental trend (Pliez, 2011). On the other hand, large-scale acquisitions of farmland – defined as the acquisition of property rights or long-term leases of portions of arable land larger than 1,000 hectares (UN Human Rights Council, 2010) – have been skyrocketing in the last decade: 'compared to an average annual expansion of global agricultural land of less than 4 million hectares in the period between 1990 and 2008, approximately 56 million hectares worth of large-scale farmland deals were announced before the end of 2009' (World Bank, 2010, xiv). Media reports and critics have qualified this phenomenon in terms of 'land grabbing' (Grain, 2012). Again, Africa has been particularly targeted by this sort of investment (World Bank, 2010). While some sources provide more conservative estimates, all seem to agree that Africa is the continent most impacted by such land deals (Nolte *et al.*, 2016).[1]

Interestingly, all available studies – most of them featuring a quantitative outlook – stress that large-scale acquisitions of farmland in Africa seem to target mostly fertile areas with abundant access to water (Cotula *et al.*, 2009; Grain, 2012; Nolte *et al.*, 2016), to the extent that land grabbing is also frequently associated with 'water grabbing' (Rullia *et al.*, 2013). The underlying explanation for this correlation is that the ambition to increase and acquire the agricultural output of fertile regions – considered as poorly exploited – is a key driver of large-scale land acquisitions. Hence, the common drivers of land grabbing identified in the available literature fail to apply in places like the Sahara Desert, due to its quintessential unproductivity. According to the *International Land Matrix Report*, places like Mauritania, Mali and Niger feature the least favourable conditions for large-scale land acquisitions, or land grabbing. They can be said to represent, then, a least-likely case (Eckstein, 1975) for the manifestation of the phenomenon at stake. And indeed, available statistics based on real estate registries report very few land deals in such areas.

However, a significant amount of anecdotal evidence suggests instead that, below the radar, rural 'land grabbing' is proceeding apace also in the dry and unproductive soils of the Sahara Desert and Sahelian savannas. One might consider this pattern of limited statistical significance in a global perspective. However, on the one hand, recent findings suggest to take with extreme caution the reliability of available statistics dealing with Africa (Jerven, 2013), even more so in inherently opaque domains such as those dealing with land deals in poorly governed areas (Cotula *et al.*, 2009; Shaw *et al.*, 2014). On the other hand, and departing from purely quantitative approaches to social investigation, such deviant cases challenge the explanatory patterns provided for in the available literature. The present contribution, then, endeavours to put forward a plausibility probe (Eckstein, 1975) for an alternative explanation. In order to make sense of 'land grabbing' taking place in areas unsuitable for agricultural purposes, such as the Sahel and the Sahara, I explore the hypothesis that opaque land deals are influenced by the investment of the profits resulting from regional drug trafficking.

In order to sustain such a claim, this contribution shall adopt the following methodology. With a view to investigating explanations, rather than correlations, the collection and analysis of qualitative evidence will be privileged. To this end, I will rely on the available literature, as well as on extensive fieldwork carried out with key stakeholders in the region between 2013 and 2016. The qualitative focus on micro-dynamics contributes to mitigating the oft-noticed challenges linked to the quantification of phenomena which are by definition hidden and opaque (UNODC, 2013). While a regional outlook shall be privileged, most of the evidence introduced in this analysis refers to Niger and Mali, given that a single-case study can provide an adequate research design for a plausibility argument.

Evidence will be treated by combining the methodological frameworks developed by Shaw and Kemp (2012) – in order to analyse the material, spatial and social factors of illegal trades and extra-legal economies that exist across the Saharan space – and that of Klute (2011)[2] – with a view to comparing this data with the biographical trajectories of key actors allegedly involved in opaque land deals.[3] The result of this investigation will then be used as a heuristic tool to understand opaque dynamics taking place in the same region in the field of urban development and real estate investment.

To this end, the chapter engages in a preliminary conceptual clarification and discusses the notions of (il-)licit and (il-)legal in the specific context herein investigated. By adopting a political economic perspective, it further discusses how illegal profits are made in the Saharan area, and how they are redistributed in the framework of local patronage networks. It eventually focuses more in-depth on how they influence land governance and real estate markets, before turning to some concluding remarks on the dynamics of territorial control in Saharan Africa.

(Il-)licit and (il-)legal from a Saharan perspective

Conventional geopolitical theories and mainstream security thinking have tended to deterministically attribute to the Sahara the 'objective' geopolitical fate of a 'buffer zone' of weak interaction (Kaplan, 1994). Against outdated geopolitical models, the present contribution builds instead on the idea that regions do not amount to bounded areas delimited by nature, but are instead social constructs enacted through practices across intrinsically porous borders (Murphy *et al.*, 2015). Recent scholarly work has come to recognise that 'the Sahara was always a borderland, in the sense of a zone constituted by its multiple interactions with neighbouring worlds, without which it would be unable to survive' (McDougall, 2012, p. 82). Within the Sahara's harsh desert environment, it is mobility, not the soil's productivity, which ensures communities' resilience. From this perspective, the Saharan space should be interpreted as a busy crossroad and a central node of cross-border trade, in which stopover towns (Daniel, 2014) and border markets (Scheele, 2012) thrive, and delineate specific patterns of economic development and land use. From this perspective, perceptions of marginality seem to mirror inaccurate outsiders' prejudices more than a careful assessment of the dynamics on the ground.

This is particularly relevant when it comes to considering the spatial aspects of extra-legal economies affecting the Saharan region. The present contribution builds on the idea that extra-legal flows across the Saharan region, such as drug, migrant and weapon smuggling, are not disembodied from their spatial dimension (Hall, 2013), nor can they be disentangled from the legal economic sphere and 'normal' social intercourses in which they take place. Interestingly, De Boer (2010, p. 257) argues that today's criminal networks are 'woven into the texture of ordinary social life, where criminal conducts intermesh with habitual social patterns'. The progressive embeddedness of the criminal economy into the 'normal'(-ised) one deconstructs the fiction relegating extra-legal economies to an independent, isolated sphere of social relations. Even today, local sources interviewed in different localities in Mali's Saharan borderlands confirm that up to 90 per cent of all the goods available there are derived from smuggling,[4] which benefits from diverging customs policies and subsidies. These, however, are grafted onto long-standing vernacular spatial practices (Bensassi *et al.*, 2015). According to Scheele (2009), traffics are so trivialised in the region that the concepts of 'fraud' and 'trade' have become synonymous in local parlance.

Within the widespread patterns of informality proliferating in the Sahara, it is often hard to isolate conducts and profiles which would perfectly fit the abstract legal category of 'organised crime'.[5] This notion, moreover, clashes with local perceptions and norms, according to which 'organised crime does not include trafficking or smuggling, regardless of the commodity, but is restricted to murder, violent crime, road banditry, burglary, and armed robbery' (Reitano and Shaw, 2014, 4). While criminalised nationally and internationally, these conducts are widely seen as unharmful and licit. The legalistic notion of organised crime, thus, seems ill-suited to capturing the specificities of Saharan extra-legal economies.

Indeed, virtually all available reports highlight the widespread social legitimacy enjoyed by 'contraband' related activities in the Saharan region, where environmental conditions are extremely harsh and jobs in the formal sector almost entirely absent (Danish Demining Group, 2014; IOM, 2014; Reitano and Shaw, 2014).

It follows that local and state authorities, formally entrusted with law enforcement duties, often prefer to adapt to, rather than challenge, these widespread norms. Anecdotal evidence collected through interviews with different local authorities from the Malian region of Gao, one of the hubs of trans-Saharan smuggling (Briscoe, 2014), largely confirm this view: 'The state has to take its own responsibility. If people here live out of traffics, it's because there's nothing else. Honestly, we do not have the choice'; 'Traffic is the main source of income in the north, all of our food comes from there'; 'We would be crazy to stop fuel smuggling. Our people would kill us!'.[6]

These observations invite one to consider with some circumspection the conspicuous claims that 'not only is organised crime an increasingly important issue for the peace and security agenda, but it is also a quintessentially African issue' (Shaw *et al.*, 2014, 3; see also UNODC, 2008). On the one hand, one does not need to underappreciate that the place of Africa in the illegal global trade is three to four times greater than its place in the legal one, and that the total value of illegal flows leaking out of the continent is supposed to be twice as much as the total flows of international development aid received by all African countries (Shaw and Reitano, 2013). On the other hand, however, the specific sociological features of African criminal cartels suggest the need to thoroughly scrutinise the appropriateness of security lenses when dealing with African 'organised crime'. Against such an approach, I argue that a focus on the political economy and on the governance of the extra-legal represents a more promising avenue to capture the specificities of the dynamics at stake.

The political economy of the extra-legal: From illegal profits to patronage networks

The present section provides a quick overview of the structure and dynamics of the regional trafficking of (legal and illegal) commodities, before analysing the financial streams they generate, and how they impact land governance.[7] Local sources[8] confirm the scholarly literature's claim (Lacher, 2012; Briscoe, 2014; Shaw *et al.*, 2014) that the infrastructure developed for the large-scale smuggling of legal goods, such as fuel and cigarettes, has formed the basis for the development of the different forms of drug trade (hashish and cocaine in particular) which have affected the region thereafter – in terms of actors and networks involved, political protections, modalities of transport, etc.

Morocco's Rif is the largest productive site of hashish in North and West Africa. In the framework of Moroccan-Algerian rivalries, in the early 2000s, Moroccan cartels developed a new trafficking route to circumvent Algeria. Existing Saharan routes across Mauritania, Mali and Niger were exploited to ship illegal commodities to Libya and Egypt, and from there to Europe and the Middle East (Scheele, 2011, 2012). In 2010, an estimated one third of Morocco's overall production, amounting to about 300 tons per year, ran through this route, generating a total income of up to 1.2 billion euros (Peduzzi, 2010), that was subsequently redistributed among producers, traffickers and armed actors performing protection rackets.

However, the real game changer of illegal trades across the Saharan region has been represented by the boom of cocaine smuggling. The 'transatlantic cocaine highway' (UNODC, 2011) was initiated with a view to connecting producing countries in Latin America to the booming consumption markets in Europe. West Africa was strategically located as an ideal hub along this route. Until 2004, available data suggests that cocaine trafficking in West Africa did not exceed three tons per year, thereby representing a negligible percentage (0.2–0.5 per cent) of the commodity's traffic worldwide (UNODC, 2011). Since 2005/6, however, seizures of cocaine in West Africa rose sharply. Between 2005 and 2008, cocaine flows in the region amounted to 40–50 tons per year (UNODC, 2008), representing 25–28 per cent of the total annual consumption in Europe (UNODC, 2008, 2011).

While subsequent figures about drug trafficking in Africa remain contested (UNODC, 2013; Perry, 2014; Raineri and Strazzari, 2015), it soon became clear that the Saharan area played a pivotal role in the articulation of regional flows. According to a senior UN officer, 'geography is the main risk factor in the Saharan space, as unchecked frontiers stretch for thousands of kilometres and it is impossible to control them. Fencing borders here, just like in Ceuta or in Mexico, is simply not an option, as space is much bigger and virtually infinite'.[9] Much literature has stressed the increasing relevance of In-Khalil, Gao, Agadez and Arlit as regional hubs of cocaine trafficking that is shipped to the desert and then transported by land along the West-East route connecting the Gulf of Guinea to Egypt (Lacher, 2012; Scheele, 2012; UNODC, 2013; Briscoe, 2014; Daniel, 2014; Global Initiative, 2015; Raineri and Strazzari, 2015). Moreover, it has been reported that a hugely profitable smuggling of synthetic drugs – including methamphetamines and counterfeited medicines – is soaring along the same route (UNODC, 2013). Several reports indicate that air shipments of cocaine have been directly targeting the unchecked Saharan lands, especially in Mali and Niger. In early November 2009, 'the burnt-out carcass of a Boeing 727 believed to have been transporting up to 10 tons of cocaine was found in the desert north of Gao' (Lebovich, 2013; see also Daniel, 2014). Yet it soon turned out that this episode – re-baptised the 'Air Cocaine' case – was nothing but the tip of an iceberg. In the subsequent months, further flights reportedly carrying cocaine were detected in north Mali (Julien, 2011; UNODC, 2013) and Niger.[10] Similar reports have surfaced in both countries until late 2015, thereby confirming that Air Cocaine was part of a well-established operational pattern.

While the significance of drug trafficking in the Saharan region is now widely recognised, its impact on local governance, and namely on land governance, is poorly studied. The immense profits generated by the trans-Saharan trafficking of illegal commodities requires one to contend with the political economy of the extra-legal in the region, and with the hybrid political order (Boege *et al.*, 2008; Hudson, 2014) fostered by illegal profits. The wealth generated by drug trafficking throughout the Saharan region is in fact unprecedented. The commercial value of all the cocaine transiting through the Saharan region is estimated, at retailers' prices, at 1.8 billion dollars. This amounts to 0.5 per cent of the global GDP of all West and Central African countries combined, a figure which is three to four times higher than the US and European equivalents (Shaw *et al.*, 2014). No alternative livelihood project has thus far been able to compete with the high-profit margins offered by participation in extra-legal economies (Reitano and Shaw, 2014). The estimated profits of a Malian drug trafficker can amount to 200 million f CFA[11] per month, about 1,000 times as much as the salaries of the security officers (including police, customs, gendarmerie and army) who are supposed to fight them. Corruption is therefore widespread: the reward for security forces' officers who agree to turn a blind-eye can amount to several million f CFA.[12]

The revenues of drug trafficking have therefore fuelled an increasingly wide network, in which the interests of different actors could be combined and fulfilled within the framework of utterly corrupt governance. Indeed, political connivances at the highest levels have been instrumental for the development of 'professional' criminal networks devoted to large-scale and long-distance narcotics smuggling in, and across, the Saharan region. What investigations in different countries have revealed (Lewis, 2014; Raineri and Strazzari, 2015) is not the helpless passivity of formal state institutions unable to fight the drug cartels hidden in their respective territories, but the key role of state authorities in the active and enthusiastic organisation of international drug trades which could have otherwise targeted different countries, and therefore redistributed drug money elsewhere. Saharan states are in fact among the poorest of the world. It is hardly surprising that local authorities struggle to capture potential resources, with little regard for the international legality of the latter. As recognised by a UNODC officer: 'the main interest of states in the region is not that customs prevent the transit of illicit goods, but rather that they help the state to raise money: and therefore, in some cases, local governments prefer to sponsor the drug trafficking in exchange for a "public" share, instead of leaving it uniquely to the private gain of the warlords'.[13] An illegal-business-friendly environment is the result of such assemblage.

The extent of the political protections offered by state authorities to drug cartels, if not the active participation of the former into the latter, is fostered by the long-standing hold to power of unaccountable political *nomenklaturas*. Local sources report allegations of the involvement of Algerian generals deployed in the south of the country in the organisation of drug trafficking across West Africa and the Sahara Desert (see also Scheele, 2011; Daniel, 2014).[14] There is evidence that François Compaoré, brother of the long-standing dictator of Burkina Faso Blaise Compaoré, has been dominating and protecting the smuggling of tobacco in the region,[15] while the regime has been cashing in a share of the flourishing kidnapping-for-ransom industry in the Sahara (Daniel, 2014).[16] In Mauritania, investigations revealed the key roles of former presidents' family members in illegal trades, including of drugs (Julien, 2011; Boas, 2014). In Niger, civil society organisations report that the army has been providing military escorts to cigarettes, drugs and migrants smugglers, to the full knowledge of the political hierarchy, in exchange for a cut of the profits and the assurance of political acquiescence.[17] Given the prospects of extracting lucrative protection rents from illegal flows, the very recruitment process into the security forces can be the object of systematised corruption (Briscoe, 2014).[18]

In other words, the real porosity of Saharan states does not appear to be a 'natural' attribute, but the result of a social construction organised territorially. State authorities across the Saharan region have in some cases directly and enthusiastically promoted the very organisation of the criminal business. In other cases, they have secured the loyalty of local and traditional elites by turning a blind-eye on their involvement in formally illegal activities locally seen as licit, such as smuggling. In particular, electoral competition has represented a unique opportunity for drug barons to buy redemption and avoid prosecution. These barons in fact have allegedly sponsored political actors with unparalleled resources, in exchange for a substantial laissez-faire policy. Reports highlighting these practices exist with regards to Mali (Briscoe, 2014) and Niger (Raineri, 2015). In the framework of state-sponsored protection rackets (Snyder and Duran-Martinez 2009), the entanglement of state institutions and criminal actors has contributed to stretching the territorial control of the state in peripheral regions (Strazzari, 2014; Vorrath, 2015). Instead of pointing to the absence of – or competition with (Felbab-Brown, 2013) – the state, available evidence suggests then that illegal economies thrive precisely where they can develop a symbiotic relationship with the former (Shaw and Reitano, 2013).

Buying sand with powder?

Scholarly literature and journalistic reports have abundantly documented how hybrid political assemblages and corrupted deals in West Africa have fostered the irregular appropriation and exploitation of land plots endowed with significant mineral wealth, such as Liberia's diamond fields, Guinea's iron mines, Cameroun's forests and Nigeria's oilfields (Reno, 2000; Global Witness, 2013; Vorrath, 2015; to name but a few). It is less obvious, however, why the relatively unproductive and arid soils of the Saharan region have been increasingly targeted by such deals in the last decade. Field observations suggest in fact that land property in the whole Saharan region has been facing a growing demand, and that its economic value of has been soaring steadily. In the present section, I will argue that drug-money-laundering represents one of the major drivers of large-scale land acquisitions and real estate investments in the Saharan area. Some anecdotal cases, which deviate from more customary trends of land grabbing, can contribute to illustrating this view.

Nioro du Sahel is a small village, situated in the drylands straddling the desert borderline between Mauritania and Mali. Interviewed in the framework of the present research, local dwellers reported that in the last few years the cost of land ownership had become exorbitant, and largely inaccessible to young peasants.[19] In the same vein, residents from the (largely desert) area north of Timbuktu reported that the price of a standard land plot of 20x20 meters, where family farming is traditionally performed, has increased tenfold in the last few years, from 300.000 f CFA to 3 million f CFA.[20] Yet nothing in the quality of the soil nor in the agricultural techniques employed seems to justify such a sharp increase of interest. While both examples refer to Mali, they illustrate a larger regional trend. In Niger, and more precisely in the inhospitable regions of Tillabéri and in the peri-urban belt of Niamey, local civil society organisations report that the value of land property titles has been subject to an exponential increase: 'land plots worth 5 million f CFA are now frequently purchased for nonsense amounts, up to 50 million f CFA'.[21]

The appetite for apparently valueless lands is testified also by another increasing trend: the fact that large expanses of arid savannah formally destined to be customary subsistence pastureland have been abusively grabbed and enclosed to set up secluded individual ranches. A famous case of this sort occurred in the region of Tahoua, in the north of Niger. The deal was particularly opaque and controversial, since Niger's law formally prohibits private land ownership in common pasturelands. Reportedly, local shepherds and nomads protested vigorously, since the abusive privatisation prevented them from crossing and exploiting the natural resources herein. Although the story made the headlines of local newspapers, public and judiciary authorities did not react, and the case was eventually silenced.[22] Yet it left behind a bitter trail of controversy hard to soothe. It remains unknown whether compensation was paid to arrange the deal, to whom, and for what amount. Yet the renewed interest in areas previously considered as marginal and unattractive is noteworthy.

How can one make sense of such an appetite for apparently valueless lands throughout the whole Saharan space? A fine-grained analysis suggests that a common thread links the few cases cited above, and can therefore indicate the road for a plausible answer to such a puzzle. What these cases have in common is the link to drug smuggling and drug profits. The area of Nioro du Sahel is allegedly crisscrossed by major flows of drug trade, and of cocaine trade in particular, connecting coastal West African countries to North Africa (Raineri and Strazzari, 2015). Similarly, in the region north of Timbuktu, where generously-financed land investments have been observed, the headquarters of a prominent Malian-Arab cartel of drug smugglers[23] is reportedly harboured. In Niger, it turned out that the businessmen responsible for the enclosure of common pasturelands were close to well-known traffickers, whose drug revenues had allegedly supported the presidential party.[24] While anecdotal and non-systematic, this evidence reveals significant patterns of consistency, and fits with the observation that, throughout the last decade, the Saharan space has become a major hub for international drug smuggling. Furthermore, it aggregates to more general trends observed in the region. Mauritanian bloggers reported that a controversial Saharawi businessman, was recently awarded 6,000 hectares of agricultural land located along the banks of the Senegal River by public authorities. This is the only fertile area of a country severely hit by food shortages, and it is therefore subject to intense competition. While mainstream explanations of the drivers of large-scale land acquisitions can contribute to illuminating this specific deal, it is worth noticing that the entrepreneur in question is suspected of being a member of a large international drug trafficking network (Attar, 2013).

One needs to observe that all the sources interviewed for the present research – including local and international law enforcement officers, criminal prosecutors, residents and smugglers – agree that the most significant source of laundered money in Mali and Niger originates from traffics, namely of drugs and cigarettes, and is directed to the purchase of land or real estate properties.[25] Indeed, illegal profits end up representing a crucial component of private and/or public investments, precisely due to the hybrid assemblage between political authorities and drug barons mentioned above. The critical field of land deals and urban development makes no exception, no matter whether it results from formal planning or informal initiatives eventually endorsed by competent authorities. Land property titles are allegedly purchased by private developers through opaque deals with corrupted politicians, both at the local and national level. The use of dirty money is reportedly hardly infrequent,[26] and – although conclusive evidence is limited – one can legitimately infer that also here the unparalleled wealth of drug revenues plays a prominent role, especially in cases where the bureaucratic machine should be lubricated and irregular procedures smoothed. The enclosure of common pasturelands or public estates is a case in point here. 'In this field, what is prohibited is not always prohibited', commented a local observer.[27] One can presume that political protection, and the land permits that go along with it, is more easily granted to the highest bidder. And no economic activity is able to outcompete the immense wealth produced by drug trafficking.

The investment in land is in fact mutually beneficial. Given the current demographic and economic trends of many Saharan states – which are experiencing a steady GDP growth and a dramatic demographic boom – land is seen as 'a very secure asset, whose value grows with each passing second'.[28] It therefore represents an ideal commodity to launder illegal profits and justify one's revenues. Marginal lands located in remote areas are particularly suitable to this end, as they are subject to less scrutiny from public authorities.[29]

This is not to say that opaque land deals are performed only as goals of money laundering. Local cultural values attach a positive social status to land ownership, irrespective of the actual economic worth of the investment. The anthropologist Judith Scheele (2012) confirms that local traffickers, who could face social contempt since they smuggle *haram* products, generally aim to invest in assets that grant one social respectability, such as cattle, land and houses. Reportedly, individuals implicated in drug trafficking used to be extremely discreet: 'one's involvement in drug smuggling was very confidential because this activity was stigmatised by the society and whomever was identified as a drug trafficker was immediately isolated and rejected'.[30]

The large availability of dirty money influences and inflates land grabbing in many different ways. The mechanisms discussed above appear to have also largely favoured the guarantors of land ownership. In the Sahelian countries, these include both traditional leaders and local public authorities at the regional or municipal levels. In the framework of patronage politics, the redistribution of drug revenues has provided disempowered elites with the resources they needed to re-establish a social legitimacy otherwise doomed to deteriorate. Anecdotal evidence reveals that in some small border villages the only available social services, albeit primitive and limited in scope, have been set up through the support of benefactors enriched by drug smuggling.[31] These include the construction of wells, the provision of employment opportunities – including perfectly legal ones – for the youth, and of healthcare for women and elders.[32]

These considerations contribute to addressing the puzzle introduced above, as they provide a plausible explanation for the major patterns of land grabbing taking place in otherwise unattractive and unfavourable areas located in the Saharan space. From this perspective, they corroborate the hypothesis of this study that drug profits have boosted opaque land deals in the region.

Building on these premises, one could legitimately stretch the argument and speculate that similar mechanisms are at play also in the field of real estate investments in urban areas. On the one hand, however, the simple analysis of price trends cannot provide an adequate support to such a supposition, because the current urban boom experienced by African and Saharan cities is fostered by many independent drivers, as the dedicated literature stressed (see for instance Pliez, 2011). In other words, African and Saharan cities provide the most, not the least favourable conditions to invest one's money, irrespective of its origin. The lack of reliable statistics and judicial proceedings[33] severely limits one's possibility to trace the origin of the conspicuous amount of money invested in urban speculation, thereby impairing the control for alterative explanations. On the other hand, a significant amount of anecdotal evidence can support the plausibility of the hypothesis that drug money has also influenced the urban boom of Sahelian cities.

In Mali, entire new neighbourhoods, made up exclusively of luxury villas, have suddenly mushroomed in the last decade, especially in Gao (Lacher 2012), in small towns in the region of Timbuktu[34] and in Bamako.[35] Significantly enough, local people have nicknamed these places "*cocainebougou*", the cocaine villages. Local sources report that 'investments in real estate remain high, and aim to launder the revenues of drug trafficking'.[36] Similarly, local observers from Niger noted that the pace of urban development in the country was quicker in the towns reputed to be at the crossroad of Saharan smuggling routes. In places like Arlit (Kohl, 2013) and most notably Agadez,[37] drug revenues allegedly fuelled an impressive urban boom. Chérife Abidine, the former MP of Agadez and close ally to Niger's President Issoufou, was particularly active in local real estate enterprises. Interestingly, he was nicknamed 'Chérife Cocaine', or 'the Boss', due to his ostensible involvement in regional drug trafficking.

Drawing on unclear regulations and opaque deals, suburban land speculation in large cities, such as Bamako and Niamey, is reportedly a well-established vehicle providing opportunities to build patronage networks. In Niamey, local observers have witnessed the explosion of the real estate portfolio of top brass of the state suspected of entertaining obscure links with local narco-traffickers (Bigot 2016). In Bamako, the urban explosion is fuelled by major schemes of peri-urban land grabbing and ambitious programmes of social housing sponsored by powerful politicians.[38] The issuance of fraudulent land titles is reportedly a common practice, and in many cases the origin of the resources invested in such projects remains unclear.[39] However, according to local actors, one can hardly disentangle real estate agencies from political patronage and criminal networks.[40] In local parlance, these are equated to a 'builders' mafia'.[41] While the link of these dynamics to drug money might be only indirect, existing literature has abundantly demonstrated the permeability of Malian political and economic elites to illegal profits and narco-trafficking (Lacher, 2012; Briscoe, 2014; Raineri and Strazzari, 2015).

In urban settings, major real estate investments result in a supply of housing for all standings which is far from proportional to the local demand, and supports the conjecture that it is designed to meet different – and unmentionable – needs. Indeed, while the commercial value of land plots, both for agricultural and residential uses, is steadily rising throughout the region, house prices and rents are subject to unpredictable changes, and often to considerable contractions, especially in big cities.[42] Interestingly, these developments give rise to unique assemblages of overlapping traffics, extra-legal economies and urban dynamics. Throughout the region, land insecurity contributes to widespread food insecurity, and both foster growing patterns of rural exodus towards regions and countries relatively better-off, including capital cities, North Africa and Europe.[43] Alongside the customary resort to informal settlement, the large supply of houses can contribute to meeting such soaring demand. In Bamako, newly built apartments resulting from public housing programmes frequently welcome nationals migrating from the rural areas. In Agadez, empty apartment blocks are currently rented to migrants en route to North Africa and Europe.[44]

Concluding remarks: Territorial control, what is it good for?

This study has aimed to corroborate the hypothesis that the dynamics of rural land grabbing and urban development in the Sahara-Sahel have been influenced by the illegal profits derived from drug trafficking across the region. While the evidence supplied herein in the framework of a least-likely case supports the plausibility of this argument, further research is needed to assess its explanatory value against competing explanations. Process-tracing – and possibly money-tracing – seem to be the most appropriate approaches to address this challenge, yet the lack of transparency and reliable data risks impairing the potential of these methodologies. Hence, the considerations sketched above – precisely due their plausibility – point to the need of more in-depth investigation, both in terms of substance and of methodology.

One can nevertheless draw some conclusions from the observations sketched above. Firstly, the cases illustrated herein suggest that the massive inflow of 'dirty money' (i.e. of financial resources derived from extra-legal activities) in fragile states is less likely to generate patterns of competition than of cooperation. The hybrid governance fostered by the assemblage of criminal actors and public authorities blurs the boundaries between legality and illegality, while ensuring a modicum of equilibrium under the aegis of state-sponsored protection rackets. Conventional security and legal paradigms seem ill-suited to capturing the specificities of this ordering. From this perspective, the analysis of the hybrid political order in Mali and in Niger invites one to de-emphasise the focus on the alleged security impact of criminal activities (more or less organised), and to in-depth study instead of its influence in the fields of economy, development and governance, given their potential to trigger major societal dynamics in the forthcoming years.

Secondly, the role of illegal profits in local governance suggests the need to reconsider the analytical paradigm through which African politics have been studied in recent years, i.e. neopatrimonialism. The emergence of state-sponsored protection rackets, in fact, seems to be furthering a transformation from a neopatrimonial governance to a politics of patronage networks. While the former focuses on the privatisation of state bureaucracies steered from the political centre, the latter emphasises the role of independent strongmen and 'godfathers' enriched by criminal profits who build their own clienteles (Utas, 2012). From a spatial perspective, this dynamic amounts to a decentralisation of governance, increasingly carried out from the marginal peripheries. While the two paradigms are not incompatible, I argue that a focus on patronage politics provides an angle through which the significance of extra-legal economies can be better assessed.

Thirdly, and lastly, the unique spatial and social features of the Saharan region underscore the emergence of a different relationship between crime and space. Building on Tilly (1985), prevailing models stress that the exercise of spatial control is a key asset, as it allows criminal organisations to perform the crucial functions of protection and extraction. Moreover, it is seen as endowed with symbolic, political and military value. However, in the vast expanses of smooth Saharan borderlands the 'seizure' and control of the space is hardly achievable, and of little significance, as every spatial unit can in principle be easily circumvented. Illegal profits, just as much as the legal ones, derive from mobility and connection, not from isolation and retreat. Spatial appropriation, then, is not an enabler, but a consequence of criminal activities, and its meaning is more economic and social than political and military. It secures one's profits, not one's protection. One could therefore infer that in the context at stake legal and illegal conducts can coexist and intermesh, rather than collide and compete, precisely because they rely on different spatial logics. Saharan criminal actors can hardly be equated to 'a state within the state', like traditional mafias. Building on a nomadic background, they seem to reject the state logic of bounded sovereignty. Borrowing John Agnew's (2002) insightful expression, one can therefore conclude that the Sahara truly is a space of flow organised territorially.

Notes

1 The International Land Coalition's web database 'Land Matrix' (available at http://www.landmatrix.org/en/) partly contributes to documenting these dynamics. However, one should keep in mind that land deals in Africa, and especially those involving revenues of dubious origin, are inherently opaque and difficult to track.

2 Interestingly, Klute's framework was developed precisely with a view to studying the informal and unwritten dynamics of political actors in the Saharan area, thereby adding further coherence to the methodology of this investigation.

3 This approach not so dissimilar from the one of Carolyn Nordstrom (2007), albeit with a smaller emphasis on ethnographic data collection, and a greater focus on the political economy of the extra-legal.

4 Interviews with local stakeholders conducted in Kayes, Timbuktu and Kidal between November 2015 and May 2016.

5 The UN Convention Against Transnational Organized Crime (UNCTOC), also called Palermo Convention, defines organised crime as 'a structured group of three or more

persons, existing for a period of time and acting in concert with the aim of committing one or more serious crimes in order to obtain [...] material benefit'.

6 Interviews with the mayors of different towns in the region of Gao, conducted locally in November 2015.

7 Due to space constraints, I will not tackle herein all sorts of traffics taking place in the Saharan region, but only those whose economic impact is more significant and directly linked to land governance. These include, namely, cigarettes, hashish, synthetic drugs and first and foremost cocaine. The smuggling of weapons and migrants, instead, will be deliberately left aside. While the former's impact on security is undisputed, its economic relevance is more doubtful. Following the collapse of Khadafy's regime, in fact, the oversupply of Libyan weapons across the Saharan space allegedly resulted in a sharp decline of selling prices and profit margins (Anders 2015). As far as the smuggling of migrants is concerned, soaring flows across the Sahara, and namely through Agadez and Gao, observed in the last years (IOM 2014) have led some scholars to put forward impressive figures of the overall economic value of this traffic, which would be worth USD255–323 million (Global Initiative 2015). While it remains partly unclear how this figure was provided, a quite uncoordinated organisation still seems to prevail, whereby profits are generated by a multitude of independent actors and widely redistributed locally. As a result, local sources from Gao and Agadez report that the individual profit margins of migrants' smugglers are incomparably lower than those obtained through drug trafficking, and do not give rise to the same kind of ostensible investments in luxury goods.

8 Interviews with traffickers from Timbuktu, Kidal and Niamey; police officers in Gao; and UN police personnel, conducted locally in November 2015.

9 Interview with a senior UN officer in charge of security in the Sahara, conducted in Dakar, October 2014.

10 Interview with Nigerien anti-organised crime prosecutor, and with former Tuareg insurgent from Agadez, conducted in Niamey in September 2015.

11 The franc CFA (Communauté Française d'Afrique) is the official currency of seven former French colonies in West Africa, including Benin, Burkina Faso, Ivory Coast, Mali, Niger, Senegal and Togo. Previously linked to the French currency, since 1999 the f CFA is exchanged at a fixed rate with the euro, whereby 1 euro = 655.957 CFA francs. Hence, 200 million f CFA amount to about 300.000 euros.

12 Interview with Gao's customs high-ranking officer, conducted locally in November 2015.

13 Interview with UN officer, conducted in Dakar in December 2014.

14 Interviews with criminal prosecutors, investigative journalists, senior UN staff, local civil society and tribal leaders from north Mali, conducted in Bamako in November 2013 and November 2014.

15 Interview with criminal prosecutor conducted in Bamako, in October 2014.

16 Judicial sources, both in Mali and in Niger, report that the former dictator Compaoré's daughter was apprehended by the police in Paris while she was shopping using the marked banknotes with whom the French secret services had paid the ransom for hostages kidnapped by AQIM in the Saharan region.

17 Interviews with Nigerian NGOs, conducted in Niamey in September 2015 and May 2016.

18 Interviews with Malian security experts conducted in Bamako in November 2013; with foot-ranking soldiers conducted in Bamako in November 2015; with the *Bureau du Vérificateur Général* conducted in Bamako in January 2016.

19 Focus group with a youth union of peasants from the department of Nioro du Sahel, conducted locally in May 2016.

20 Interview with Arab intellectual from Timbuktu, conducted in Bamako in May 2016.

21 Interview with Transparency International, conducted in Niamey in September 2015.

22 Interviews with residents from the region, former Tuareg combatants and local authorities, conducted in Niamey and Tahoua in September 2015 and May 2016.

23 Interview with Arab leader from Timbuktu, conducted in Bamako in May 2016. See Daniel (2014).

24 Interviews with local authorities, residents from the region of Tahoua and local NGOs, conducted in Niamey in September 2015.

25 Interviews conducted in Bamako and Niamey, between November 2014 and January 2016, with Malian criminal prosecutors of the PENI and of the judicial pole of the economic and financial crimes divisions, Malian criminal police, UN experts on organised crime, Transparency International section in Niger, small traffickers from Agadez and residents of Gao, Timbuktu and Agadez. While some sources claimed their inability to answer this question, it is noteworthy that none of those interviewed for the present research has explicitly rejected this view.

26 Interviews with: UN specialist in organised crime, conducted in Bamako in December 2014; CENTIF, conducted in Bamako in November 2015; and Malian lawyer specialised in land disputes, conducted in Bamako in December 2016.

27 Interview with Malian lawyer specialised in land disputes, conducted in Bamako in December 2016.

28 Interview with Malian lawyer specialised in land disputes, conducted in Bamako in December 2016. Available quantitative data confirm this view: see Nolte *et al.* (2016).

29 Interview with Malian CBOs dealing with urban land acquisitions, conducted in Bamako in December 2016.

30 Interview with a tribal leader of Arab origins living nearby a drug-trade crossroads between Mali, Niger and Burkina Faso, conducted in Bamako in November 2015. Yet, things appear to have radically changed in the last years, as traffickers are now easily identifiable by the sudden signs of the visible wealth they boast. As a youth leader from Kidal interviewed in November 2015 confirmed: 'drug trade is now very gossiped because of the exorbitant expenses afforded by alleged traffickers. Recently, a drug baron from Gao has purchased a 600 million f CFA worth villa, another has spent 80.000 dollars for his wedding'.

31 The newly appointed governor of the region of Taoudenni, interviewed in the framework of the present research in Bamako in January 2016, acknowledged that in vast areas of the region of Taoudenni the state was 'completely absent, and non-state actors endowed with considerable resources, including traffickers, might have filled this gap'.

32 Interviews with youth organisations from Timbuktu, Kidal and Gao conducted in Bamako in November 2013, and with former combatant from north Niger, conducted in Niamey in September 2015. Noteworthy, the strategy of social entrenchment pursued by drug barons, attested by the literature focusing on Latin American cartels, here combines smoothly with the specific social structure of African rural areas.

33 Both in Mali and in Niger, the amount of judicial proceedings currently underway or judged concerning crimes of corruption or money laundering is very limited and actually very opaque, especially concerning drug revenues. Albeit official statistics are lacking, anecdotal evidence suggests that no more than three or four cases have been trialled in Mali, as well as in Niger, in the last years. In Mali, many cases are stuck at the stage of inquiry, due to the lack of capacity or political determination. In Niger, the executive retains the authority to interfere with the investigations started by other competent bodies. The non-execution of judgements is also frequent. The challenges faced by law enforcement apparatuses can be considered as a further indicator of the economic and political impact of the profits derived from illicit trades in the region.

34 Interview with local researcher from Timbuktu, conducted in Bamako in May 2016.

35 Interview with UN expert in organised crime, conducted in Bamako in November 2014.

36 Interview with resident of Gao, conducted in Bamako in May 2016.

37 This view has been confirmed in the framework of several interviews, including with a professor of geography at the University of Niamey; two residents of Agadez; one local smuggler; and a EU security expert, conducted in Niamey in September 2015.

38 Interview with regional administrators, with criminal prosecutor from the PENI, and with Malian CBOs dealing with urban land acquisition, conducted in Bamako in November 2015.

39 Interview with Malian lawyer specialising in land disputes, conducted in Bamako in December 2016.
40 Interviews with administrators from the region of Gao; Malian CBOs dealing with urban land acquisition; criminal prosecutor specialising in economic and financial crimes, conducted in Bamako between November 2015 and January 2016. The criminal prosecutions concerning the Malian real estate agencies *Banga Immobilier* and *Kindy-Mali* represent cases in point here. Interestingly, both cases were concluded with the substantial impunity of the alleged perpetrators.
41 Interviews with key stakeholders of Malian civil society and community-based organisations, conducted in Bamako between November 2013 and May 2016.
42 Interview with Malian CBOs dealing with urban land acquisition, and with the Malian Cellule Nationale de Traitement des Informations Fiancières (CENTIF), conducted in Bamako in November 2015.
43 Interviews with peasant unions and local authorities, conducted in Nioro du Sahel, Bamako, Niamey and Tabalak in May 2016.
44 Interview with local and international experts on migration, conducted in Niamey in September 2015.

References

Agnew, J. 2002. *Place and Politics in Modern Italy*. Los Angeles: University of California Press.

Anders, H. 2015. Expanding arsenals. Insurgents arms in northern Mali. In: Small Arms Survey ed. *Weapons and the World*. Geneva: Small Arms Survey, 156–185.

Attar, A. 16 February 2013. Mauritanie: fin de parcours pour Mohamed Ould Abdel Aziz?. *Afrik.com*. Available from http://www.afrik.com/mauritanie-fin-de-parcours-pour-mohamed-ould-abdel-aziz (Accessed in August 2016).

Bensassi, S., Brockmeyer, A., Pellerin, M. and Raballand, G. 2015. *Commerce Algérie-Mali: la normalité de l'informalité*. Washington DC: World Bank.

Bigot, L. 10 October 2016. Au Niger, l'armée affaiblie par la paranoïa de son président. *Le Monde Afrique*. Available from http://www.lemonde.fr/afrique/article/2016/10/10/au-niger-l-armee-affaiblie-par-la-paranoia-de-son-president_5011114_3212.html (Accessed in December 2016).

Boas, M. 2014. Guns, money and prayers: AQIM's blueprint for securing control of northern Mali. *CTC Sentinel*, *7* (4), 1–6.

Boege, V., Brown, A., Clements, K. and Nolan, A. 2008. On hybrid political orders and emerging states: State formation in the context of 'fragility'. In: *Berghof Handbook for Conflict Transformation*, Online Version, October 2008.

Briscoe, I. 2014. Crime after jihad: armed groups, the State, and illicit business in post-conflict Mali. *Clingendael Report*. The Hague: The Clingendael Institute.

Cotula, L., Vermeulen, S., Leonard, R. and Keeley, J. 2009. *Land Grab or Development Opportunity? Agricultural Investment and International Land Deals in Africa*, London/Rome: IIED/FAO/IFAD.

Daniel, S. 2014. *Les Mafias du Mali*. Paris: Descartes et Cie.

Danish Demining Group. 2014. Evaluations des risques sécuritaires aux frontières. Région du Liptako-Gourma: Mali, Burkina et Niger, DDG.

Eckstein, H. 1975. Case study and theory in political science. In: Greenstein, F. and Polsby, N. eds. *The Handbook of Political Science*. Reading: Addison-Wesley Professional, 79–137.

Felbab-Brown, V. 18 July 2013. A state-building approach to the drug trade problem. *Brookings Institute Op-Ed*. Available from https://www.brookings.edu/opinions/a-state-building-approach-to-the-drug-trade-problem/ (Accessed in September 2016).

Global Initiative against Transnational Organised Crime. 2015. Libya: a growing hub for Criminal Economies and Terrorist Financing in the Trans-Sahara. *Policy Brief.* May 2015.

Global Witness. 2013. Logging in the shadows: How vested interests abuse shadow permits to evade forest sector reforms. An analysis of recent trends in Cameroon, Ghana, the Democratic Republic of Congo and Liberia. London: *Global Witness Report.*

Grain, 2012. *Squeezing Africa Dry: Behind Every Land Grab Is a Water Grab.* Barcelona: Grain.

Hall, T. 2013. Geographies of the illicit: globalization and organized crime. *Progress in Human Geography*, *37* (3), 366–385.

Hudson, R. 2014. Thinking through the relationships between legal and illegal activities and economies: spaces, flows and pathways. *Journal of Economic Geography*, *14* (4), 775–795.

IOM, 2014. *Fatal Journey. Tracking Lives Lost during Migration*. Geneva: International Organization of Migration.

Jerven, M. 2013. *Poor Numbers. How We Are Misled by African Development Statistics and What to Do about It*. Ithaca: Cornell University Press.

Julien, S. 2011. Le Sahel comme espace de transit des stupéfiants. Acteurs et conséquences politiques. *Hérodote*, *142* (6), 125–142.

Kaplan, R. 1994. The coming anarchy. How scarcity, crime, overpopulation, tribalism, and disease are rapidly destroying the social fabric of our planet. *The Atlantic Monthly*, *273* (2), 44–65.

Klute, G. 2011. From friends to enemies: Negotiating nationalism, tribal identities, and kinship in the fratricidal war of the Malian Tuareg. *L'Année du Maghreb*, 163–175.

Kohl, I. 2013. Afrod, le business touareg avec la frontière: nouvelles conditions et nouveaux défis. *Politique Africaine*, *132* (4), 139–159.

Lacher, W. September 2012. Organized crime and conflict in the Sahel-Sahara region. *The Carnegie Papers*, Washington DC: Carnegie Endowment for International Peace.

Lebovich, A. 15 March 2013. Mali's bad trip. Field notes from the West African drug trade. *Foreign Affairs*.

Lewis, D. 31 January 2014. Insight: Surge in cocaine trade undermines Conde's bid to revive Guinea. *Reuters*. Available from: http://www.reuters.com/article/us-guinea-drugs-insight-idUSBREA0U0EG20140131 (Accessed in May 2016).

McDougall, J. 2012. Frontiers, Borderlands, and Saharan World-History. In: McDougall J., Scheele J. eds., *Saharan Frontiers: Space and Mobility in Northwest Africa*. Bloomington: Indiana University Press, 73–90.

Murphy, A., Entrikin, N., Paasi, A., Macleod, G., Jonas, A. and Hudson, R. 2015. Bounded vs. open regions, and beyond. Critical perspectives on regional worlds and words. In: Paasi A. and Jones M. eds., *Regional Worlds and Words: Advancing the Geography of Regions*. London: Routledge, 6–15.

Nolte, K., Chamberlain, W. and Giger, M. 2016. *International Land Deals for Agriculture. Fresh Insights from the Land Matrix. Analytical Report II.* Rome: International Land Coalition.

Nordstrom, C. 2007. *Global Outlaws. Crime, Money, and Power in the Contemporary World*. Los Angeles: University of California Press.

Peduzzi, J.-L. 2010. Physionomie et enjeux des trafics dans la bande sahélo-saharienne. In: IFRI, *Le Maghreb dans son environnement régional et International*. Paris: IFRI.

Perry, A. 20 November 2014. Blood Lines: How Europe's cocaine habits funds beheadings. *Newsweek*. Available from: http://europe.newsweek.com/blood-lines-how-cocaine-nights-fund-beheadings-285545?rm=eu (Accessed September 2016).

Pliez, O. 2011. *Les cités du désert: des villes sahariennes aux saharatowns*. Marseille: Presses Universitaires Marseille.

Rafei, L. 29 October 2014. Africa's urban population growth: trends and projections. *The World Bank Data Blog*. Available from: http://blogs.worldbank.org/opendata/africa-s-urban-population-growth-trends-and-projections (Accessed December 2016).

Raineri, L. December 2015. Il Miracolo della Pax Mafiosa in Niger. *Limes*, pp. 83–94. Available from: http://www.limesonline.com/cartaceo/il-miracolo-della-pax-mafiosa-in-niger?prv=true&refresh_ce (Accessed 30 June 2017).

Raineri, L. and Strazzari, F. 2015. State, secession and jihad: The micro-political economy of conflict in North Mali. *African Security*, *8* (4), 249–271.

Reitano, T. and Shaw, M. 2014. People's perspectives of organised crime in West Africa and the Sahel. *ISS Paper* 254, Institute for Security Studies, April 2014.

Reno, W. 2000. Shadow states and the political economy of civil war. In: Berdal M. and Malone D. eds. *Greed and Grievance. Economic Agendas in Civil Wars*. London: Lynne Rienner, pp. 43–68.

Rullia, M. C., Savioria, A. and D'Odorico, P. 2013. Global land and water grabbing. *Proceedings of the National Academy of Sciences*, *110* (3), 892–897.

Scheele, J. 2009. Tribus, etats et fraude: la région frontalière algéro-malienne. *Etudes Rurales 184* (2), pp. 79–94.

Scheele, J. 2011. Circulations marchandes au Sahara, entre licite et illicite, *Hérodote*, *142* (6) 143–162.

Scheele, J. 2012. *Smugglers and Saints of the Sahara: Regional Connectivity in the Twentieth Century*. Cambridge: Cambridge University Press.

Shaw, M. and Kemp, W. 2012. *Spotting the Spoilers: A Guide to Analyzing Organized Crime in Fragile States*. New York: International Peace Institute.

Shaw, M. and Reitano, T. 2013. The evolution of organised crime in Africa. *Institute for Security Studies Paper*, *244*, April 2013.

Shaw, M., Reitano, T. and Hunter, M. 2014. Comprehensive assessment of drug trafficking and organized crime in west and central Africa, *Report to the African Union*, January 2014.

Snyder, R. and Duran-Martinez, A. 2009. Does illegality breed violence? Drug trafficking and state-sponsored protection rackets. *Crime Law and Social Change*, *52*, 253–273.

Strazzari, F. 2014. Captured or capturing? Narcotics and political instability along the "African Route" to Europe. *The European Journal of Organized Crime*, *1* (2), 5–34.

Tilly, C. 1985. War making and state making as organized crime. In: Evans, P., Rueschemeyer, D. and Skocpol, T. eds., *Bringing the State Back In*. Cambridge: Cambridge University Press, 169–191.

UN Human Rights Council. 2010. Large-scale land acquisitions and leases: a set of minimum principles and measures to address the human rights challenge. *Report of the Special Rapporteur on the Right to Food*, 21/10/2010, [A/HRC/13/33/Add.2].

UNODC. 2008. *Drug Trafficking as a Security Threat in West Africa*. Vienna.

UNODC. 2011. *The Transatlantic Cocaine Market*. Research Paper, Vienna.

UNODC. 2013. *Transnational Organized Crime in West Africa: A Threat Assessment*, Vienna.

Utas, M. (ed.) 2012. *African Conflict and Informal Power, Big Men and Networks*. London: Zed Books.

Vorrath, J. 2015. Organized crime and development. Challenges and policy options in West Africa's fragile states. *SWP Research Paper* 9, Berlin, December 2015.

World Bank. 2010. *Rising Global Interest in Farmland. Can it yield sustainable and equitable benefits?*. Washington DC, World Bank.

3 Invisible journeys across India–Bangladesh borders and bubbles of corrupt networks

Stories of cross-border rural–urban migration and economic linkages

Hosna J. Shewly and Md. Nadiruzzaman

Introduction

Illegal movement of people across international borders and the invisible presence of illegal migrants in various megacities' economic activities largely depend on economic globalisation, war, destitution and a state's capacity to rule its international borders. Unlike south–north migration, cultural similarity and geographic proximity are significant migration drivers for south–south migration (Nawyn, 2016, p. 83; Samaddar, 1999). Such factors are also central for ever-evolving illegal cross-border networks and migration. And, it needs to be acknowledged that simple macroeconomic differences between migration sending and receiving countries can only portray a partial picture of the complex realities that drive migration (Van Hear *et al.*, 2012). The rise of cross-border illegal movements not only raises academic curiosity but also generates political rhetoric between migration sending and receiving countries. Bangladeshi migrants in India are a matter of huge bilateral controversy at state level, while India, without reference to any valid survey, expresses concerns about the influx of millions of Bangladeshi illegal migrants that Bangladesh absolutely nullifies. Thus, the existence of illegal migrants is highly disputed bilaterally, as are their eventful stories.

Bilateral migration statistics between India and Bangladesh offer fascinating evidence. It is reported that 500,000 Indians illegally work in Bangladesh, while India claims that annually 25,000[1] Bangladeshis enter India with tourist visas who never return (Jamaluddin, 2009). It is worth mentioning here that Bangladesh was fifth among the top fifteen remittance sending nations to India in 2013, after the UAE, Saudi Arabia, USA and UK (The Economic Times, 2014). Significantly, however, illegal Bangladeshis in India have long been a concern among Indian politicians and academia. As part of security concerns, India fenced more than 3,000 km of its land border with Bangladesh and border guards are vigilant round the clock. Unsurprisingly, such measures could not stop cross-border movements. Besides, the number of people migrating to another country does not distinguish the patterns, process and drivers of migration. Here, in this chapter, we are concentrating on short-term and circulatory migration of people who are vulnerable to natural disasters.

This ethnographic research builds on experiences of many cross-border trespassers, brokers and analyses oral stories of their journey. This research seeks to understand corrupt spaces and flows from retrospective memories of peoples' journey across the India–Bangladesh border – processes of their migration decision, networks, destinations, challenges, expectations and survivals in everyday life. It is not the growing ease of travel, but growing cross-border illegal networks that contribute mostly to such migration. The focus on *journeying* and methods of illegal and provisional migration from one country's coastal zone to the other country's megacities can represent corrupt spaces and flows from three perspectives – organised networks of illegal migration, corrupt government agencies/agents in different scales/locations and different bubbles of economies involved in it. Thus, this chapter theoretically contextualises corrupt spaces and flows through short-term and circulatory migration. In doing so, it also contributes to the cross-section of border and migration literature by showing, (i) the cross-border *journey* of migration as a significant methodological aspect in understanding the process of migration; (ii) circulatory illegal migration, a less attended but important part of migration; and (iii) positive aspects of circulatory illegal migration in migrant's livelihoods and their places of origin.

The structure of the chapter is as follows. It begins with a theoretical focus on actors of legal and illegal border crossings and migration. The following section will then concentrate on academic scholarship on mobilities and migration across the India–Bangladesh border. Then, the chapter moves onto the methodological aspects of this research followed by an empirical section on illegal movements across India–Bangladesh borders. A discussion section will analyse the connections and contributions of the empirical findings to existing knowledge on illicit/illegal networks. And, finally the conclusion summarises the findings.

International borders, illegal networks and circulatory migration

Here, in this chapter, the illegal involves a range of individual and networked actions/activities related to illegal human migration movements across India–Bangladesh borders and big and growing cities which create a complex impact on traditional aspects of state authority and control over international borders and mobility. Illegal migrants are generally attracted to rising Indian megacities where they have better employment opportunities, hence our focus is on big cities. Cross-border illegal movement and migration have long been considered as key focuses in international security, border, migration and mobilities literature. Here, we focus on various actors who facilitate or restrict cross-border illegal journeys and the economies involved in them.

A vast majority of interdisciplinary literature considers border crossing points and state border agents as a centre of attention, examining the effectiveness of border security measures to curtail illegal movement, especially in post 9/11 contexts. Scholars have shown border agents are most powerful actors in deciding border crossers' fate and creating a space of exception where human and refugee rights are at stake (Salter, 2008; Mountz, 2008; Lyon, 2003). The use of advanced technology, identity documents and delocalisation of border checks have also developed a new network of actors and algorithm methods managing the international border (see Balibar, 2004; Amoore, 2006; Vaughan-Williams, 2009; Walters, 2006). Nevertheless, border walls and fences perform new materialities of security paradigms, although critical scholarship questions whether these are as effective as expected or merely politically choreographed ineffective missions by the state elites (see Jones, 2012). Ironically, a vast majority of state borders are unguarded or thinly guarded, while overwhelming security measures are taken at the border checkpoints (see Johnsons and Jones, 2016). While these important critical scholarships reflect the grey zones of border security networks and worries about border securitisation intentions, the focus remains on state actors and border trespassers.

Illegal actors and their networks have also received diverse theoretical attentions in social science literature. Scholars consider the oppositional aspects of legal and illegal or/and often focus on how legal economies can fight against illegal economies to stop trafficking (see Shelley and Bain, 2015). Others have shown how ever growing transnational smugglers, human traffickers or drug dealers exploit people and find ways through the gaps in border security measures which are often prominent in conflict or war zones (Niam, 2006; Herbert, 2014). Another academic centre of attention, on the other hand, is on borderland realities and the nexus between legal and illegal. As such, academics have theorised the zones of ambiguity and illegality in the borderland. Heyman and Smart (1999, p. 1) argue that the 'state law and eviction of state law should be studied together'. Besides, these illegal networks are not always centralised organised groups but rather fluid ones involving a vast population of participants for mutual advantage (Campbell, 2013). Our research findings echo scholars who have shown that illegal actors are not isolated but rather connected to legal actors, often border security agents.

Here, we show the 'circuits' of corrupt places and economic activities through illegal migrants' circulatory journey across India–Bangladesh borders. This can provide a wider and meaningful interconnected picture of the different stakeholders, including state and illicit actors across borders. Understanding circulatory migration through migrant journeys – to a migrant receiving country and further journeys back to the origin country – and the impact of such migration on their livelihood and wellbeing contributing to the local economy are under-theorised domains of international migration and border literatures. It provides an opportunity to understand the associations between 'economic flows and the places through which it passes' (Hall, 2013, p. 379). The following section shows how mobilities and migration across this border have been examined in the literature.

Mobilities and migration across the India–Bangladesh border

The India–Bangladesh border, the fifth longest land border (4,095 kilometres) of the world, is also considered to be one of the most dangerous borders of the world. On average, Indian border guards, Border Security Force (BSF), kill 50 Bangladeshis every year (see BBC Bangla 2016). Human Rights Watch (2010) identifies BSF as a 'trigger happy' force because of their aggressive use of power to shoot civilians at the Bangladesh border. And Jones (2009, p. 787) defines BSF as 'agents of exception' because of their securitisation process in the borderland by converting farmlands into spaces of exception[2]. Still, diverse mobilities and migration across this border have continued since the partition of 1947.[3] No-man's land does not apply to this heavily populated borderland, as local cultivators own and cultivate all the lands up to zero lines of the border as observed during our participant observation (also see Van Schendel, 2005; Jones, 2009). Mundane social and agricultural activities around the zero line, thus, not only provide easy hideouts for smugglers and traffickers in disguise, but also accelerate border casualties when people accidentally enter India.

Bengal was a single administrative, social and cultural entity before the partition of India in 1947 and the division of British India into India and Pakistan coincides with the creation of an international border through Bengal. Staying in Delhi, without any physical survey and only using some outdated maps, Sir Cyril Radcliffe decided the fate of voiceless millions living in an active delta (for detail, see Van Schendel, 2005; Chatterji 1999; Hodson 1985). It is worth mentioning here that the international border through Bengal did not strictly follow the religion criteria, as Van Schendel (2005) shows only 26 per cent of the borderline separated a Muslim majority area in East Pakistan from a Hindu majority one in India. Such creation of the border triggered an extraordinary movement of people across the Bengal border to avoid violence and brutality. A growing scholarship on the partition consequences shows mass displacement, minority identity and shift of Hindus to west Bengal (see Das, 1995; Feldman, 2003; Banerjee, 2010). A gap still remains in the literature about the Muslims' journeys to east Pakistan (the only exception is Rahman and Van Schendal, 2003). Beyond this dominant discourse of violent displacement and the vulnerability of Hindu minority identity, Sanyal's (2014) take on hegemonic roles of refugee Hindus in west Bengal and the construction of 'Hindu space' by uprooting Muslims not only provides a new insight into post-migration actions, but also shows territorial rights based on religion. Not all post-partition migrations are forced, there are numerous cross-border labour migrants and cross-border settlers after marriage as well as migration for better living conditions or maintaining status with in society (Rahman and Van Schendal, 2003; Sanyal, 2009). Some permanent migration is cumbersome to distinguish as it happens slowly, invisibly and unofficially. For example, the Bangladesh Bureau of Statistics (BBS) shows Hindus were 22 per cent in the 1951 census, falling to 14 per cent in 1974, and even lower, to only 8.4 per cent in the 2011 census (*The Hindu*, 2016).

Muslims migrating to India, especially to northeast India, is another concern in India leading to political rhetoric and national election agendas for removing illegal immigrants to Bangladesh. Indian political elites define 3.2 million Bangladeshis as living in India (see Sur, 2014). The idea of fencing the border was first proposed in India by the politicians of Assam in 1964 before the independence of Bangladesh. There was a protest in Assam that illegal immigrants from East Pakistan were causing a remarkable change in the local demography (tribal-nontribal ratio). Soon after the suggestion of completely sealing the border, the government of India decided to prevent infiltration by putting barbed wire fencing in selected areas (Bhasin, 2003). This was primarily a political statement and the fencing project resumed after a violent anti-foreigner movement in Assam in 1979. The movement was for the deportation of all Bengali and Hindi speaking people settled there from Bangladesh and other parts of India. Similarly, other provinces of India adjacent to Bangladesh, West Bengal and Tripura wanted government action to stop infiltration from Bangladesh. Following this demand, the government considered the erection of a fence in West Bengal, Tripura and Assam to cover a 3,200 km border (Bhasin, 2003). India's fencing project covered construction of single to double wired composite fences fitted with sophisticated electronic devices, especially on the India-Pakistan border. The project included 2,800 km of border roads and 24 km of bridges along the India–Bangladesh border (Van Schendel, 2005).

Scholars have theorised illegal migration across the India–Bangladesh border from the perspectives of the state's territorial sovereignty, paper citizenship, or demographic invasion (Samaddar, 1999; Sadik, 2009). In a very well-articulated book on 'paper citizens', Sadik (2009, p. IX) makes a powerful argument that immigrants might be illegal or unauthorised, but they are seldom undocumented. He shows how illegal migrants from Bangladesh are gaining and performing citizenship in India's megacities using fake documents. While the literature is rich in theorising diverse kinds of migration from Bangladesh to India since partition, other significant aspects of illegal human movement remain unexplored; such as, the material benefits of all actors and the hidden political economy which stimulates the whole process and keeps all the actors in this business. Most importantly, the temporary nature of illegal migration and migrants' journeys back to their homes have been entirely overlooked in this rich scholarship on borders and migration in the region. Therefore, tens of thousands of people, who are continuously moving across the border, their stories, challenges, survival strategies, sighs, successes, economic contribution and everything, remain unaccounted. This research is an endeavour to document their circulatory migration journey.

Methodology and people under study

The field research followed two phases. In its first phase, both the authors conducted separate ethnographic field research from September 2009 to April 2010 on mobility of the northwestern borderland enclave dwellers in India and Bangladesh and on vulnerabilities of cyclone-wrecked communities in two coastal villages in southern Bangladesh. As part of their PhD projects, the first author conducted four in-depth interviews and ten informal group discussions with illegal migrants in a Delhi slum. And, the second author conducted several interviews with returned migrants in his field sites. The authors had their joint fieldwork for ten weeks (February–April 2015) in two villages of the southwestern coast. These villages were chosen as they have very strong India connections and, most importantly, the second author has already gained trust within these coastal communities for maintaining continuous engagement since 2009 through ethnographic PhD fieldwork and two postdoctoral researches. Living with these communities for a relatively long period of time, working there as a school teacher, understanding the local power dynamics, participating in their social and familial events, having been distinguished (as harmless) from other 'outsiders' such as NGO workers, government officials, journalists and philanthropists, the second author was in an advantageous position to use observations and to better understand the local context. The names of villages were anonymised to protect the identity of the respondents.

Rather than being guided by a list of predetermined questions, we preferred to be a part of the setting to be studied with an objective of participating in the wider detail of the subject matter. We gathered data in two different ways: (a) observations (Arens and Beurden, 1977) and (b) learning through talking to people (Crang and Cook, 2007, p. 16), in this case informal in-depth interview at household and community level. We maintained a research diary to take notes. We spent time at local tea stalls, local government council office and local market places and such public places.

Illegal journeys of migrants

This empirical section strives to elaborate on why, where and how people migrate. According to UNEP's Geo Assessment Report (2016), more than 42 million people in the Asia and Pacific region were displaced during 2010–11 due to extreme weather events. Bangladesh is one of the most susceptible to these environmental stresses in the whole region. The southern coast of Bangladesh, our main research site, is often referred to as the Climate Change Ground Zero[4] because it is highly susceptible to sea level rise, increased salinity, arsenic contamination, tidal surges, floods and water logging. High population growth, reduced arable land, inadequate income earning opportunities and changed land use together force local people into subsistence livelihoods. Income earning opportunities have shrunk further with challenged access to resources, particularly for the grassroots. This changing environment of scarcity of livelihood opportunities triggers migration decisions. Faruk (2015) estimates the number of this migration could reach up to 15 million in Bangladesh by 2050.

In Bangladesh, 54 per cent of coastal communities are functionally landless and more than 30 per cent are absolutely landless[5] (Jentoft *et al.*, 2010). Fishing has always been the occupation of last resort (Allison and Ellis, 2001; Béné, 2003; Deb, 2009), an open offer from nature to anyone, whose other livelihood options are diminished (Alam, 2001). Table 3.1 shows a dramatic increase of fishers over the last few years in one of our research sites. Over the last few decades, land ownership has declined because of embedded economic polarisation in the society as well as riverbank erosion along one of the research sites. Though land erosion was not a problem at other research sites, increasing population pressure on a small piece of arable land drove many to find alternative options for making their own living. Livelihood options, alternative to cultivation, available around our field sites are mainly wage-earning in farmlands and from local development

Table 3.1 Change in dependence on fishery resources (Upazila BBS Office)

Year	*2007–08*	*2008–09*	*2009–10*	*2010–11*	*2011–12*	*2012–13*	*2013–14*	*2014–15*
No. of fishing-dependent families	450	1,000	2,000	3,250	3,250	3,250	3,250	3,246
No. of fishers	925	1,965	2,500	5,290	5,290	5,290	5,290	5,284

works, fishing in local open water bodies and collecting timber and non-timber resources from the Sundarbans. Otherwise, temporary or permanent economic migration is also a choice (Rigg, 2007). As mentioned earlier, there is no systematic shift from one kind of livelihood opportunity to another, nor do they often pick one from a range of choices; rather people take on whatever is available to them (Ellis, 2000). However, decline in one livelihood certainly puts pressure on other available opportunities, as options are limited.

Migration is one of those limited opportunities. Data from a very recent fieldwork (February–April 2015) shows that 25 households have permanently moved away from the studied river island (out of 170 households) since the devastation of Cyclone Sidr (2007), and 22 of them have moved to the mainland across the river, where they have their ancestral roots and kinship network. More importantly, out of these 25 migrated households, 20 have migrated over the last three years. Combining both the field sites, until March 2015, a total of 368 people migrated from their ancestral home, out of which 161 people permanently settled elsewhere and 207 went away as temporary economic migrants. Interestingly, more than half of the total migrants (220 out of 368 people) have moved away from their home very recently, within less than a decade. Besides, the number of temporary economic migrants, both nationally and internationally, has also sharply increased. Migration is certainly a signal of what is happening on the ground. This could be due to a diminishing sense of place – people gave up and moved on. It also could be a sign of inhabitants' positive desire to change their wellbeing with the support of remittances (see Black *et al.*, 2011).

As mentioned earlier, we interviewed people from two villages who have very strong connections to India. Each village is divided into eight to nine clusters depending on the concentration of houses. These clusters of houses are called 'para', where households are normally tied within an ancestral kinship network and have fair ideas of their neighbours' present locations. Informal group discussions were conducted in these clusters, to estimate the number of migrants and their destinations. It was interesting to see two distinctive characteristics between the two villages in close proximity. In one village, almost one in six households rely on remittances from India. The other village, a few miles down the coast, also has dependence on remittance income, but they are internal, mainly from two big cities, Dhaka and Chittagong. We found that people often move to a new place through their networks and that is probably one of the main reasons for these two villages, despite being in very close proximity, having two different migration destinations.

This research builds on stories and experiences of folks who have been frequently trespassing the India–Bangladesh border for many years. A significant portion of these displaced people happen to trespass the border and move to urban slums in Mumbai, Delhi, Kolkata, Hariyana, Bangalore, Goa and other Indian cities. They have their own social networks set along the way to their destinations. Being trespassers, their legal work permit gets repudiated, which increases their attraction to employers as cheap labour. Below is a brief story of Ilias who rode a motorbike for the second author during his field visits since 2009.

Ilias, a motorbike rider and small trader at the local Upazila (sub-district) market, leads a solvent life with his wife, two children and elderly parents. Things were very different when Ilias was a teenager. He was one of three brothers, and his father was a daily wage earner. They used to squeeze into a small hut on government land and hardly had three square meals on a regular basis. Being the eldest, Ilias was taken out from school when he was just 14 and engaged with his father in manual labour to raise the family income. Unable to cope with this, Ilias moved to India with the help of a broker in exchange for two hundred and fifty taka (approximately US$3). Since then, for the last 20 years, he has travelled to India many times, working in different cities across India. He has had positive experiences in India, which inspired his other friends, who later joined him in successive journeys. Now, he has his own land, house, transport and small business. He has contacts in different border points as well as in India, which can get others through and find a job for them in India. We were 10–12 people listening to Ilias's story on his rooftop on an autumn evening, where other than the two authors, all of them had stories like Ilias and several of them had travelled together to India at different times.

Border trespassing is coordinated by a network of brokers from a home village to the host employer. The first-time travellers are transferred from one broker to the other at different points. Travellers pay money to the first broker, who manages and negotiates contracts with other brokers and local border guards. Illegal trespassers are locally called *dhur*. During the time of our field visit in early 2015, the average rate per *dhur* transfer was 30–40 US dollars. One broker handles 15–20 *dhur* and they all march to the border together. At the border, all local brokers hand over their *dhur* to a different set of brokers, who negotiate the price with border guards across the border, and establish contact with brokers on the other side. For each *dhur*, border guards receive 10 US dollars; the brokers are not very honest in making such deals; as a broker confesses, 'if we pay for ten *dhur*, we take 15 across the border. During the rush of crossing border gates, border guards could not count the actual number of crossers' (Interview: 25 March 2015). The southwestern section, like most parts of India–Bangladesh border, is controlled by barbed wire fences, watch towers and regular patrols. And border gates are fully operated by Indian border security forces.[6] Border transfers always take place under the cover of darkness in the transition between two shifts of duties of border guards. People run across marshlands risking their lives to secure their living. Very often, a couple of hundred *dhur* cross the border in one transfer.

Not all of them are successful in this race. Those that make through the crossing complete the rest of their journey with their brokers on the other side of the border. Often female migrants become targets for sexual assault by border guards. Niaz explains:

> [I]n my third or fourth trip to India, a young couple were travelling with us. In a dark night, we arrived in an open field along the border, waiting for the broker's signal to cross the border. Suddenly, the broker alarmed us that border force is approaching and told us to run. While all of us were scattered, running for our own life, the lady got missing from the back. She never turned up. Her husband was screaming like a mad. We all knew, she became a prey to border guards.
>
> (Interview: 1 March 2015)

We heard similar stories a number of times from different *dhur*. One of them even noticed such negotiation between the broker and the border guards.

This southern part of the border divides a deltaic coast and the Sundarbans, the largest mangrove forest in the world. Thus, natural features, such as rivers, marsh and and low-lying areas, are not suitable for installing barbed wire fences. In such areas, border movements are controlled by border security patrolling. Munni, a housewife and mother of a six-year-old girl, in her first ever trip to India, was with a group of *dhur* who were using a river route. Suddenly, they recognised a patrol boat nearby and all of them jumped into the water and hid under water plants. After staying in the water for several hours, when they had an all clear signal from their broker, they boarded back on to the boat and headed towards the land. On the other side of the border, they walked until dawn to reach to a local transport terminal. From there, the *dhur* team travelled via Sealdah, to Hawra and finally to Bangalore. From Bangalore, the team were split up and sent to their pre-set jobs. Munni joined as a domestic maid in an apartment block and worked for six years with the same landlord. During that time, she used to come back at least twice every year through those illegal routes. Within the first two years of her work and travel back and forth, she became a broker of *dhur*. She took her husband and two of her brothers on her second trip and hooked them up with a scrap recycling business.

From domestic work, Munni saved 1,000 US dollars every year. She also had additional commission from working as broker. After six years of work, she and her husband together saved 15,000 US dollars. They invested a portion of that money to buy land and build a house for themselves. The rest of the money they invested in buying agricultural lands, which they lease out to landless farmers. For the first time, Munni's parents, who were the primary carers for her daughter, Asma, moved to a self-owned property. Asma is now 13, and Munni decided to settle back home to give more time to her daughter. Her husband, Selim, will work in India for another few years and then will settle back home. He wishes to run in the next local government election as a council member for his *ward* (village).

Nowadays, Munni goes on and off to India if she can organise clients, a team of *dhur*. She guides them to their destinations and comes back home. The most unique part of it, which supposedly drives clients or *dhur* to this career path, is that a *dhur* does not have to pay the initial transfer cost (30–40 US dollars) upfront. There is an arrangement of paying this service charge later in instalments as soon as the *dhur* is in a job. Thus, in many cases, this is an initial investment for brokers, which gives them a regular income later. Also, as many of the *dhur* informed us, they could not afford to pay 30–40 US dollars, when they first signed up to this job. A secured job at a destination and a flexible payment system together make this type of arrangement very attractive. For many of these *dhur*, Dhaka and Chittagong, the two largest employment hubs in Bangladesh, are very far and difficult for them to reach, since they do not have any contacts to these two cities. On top of that, in their view, as Indian currency is stronger than the Bangladeshi taka, they can see the tangible growth of their assets, when they send/bring remittances to Bangladesh.

Once they are on the Indian side of the border, since they do not have legal work permits, they are cheap labour and thus have a high demand in the labour market. Female *dhur* normally get engaged in domestic work. Their illegal presence helps raise their attraction in the job market, particularly to their landlords. Being illegal migrants, they refrain from exposure on the open job market, which allows their employers (landlords) to offer a cheap long-term deal. Again, for migrants, domestic jobs are hassle free, as security forces do not crack down on them. In construction industries and factories in growing cities, a *dhur* can be more easily exploited than a genuine permit holder. Their complexion and physical appearance are similar to Indians. They can easily blend in with the rest of the population. However, they are often chased by the special security forces and by the police, particularly when they are identified by local police's informers. These informers' generally work as a connection between the city police and *dhur*. They negotiate a regular bribe deal with city police for not arresting illegal migrants, keep city police informed about illegal migrants who have not signed up to this regular bribe payment system, and negotiate a deal to bail illegal migrants out from police custody. The majority of informants mentioned that if they miss this regular payment, they become victims of the city police. If they are caught by the special security forces, they are eventually deported to Bangladesh. In the case of their being arrested by the police, they end up in jail. There is a network of brokers who help to bail them out from jail.

There are also bubbles of fake brokers who take advantage of people's helplessness. When Amol, an illegal Bangladeshi migrant, was arrested in Delhi in 2010, he contacted a broker for 30,000 taka (US $375). Amol's family borrowed this money with high interest rate from a loan shark. On receipt of this money, the broker did nothing. Amol served two years jail sentence under the Foreigner's Act and then was deported back to Bangladesh. He came back home jobless and with a burden of huge debt.

From migrants' personal accounts, there are both positive and negative stories and it is hard to tell which is higher in number. However, two things were echoed very commonly across all informants: i) their migration decision at the very first instance is triggered by desperation; and ii) all through the journey, they live an anxious, alert and vigilant life. They understand there are challenges, including the worst one of becoming a victim of border shooting, still they hope for sufficient savings to begin a better life back in home.

Discussion

Human mobility from stressed habitats is inevitable (Adger *et al.*, 2009; Faruk, 2015; Islam *et al.*, 2014; van Hear, *et al.*, 2012). Oliver-Smith and Shen (2009) reviews 321 research works on global migration, published between 1958 and 2008. Interestingly, those research works have major focuses on different migration drivers, particularly environmental stresses, war and economic challenges. About one-fourth of those papers are in-depth case studies on Bangladesh. This signifies the reason for migration being such an important topic for this country. Warner *et al.* (2012) led a research project, titled, *Where the rain falls*, in eight countries to understand the relationship between food security, rainfall and population mobility. This research was conducted on small geographic locations in each country. In Bangladesh, its research sites were the two small local government units (Union[7]) of Kurigram, a northern district, which have a strong mobility network with Munshiganj, a central district (Ahmed *et al.*, 2012). Lu *et al.* (2016) have shown this migration pattern at national level. They used cell phone data and analysed anonymised call data record to understand population movements across Bangladesh over a two year period. All other research on migration is either on internal migration or on international labour migration. This chapter introduces illegal cross-border circulatory migration, which is not a new trend, but has rarely been addressed earlier in migration literature.

As we see in theoretical and historical background discussion, existing literatures have concentrated around the beginning or at the end of their journey – why do people migrate (Adger *et al.*, 2009; Faruk, 2015; Islam *et al.*, 2014; Oliver-Smith and Shen, 2009; van Hear, *et al.*, 2012) or how migrants are doing (Banerjee, 2010; Sadik, 2009; Sanyal, 2009). There is hardly any attention to migrants' journeys to their desired destinations. The description of journeys, as outlined in this chapter, joins these two ends together. As shown in this chapter, illegal migrants' journeys are the most significant aspect of illegal migrationhood, as Niaz, Amol, Munni and others feel and experienced risk, uncertainty, disappointment, achievement and/or emotional strain. At the heart of the unauthorised journey, there are several actors who encourage/lure, facilitate/exploit and, most importantly, control such journeys. A central focus on why, when and how a journey actually happens, can reveal rich experiential aspects of actors involved in it which can be a very useful concept and methodological approach for the scholars working on migration, mobilities and corrupt networks and flows.

Circulatory migration journeys provide several grey areas in relation to licit/illicit and legal/illegal practices and perceptions as such 'the threshold between legal and illegal are not clearly definable' (Chiodelli *et al.* 2017, p. 5). Firstly, local construction of licitness over illegality. Although unauthorised migration is illegal, people in the research sites consider it socially legitimate though risky. For example, people were open and frank sharing their circulatory migration journeys in public places like local tea stalls and everybody knew about others' whereabouts. On the contrary, when we met a broker, who is now an elected member of a local council, he took us in the middle of a rice field so that none could hear us. Later, we met him in a different place away from his locality, while he was more open and was not seemingly worried about anyone overhearing us. From several such observations, it appeared to us that licitness and illicitness are subjective and relationally defined (Chiodelli *et al.* 2017) and are influenced by individual's socio-political circumstances and their judgement on the interface of licit and illicit activities. Most decisively, it is not all what the state decides to be legal or illegal, rather how the people construct licit and illicit for their livelihood (Van Schendel and Abraham, 2005). In addition, the borderland's historic and economic circumstances, and borderlanders' perception of legal/illegal and licit/illicit are important factors in this consideration. Seven decades on from partition, still borderland people are not keen visiting friends and families on other sides of the borders with visas. To them, it is irrational and unnecessary to make a 150-mile trip to Dhaka to process a tourist visa (which can be refused) to meet their friends and families living just a hundred yards away across the border.

Secondly, this chapter brings, (i) a grey zone where legal and illegal constitute intrinsic parts of corrupt networks and flows at local, national and international scales; this grey zone connects local *dhur* with Indian mega city employers through different layers of legal and illegal actors; and, (ii) ambiguous responses from the nation-state whose territorial sovereignty has been invaded by this parallel process and actors of corrupt networks. Corrupt state agencies are accomplices and the states have not taken any initiative to stop employers from offering jobs to any *dhur*. Instead, big corporates and builders take benefits out of it, by employing *dhur* at a minimum rate. To the people, it is also a matter that state agents including border guards, city police, etc. are part of this network. Raineri (2017, this volume) explains drug trafficking in the Sahara desert, where drug traffickers are the nodes of a large network and are apparently static. The nodes operate their own gangs to get connected with other nodes. In our case, the setup is completely different. Here, we see institutions, such as border guards, law enforcing agencies and employers, are the nodes that *dhur* weave through. As we see, from our interviews, stories and field notes, they have repeated experience of completing this circulatory migration and their main objective was to develop their material wellbeing. We see this common trajectory to all the cases we explained in the earlier section.

And finally, it reveals that the illegal migrants also use their agency. Unlike forced refugee migration, these people negotiate and make their way out through corrupt networks and flows. It reflects their agency rather than completely being held within the illegal actors' hands. Furthermore, such journeys are an agency of change and a transformative event for the life of migrants (Benezer and Zetter, 2015, p. 303). Significantly, however, a successful circulatory illegal migration very often encourages other journeys and roles in the corrupt networks and flows. As such, Munni has turned to a broker from a *dhur*. From a subject of illegal flows, she became an agent of corrupt networks. This is also linked to local constructions of licitness. Perhaps, subject and agent transformation is higher in this case because of such circulatory illegal migration is not considered illicit in the borderlands.

Conclusion

This chapter has shown the circuits of corrupt spaces and flows through eventful journeys of circulatory migrants across India–Bangladesh border. It shows how different fluid actors participate in these circuits. This research, thus, shows the tensions between strict state surveillances across the borders on illegal human movement and a thriving business of illegal migration. At the same time, it represents a 'systematic symbiotic relationship between legal and illegal' (Hudson, 2014, p. 775). As mentioned earlier, we need to keep in mind that state ascribed borders and the concepts of licit and illicitness are not same in the borderland. People have their own perceptions, practices and necessities, which drive many to cross international border illegally.

This chapter tells the story of circulatory migration journeys from Bangladesh to India, where *dhur* use their knowledge on different corrupt places and weave through those places to benefit their livelihood and wellbeing. The stories of Munni and Ilias demonstrate how their drive for an 'illegal' circulatory migration has paid off in their life and wellbeing. Though we have consistently used 'illegal' while describing their journey, their world view on 'corrupt spaces' may differ from how the state defines it. To them, everyday challenges and anxiety that they have been facing are even worse than the risks they take to cross the border. To them, the state does not mean much, as they are marginalised, cornered and abandoned in terms of their social safety nets and wellbeing. Their stories also unmask the unexplored aspects of circulatory migration and challenges stereotypes of Bangladeshi Muslim migrants permanently settling in to India.

The people living in the Bengal borderlands exist below the poverty level and the principal economic activities include agriculture, wage labour and trade. Borderlands between India and Bangladesh are completely impoverished, threatened, marginalised and economically deprived (see Van Schendel, 2005). As we see in the above empirical section, an established network of *dhur* and brokers has existed for long time. As long as this impoverished nature of the borderland exists, illicit networks will potentially lure the marginal communities to become part of such networks.

Notes

1 This figure is about Bangladeshis who visit India to obtain a legal permit and do not come back. However, there is another group who cross the border illegally with an intention to work in India. There is no valid referenced data on them. In different Indian literatures and newspapers, there are anecdotal estimate of 1–2.5 million illegal Bangladeshi migrants working in India.

2 India–Bangladesh border, in many areas, runs through agricultural lands and settlements. As a part of the securitisation of the border, the BSF increasingly exercised their ability to violently impose their authority in the political border.

3 The end of British rule in 1947 led to a division of India first and foremost on the basis of religion. The demand of Pakistan was the outcome of three factors-such as continuing religious feuds, the uneven economic development providing some real basis of fears of 'Hindu Imperialism' and dispute between the Congress and the Muslim League over power sharing in postcolonial India. Partition and the cartographic procedure to divide Bengal followed 'religion and other factors' criteria. The 'other factor' was vague and contributed to disputes over the demand of territory within the boundary commission. Ultimately, the Commission failed to agree upon the best way to divide the united Bengal which, eventually, led Radcliffe, the Chairman of the Commission, to take the responsibility of bisecting Bengal. For detail on partition procedures and its consequences see Van Schendel (2005), Chatterji (1999), Hodson (1985).

4 http://asiafoundation.org/in-asia/2010/04/21/from-bangladesh-climate-change-ground-zero/

5 If a household possesses less than half an acre of agricultural land, that is considered insufficient to produce enough to maintain a household living. This group is called functionally landless. And absolute landless are households who do not have any agricultural land whatsoever. Both of them are considered extreme poor groups and are entitled to apply for government lands.

6 The BSF and the Border Guards Bangladesh (BGB) defend the respective sides of the border, which is carried out from the Border Outposts (BOPs). For BGB, a BOP normally comprises 15–20 foot soldiers and for BSF the number is 20–25 soldiers (Chowdhury, 2003, Jamwal, 2004). On an average, the distance between BOPs varies from 10–20 km on the Bangladesh side, and 5–6 km on the Indian side. The border between these two countries is demarcated by border pillars. Indian Government-erected border fencing is considered a defence structure; this fence is not allowed inside the no-man's-land, which is 150 meters in each direction from the border line. Therefore, border fences are built in Indian Territory, off the no-man's-land. Thus, BSF have a complete control on border gates.

7 The Union is often abbreviated as UP (*Union Parishad*), the lowest tier of the Local Government structure in Bangladesh. A UP is divided into nine areas called *wards*. A Member is elected from each *ward* to sit on the UP.

References

Adger, W.N., Dessai, S., Goulden, M., Hulme, M., Lorenzoni, I., Nelson, D.R., Naess, L.O., Wolf, J. and Wreford, A. 2009. Are there social limits to adaptation to climate change?. *Climatic Change*, *93* (3–4): 335–354.

Ahmed, A.U., Hassan, S.R., Etzold, B. and Neelormi, S. 2012. 'Where the Rain Falls' project, case study: Bangladesh. Results from Kurigram District, Rangpur Division. Report No. 2, Bonn: United Nations University – Environment and Human Security (UNU – EHS).

Alam, M. 2001. *Slaves of Water: Indigenous Knowledge of Fisheries on the Floodplain of Bangladesh*. Unpublished PhD Thesis, Durham University.

Allison, H.A. and Ellis, F. 2001. The livelihoods approach and management of small-scale fisheries. *Marine Policy*, *25* (5): 377–88.

Amoore, L. 2006. Biometrics borders: Governing mobilities in the war on terror. *Political Geography*, *25* (3): 336–351.

Arens, J. and van Beurden, J. 1977. *Jhagrapur: Poor Peasants and Women in a Village in Bangladesh*. Orient Longman.

Balibar, E. 2004. *We the people of Europe? Reflections on transnational citizenship*. Princeton, NJ: Princeton University Press.

Banerjee, P. 2010. *Borders, Histories, Existences: Gender and beyond*. New Delhi: Sage Publications.

BBC Bangla. 20 December 2016. Shimanta Bangladeshi Hottar Ghotonaottonto Udbagar Bishoy. Available at: http://www.bbc.com/bengali/news-38375869?ocid=socialflow_facebook. (Accessed on 20 December 2016.)

Béné, C. 2003. When fishery rhymes with poverty: A first step beyond the old paradigm on poverty in small-scale fisheries. *World Development*, *31* (6): 949–75.

BenEzer, G. and Zetter, R. 2015. Searching for directions: Conceptual and methodological challenges in researching refugee journeys. *Journal of Refugee Studies*, *28* (3): 297–318.

Bhasin, A.S. (ed.) 2003. *India–Bangladesh relations: Documents 1971–2002*, vol. *1*. New Delhi: Geetika Publications.

Black, R., Bennett, S.R.G., Thomas, S.M. and Biddington, J.R. 2011. Climate change: migration as adaptation. *Nature*, *478* (7370): 447–449.

Campbell, P.B. 2013. The illicit antiquities trade as a transnational criminal network: Characterizing and anticipating trafficking of cultural heritage. *International Journal of Cultural Property*, *20* (2): 113–153.

Chatterji, J. 1999. The fashioning of a frontier: The Radcliffe line and Bengal's border landscape, 1947–1952. *Modern Asian Studies*, *33* (1): 185–242.

Chiodelli, F., Hall, T., Hudson. R. and Moroni, S. 2017. Grey governance and development of cities and regions: the variable relationship between (il)legal and (il)licit. In F. Chiodelli, T. Hall and R. Hudson (eds.) *The Illicit and Illegal in the Governance and Development of Cities and Regions: Corrupt Places*. London: Routledge.

Chowdhury, A.S. 2003. Bangladesh–India border issues and management. *NDC Journal*, *2* (1): 57–71.

Crang, M. and Cook, I. 2007. *Doing Ethnographies*. London: Sage Publications Ltd.

Das, V. 1995. *Critical Events: An Anthropological Perspective on Contemporary India*. New Delhi: Oxford University Press.

Deb, A.K. 2009. *Voices of the Fishantry: Learning on the Livelihood Dynamics from Bangladesh*, Unpublished PhD Thesis, University of Manitoba.

Ellis, F. 2000. *Rural Livelihoods and Diversity in Developing Countries*. Oxford: Oxford University Press.

Faruk, A.K.M.I. 2015. Climate change induced migration in bangladesh. IUCN. https://www.iucn.org/content/climate-change-induced-migration-bangladesh (Accessed on 2 December 2016).

Feldman, S. 2003. Bengali state and nation making: Partition and displacement revisited. *International and Social Science Journal*, *55* (1): 111–121.

Hall, T. 2013. Geographies of the illicit: Globalisation and organised crime. *Progress in Human Geography*, *37* (3): 366–385.

Herbert, M. 2014. Partisans, profiteers and criminals: Syria's illicit economy. *The Fletcher Forum of World Affairs*, *38* (1): 69–86.

Heyman, J.M. and Smart, A. 1999. States and illegal practices: An overview. In J. Heyman (ed.) *The States and Illegal Practices*, 1–24, Oxford and New York: Berg.

The Hindu. 2016. Bangladesh's Hindu's number 1.7 crore, up by 1p.c in a year: Report. 23 June.

Hodson, H.V. 1985. *The great divide: Britain-India-Pakistan*. Karachi: Oxford University Press.

Hudson, R. 2014. Thinking through the relationships between legal and illegal activities and economies: Spaces, flows and pathways. *Journal of Economic Geography*, *14* (4): 775–795.

Human Rights Watch. 2010. Trigger happy: Excessive use of force by Indian troops at the Bangladesh border. Available at: https://www.hrw.org/sites/default/files/reports/bangladesh1219_brochure_web.pdf.

Islam, M.N., Sallu, S., Hubacek, K. and Paavola, J. 2014. Limits and barriers to adaptation to climate variability and change in Bangladeshi coastal fishing communities. *Marine Policy*, *43 (January)*: 208–216.

Jamaluddin, S. 2009. Bangladesh–India economic tie. *The Financial Express*, 26 July.

Jamwal, N. S. 2004. Border management: Dilemma of guarding the India–Bangladesh border. *Strategic Analysis*, *28* (1):5–36.

Jentoft, S., Onyango, P. and Islam, M.M. 2010. Freedom and poverty in the fishery commons, *International Journal of the Commons*, *4* (1): 345–66.

Johnsons, C. and Jones, R. 2016. *Placing the Border in Everyday Life*. New York and London: Routledge.

Jones, R. 2009. Agents of exception: Border security and the marginalisation of Muslims in India. *Environment and Planning D: Society and Space*, *27* (5): 779–797.

Jones, R. 2012. *Border Walls: Security and the War on Terror in the United States, India and Israel*. New York: Zed.

Lu, X., Wrathall, D., Sundsøy, P.R., Nadiruzzaman, M., Wetter, E., Iqbal, A., Qureshi, T., Tatem, A., Canright, G., Engø-Monsen, K. and Bengtsson, L. 2016. Unveiling hidden migration and mobility patterns in climate stressed regions: A longitudinal study of six million anonymous mobile phone users in Bangladesh. *Global Environmental Change*, *38* (May): 1–7.

Lyon, D. 2003. *Surveillance after 9/11*. Cambridge: Polity.

Mountz, A. 2008. The enforcement archipelago: Detention, haunting, and asylum on islands. *Political Geography*, *30* (3): 118–128.

Nawyn, S. J. 2016. Migration in the global south: Exploring new theoretical territory. *International Journal of Sociology*, *46* (3): 81–84.

Niam, M. 2006. *Illicit: How Smugglers, Traffickers and Copycats Are Hijacking the Global Economy*. London: William Heinemann.

Oliver-Smith, A. and Shen, X. 2009. *Linking Environmental Change, Migration & Social Vulnerability*. United Nations University – Environment and Human Security (UNU-EHS).

Rahman, M. and Van Schendal, W. 2003. "I am not a refugee". Rethinking partition migration. *Modern Asian Studies*, *37* (3): 551–584.

Raineri, L. 2017. Drug trafficking in the Sahara Desert: follow the money and find land-grabbing, in F. Chiodelli, T. Hall and R. Hudson (eds.) *The Illicit and Illegal in the Governance and Development of Cities and Regions: Corrupt Places*. London: Routledge.

Rigg, J. 2007. *An Everyday Geography of the Global South*. London: Routledge.

Sadik, K. 2009. *Paper Citizens: How Illegal Immigrants Acquire Citizenship in Developing Countries*. Oxford: Oxford University Press.

Salter, M.B. 2008. When the exception becomes the rule: Borders, sovereignty and citizenship. *Citizenship Studies*, *12* (4): 365–380.

Samaddar, R. 1999. *The marginal nation: Transborder migration from Bangladesh to West Bengal*. Delhi: Sage Publications.

Sanyal, R. 2009. Contesting refugeehood: Squatting as survival in post-partitioned Calcutta. *Social Identities*, *15* (1): 67–84.

Sanyal, R. 2014. Hindu space: Urban dislocations in post-partitioned Calcutta. *Transactions of the Institute of British Geographers*, *39* (1): 38–49.

Shelley, L. and Bain, C. 2015. Human trafficking: Fighting the illicit economy with legitimate economy. *Social Inclusion*, *3* (1): 140–144.

Sur, M. 2014. Divided bodies: Crossing the India–Bangladesh border. *Economic and Political Weekly*, *XLIX* (13): 31–35.

TNN. 2014. India's highest amount of remittances comes from the gulf. *The Economic Times*. 01 December. Available at: http://articles.economictimes.indiatimes.com/2014-12-01/news/56614713_1_remittances-bangladesh-and-nepal-fdi (Accessed on 10 December 2016).

UNEP. 2016. GEO-6 Regional Assessment for Asia and the Pacific. United Nations Environ ment Programme, Nairobi, Kenya. http://uneplive.unep.org/media/docs/assessments/GEO_ASSESSMENT_REPORT_ASIA_Wam.pdf. (Accessed on 2 December 2016).

Van Hear, N., Bakewell, O. and Long, K. 2012. Drivers of migration. Migrating out of poverty. *RPC Working Paper 1*. Available at http://citeseerx.ist.psu.edu/viewdoc/dow nload?doi=10.1.1.372.8319&rep=rep1&type=pdf. (Accessed on 15 December 2016.)

van Schendel, W. 2005. *The Bengal Borderland: Beyond State and Nation in South Asia*. London: Anthem Press.

van Schendel, W. and Abraham, I. (eds.). 2005. *Illicit Flows and Criminal Things: States, Borders and Other Side of Globalisation*. Bloomington and Indianapolis: Indiana University Press.

Vaughan-Williams, N. 2009. *Border Politics: The Limits of Sovereign Power*. Edinburgh: Edinburgh University Press.

Walters, W. 2006. Border/control. *European Journal of Social Theory*, *9* (2):187–203.

Warner, K., Afifi, T., Henry, K., Rawe, T., Smith, C. and De Sherbinin, A. 2012. An 8-Country Study to Understand Rainfall, Food Security and Human Mobility, Where The Rain Falls: Climate Change, Food and Livelihood Security, and Migration, Global Policy Report. Bonn: United Nations University – Environment and Human Security (UNU – EHS). https://www.files.ethz.ch/isn/156058/WTRF_Global_Policy_Report_smaller.pdf (Accessed on 15 March 2016).

4 Gangsters, guerrillas and the rise of a shadow state in East Timor

James Scambary

Introduction

In 1999, in a UN sponsored referendum, the people of East Timor voted for independence from Indonesia, after 24 years of occupation and nearly 400 years of Portuguese colonialism before that. The UN Security Council mandated the establishment of the United Nations Transitional Administration of East Timor (UNTAET) to manage East Timor's transition to full statehood. Its scope of responsibilities was comprehensive, including humanitarian assistance, establishing new security forces and building the foundations of a new democratic state. By the end of 2005, with the mission being classed as a success, the international presence had been substantially scaled down.

Between April and June 2006, a rapid series of events – that took most observers completely by surprise – resulted in East Timor rapidly traversing the full discursive spectrum from UN success story to state failure. In what is now popularly referred to as the 'Crisis', a protest by a group of sacked soldiers outside the national parliament descended into a riot, leading to a series of armed confrontations between the army, the police force and sundry paramilitary groups. This initial series of events then served as a catalyst for a wider communal conflict.[1] Assuming the appearance of an ethnic and political divide between people from the east and west of the country,[2] this conflict was conspicuous for the involvement of a wide variety of gangs, martial arts groups (MAGs) and other informal security groups (ISGs). An estimated 135,000 people fled their homes and at least 37 were killed (UN, 2006).

The UN state-building project and East Timor's Crisis have been the subject of an ongoing and prodigious academic debate, serving as a sort of test tube for a profusion of state-building theories focussed on critiques of the UN's performance. Informed by a range of internationally influential normative frameworks, such as the work of Collier and Hoeffler (2004), explanations for the Crisis have rarely departed from a narrow range of macro-level factors such as flawed, top-down UN state-building models, ethnicity, economic disadvantage and an attendant 'youth bulge'. More than a decade later, the Crisis is now viewed as a historic object lesson in state-building, a sort of distant democratic rupture in the transition to modern statehood. Democratic elections and an impressive array of rational legal institutions are seen as milestones of progress towards full statehood (see, for example, Kingsbury, 2014). Its considerable oil revenues have been used to fund a massive construction boom, with potentially fractious groups bought off through pensions, contracts or state employment. ISGs and conflict are largely viewed as a phenomenon of the past, as a sort of brief 'explosion' of urban unemployed youth despair and frustration.

Such macro-level, state centric frameworks take little account of the social, cultural and historical context for these events, and tells us even less about how East Timor's politics work or about the state of its democracy. As this chapter will argue, it is more useful to view the state of East Timor ethnographically – as being comprised of a network of personal relationships and alliances. Rather than being marginalised, informal and illicit groups and local level actors – particularly ISGs – form the very foundations of this network. In this view, rather than a passing democratic rupture, the 2006 Crisis must be seen as an integral process in the consolidation of current contours of power. The clandestine, informal power structures of the war of resistance have now essentially been replicated with the former resistance army commander, ex-President and Prime Minister and now all-powerful Minister of Planning and Strategic Investment, Kay Rala 'Xanana' Gusmão, at its head.

This chapter details how a specific set of social, political and economic factors have driven the emergence of a clientelist, neo-patrimonial state in newly independent East Timor. It analyses how a command style of government and complex systems of reciprocal obligation embedded in an array of parallel, informal and illicit networks have undermined formal rational legal institutions, processes and structures, with critical consequences for future development and stability.

To capture these different and largely informal processes, I will adopt a political economy approach – an approach that examines the formal or informal economic, political, social and cultural characteristics of a society and the interactions between them (Leftwich, 2008) – the 'rules of the game' that shape the exercise of power and distribution of resources (Peake and Dinnen, 2014). A political economy approach allows for a greater focus on the key actors within the decision-making process and their networks of relationships down to the village level.

The data drawn upon here is the product of ten years of research for a range of different research projects and consultancies funded in part by the World Bank, the New York Social Science Research Council and the (now disbanded) Australian Aid Agency, AusAID. Key informant interviews with the leaders and members of ISGs form the primary source of information, in addition to interviews with various agencies who have interacted with these groups in some way such as through peacekeeping missions, including local and international NGO's, UN officials and police (UNPOL). Longitudinal analysis of UNPOL data and conflict incidents contained in daily media monitoring reports is also utilised. The analysis is also informed by four years of living in East Timor between 2003–2006.

This chapter proceeds in five parts. The first part is comprised of a discussion of the different theoretical conceptualisations of the Timorese state – and clarification of key terms such as clientelism. It then proceeds to a discussion of the origins and nature of contemporary ISGs, followed by an examination of the networked nature of East Timorese society. The fourth section is comprised of a description of the events that led to the formation of the current government and emergent clientelist relationships with ISGs and veterans' groups. The chapter concludes with a discussion of the implications for the future.

Dominant narratives

Perhaps due to the extended UN presence, there has been an ever-proliferating scholarship on state-building processes in East Timor, both before, but particularly after the 2006 Crisis, and continuing to this day – there were at least eight books published on this topic between 2014–2016 alone (see, for example, Beuman, 2016). Much of this commentary reflects wider, positivist oriented frameworks in international scholarship on conflict. A common theme to this scholarship is a search for a single or set of 'pathogens' (Cramer, 2006: 94) or 'root causes' (Woodward, 2007: 145) that sparked the conflict. Woodward divides the most commonly identified root causes into three main arguments: the 'economic argument', which cites low overall GDP per capita, dependence on primary commodity exports – thereby creating a conflict trap of low or non-existent economic growth after war, and a large pool of unemployed young men; the 'political-regime argument', which posits that civil war is caused by authoritarian rule, the absence of democracy or that it is 'partial democracies' and a particular sequence of democratisation that is most prone to political instability and even violence; the 'cultural argument', which cites cultural difference, often summarised, however, as 'ethnic conflict' as a the key source of friction (2007: 150–151). Explanations for the Crisis have largely fallen within these three categories, including latent ethnicity, East Timor's semi-presidential system, a perceived poor fit between indigenous structures and imported western systems, flaws in the type of state-building model adopted by the UN (see, for example, Richmond and Franks, 2008) to the perils of natural resource wealth – the 'resource curse' (see, for example, Cotton, 2007).

Conflict, in this framework, is understood as the independence struggle and the subsequent civil conflict of 2006, rather than the endemic sub-national conflict that has dogged the country since independence. Indeed, there has only been one study completed on sub-national conflict, and that was in 2007 (Gunter 2007). Normative, econometric frameworks of such influential theorists as Collier and Hoeffler (2004) were pervasive in accounts of the Crisis (see, for example, Shoesmith, 2007), and continue to inform current scholarship (see, for example, Kingsbury, 2014). As Richards points out, these frameworks are deeply rooted within European thought of the seventeenth and eighteenth centuries (2005: 4) and are now dated, highly contested and even superseded (Woodward, 2007: 154). However, such analysis continues to dominate contemporary policy approaches and academic discourse.

There is also an implicit geo-spatial and social dichotomy in state-centric frameworks, which counterposes the state to society, and the 'modern' urban capital to the 'traditional' rural countryside. Discussions continue to pose an opposition between the 'liberal' – taken to mean the UN imposed state building model – and 'local' or customary practices, articulated as a sort of new 'hybrid' order. The assumption is that there is or was a void, created by the UN state-building model, that must be bridged through a rapprochement between the informal 'local' practices and formal, national systems (see, for example, Wallis, 2013).

Jones (2010) contends that an overemphasis on the centrality of the UN intervention ignores the fact that the state actually has very little presence on the majority of people's lives in East Timor. Jones contrasts neo-Weberian institutionalists, who believe that 'modern' state institutions can be grafted on to societies reductively labelled as 'traditional', with neo-liberals who believe that better institutional design could have prevented the Crisis. As Jones asserts, these approaches assume that institutions have magical powers that they simply do not possess, and do not take account of human agency. Struggles for power and resources, Jones believes, would characterise any post-conflict scenario, and the UN was only one of many players in a highly contested process of state formation (2010: 566).

Hindsight is a wonderful thing, yet such a reliance on dominant state-centric frameworks and narratives ensured that no outside observers saw the 2006 Crisis coming. Given that the UN presence had already been considerably scaled down and had to be remobilised, this was a costly oversight. Now, a similar dominance of such frameworks has failed to detect the entrenchment of an increasingly pervasive set of parallel, informal networks that operate as a sort of shadow state. William Reno coined the term 'shadow state' to encapsulate the establishment of a rigidly organised but informal patronage system that facilitates rulers' control over resources, while binding potential rivals into lucrative exchange relationships (Reno, 1995).

While it is a contested term, clientelism seems to best encapsulate how this patronage system operates on the ground. Clientelism in East Timor does not approach the sophistication of Indonesian party machine politics, whereby professional brokers are paid to mobilise the vote for political party candidates at election times, as described, for example, by Aspinall (2014). Neither, on the other hand, does it resemble the Melanesian style of direct relations between politicians and their constituents where cash and resources such as development projects are disbursed through a swag of slush funds. Given the debate around this term, and East Timor's still emergent form of this phenomena, a broader, simplified definition will be utilised. Erdman and Engel (2007), in distinguishing between patronage and clientelism, employ a group versus individual distinction, defining patronage as the politically motivated distribution of favors or goods not to individuals, but to larger groups. Under clientelism, brokers mediate the exchange between the 'little man' and the 'big man' (107). Through this network of brokers, the political center is linked with larger groups in the countryside. This definition seems apt for the network of veterans, 'big men' and underworld figures that will be described below. Politicians' links with individual leaders of ISGs give them access to and influence over a considerable pool of voters at elections, right down to village level, and also the muscle required for political violence. These brokers are rewarded through construction contracts and other state resources such as jobs or cabinet positions. East Timor's over-dependence on oil revenue, as will be described in the next section, and powerful veterans' lobby also meets Robinson and Verdier's characterisation of clientelist states – that is, states that lack a developed indigenous private sector and the presence of entrenched pressure groups (Robinson and Verdier, 2013).

Gusmão's executive style decision-making process, as will be described below, could best be described as neo-patrimonialist – a lack of distinction between office and office holder masked behind discourses, juridical norms and institutions that nourish the illusion of a legal-bureaucratic logic (Brinkerhoff and Goldsmith, 2002: 2).

Informal foundations

East Timor does not exist within a vacuum, but within a specific geographic (Figure 4.1), historical and cultural context. East Timor bears many similarities with other societies in the region such as Papua New Guinea (PNG) to the east, where, as Morgan (2005) observes, pre-existing informal social structures and practices pervade the state at every level – a statement he believes applies to the wider region. Informality is at the core of the East Timorese state. Decades of war, a very recent clandestine resistance history and still vibrant traditional social structures, rather than any nascent UN and Weberian legal-rational institutions and principles, still largely determine social and political behaviour, and also act to blur western concepts of legality.

After 400 years of colonial rule by the Portuguese and 24 years of Indonesian occupation, East Timor has never had a state. While historically there were a

Figure 4.1 East Timor in the Asia Pacific.

Source: Drawn by Maddalena Falletti

number of kingdoms, these were often ephemeral, given frequent inter-clan fighting and in most cases, highly localised (see, for example, Hägerdal, 2012). East Timor's society largely conforms to a segmentary pattern of ancestral lineage-based descent groups, centred on geographically specific landholdings and boundaries. The rigidly hierarchical guerilla resistance force, *Forças Armadas de Liberatação National de Timor Leste* (Armed Forces for the National Liberation of East Timor – FALINTIL), and clandestine resistance network, was the closest thing East Timor had to a national level structure. Guerrilla and clandestine leaders still retain high personal prestige and authority either for their feats of bravery during the war, their positions as heads of extended families, or both. As Blunt (2009) claims, resistance leaders were accorded an honorary sacred status that has endured into the independence period. This culture is also reflected in the fact that two former guerrilla leaders are now the most powerful men in the country: Gusmão, previously the supreme commander of the armed resistance movement, and President Francisco Guterres 'Lu-Olo'. Gusmão is still widely revered and also feared (ICG, 2013).

Kinship and clandestine resistance ties are the two main forms of reciprocal relationship that bond people in East Timor. According to McWilliam (2005), the rural clandestine networks known as *nucleos de resistencia popular* were built around these close-knit extended family relationships. So tight were these networks, they not only survived Indonesian repression, resettlement and attempts to socially remould Timorese society, but also enabled the resistance movement to regroup and revive in 1983 after near annihilation (McWilliam, 2005).

National level political leaders and actors can also be intricately linked with ISG leaders through kinship or wartime activism in diaspora clandestine movements – ties that are often invisible except to the actors involved (Scambary, 2013). Many elites studied in Indonesia, and there is a core group of powerbrokers within the ruling party who were prominent in organising street violence during the 2006 Crisis, who are both members of the student activist group *Resistência Nacional dos Estudantes de Timor Leste* (National Resistance of East Timorese Students – RENETIL), and the *Partidu Democratica* (Democratic party – PD). Both organisations were founded by the now deceased Fernando De Araujo when he was a student in Indonesia. The PD is now part of the current governing coalition. A number of its members are also members of *Persaudaraan Setia Hati Terate* (PSHT – the Faithful Fraternity of the Heart), (further discussed below), which therefore acts as a sort of informal network binding together former pro-independence activists who studied in Indonesia (Scambary, 2015). There are also powerful kinship bonds that link different members of these groups. The former leader of PSHT, Jaime Lopes, jailed for his part in the violence of 2006, is the blood cousin of De Araujo, who both come from the same village.

Informal security groups

There is also the influence of its closest neighbour and former coloniser, Indonesia. As Blunt (2009) asserts, 24 years of Indonesian occupation left indelible marks on bureaucratic practice and public expectation in East Timor. One major legacy is corruption, but another is a range of ISGs – a disproportionate number and variety for a largely agrarian society of little over one million people. The term 'informal security groups', while acknowledging its limitations, is used here as a catch-all phrase to describe an almost unclassifiable broad spectrum of groups, from anti-social or militant groups to relatively benign youth groups, with the common denominator being that they are all in some way involved in providing security, while paradoxically often being a source of insecurity.

There is little evidence to support the portrayal of Timor's many ISGs as of recent provenance, urban centred and born of poverty and despair. Most contemporary ISGs in East Timor can trace their existence back to the Indonesian occupation, even up to three decades before the Crisis. The war of resistance spawned a profuse variety of ISGs, ranging from mass membership, national level MAGs and millenarian movements to street corner gangs. While FALINTIL was demobilised, these groups were not.

There are more than two-dozen different types of resistance era remnant groups found on a national basis in East Timor. They fall into three rough categories of MAGs, veterans' and millenarian movements – a belief in restoring lost traditions from an imagined golden era to effect the return of perceived former benefactors (Keesing, 1981: 407-408). The latter two are interchangeable categories as the three main groups – Sagrada Familia, COLIMAU 2000 and the *Conselho Popular Defesa de Republica Democratica de Timor-Leste* (Popular Defence Committee-Democratic Republic of Timor-Leste – CPD-RDTL) – are a mixture of both. COLIMAU 2000 for example, founded during the Indonesian occupation, began as a syncretic millenarian movement, called *Sagrada do Coração de Jesus* (Sacred Heart of Jesus) (Kammen, 2009: 400).

As one security sector reform report noted, these groups had their inception at a time of violence and lawlessness; many of them engaged in rackets such as cross-border smuggling, theft, illegal logging and extortion (Centre for Defence Studies, 2000). These activities continued well into the independence period (ICG, 2004). Cornelio Gama (also known as L7), for example, the leader of Sagrada Familia and, briefly, Member of Parliament (MP), was arrested but later released for smuggling in 2010 (Timor News online, 2010).

While East Timor's resistance struggle spawned a multitude of groups, so did the Indonesian military's counter insurgency strategy. In recognition of the value of East Timor's youth to the resistance movement, the Indonesian military began setting up groups to co-opt them – as it did in Indonesia – a practice well documented by Ryter (1998). As described by Wilson (2002), the Commander of the Indonesian Special Forces *Komando Pasukan Khusus* (KOPASSUS), Prabowo Subianto, was instrumental in setting up the MAG peak body in Indonesia, the *Pencak Silat* Association (IPSI) and he continued this strategy in East Timor, establishing about half a dozen groups. The MAGs are now a ubiquitous feature of the post-independence landscape and comprise the chief sources of, or vehicles for communal tensions. There are some 15–20 MAGs and the number of registered members is probably around 20,000, with as many as 45,000 unregistered members. According to Ostergaard (2005), up to 70 per cent of Timorese young men are active in MAGs.

One of these MAGs is PSHT – also the biggest and most violent group (Figure 4.2). Apart from organised violence, PSHT is also reputed to be heavily involved in extortion rackets and providing security for the many Chinese brothels that dot the Dili landscape. It still has strong links with its parent body in Indonesia, which is also suspected of involvement in organised crime (Maksum *et al.*, 2007). High-ranking leaders are often well-educated and employed in senior positions in government – including at least one Minister – and even in international agencies such as the UN. Their members can also be found throughout civil society organisations and in security company rosters, the police force and army – further blurring the lines between ISGs, the state and definitions of legality. Police are in fact frequently accused of siding with one group against another during MAG clashes. In one clash just before Christmas, 2011, for example, which resulted in two fatalities, as many as ten national police (PNTL) members were accused of being involved (Timor-Leste Subscriber News December 22, 2012). In 2014, as part of an initiative to purge the PNTL of active MAG members, 801 PNTL members handed over their MAG uniforms (Timor-Leste Subscriber News, 2014), although few believe this changes their loyalties to MAGs in any way.

While small, fluid and highly localised, there are also a number of vertically and horizontally connected former resistance leaders, or 'big men', with the status and authority who can mobilise these groups when required on behalf of elites. These 'big men' figures are part of a national network which also includes

Figure 4.2 PSHT members.

Photo: J. Scambary

paramilitary leaders and veterans who connect the state with extended descent groups and clandestine networks at a local level. Many of these such figures are also involved in illicit activities such as extortion, theft and human trafficking.

These are not just random groups of bandits or rebels, however. Many have a distinct geographic, spatial and kin-based nature, constituting coherent if informal networks. Rather than being gangs of alienated, delinquent youth, as popularly portrayed, they are deeply embedded within their local communities. Groups like COLIMAU 2000 and CPD-RDTL are endemic to particular rural areas, reflecting their descent-group based nature, with strongholds based on the natal regions of their respective leaders. While MAGs are generally portrayed as urban groups, they are just as prevalent in rural areas. Their membership also tends to be descent-group based, so that one entire village or extended family might belong to one MAG, and a corresponding political party (Scambary, 2013). Clan feuds, often glossed as MAG conflicts, frequently cause significant damage and fatalities, with up to 100 houses burned down and up to ten people at a time being killed. In contrast to depictions of poor, illiterate youth arriving in the city who are unable to find work, join MAGs and engage in crime, usually they have already signed up before they arrive, and quite often are already well indentured in violence. Such dynamics render such groups ideal for both mobilising the vote at election time and also for political violence.

Attitudes to crime, violence and corruption

That so many such groups exist in East Timor cannot be attributed to the Indonesian occupation alone, but to wider attitudes towards violence, crime and corruption. Community attitudes to predatory practices such as extortion, for example, are complex and ambivalent. Many groups in Dili sustain themselves through 'donations' or 'taxes' (as the practice is benignly referred to locally) on local businesses or community members. The prevalence of this practice is confirmed by one report on crime and violence in Dili which found that 50 per cent, and in some areas 100 per cent, of local businesses reported being subject to extortion (World Bank, 2010). In many cases, the community instigates extortionate demands collectively, as a form of rent-seeking. There is a widespread expectation, in rural areas as well as the city, that any new business, especially if it is a 'wealthy' international agency, owes 'compensation' to the local community in return for the use of 'their' land (sometimes they might have no actual legal claim to the land).

There is a similar ambivalence towards violence, whereby an offence is defined not so much by the act itself, but in the social context in which it occurs, and the relationship that the people involved have to each other (Banks 2000: 37). It is not what you do, then, but whom you do it to. Violence is widely condoned as a means to an end, in the name, for example, of putative redistributive or restorative justice. Payback traditions are also still very strong and constitute a significant source of violent disputes (Scambary, 2013).

Similar attitudes pertain to corruption. East Timor's society is based on reciprocal exchange obligations. Corruption is widely perceived as failure to share rather than as wrongdoing. It is not the act itself that is problematic, but who is, or who is not benefitting. A widespread and, as it proved, potent sentiment, prior to the 2006 violence, was that the ruling party *Frente Revolucionária do Timor-Leste Independente* (Revolutionary Front for East Timorese Independence – FRETILIN) was sitting on a large pile of cash, but was only sharing it with its supporters and family members in the eastern districts. The reality was that the FRETILIN government at the time was largely reliant on donor funds – oil revenues had not at that point come on-stream, so it only had a tiny fraction of the current administration's budget (IMF, 2005). Morgan's observation that Melanesians deride politicians for corruption and profligacy, but participate in behaviour that contributes to state malfunctioning, is also apt here (2005). In a 2011 corruption survey, over half the population thought that corruption was a serious problem (East Timor Anti-Corruption Commission, 2011), and yet the ruling coalition increased its vote at the next election.

Networked politics

The blend of informality and the illicit also permeate East Timor's politics. In Schumpeter's much quoted formula, multiparty elections at regular intervals are a hallmark of a successful democracy (1953). As can be seen throughout the South East Asian and Asia Pacific regions (see, for example, Mietzner, 2015; Hutchcroft, 2013); however, the existence of a competitive party system is not necessarily evidence of an open, vibrant policy debate, and fraud is not the only way that the electoral process can be manipulated.

East Timor's politics can be characterised as competing networks of patronage and reciprocity, with access to state resources the chief objective of incumbency (Blunt, 2009). Complex alliances derived from kinship or clandestine resistance era networks are still far more critical factors in social and political action than ideology or legal rational principles. While some parties in East Timor, like FRETILIN, for example, have greater broad-based appeal than others, most parties have a distinct regional support base. Voting still tends to follow kinship lines, with parties largely serving as electoral vehicles for ambitious local personalities. As observed by Feijo (2016: 197), most parties tend to poll well only in the natal region of their leaders.

Voters are mobilised at election time through traditional authorities and local or regional 'big men' figures, like the politicians as described above, for example, or resistance veterans who in many cases are also the heads of descent groups. Whole villages have been known to switch allegiances at the behest of these leaders (Timor-Leste Subscriber News, 2010). Therefore, if you buy the leader, through the award of government contracts, for example, you buy the village to some extent.

The local and the national are also intricately connected in East Timorese politics. National level political allies – or adversaries – based in the country's capital Dili, may originate from rural villages less than a few kilometres apart. Many, if not most people living in the capital Dili have residences and landholdings in rural areas and visit them frequently. Constant cyclical and circular population movements (there are at least five significant circular population movements per year in East Timor, including public holidays and the dry season) further enhance linkages between the urban capital with rural areas, and also between people.

Therefore a rural–urban divide certainly exists in terms of service delivery – services such as water and sanitation or public health services tend to deteriorate even metres beyond the gates of the national parliament, let alone in rural areas. But in social terms, such population movements and personal networks render orthodox local and national or liberal and local dichotomies largely meaningless.

The April/May 2006 Crisis

These networks were all effectively mobilised during the 2006 Crisis and subsequent elections. The 2006 Crisis is generally understood to have been sparked by the sacking of 591 soldiers in March that year for refusing to obey orders and return to barracks.[3] This group became collectively known as the Petitioners – a group of soldiers, of predominantly western origin, who signed a petition alleging discrimination by the *FALINTIL-Forças de Defesa de Timor Leste's* (F-FDTL) (UN, 2006). The violent demonstration in support of their protest on April 28 was to prove a lightning rod for existing tensions, and the emergence of a range of new and existing disaffected groups. The broad outline of the main events of the Crisis, following the chronology established by the Report of the United Nations Independent Commission of Inquiry, is set out below (UN, 2006).

1. March 16: Dismissal of 591 soldiers from the F-FDTL for desertion.
2. April 24: Group of sacked soldiers known as the Petitioners and their supporters stage demonstrations outside Parliament.
3. April 28: Demonstration turns into riot and two people are killed.
4. May 23: Five killed in armed confrontation between the F-FDTL and paramilitary group comprised of ex-national police and military police.
5. May 24–25: Nine killed when Petitioners and affiliated paramilitary group attacks national F-FDTL headquarters.
6. May 25: Nine police killed in confrontation between the F-FDTL and police; the police force largely disintegrates in Dili.
7. Wider communal violence erupts, taking the form of regionally based 'ethnic violence'.
8. June 26: Prime Minister Mari Alkatiri resigns and Foreign Minister Jose Ramos Horta appointed as interim Prime Minister.[4]

There was a clearly orchestrated pattern to the early stages of this conflict. There was a rapid sequence of armed attacks on the military, followed by a period of concerted mob violence targeting selected areas dominated by FRETILIN supporters from the eastern regions of the country (Scambary, 2009). Mobs comprised of local gang or clan members – mostly trucked in from rural areas – were organised through clandestine networks. A number of rural and Dili-based big-men figures were key to organising these mobs, while the larger, national based groups such as the veterans' groups and PSHT were coordinated under the umbrella of a political front group, the 'National Front for Justice and Peace' (FNJP). The FNJP[5] was primarily a creation of opposition parties. Both its key leaders, Vital Dos Santos and Major Augusto Tara Araujo for example, went on to become Members of Parliament in the governing coalition, the Parliamentary Majority Alliance (AMP) (East Timor Legal News, 2008).

Emergent clientelist patterns

Against the backdrop of ongoing violence, elections proceeded for a new president and Parliament in 2007, involving a number of long-established political parties in East Timor. The two main ones were FRETILIN, which traces its lineage back to the brief-lived period of independence before the Indonesian invasion in 1975 and comprised the main resistance movement, and the *Congresso Nacional da Reconstrução Timorense* (National Congress for Timorese Reconstruction – CNRT), which was created in 2007 to act purely as a political vehicle for Gusmão (Shoesmith, 2011). CNRT's rapidly assembled party list in 2007 consisted of those loyal to Gusmão and opposed to FRETILIN, rather than because of any policy or technical competency.

CNRT ran a crudely populist election campaign, featuring glossy posters of high-rise developments, gleaming shopping malls and modern highways. Their main policy was to start spending the oil revenue immediately, which they quickly proceeded to do once they came to power. Their victory was not just achieved through advertising though. The veterans' groups value lay not just in their contribution to destabilising the FRETILIN government, but also for their networks, as described earlier, which are still quite extensive and cohesive.[6] A number of big man style figures were also mobilised in support. Gusmão recruited the paramilitary leader Vicente Conceiçao (aka Railos) as campaign coordinator in the 2007 parliamentary elections, a move that both rewarded him for his part in the destabilisation of the FRETILIN government, but was also no doubt a recognition of his considerable extended family networks in Liquisa District (ICG, 2007). Railos' appointment is controversial, given that he was recommended for prosecution by the UN Commission of Inquiry into the violence of 2006 for leading an armed attack on the national army headquarters (UN, 2006).

The 2012 election was particularly revealing of the increasing entrenchment of clientelist relations. A European Union (EU) election observer team noted a large number of anomalies with this election. As their report confirmed, the CNRT campaign relied heavily on non-party structures, but particularly on veterans' structures – some of which, as they observed, appeared to overlap with the state agencies handling veterans' affairs, including their pensions. As the report claimed, these structures were headed by individual veterans who have benefited from government contracts. As the report also politely noted, although legal in Timor-Leste, this is not in line with international best practice for democratic elections (European Union, 2012). The day after the 2012 election campaign began, the government announced that it would begin paying the pensions due to more than 27,000 veterans and their families, worth around USD $46 million. This figure rose to USD $105 million in the 2017 budget. In addition to this handout, veterans received $78 million in contracts – awarded without a tender process – for projects related to the national electrification scheme (La'o Hamutuk, 2013).

The Government also moved quickly to reward party loyalists and militants. Apart from their value to the destabilisation of the previous Government, there was also a realisation that many of these groups and individuals were potential sources of future instability. Therefore, in addition to the veterans, a number of prominent underworld figures, some of them key to the 2006–2007 violence, also profited from lucrative government contracts. The paramilitary leader, Railos, for example, was awarded a number of government water and sanitation projects, and is now a successful businessman. Like the veterans, many such figures have little or no business experience or acumen, so they merely act as brokers, attracting Government contracts and then sub-contracting them for a fee or percentage.

Two senior PSHT leaders were given posts: Bendito Freitas, the PSHT spokesperson was appointed as Secretary of State and later, Minister of Education (although he has since been rotated out of that post). The PSHT president, Jaime Lopes, became the Secretary of State for Land and Property. The appointment of Lopes is particularly controversial. Lopes was jailed for six months in February 2007 after international forces found over 400 mostly homemade weapons in his and his group members' houses nearby (UN, 2007). Given his criminal record, according to a local NGO, the Judicial Systems Monitoring Program, his appointment is also possibly unconstitutional (East Timor Legal News, 2012). Constitutionality aside, such appointments spoke loudly about attitudes towards the rule of law. Indeed, rather than receiving a lengthy jail term, most organisers or perpetrators of the 2006 violence now have lucrative contracts, government jobs or seats in Parliament.

Centralisation of power

After the 2007 election, Gusmão appointed 44 ministers, vice ministers and secretaries of state, adding another nine appointments after the 2012 election (Tempo Semanal, 2012). This is for a country of little over one million, with half the population under the age of 15 and over 80 per cent living in rural areas engaged in largely subsistence agriculture. In the classic pattern of clientelist based systems, supporters and their families were also rewarded through employment in the public sector. After 2008, civil service numbers increased by nearly 70 per cent, with an attendant 33 per cent increase in salaries (Everett, 2012).

Gusmão also centralised all decision-making within his office, in a neo-patrimonial style which many have likened to his resistance era commander-in-chief role. According to a confidential 2008 US Embassy cable, for example, Gusmão operates with a small coterie of non-elected advisers or confidantes. The members of this group are typically figures from the clandestine resistance well known to Gusmão (US Embassy, 2008). They also serve as brokers for foreign firms, so they have a vested interest in poor spending decisions and lack of budgetary oversight.

Despite stepping down from power early in 2015, Gusmão's new position as self-appointed head of his own self-designed Ministry of Planning and Strategic Investment (popularly dubbed the 'ministry for everything') means that he continues to maintain total control over the capital budget and the three main regulatory bodies overseeing infrastructure spending (RDTL, 2015). Indeed, a cursory scan of government project documents reveals that Gusmão's Ministry is now listed as both the financing institution and project owner for nearly all projects around the country. This is the case for projects ranging in size from a public toilet to multimillion road projects (RDTL Procurement Portal, 2015).

Such a centralisation of power has been disastrous for state finances. A raft of extravagant white elephant projects is now underway, including a special economic zone and a 'resources corridor' along the south coast which will include a four-lane highway in a region where, on current trends, wandering goats would constitute the main traffic. Embarked on without any real feasibility study or planning, these projects could potentially bankrupt the state – production from current petroleum fields peaked in 2012, and is forecast to end in 2020, while the prospects for new development remain bleak (ADB, 2015). Unless current spending trends are reversed, East Timor will run out of money in less than a decade.

A shadow state

Despite all the bells and whistles of a democratic state, such processes and structures merely provide a façade for a system that is increasingly less democratic and inclusive. Bloated structures – with attendant complex organograms on PowerPoint wheeled out at donor meetings – create a mirage of functional ministries. But as embodied by the USD $40 million extravagant, multi-storey Ministry of Finance building, they are largely empty shells (Figure 4.3). There are few competent or qualified ministers or senior functionaries and even fewer qualified staff; one 2014 study found that many civil servants still lack even basic skills in literacy and numeracy (Goldfinch and Derouen, 2014: 101). A range of recent press reports paint a picture of declining or even collapsing service delivery such as essential medicines (Quintão, 2017).

Equally, elections – without any real policy debate to differentiate between parties, and contests being largely decided by clan based affiliations, pork barrelling and clientelist networks – do not really conform to modern notions of democracy. Such practices are viewed as problematic in PNG (see Haley, 2015), for example, and it is difficult to see why they are not viewed as such in East Timor.

Gusmão's executive style decision-making process, without recourse to parliamentary processes, or even consultations with relevant ministries or advisers, renders the whole political apparatus largely redundant. Indeed, the 2017 budget was approved unanimously, so Parliament largely serves as a rubber stamp (RDTL, 2016).

Figure 4.3 The Ministry of Finance building.

Photo: J. Scambary

Such developments should be cause for alarm. As normative state-centric frameworks and dominant narratives failed to predict the 2006 Crisis, they are now therefore also in danger of missing the next unfolding crisis. The current status quo, devoid of any meaningful checks and balances, has set the country on a self-destructive path that may bankrupt the state, with critical consequences for stability and future generations.

Conclusion

This chapter has described the emergence of an informal, shadow state built on a parallel set of informal and illicit networks that largely bypass or supersede the Weberian rational principles and structures set in place by the UN and other external agencies.

Nonetheless, informed by influential macro-level theoretical frameworks in international state-building and conflict analysis literature, dominant narratives in academic and development discourse have cast the State of East Timor as being a nascent post-conflict democratic nation in transition to modern statehood. In this framework, violent groups such as MAGs and veterans' groups are portrayed as an urban phenomenon, products of poverty and despair, but now largely a thing of the past. The 2006 Crisis is viewed as a sort of temporary reversal or birthing pain, blamed on the tensions between indigenous structures and the top-down 'liberal' model imposed by the UN. These tensions are now rather optimistically viewed as being slowly overcome through new hybrid forms of local governance (Wallis, 2013).

As argued here, such frameworks cannot account for the range of opaque, informal processes and relationships that drive politics in such small island segmentary societies, or even larger South East Asian countries in the region. Due to its historical and cultural context, the state of East Timor was at its very inception grounded in informality. The plethora of rational legal institutions created under the aegis of the UN administration, rather than being central to its political trajectory, has had a largely peripheral influence as a consequence. The 2006 Crisis had little to do with the UN state-building process. It was not a temporary democratic rupture but an integral process in entrenching the former clandestine resistance command structure and the full range of parallel, illicit and informal behaviour and relationships that entails. It is this set of behaviours and relationships, permeating down to village level in rural and urban centres, that comprise the current state of East Timor. The central role played by a range of informal and illicit groups in the formation and perpetuation of this shadow state place violence and illegality at its very heart.

This is not a permanent state of affairs, however. The state in East Timor does not have a monopoly on formal violence, as in Schumpeter's oft-quoted definition of statehood (1954), but relies instead on a very unstable alliance of informal networks. The cohesiveness of this alliance rests on Gusmão's central authority. Once he departs the scene, as he eventually will, there is no leader who has the authority to hold these disparate elements together. What may follow Gusmão's departure is a more fragmented and individualistic Melanesian style of patronage and corruption, like PNG's, where individual politicians still loot the public treasury but respond to a narrow, localised descent group based constituency (Allen and Hasnain, 2010). East Timorese politics may also come to resemble its Melanesian neighbours as without Gusmão, his party and governing coalition, built entirely around his prestige and authority, may fragment, resulting in highly fluid and opportunistic party alliances – as is already becoming the case – and constantly changing governments.

However, as stated, if current unsustainable spending trends continue, East Timor is now on track for bankruptcy. It was patronage that held the country together after 2006. With no money to keep these disparate groups onside, should another significant conflict break out, it will be difficult to see how they will put the genie back in the bottle next time.

Notes

1 The term conflict is used throughout this chapter to denote violent conflict. Terms such as 'tensions' or 'disputes' will be used for non-violent conflict. Conflict is also used here to denote group conflict, rather than individual violence such as gender-based violence.

2 East Timor has 13 districts: nine to the west of Dili, four to the east. Manatuto District, although in the east, was adopted in 2006 as a western district for political reasons. There is little historical basis for such an arbitrary division, but the complexities are further explored in the following chapter.
3 Many of that number were dismissed for sundry disciplinary reasons; some had been absent for years, having returned to their home villages or taken second jobs.
4 The conflict did not end, however, with the resignation of the Prime Minister, Mari Alkatiri, or even in May, as nearly all accounts seem to suggest. After this initial first phase, with communal violence lasting for another four months, another, far more widespread conflict erupted, but with far more localised patterns of violence spread beyond Dili to rural districts (see Scambary, 2009, for more details).
5 The FNJP later became the National Movement for Unity and Justice.
6 In 2005, I coordinated a national radio documentary project on women's role in the resistance, and it was clear from our research interviews in nearly all districts that these networks were still very much intact – people even continued to use their codenames in many cases.

References

Allen, M. and Hasnain, Z., 2010. Power, pork and patronage: Decentralisation and the politicisation of the development budget in Papua New Guinea. *Commonwealth Journal of Local Governance*, 6: 7–31.

Asian Development Bank (ADB), 2015. Asian Development Outlook 2015: financing Asia's future growth. Manila: Asian Development Bank.

Aspinall, E., 2014. Indonesia's 2014 Elections: Parliament and Patronage. *Journal of Democracy*, 25 (4): 96–110.

Banks, C., 2000. Developing Cultural Specificity for a Cultural Criminology. In: Banks, C. (ed) *Developing Cultural Criminology: Theory and Practice in Papua New Guinea.* Sydney, Sydney Institute of Criminology.

Beuman, L., 2016. *Political Institutions in East Timor: Semi-Presidentialism and Democratisation.* London: Routledge.

Blunt, P., 2009. The political economy of accountability in Timor-Leste: Implications for public policy. *Public Administration and Development*, 29: 89–100.

Brinkerhoff, D. and Goldsmith, A., 2002. Clientelism, patrimonialism and democratic governance: An overview and framework for assessment and programming. U.S. Agency for International Development. Office of Democracy and Governance. Washington, DC: US Agency for International Development.

Centre for Defence Studies (CDF), (2000). Independent Study on Security Force Options and Security Force Reform for East Timor. London: CDF, Kings College.

Collier, P. and Hoeffler, A., 2004. Greed and grievance in civil war. *Oxford Economic Papers*, 56 (4): 563–595.

Cotton, J., 2007. Timor-Leste and the discourse of state failure. *Australian Journal of International Affairs*, 61 (4): 455–470.

Cramer, C., 2006. *Civil War is not a Stupid Thing: Accounting for Violence in Developing Countries.* London: Hurst & Co.

Democratic Republic of Timor-Leste (RDTL), 2012. State budget 2012: Budget overview. Dili: Democratic Republic of Timor-Leste Ministry of Finance. (Author's private copy) Democratic Republic of Timor-Leste (RDTL), Procurement Portal http://www.eprocurement.gov.tl/public/indexeprtl?&lang=en (accessed on December 12, 2015).

Democratic Republic of Timor-Leste (RDTL), 2015. Structure of the VI Constitutional Government. Available at: http://timor-leste.gov.tl/?p=13&lang=en (accessed on September 8, 2015).

Democratic Republic of Timor-Leste (RDTL), 2016. 2017 General state budget approved unanimously in final vote. Press release, Minister of State and of the Presidency of the Council of Ministers, December 9, Dili. Available from: http://timor-leste.gov.tl/?p=16926&lang=en&lang=en (Accessed on January 12, 2017).

East Timor Anti-Corruption Commission, 2011. Corruption Perception Survey 2011, Dili. Dili: East Timor Anti-Corruption Commission.

East Timor Legal News, 2012. Civil society does not agree with the ex-prisoner's involvement in government. *East Timor Legal News*, August 10. Available from: http://www.easttimorlawandjusticebulletin.com/2012/08/civil-society-does-not-agree-with-ex.html (accessed on November 12, 2013).

Erdmann, G. and Engel, U., 2007. Neo-patrimonialism reconsidered: Critical review and elaboration of an elusive concept. *Commonwealth & Comparative Politics*, 45 (1): 95–119.

European Union, 2012. European Union Election Observation Mission, Timor-Leste 2012: Final Report on the Parliamentary Election. Brussels: European Union. (Author's private copy).

Everett, S. 2012. Oil in Timor-Leste – A Kick-Start or a Kick-Back? The Asia Foundation, Dili, February 22, 2012. Available at: http://asiafoundation.org/in-asia/2012/02/22/oil-in-timor-leste-a-kick-start-or-a-kick-back/.

Feijo, R., 2016. *The Dynamics of Democracy in Timor-Leste: The Birth of a Democratic Nation 1999-2012*. Amsterdam: Amsterdam University Press.

Goldfinch, S. and DeRouen, K., 2014. In It for the long haul? Post-conflict state-building, peacebuilding, and the good governance agenda in Timor-Leste. *Public Administration and Development*, 34: 96–108.

Gunter, J., 2007. Communal conflict in Viqueque and the charged history of '59. *The Asia Pacific Journal of Anthropology*, 8 (1): 27–41.

Hägerdal, H., 2012. *Lords of The Land, Lords of The Sea: Conflict and Adaptation in Early Colonial Timor, 1600–1800.* Boston: Brill, Leiden.

Haley, N., 2015. Assessing the shift to limited preferential voting in Papua New Guinea: Electoral outcomes. In Brief 2015/30a, State, Society & Governance in Melanesia Program (SSGM), Canberra: ANU College of Asia & the Pacific.

Hutchcroft, P., 2013. Linking capital and countryside: Patronage and clientelism in Japan, Thailand, and the Philippines. In Diego Abente Brun and Larry Diamond (eds) *Political Clientelism, Social Policies, and the Quality of Democracy*. Baltimore: Johns Hopkins University Press.

International Crisis Group (ICG), 2004. David and Goliath, Timor Leste and Indonesia: Is all well? Or is it not as well as it looks? (Unpublished briefing). International Crisis Group. Jakarta/Brussels. (Author's collection).

International Monetary Fund (IMF), 2005. Country Report: Timor-Leste. 5 (245). Washington, DC.

Jones, L., 2010. (Post-) Colonial state-building and state failure in East Timor: Bringing social conflict back in. *Conflict, Security & Development*, 10 (4): 547–575.

Kammen, D., 2009. Fragments of utopia: Popular yearnings in East Timor. *Journal of Southeast Asian Studies*, 40 (2): 385–408.

Keesing, R., 1981. *Cultural Anthropology: A Contemporary Perspective.* New York: Holt, Rhinehart and Wilson.

Kingsbury, D., 2014. Democratic consolidation in Timor-Leste: Achievements, problems and prospects, *Asian Journal of Political Science*, 22 (2): 181–205.

La'o Hamutuk, 2013. Presentation, 'The national impact of benefits for former combatants'. March. Accessed September 28, 2013. Available from: http://www.laohamutuk.org/econ/pension/VetPension6Mar2013en.pdf — 2011. 'Power Plant and National Electrical Grid 2008–2009: Mega-project or Mega- problem?' http://www.laohamutuk.org/Oil/Power/ 08PowerPlant.htm (accessed on May 17, 2013).

Leftwich, A., 2008. Developmental states, effective states and poverty reduction: The primacy of politics. Paper prepared for the United Nations Research Institute for Social Development (UNRISD) project on Poverty Reduction and Policy Regimes.

McWilliam, A., 2005. Houses of resistance in East Timor: Structuring sociality in the new nation. *Anthropological Forum*, 15 (1): 27–44.

Maksum, A., Tjahyono, I. and Purbodjati, M., 2007. *Konflik kekerasan antar kelompok perguruan pencak silat studi kasus di daerah Madiun* (Violent conflicts between martial arts groups in Madiun area: a case study). Surabay: Negeri Surabaya University Click here to enter text. (Author's collection).

Mietzner, M., 2015. Dysfunction by design: Political finance and corruption in Indonesia. *Critical Asian Studies*, 47 (4): 587–610.

Morgan, M., 2005. Cultures of dominance: Institutional and cultural influences on parliamentary politics in Melanesia. State Society and Governance Discussion Paper 2005/2. Canberra: ANU.

Oliveira, V., 2016. 'Empty Ministry of Finance Building a Waste of Money', says MP. *The Dili Weekly*, June 06. Available from: http://www.thediliweekly.com/en/news/capital/13808-edifisiu-mf-abandonado-mp-44-086-mil-fakar-saugate-deit.

Ostergaard, L., 2005. Timor-Leste youth social analysis mapping and youth institutional assessment. *World Bank*. Dili (Author's collection).

Peake, G. and Dinnen, S., 2014. Transnational crime in the Pacific – a conversation starter, state, society and governance in Melanesia. In Brief Discussion Paper 2014/16, Canberra: ANU.

Quintão, P., 2017. Government lacks proper system to monitor medication stocks. *The Dili Weekly*, January 31. Available from: http://www.thediliweekly.com/en/news/health/14296-government-lacks-proper-system-to-monitor-medication-stocks (accessed February 2, 2017).

Reno, W., 1995. *Corruption and State Politics in Sierra Leone.* Cambridge: Cambridge University Press.

Richmond, O. and Franks, J., 2008. Liberal peacebuilding in Timor Leste: The Emperor's New Clothes? *International Peacekeeping*, 15 (2): 185–200.

Robinson, J. and Verdier, T., 2013. The political economy of clientelism. *Scandinavian Journal of Economics*, 115 (2): 260–292.

Ryter, L., 1998. Pemuda Pancasila: The last loyalist men of Suharto's free order. *Indonesia*, 66: 44–73.

Scambary, J., 2009. Anatomy of a conflict: the 2006–7 communal conflict in East Timor. *Conflict, Security and Development*, 9 (2), 265–288.

Scambary, J., 2013. Conflict and resilience in an urban squatter settlement: Dili, East Timor, *Urban Studies*, 50 (10): 1935–1950.

Scambary, J., 2015. In search of white elephants: The political economy of resource income expenditure in Timor-Leste. *Critical Asian Studies*, 47 (2) 283–308.

Scambary, J., Da Gama, B., and Barreto, J., 2006. 'Survey on gangs and youth groups of Dili, Timor-Leste', AusAID, September. Available from: www.etan.org/etanpdf/2006/Report_Youth_Gangs_in_Dili.pdf.

Schumpeter, J., 1954. *Capitalism, Socialism and Democracy* (4th edition). London: Allen & Unwin.

Shoesmith, D., 2007. Timor-Leste: Interpreting violence in a post-conflict state. In: Shoesmith, D. (ed.) *The Crisis In Timor-Leste: Understanding the Past, Imagining the Future.* Darwin: Charles Darwin University Press.

Shoesmith, D., 2011. Political parties and groupings of Timor-Leste. *Australian Political Parties for Democracy Program, 3rd ed.* Sydney: Australian Labour Party International.

Tempo Semanal, 2012. 'Breaking news: *Tempo Semanal* exclusive: Fifth constitutional government.' August 3.

Timor News online, 2010. L-7 Calls on PNTL to Explain Motive of Seizing His Car. 13 July.

Timor-Leste Subscriber News, 2014. 801 of PNTL members handing (sic) over their martial art uniforms. January 16.

Timor-Leste Subscriber News, 2012. Ten PNTL officers involve in martial arts activities. January 25.

Timor-Leste Subscriber News, 2010. Three parties' followers affiliate to CNRT. December 6

United Nations (UN), 2006. Report of the United Nations Independent Special Commission of Inquiry for Timor-Leste. Geneva: The UN. Available from: http://www.ohchr.org/Documents/Countries/COITimorLeste.pdf (Accessed on July 7, 2008).

US Embassy, 2008. Major Projects and Government Procurement in Timor-Leste. Available from: http://www.Laohamutuk.org/reports/Wikileaks/2008Dec31Infrastructure.pdf (Accessed on August 6, 2008).

Wallis, J., 2013. A liberal-local hybrid peace project in action? The increasing engagement between the local and liberal in Timor-Leste. *Review of International Studies*, 38, 735–761.

Woodward, S., 2007. Do the root causes of civil war matter? On using knowledge to improve peacebuilding interventions. *Journal of Intervention and State-building*, 1 (2): 143–170.

World Bank, 2010. Violence in the city: Understanding and supporting community responses to urban violence. World Bank Conflict, Crime and Violence Social Development Department, Washington DC. Available from: http://siteresources.worldbank.org/EXTSOCIALDEVELOPMENT/Resources/244362-1164107274725/Violence_in_the_City.pdf (Accessed on October 24, 2011).

5 Criminal networks, youth street groups and illicit territorial regulation in Moscow and Tbilisi

Svetlana Stephenson and Evgenia Zakharova

Introduction

This chapter analyses the relationships between neighbourhood peer groups and members of criminal networks in post-Soviet urban spaces. Neighbourhood peer groups are widely present in urban areas across the former Soviet Union. Evidence collected in Bishkek (Nasritdinov and Schröder 2016), Moscow, Kazan (Stephenson 2008, 2012, 2015) and other cities across the Russian Federation (Gromov 2009, Karbainov 2009, Golovin and Lurie 2008) shows that these quasi-kin groups tend to unite young male residents aged around ten to18 and living in peripheral areas of large cities, and most of the youth in medium-sized cities and small towns, while in Yerevan (Ponomareva 2014, 2015) and Tbilisi (Zakharova 2010, 2012, 2015) they tend to unite the majority of boys and young men in these cities.

These groups, rather than collections of marginalised and stigmatised delinquents (Anderson 1999, Sánchez-Jankowski 1991, Whyte 1993), are neighbourhood organisations. They are multi-ethnic groups that have traditionally united the young residents irrespective of their social backgrounds, with major distinctions drawn between those young people who participate in the street lifestyle and those who withdraw into the space of home. Their social composition reflects the specific character of Soviet urbanisation that was associated with relatively low residential social differentiation, a situation that is currently changing as a consequence of housing privatisation and marketisation.

The groups are commonly regarded, by adults and young people alike, as "schools of life" for young men, where they remove themselves from the sphere of school control and parental discipline at least for the time that they spend outdoors. In character contests and ritual fights with "enemies" from neighbouring streets they learn to be "real men". Here they become fearless warriors, defenders of the local space, loyal friends. In other words, they acquire qualities relating to conceptions of hegemonic masculinity (Messerschmidt 2012), an ideology that legitimises the existing system of gender inequality. Rather than anomic social actors lashing out at a world in which they have no stake, or members of deprived ethnic and racial minorities, young people see themselves as the key local reputational group that upholds the social order in the community (Collins 2008, Suttles 1968, p. 229).

The groups differ in the extent of their use of violence and criminal activities, inclusion of girls and young women (with territorial groups in the Caucasus limiting themselves entirely to boys and young men), the presence or absence of leaders and other features of social organisation (such as internal discipline, style of clothes and group insignia).

The groups tend to have a street code of conduct, a set of moral instructions that create cultural unity in the group and establish their social order. The authors' interviews with members of street organisations in Moscow and Tbilisi show that the key instructions are very similar. Group members should behave as honourable warriors, who never lose face publicly or let down their group. If challenged, they should respond violently to any perceived assault on one's dignity, and defend the honour of the group in street altercations. They should refrain from assaulting women, young children and elderly people. They are expected to demonstrate control and integrity, refrain from making empty threats or accusations and behave confidently and decisively in any street interaction. They should be able to present themselves as the masters of the street (while placing non-street young men in positions of inferiority), and act as experts in its law.

A persistent feature that researchers encounter in many urban areas in the post-Soviet region is the links between young men and representatives of the criminal networks of thieves-in-law and their associates. These links, which were noted by authors writing about the youth culture in the Soviet Union (Raleigh 2006, Kozlov 1998), remain a feature of post-Soviet societies. The associations between members of street groups and adult members of the criminal networks living in the community go far beyond older criminals acting as tutors in criminal behaviour, as posited in classical criminological theory (see, for example, Sutherland and Cressey 1970, pp. 77–9). Nor are the youth groups we discuss here a part of organised crime groups and mafias as in some American and Italian criminal organisations (Hagedorn 2015, Paoli 2003), although some of the members may aspire to illegal careers. Instead, as we will show, these young group members participate together with members of criminal networks in the illicit governance of their areas. While young people police their local territory and fight against "intruders" from the neighbouring streets and quarters, and in the Caucasus control the reputation of local girls and young women (Ponomareva 2014, Zakharova 2010), the adult criminals act as agents of alternative justice. Between themselves, as we will argue, members of adult criminal and street networks in these areas form patron-client relationships, where ex-convicts act as agents of moral authority for members of youth peer groups, provide protection, supply specialist expertise in violence and act as mediators in conflict. These relationships are both a product of the Soviet high incarceration society, and, as we will explain, local historical and cultural traditions. They have also emerged as a result of a low degree of trust in formal justice in the Soviet and post-Soviet space.

The spatial dimensions of grey governance in Soviet and post-Soviet societies and the customary and socially sanctioned practices of territorial control by non-state actors have not as yet been sufficiently explored. The attention of researchers has been largely directed at the role that members of criminal communities played in the Soviet-era and post-Soviet shadow and criminal economies, their penetration into the structures of legal power and their role in compensating for the weakness of institutional regulation of economic activities (for example, Volkov 2002, Sokolov 2004, Slade 2013, Kupatadze 2012).

In this chapter, we address the illicit territorial governance by street youth groups and criminal communities by looking at the relationships between the members of youth street organisations and criminal groups in Moscow and in Tbilisi. Research in the southeastern administrative area (*okrug*) of Moscow,[1] conducted by Stephenson in 2006, included 23 in-depth interviews with young people aged 12–17 who were members of neighbourhood groups from across the area. The research took place in participants' homes and on the streets, and access to interviewees was achieved using the snowballing technique. The project team also conducted six focus groups with the members of territorial groups, in which 42 young people took part.[2] All interviewees gave their informed consent. Interviews were also conducted with the parents of the young people who participated in the study and local community members. We also use the analysis of the data collected by Zakharova in areas across Tbilisi, the capital of Georgia, between 2007–2012, where around 100 semi-structured and in-depth interviews were conducted with men aged 18–30 who had been members of youth street groups in the recent past, and with community members.

The chapter is organised in the following way. We first discuss the origins and the social and cultural influence of the Soviet and post-Soviet criminal communities of thieves-in-law. We then move on to analyse the patron-client relationships between the thieves and youth groups, and the role of professional criminals in the local social regulation. We proceed to analyse the case studies conducted in Moscow and Tbilisi. The chapter concludes with discussion of the interplay between the illicit systems of regulation and local social and cultural traditions, and of the changing relationship between formal state regulation and the alternative street systems.

The comparison between Moscow and Tbilisi can offer, we argue, many important insights into the spatial dimensions of grey governance. Both Moscow and Tbilisi are capital cities of independent states that until 1991 had been a part of the Soviet Union. The generating factors that produce the street-criminal nexus in both cities are similar. Both have a presence of street corner societies whose members exercise informal social control over their turf. In both cities one can find areas where members of criminal communities have taken residence, and where they aspire to achieve wider social acceptance, forming reciprocal relations with young people and other members of the community. At the same time, there are locally specific factors that can account for substantial differences in the practices of illicit social regulation in both cities. We outline some of these, such as particular urban residential patterns, historical traditions of informal mediation and culturally embedded practices of youth group violence.

Thieves-in-law and their social and cultural influence

The criminal network of "thieves-in-law" (*vory-v-zakone*, professional criminals) emerged in the conditions of the Soviet high incarceration regime, where the prisons and labour camps, with their huge intakes and customary lengthy sentences, produced this highly organised alternative society (Oleinik 2003, Efimova 2004, Chalidze 1977).[3] The thieves effectively created "extra-state entities" in prisons and penal colonies (Holzlehner 2014, p. 136). They represented a top caste in the prisons and set the law and rules of behaviour for the other inmates. Both inside and outside prison, the thieves acted as the figures of moral authority and agents of informal social regulation for the majority of criminals. In Georgia, according to Gurov (1995, p. 159), 80–100 per cent of prison inmates regarded the thieves as their unofficial leaders, while in Russia this figure was lower, at about 50 per cent (Kupatadze 2012, p. 54). The thieves had had their own hierarchy, with the "crowned" thieves and their associates, so called *avtoritety* ("authorities") at the top, and their own moral code, the *poniatiia* (understandings). They also developed complex rituals, together with their own body language of tattoos. The code prohibited them from working, serving in the army or having any other association with the state authorities (Chalidze 1977, p. 74; Serio and Razinkin 1995, p. 73).

In the Soviet Union, the thieves participated in the criminal regulation of the shadow economy that compensated for the inadequacies of the state planning system and the perpetual shortages that it created (Ledeneva 1998). This massive shadow economy that began to develop in the country from the end of the 1950s, involved off-the-books production and distribution of goods (Grossman 1977). The so-called *tsekhoviki* (illegal entrepreneurs) and *spekul'anty* (speculators) organised production of illegal goods in legitimate companies or sold legitimate goods in the black market, bypassing state shops. The thieves provided *tsekhoviki* and other black marketeers with investment capital or organised the transportation and sale of illicit goods, often under the patronage of party bureaucracy and the police (Sokolov 2004, Cheloukhine 2008).

Among the Soviet republics, Georgia had a particularly strong contingent of thieves-in-law. In the early 1990s a third of all thieves-in-law in the USSR were of Georgian origin (Glonti and Lobzhanidze 2004, p. 45). The strength of organised crime in Georgia may reflect the scale of its shadow economy compared to the other Soviet republics (Glonti and Lobzhanidze 2004, p. 53), with Georgia topping the league (Slade 2013, p. 38). According to some estimates, the shadow economy in Georgia made up over 25 per cent of the Republic's GNP (Mars and Altman 1983, p. 546). Georgian thieves were quick to appreciate both the economic potential and vulnerability of illicit entrepreneurs. Using their violent skills and reputation for effective enforcement, they started to offer them protection, helping to resolve disputes, providing information and enforcing decisions. They also protected the illegal markets in stolen goods, prostitution and other criminal operations. These actions went alongside their own criminal activities such as theft, burglary and armed robbery (Slade 2013, ch. 3).

The thieves' influence stretched far beyond the world of prison and the shadow economy. In the communities where they settled after release, they acted as conflict mediators and informal judges (Handelman 1994, p. 36). Prison norms were well known (if only vicariously) to all strata of the Soviet society, and, according to Abramkin, they resonated with popular conceptions of justice, as opposed to the formal state law, as they were seen as embodying the values of brotherhood and fairness, and respect for the "crowned" thieves, who acted as sources of traditional authority in the prison society (Abramkin 2007).

While in Russia in the late Soviet period the influence of criminal culture was particularly strong in working class areas (Stephenson 2015, ch. 1), a situation that continues to this day, in Georgia respect for the "thieves' world" (the common name for the thieves' societies) could be encountered in all sections of the population. For example, the artistic intelligentsia sympathised and made contacts with the thieves. It is sometimes argued that the Georgian intelligentsia found in criminal society a kind of countercultural utopia opposed to the norms embodied in the oppressive state. Many members of oppositional intelligentsia saw the thieves as heroic fighters against the Soviet state power, and were happy to mix with them socially, at various family celebrations and dinner parties (Manning 2009, p. 77). However, there is also evidence of a patron-client nature to their relationship. Famous actors, film and theatre directors, artists, writers and poets could also be personally involved in the shadow economy. They paid thieves-in-law protection money because they realised that if the thieves were known to be involved in their illegal business, nobody would dare to touch it (gamtsemlidze n.d.).

The prestige of the "thieves' world" and its representatives was particularly high among the members of the Soviet neighbourhood youth groups. As authors who studied the influence of the criminal culture on the Soviet youth culture showed, starting from the mid-1950s, when millions of prisoners began to come back from the GULAG, young people started learning prison folklore, poems and songs, looking for role models among the ex-convicts and creating groups and societies where they played out their fantasies about the world of brotherhood and justice that they believed to exist among the thieves (Dobson 2009, Tsipursky 2009, Raleigh 2006). At the same time thieves also saw their role in spreading their law among the wider public and "educating" young people who lived in "their" territories (Razinkin 1995; Oleinik 2003, p. 35, p. 73).

The influence of the thieves' world on youth groups in both Russia and Georgia reached its peak in the end of the 1980s and the beginning of the 1990s. In the 1990s both Russia and Georgia saw the rise of new criminal groups – the so called "bandits". In Russia these were racketeering gangs who had not been grounded in the world of prison and were often organised by ex-sportsmen, army and police veterans (Volkov 2002) or evolved out of youth street groups (Stephenson 2015). Like thieves, they became involved in extortion and protection rackets typical of classical mafias (Varese 2001), but they soon developed a range of other criminal activities – including real estate fraud, money laundering, the illegal drug trade – and started to appropriate legal businesses. Their organisations were much less hierarchical; they were open to people without criminal records as long as they promised loyalty to the bandits' *bratva* (brotherhood). They were much more pragmatic and entrepreneurial in their orientations and less concerned about building wider social acceptance than the thieves' groups. In Georgia the bandit groups were associated with the Mkhedrioni movement, a heavily armed paramilitary group headed by Djaba Ioseliani (commonly referred to as a thief, although this is sometimes disputed). Members of Mkhedrioni, who did not subscribe to the thieves' code of honour, competed for spheres of control with the old-school thieves. Mkhedrioni became a magnet for sections of Georgian youth who saw membership of this organisation as their only chance of survival in conditions of profound economic crisis and devastation brought about by civil war and the Georgian-Abkhasian conflict. Although Mkhedrioni was outlawed by President Shevardnadze in 1995, the thieves' influence on the streets continued to wane.

In the late 1990s and early 2000s, with the strengthening of the state in Putin's Russia, and following President Saakashvili's vigorous campaign to eradicate thieves-in-law in Georgia between 2004 and 2013, the criminal organisations were substantially weakened (Volkov 2002, Slade 2013). Nevertheless, they retained their cultural influence on the world of the streets and were still involved in the local systems of patron-client relations with members of local communities (in Georgia acting mainly from abroad).

Patronage systems and illicit social regulation

The participation of agents of organised violence and criminality in informal social regulation is not exclusive to the post-Soviet countries. Representatives of Italian mafia families not only provide "protection" to businesses, but also mediate in disputes, help residents return stolen property and generally substitute for slow or inefficient legal justice (Blok 1974, Arlacchi 1988, Catanzaro 1992, Paoli 2003). Criminal gangs in North and Latin American cities may also play a similar role in informal governance in areas where the state is either weak or corrupt (Venkatesh 2000, Arias and Rodrigues 2006, Rodgers 2006), and similar processes have been observed in other countries of the developing world (see Scumbary, this volume). In the post-Soviet space, members of thieves' and bandits' criminal organisations have similarly been shown to use their own, alternative legal system to resolve conflicts, help businessmen and residents secure loans, investigate crimes and mediate between members of the community and state authorities (Varese 2001, Volkov 2002, Stephenson 2015).

While institutional sociologists tend to see this relationship as one of exchange of services in return for payment (Gambetta 1993), we would suggest that it can be seen as a form of patronage. The criminals have the power of violent enforcement that the residents (including the young people) lack, and they either use it in exchange for a payment or subsequent favours, or in return for symbolic gifts and respect, thereby confirming their informal power and prestige and earning the loyalty of the community in which they live.

As John Levi Martin argued in his book, *Social Structures*, patronage relationships, in which the patrons protect their clients and assist them in pursuing their interests in return for support and loyalty, do not constitute a form of economic exchange. Instead, they represent a form of reciprocal obligations, albeit between unequal parties. These relationships often exist in settings where "there is a strong anarchic component to social life" (Martin 2009, p. 195), usually where the state is either weak or does not reach. These include the sphere of illegal activities and spaces "where kin groups are unable to fully protect people against violence" (Martin 2009, p. 195). The space of the street is precisely such a place of indeterminacy and danger, where the illicit and violent behaviour of the members of quasi-kin groups exists outside the sphere of state regulation. Going to the police for help is widely seen as inappropriate and damaging for young people's street reputations, and young people turn instead to patrons from the criminal networks. Older residents may also look for protection from the underworld, as both in Russia (Taylor 2011, p. 114) and in Georgia (Zakharova 2010, p. 117), law enforcement authorities are widely seen as inefficient and corrupt, while in Georgia they are also widely seen as hostile and alien to the society.

Criminal mediation has also been linked to long-standing traditions of informal conflict resolution (cf. Scumbary, this volume). In Russia traditional forms of mediation used by the peasant community have long since disappeared, but in the Caucasus such mediation remained a vital alternative to state justice both in Soviet and post-Soviet times (Babich 2001, Jalabadze and Janiashvili 2016). In the data from the North Caucasus, mediator-based conflict resolution is described as a way to reach reconciliation before the blood feud mechanism would be triggered (Albogachieva 2014, pp. 96–97; Bersanova 2014, pp. 117–119; Babich 2014, pp. 65–91). At the same time, in Russia the cultural traditions of arranged group territorial fights between youth groups create a need for their own adjudicators and "dispatchers" of violence (Stephenson 2012).

In what follows, we analyse the relationship between members of youth street organisations and their criminal patrons, as well as wider systems of informal social regulation in the two cities.

The role of criminal groups in illicit social regulation in the Moscow periphery

While older Moscow residents remember the whole of the city being divided into different groups' territories up to the 1960s, nowadays these groups tend to be concentrated in peripheral urban areas. These areas were built to support manufacturing that was largely sited in industrial belts surrounding the centre, and where dense housing projects were constructed (Becker *et al.* 2012, p. 36). This is where young people who actively participate in the street culture can encounter the ex-prisoners who return home after release, and where a specific street-criminal nexus can be found.

In these areas, young people's social identities and distinctions can become profoundly influenced by the criminal culture. Group participants call themselves *patsany* (lads). Non-members have derogatory names, such as *lokhi* (suckers) or *botaniki* (botanists), taken from the prison argot. The latter term derives from the humiliating name given by criminals to the political prisoners in the GULAG whom they viewed as a bunch of scientists with useless skills. Young people who are subjected to systematic street or school extortion are known as *terpily* (sufferers), again a term that derives from prison culture. Street young people believe that their code of *poniatiia* ("understandings", another prison concept) directly derives from the criminal law. Those young men who engage in extreme violence (*bespredel*, a prison term meaning lawlessness, neglect of *poniatiia*) are known as *bespredelschiki* and are shunned by the street groups.

In interviews and focus groups, young men described the ex-convicts as people with moral authority who took it upon themselves to maintain "order". As one informant said, "These are people who have done time, they have an understanding of life. They make sure that there is order in the territory, that we are not at each other's throats." (interview with a 15-year-old man, Moscow, 2006).

There was evidence that the adult ex-convicts living in the communities supported the youth in their attempts to keep their territory "strong" and acted as dispatchers and regulators of violence. In many urban areas across Russia the strength of the territory is determined in a key ritual of youth collective life called *strelka* (arranged fight). Some researchers see this ritual as transposed into cities from rural communities, where these practices formed a core part of village life (Morozov and Sleptsova 2004, Bernshtam 1988, Kabanov 1928), and may reflect a particular character of Russian urban development where the rapidly expanding cities were incorporating neighbouring villages. Moscow was no exception: for example, in 1960 alone, according to Lappo, it incorporated 155 villages. In the resultant "symbiosis" between urban and rural areas, rural social and cultural traditions lingered for a long time (Lappo 2006).

Street groups use *strelki* as a means of settling disputes and confirming territorial boundaries with other groups. The young men agree in advance on the approximate number of fighters and whether weapons (such as chains, clubs or knuckledusters, but never guns or knives) are allowed. If a group is defeated, the reputation of the territory suffers and it can even lose access to important places, such as night clubs, cinemas or stadiums. Ex-convicts can be consulted on organisation of *strelki* and mobilise additional fighters in return for a symbolic gift (often a crate of beer). They can also provide advice on other practices and rituals of violence as well. As one of the informants explained:

> Let's say, our leader has agreed a fight with one hundred people on each side, and we have trouble gathering them. We would always go to [ex-convicts] to ask to make up the numbers. Sometimes they would agree to get them from neighbouring districts. Or they can investigate in advance, who would come from the other side, what would they bring, would there be weapons or not. We can also ask them for advice on what to do if one of our lads was attacked by several lads from outside.
>
> (Focus group, 17-year-old man, Moscow, 2006)

While the leaders of the groups were supposed to have wide social networks in the territory, including having contacts with ex-convicts, ordinary members sought such contact in situations when they were personally threatened and needed to improve their street credibility and find protection in conflict with youths from other neighbourhoods. Young men who were not "lucky" enough to have a neighbour or a relative who had done time, spoke of attempts to get introduced to ex-convicts, hoping to acquire patrons who would help them stay safe. As violent physical conflict is often preceded by an investigation of who is who in the local reputational system, and what kind of connections one has, the ability to drop the right name can be a matter of life and death. The ability to refer to such a patron in a crisis situation did not presuppose any strong relationship with the latter, nor did it entail any subsequent payment.

Interviews showed that the role of ex-convicts in local social regulation was not limited to the sphere of violent support and expertise. They gave small loans to young people (and older neighbours), investigated crimes in the area (such as the theft of a car or a bicycle) and helped, for a fee, to return stolen property. Interviews with young people and community members showed, however, that such services are only provided to people known personally to the ex-convicts.

As one informant reported:

> We have Uncle Sasha Medvedev, he is a thief-in-law. He is 46 years old, he spent time, you can see from his tattoos. He used to be a pickpocket of the highest level. He sits outside the entrance door on a bench with other ex-convicts, playing dominoes and drinking beer. The lads come to him for advice. He looks after order. If we win in a *strelka* he praises us and gives us beer. He can lend you some money too. He is like a father to us. He can also help if a car is stolen, or somebody has burgled a flat, but only if he knows you.
>
> (Interview with a 14-year-old male, Moscow, 2006)

The bonds between members of the criminal networks and youth groups are strengthened through the practice of "warming up the *zona*" (a collective name for prisons and labour camps). Young people collect money, food and clothes to help incarcerated inmates, who include both members of the local street groups who serve time and adult convicts who are not personally related to young people. This is seen as an important obligation, and protection against risk, as, in case these young men themselves are incarcerated, their own "names" would be known and they could rely on positive treatment in prison.

A minority of young men, so called *initsiativshchiki* (initiative-takers), actively seek to join criminal groups, liaising with former convicts and members of criminal networks in their areas, and building their criminal reputations through small-scale racketeering, burglary and other forms of acquisitive crime. The ex-convicts provide advice to these young men on where and how to start their projects of racketeering or burglary (advising them on which local markets or street kiosks do not have their own protection so it would be safe to offer "protection" or commit burglaries). In return, the lads give the older tutors "gifts" (which could constitute 10–30 per cent of their incomes from crime). Young people reported that they could also be asked to help the criminals to punish disobedient businessmen who refuse to pay their protection money.

Here is one typical account:

> They asked us sometimes, although we did not always agree, to trash a street kiosk or beat up the owner. Sometimes it was a shop, and we were reluctant

> to go there because the police could easily nick us there. Normally, however, these requests concerned street markets, this was much safer, we would enter the market in a crowd and start destroying the stalls we were told to attack. So that people who traded there got lost.
>
> (focus group, a 17-year-old male, Moscow, 2006)

While the influence of criminal organisations on Moscow youth communities is on the wane, apart from the peripheral areas described here, in other, more deprived regions, such as in the Zabaikal'e region in Siberia, young members of the so-called Convicts' Movement (Arestantskoe Urkaganskoe Edinstvo, AUE) learn the prison code, collect money, food and clothes to help incarcerated inmates and provide services to adult criminals (Petelin 2016). Similar networks have been found to operate in 17 regions of Russia (Loriia 2016).

The role of criminal groups in illicit social regulation in Tbilisi

In urban Georgia the "street" as a social system functions primarily in the form of peer groups of young people which in Georgian slang were given the special name *birzha* (pl. *birzhebi*), a (labour) exchange, presumably by analogy with the other meaning of this word which describes a special place in public where workers seeking a job gathered to wait for an employer (e.g. cabmen's *birzhebi*). These groups are formed locally from the men who live in the same urban quarter or on the same street. Unlike Moscow, though, street life has been present throughout the urban territory. Different urban quarters (*ubani*) have their own *birzhebi*, which may have slightly different slang, manner of dress and traditions. Similar to Russian street peer groups, these are associations of young men that tend to lack formal leadership or ritualised procedures of admission and exit. As in Russia, in Georgia involvement in street culture traditionally did not correlate with ethnicity or class. An academician's son participating in a street gang or a university professor offering to resort to street methods of conflict resolution represent recent examples from everyday life (forumi, 2016; interview with a 47-year-old male, Tbilisi, 2007). Until relatively recently, in Georgian society participation in street peer groups was also regarded as a possible way to build a career in the thieves' world, for instance, one of the interlocutors recounted how his father, seeing his son's strong involvement in the street life, had once asked him anxiously: "Are you going to become a thief?" (interview with a 22-year-old male, Tbilisi, 2011).

In another similarity with Russia, the street code in Georgia is associated with the normative ideas of hegemonic masculinity also found in the prison culture. As one informant said, "Men's and thieves' understandings have very much in common. Or at least they used to have … If you are a man you won't stay under *abaroti* [i.e. needing to respond to insult]" (interview with a 22-year-old male, Tbilisi, 2011).

The street culture offers ready socialisation models to a teenager, ascribing to him this or that social status. These statuses have special terms in street slang. The street frame of reference rests upon three main positions: *dzveli/kai bichi* (old lad/

good lad), *patiosani/vazkhatsi bichi* (honest, decent lad/manly lad) and *chmori/kle* (in Georgian offensive slang "weakling"/"dick"). The two main positions that represent the top and the bottom rungs of the street social ladder are *dzveli/kai bichi* and *chmori/kle*. In its primary meaning the term *dzveli bichi* denotes someone whose ultimate life purpose is to become a thief-in-law and who builds his street career and defines his life priorities accordingly. These street youths seek contacts with a thief, as they need these relationships both for building their criminal careers and for winning street authority. In its ultimate expression this status implies acquisition of prison experience, which is considered to be a "pass" to the thieves' world and can lead to eventual entry into the elite of this society, to a position of a "crowned" thief. A *dzveli bichi* is on a special life mission, of serving an idea (the "thieves' truth") that requires strict self-discipline and knowledge of the tiniest details of the street code and its "primordial" foundations in the thief's code. "What life do you live?" (*ra tskhovrebit tskhovrob*?) – "A thief's life" (*kurduli tskhovrebit*), would be a proper street exchange about status. *Dzveli/kai bichi* also act as enforcers for the thieves in their protection business.

> A thief doesn't interfere himself, he acts via *kai bichebi*, who are all over him all the time … It may be below the thief's dignity to meet with somebody who is a nobody and he sends them *kai bichebi* [that are close to him] like "I am from such-and-such thief, he is asking for a share."
>
> (interview with a 29-year-old male, Tbilisi, 2011)

One special person who is particularly close to the thief is the *makurebeli* (supervisor, a term taken from the prison culture) of an *ubani*, school or university. The authority of such *makurebeli* was reinforced by their contacts in the thieves' world, and in turn the *makurebeli* reported to the thieves and implemented their instructions. For instance, the *makurebeli* was responsible for the money of *obshiaki* (funds) collected for prisoners in their neighbourhoods.

The image of the *dzveli bichi* is associated with "black" (i.e. thief's) style and looks. This style determines gait, clothing, manner of speaking and is easily recognised by anyone who was socialised in Georgian culture.

Dzveli bichi status provides basic features for the hegemonic masculinity model in Georgian urban culture. In terms of its significance for the young men this role model has no alternatives. The *dzveli bichi* is a central representative of the Georgian street culture. He is seen as a person free from control or pressure of any authorities besides those who are part of the street frame of reference, who is only bounded by a strict behavioural code and obligations of respect and loyalty to those equal to him in status. He should choose a life course that is strictly dissociated from the life scenarios provided for a man by the state. As a faithful follower of the prison norms, a *dzveli bichi* must not do army service, study in state institutions of higher education or "work for a salary". In Soviet times, he certainly could not be a member of the Communist youth organisations (young pioneers and Komsomol), or Communist party member. The status and the image of the *dzveli bichi* was so attractive as a masculine model and an image of a person symbolising resistance to state institutions that many teenagers seeking popularity in the street or with girls adopted its surface features while not aspiring to live a "thief's life".

Street experience and the absence of any known "faults" (violations of the thieves' rules) are the chief requirements one has to meet to qualify for this status. Any claim to it should be legitimated by a thief-in-law: "Two jerks and a thief sit in one room. The thief is asking about one of the guys: 'He is ours, from the *ubani*, isn't he?' They answer him 'yes, he's *kai bichi*'. By silently accepting this he fixes his status. In other words, in such a situation the naming of the status by a thief has a crucial meaning" (interview with a 52-year-old male, Tbilisi, 2012). At the same time, on the neighbourhood level confirmation of the status by already acknowledged *dzveli bichebi* is highly important. If something incompatible with *dzveli bichi* status becomes known about the person, his status may be reduced to the bottom rung, to the level of *chmori/kle*. Lowering to this status may be made by a thief-in law by means of verbal *gapucheba* (spoiling), reminiscent of prison degradation rituals.

Chmori/kle is the status given to those incapable of confronting challenges or standing up for themselves and for the persons, damage to whose reputation is equated with the harm to their own honour (street friends, relatives, neighbours etc.) The status of *chmori/kle* is also associated with homosexuality, and this meaning is adopted from prison culture. Those considered under *kle* category are victimised by those having *dzveli bichi* status, with the aggression most frequently taking the form of mockery, insults, extortion and exploitation. The status of *patiosani bichi* is ascribed to those who are capable of standing up for themselves, are familiar with the street code and take into account its chief requirements, but do not lead a street life and do not attempt to establish themselves in the street. In contrast to the *dzveli bichi*, for the *patiosani bichi* the street is secondary or even unimportant as a social arena, as they pursue career scripts set out by family and the educational system. Similar to Russia, there is also a street status of *besprideli* or *bespridzelniki* (people involved in lawless behaviour). "*Bespridzelniki* were such jerks who were looking for such situations, were asking for trouble, to hit, to cut somebody" (interview with a 28-year-old male, Tbilisi, 2011).

The role of the thieves in illicit social regulation has been much more substantial in Tbilisi than we observed in peripheral Moscow areas. Furthermore, in Tblisi the degree of the thieves' influence seems not to be dependent on a centre-periphery distinction, although two neighbourhoods do stand out in this respect. The first of these, Nadzaladevi (Nakhalovka), is an industrial district that emerged chaotically in the end of the nineteenth century around railroad workshops and is known for the particularly profound influence of the thieves. In contrast, the second neighbourhood, Vake, is an area where members of the Soviet elite settled, with a reputation for being "innovatory" or "less conservative". Here the thieves have not enjoyed the same respect as elsewhere – for example, it is said that money for criminal funds, *obshchiaki*, is not collected in Vake (interview with a 30-year-old male, Tbilisi, 2011).

Relying on the knowledge of the code and on their status as "men of honour", thieves-in-law and their associates (so called "authorities") provided an arbitration service to representatives of the local population regardless of economic or social distinctions, mediating in a variety of conflicts, with the exception of domestic ones. The thieves and their associates helped return stolen possessions, ensure debt repayment and fulfillment of other obligations to any resident of their *ubani* who requested this service:

> In case of something serious, a bet, in this case to safeguard oneself against the situation when they won't be able to pay off, it was like 'why not to get a thief or some authority involved' ... and they got an authority involved and he got a share too, but he also controlled that they would get in time what they had owed.
>
> (interview with a 29-year-old male, Tbilisi, 2011)

The clients could be men or women. For instance, if a woman preferred to decide her issue with the help of street arbitrators she could do this through an intermediary (e.g. her male relative) who had a good understanding of street power relationships. The threat to "get the people involved" was a common way of exerting pressure in conflict situations.

The choice between the two normative fields (that is the formal legal system and the street code) was relatively free, but according to the street code in each particular case it had to be irrevocable: if the case was initiated street-wise it had to be finished in the same way. The explanation is quite rational,

> Let's say I've lent you money, you don't pay me back … The person from their side whom I will talk to … has to be a member of my world too. And the transit from here to there makes problems for both sides, and then in the investigation they will be like: 'Who have you met?' – I think you understand what I mean. And there is a kind of a dogma that if you trouble somebody from the street you mustn't go, mustn't trust any executive body … And where does this stem from … But yes, it is reasonable .
>
> (Interview with a 22-year-old male, Tbilisi, 2011)

According to the interview data, it was relatively late that the thieves began to charge a fee for their arbitration service:

> When the term "my thief, your thief" emerged, I mean during the street negotiation, just imagine, what is it like "my thief", I mean that I pay him money and you pay yours, these are not thieves any longer. Formerly [the thieves] were not paid [for mediation]. But when I was a child [1990s–early 2000s] they already were. There were for example the "hundred dollar thieves".
>
> (interview with a 21-year-old male, Tbilisi, 2009)

There was a norm according to which the thief took 20 per cent of the sum whose payment he had to guarantee. However, in practice the compensation depended on the specifics of the case and the relationship between the mediator and the conflict party.

The street method of conflict resolution is often seen as the one which enables people to refrain from aggravating the situation further and de-escalating the conflict. It is used to control street violence or mediate in business disputes.

> I remembered Vakhtangovich, he is this kind of a guy, he's got a big company, he's a businessman, he knows what's what, that sort of thing. But when it happened that he needed something, he had to get money [to get his money back] he again came to an "authority". And he did this because he didn't want to push him [the debtor] into even more serious problems – you even go to meet his, this guilty person's, needs. And if the police came to him, this guy would face the music. He would be jailed and so on. And here if an "authority" holds you accountable, at least, he won't imprison you. You are guilty and that's it.
>
> (Interview with a 22-year-old male, Tbilisi, 2011)

The use of street code and street mediation is currently diminishing. Previously the code was almost impossible to ignore: for instance, in the Soviet period if a conflict occurred between a Komsomol member who did not participate in street life and someone who shared the street culture, it was yet settled according to the thieves' rules. However, as a result of Saakashvili's reforms and propaganda campaigns against the thieves' world, formal means of conflict resolution have become more widely practiced. With strengthening of the state and economy, the street career ceased to be as promising as it used to be in the 1990s and early 2000s. As a result, the street culture described above, with its pronounced street-criminal nexus, began to wane.

Conclusion

Having outlined the relationships between street peer groups, local communities and criminal societies in post-Soviet Moscow and Tbilisi, what lessons can we draw? The main lesson, it seems, is that high incarceration societies create resilient prison cultures that can have a profound impact on mainstream society and particularly on the world of street peer groups. This impact is not limited to deliberate indoctrination of young people by criminals and/or their recruitment into gangs and organised crime groups. Young people's individual and collective identities and, for some, street career strategies become shaped by encounters with the denizens of the penitentiary. Prison normative systems affect dominant masculinity constructions, creating a lasting effect on perceptions of "proper manhood" that can, as Marina Yusupova has shown, outlive the street experience and inform the gender ideologies of adult non-criminal men (Yusupova 2015).

In the community, ex-convicts can fill the regulatory vacuum and participate in conflict resolution. They form patron-client relations with young people and other members of the local communities, regulating violence, mediating in conflicts and creating a regime of illicit regulation. This regime, in which the criminals may often behave in a predatory and opportunistic way, can also have positive social and economic benefits, compensating for the inefficiency or absence of state regulation.

The influence of the networks moulded in the Soviet prisons intersects with traditional forms of regulation of popular violence. In Russia these took the form of organised group fights that confirmed the local reputation of male fighters and set territorial borders; in Georgia they were traditions of informal resolution of conflicts that helped prevent conflict escalation. We have seen that adult criminal mediators play a major role in regulation of territorial violence in those areas of Moscow where the street remains the key place of male socialisation, while playing a relatively limited role in conflict mediation at the community level. In contrast, while territorial practices of organised violence are less important in Tbilisi, criminal mediation has, until relatively recently, been a core practice of local conflict resolution.

The Soviet and post-Soviet systems of formal regulation and highly repressive penal policies have coexisted with locally specific traditions of informal, illicit and criminal social regulation. These alternative systems of regulation have been particularly strong in areas where the state penetration was low and inefficient and/or where there was a strong cultural resistance to state power. Among such spaces was the space of prison, where inmates created their alternative orders, and the space of the streets, colonised by local street corner societies. The intersection of these orders produced complex ground-level social systems of reciprocity and authority.

In both societies the increasing privatisation of public space and growing social differentiation have led to a decrease in the importance of the street social systems, particularly in more affluent areas, while the strengthening of the state undermines the power and prestige of criminal groups. Nevertheless, the street remains an important arena of local life and continues to be the place for identity formation for young men. Encounters with the representatives of prison society and with the "truths" that they've learned while in incarceration continue to shape their views of themselves and the world around them.

Notes

1 The southeastern *okrug* of Moscow is an old industrial region. The main housing construction in the territory dates back to the 1980s, when residential quarters of high-rise buildings were built for migrants coming to work in the local industry. The territory is divided into industrial zones and "dormitory" areas with high population density (this is where the youth street groups are based). Since the start of the market reforms, many large industrial enterprises in the territory have gone through several waves of redundancies. Nevertheless, the territory still has the highest concentration of industry among the Moscow regions. The average price of housing here is lower than in other Moscow regions and the area still attracts significant migration.

2 The focus groups took place in the school for juvenile delinquents in the southeastern *okrug* of Moscow. The school is an "educational institution of a closed type". It belongs to the Moscow city department of education. Its students are referred to it by courts for minor offences (mainly hooliganism and theft), as an alternative to criminal punishment.

3 Incarceration rates in the USSR were consistently the highest in the world, although they differed by year. For example, 780 per 100,000 people were incarcerated in 1936; 1,500 in 1941; 2,700 in 1953; and 847 in 1986 (Luneev, 2006, quoted in Yusupova, 2015, p. 58).

References

Abramkin, V. 2007. "Bratstvo kak strategiia"'. *Smysl* 11:105–107.

Albogachieva, M.S.-G. 2014. "Primiritelnye komissii v Ingushetii: istoriia i sovremennost"." In *Traditsionnye praktiki uregulirovaniia konfliktov. Materialy ezhegodnogo seminara 2010–2014 gg.*, edited by A. Konovalov, 92–114. Moscow: MOO Tsentr "Sudebno-pravovaia reforma".

Anderson, E. 1999. *Code of the Street: Decency, Violence, and the Moral Life of the Inner City*. New York, London: Norton.

Arias, E.D. and Rodrigues, C.D. 2006. "The myth of personal security: Criminal gangs, dispute resolution, and identity in Rio de Janeiro's Favelas". *Latin American Politics & Society*, 48 (4): 53–81.

Arlacchi, P. 1988. "Some observations on illegal markets". In *The New European Criminology*, edited by V. Ruggerio, N. South and Taylor I., 203–215. London: Routledge.

Babich, I.L. 2001. "Mekhanizmy formirovaniia pravovogo pliuralizma na Kavkaze (na primere Kabardino-Balkarii i Severnoi Osetii)". In *Sotsialnaia organizatsiia i obychnoe pravo. Materialy nauchnoi konferentsii 24–26 avgusta 2000 g*, edited by A.N. Manuilov, 7–25. Krasnodar.

Babich, I.L. 2014. "Vozrozhdenie instituta mediatorstva v gorskikh soobshchestvakh Severnogo Kavkaza v sovetskie i postsovetskie gody (1950–2000 gg.)". In *Traditsionnye praktiki uregulirovaniia konfliktov: Materialy ezhegodnogo seminara 2010–2014 gg.*, edited by A. Konovalov, 65–91. Moscow.

Becker, C., Mendelsohn, J.S. and Benderskaya, K. 2012. *Russian Urbanization in the Soviet and Post-Soviet Eras*. London: Human Settlements Group, International Institute for Environment and Development, working paper 9. Available at: http://www.iied.org/pubs/display.php?o=10613IIED, accessed 6 November 2016.

Bernshtam, T.A. 1988. *Molodezh v obriadovoi zhisni russkoi obshchiny XIX – nachala XX veka: Polovozrastnoi aspekt traditsionnoi kultury*. Leningrad: Nauka.

Bersanova, Zh.Kh.-A. 2014. "Obychai krovnoi mesti i praktika primireniia v sovremennoi Chechne". In *Traditsionnye praktiki uregulirovaniia konfliktov. Materialy ezhegodnogo seminara 2010–2014 gg.*, edited by A. Konovalov, 115–123. Moscow.

Blok, A. 1974. *The Mafia of a Sicilian Village, 1860–1960: a Study of Violent Peasant Entrepreneurs*. Oxford: Blackwell.

Catanzaro, Ra. 1992. *Men of Respect: A Social History of the Sicilian Mafia*. New York: Free Press; Toronto: Maxwell Macmillan Canada; New York: Maxwell Macmillan International.

Chalidze, V.I. 1977. *Criminal Russia: Essays on Crime in the Soviet Union*. New York: Random House.

Cheloukhine, S. 2008. "The roots of Russian organised crime: The old-fashioned professionals to the organised criminal groups of today". *Crime, Law and Social Change*, 50: 353–374.

Collins, R. 2008. *Violence: A Micro-Sociological Theory*. Princeton, NJ: Princeton University Press.

Dobson, M. 2009. *Khrushchev's Cold Summer: Gulag Returnees, Crime, and the Fate of Reform after Stalin*. Ithaca, NY: Cornell University Press.

Efimova, E. 2004. *Sovremennaia tiur'ma. Byt, traditsii i fol'klor*. Moscow: O.G.I. tbilisis forumi. 2016. "90 tslebis kriminaluri tbilisi da saqartvelo, e,ts., sadzmoebi", https://forum.ge/?f=29&showtopic=34820902&st=345.

Gambetta, D. 1993. *The Sicilian Mafia: The Business Of Private Protection*. Cambridge, MA: Harvard University Press.

gamtsemlidze, dato. n.d. "qvelmoqmedeba da gadasakhadebi". http://experti.ge/kvelmokmedeba_dagadasaxadebi.htm.

Glonti, G. and Lobzhanidze, G. 2004. *Professional'naia prestupnost' v Gruzii: vory v zakone*. Tbilisi: TraCCC.

Golovin, V. V. and Lurie, M.L. 2008. "Ideologicheskie i territorialnie soobshchestva molodeozhi: megapolis, provintsialnii gorod, selo". *Etnograficheskoe Obozrenie*, 1: 56–70.

Gromov, D.V. 2009. "Podrostkovo-molodeozhnye ulichnie gruppirovki kak ob'ekt etnograficheskogo issledovaniia". In *Molodeozhnye ulichnye gruppirovki: vvedenie v problematiku*, edited by D.V. Gromov, 8–72. Moscow: IEA RAN.

Grossman, Gregory. 1977. "The 'second economy' of the USSR". *Problems of Communism*, 26 (5): 25–40.

Gurov, A.I. 1995. *Krasnaia mafia*. Moscow: MIKO Kommercheskii vestnik.

Hagedorn, J.M. 2015. *The Insane Chicago Way: The Daring Plan by Chicago Gangs to Create a Spanish Mafia*. Chicago: The University of Chicago Press.

Handelman, S. 1994. *Comrade CRIMINAL: THE THEFt of the Second Russian Revolution*. London: Michael Joseph.

Holzlehner, Tobias. 2014. *Shadow Networks: Border Economies, Informal Markets and Organized Crime in the Russian Far East*. Berlin: LIT.

Jalabadze, N. and Janiashvili, L. 2016. "Traditional law and blood feud: Svan legal practice in Soviet times and in contemporary Southern Georgia". In *State and Legal Practice in the Caucasus: Anthropological Perspectives on Law and Politics*, edited by Stéphane Voell and Iwona Kaliszewska. London: Routledge, 37–50.

Kabanov, S.F. 1928. *Bor'ba s ugolovnoi prestupnost'iu v derevne*. Moscow: Izdatel'stvo NKVD RSFSR.

Karbainov, N.I. 2009. "'Ei, khunkhuz, kuda idiosh? Zdes' bratva, i ty umriosh!': 'ulichnye voiny' v Ulan-Ude." In *Molodezhnye ulichnye gruppirovki: vvedenie v problematiku*, edited by D.V. Gromov. Moscow: IEA RAN, 132–148.

Kozlov, A.S. 1998. *"Kozel na sakse": i tak vsiu zhizn´*. Moscow: Vagrius.

Kupatadze, A. 2012. *Organized Crime, Political Transitions, and State Formation in Post-Soviet Eurasia*. Houndmills, Basingstoke, Hampshire; New York, NY: Palgrave Macmillan.

Lappo, G.M. 2006. Rossiiskii gorod - simbioz gorodskogo i sel'skogo. *Demoscope Weekly* (221–222). Accessed 22 November 2016.

Ledeneva, A.V. 1998. *Russia's Economy of Favours: Blat, Networking, and Informal Exchange, Cambridge Russian, Soviet and Post-Soviet Studies*. Cambridge, UK: Cambridge University Press.

Loriia, E. 2016. "Detei zatsavliaiut sdavat' den'gi na obshchak dlia zony". *Izvestiia*. Available at: http://izvestia.ru/news/621939#ixzz4EGOpbbU5. Accessed 8 November 2016.

Luneev, V. 2006. "Prestuplenie i nakazanie v Rossii". *Demoskop Weekly*, issue 239–240. Available at: http://demoscope.ru/weekly/2006/0239/tema07.php. Accessed 5 January 2017.

Manning, P. 2009. "The city of balconies: elite politics and the changing semiotics of the post-socialist cityscape". In *City Culture and City Planning in Tbilisi: Where Europe and Asia Meet*, edited by K. Van Assche, J. Salukvadze and N. Shavishvili, 71–102. Lewiston, NY, Lampeter: Edwin Mellen Press.

Mars, G. and Altman, Y. 1983. "The cultural bases of Soviet Georgia's second economy". *Soviet Studies* 35 (4): 546–560.

Martin, J.L. 2009. *Social Structures*. Princeton, NJ: Princeton University Press.

Messerschmidt, J. 2012. "Engendering gendered knowledge: assessing the academic appropriation of hegemonic masculinity". *Men and Masculinities*, 15 (1): 56–76.

Morozov, I.A., and Sleptsova, I. S. 2004. *Krug igry: prazdnik i igra v zhisni severorusskogo krest'ianina (XIX-XX vv.)*. Moscow: INDRIK.

Nasritdinov, E. and Schröder, P. 2016. "From Frunze to Bishkek: Soviet territorial youth formations and their decline in the 1990s and 2000s". *Central Asian Affairs*, 3:1–28. doi: http://dx.doi.org/10.1163/22142290-00301001.

Oleinik, A.N. 2003. *Organized Crime, Prison, and Post-Soviet Societies*. Aldershot: Ashgate.

Paoli, L. 2003. *Mafia Brotherhoods: Organized Crime, Italian Style*. Oxford: Oxford University Press.

Petelin, G. 2016. "Urkagany vsiali shkoly pod kontrol". (February 2). doi: www.gazeta.ru/social/2016/02/02/8053655.shtml.

Ponomareva, E.Ya. 2014. "Konstrukty i praktiki maskulinnosti v ulichnykh podrostkovo-molodyozhnykh soobschestvakh g.Yerevana (Armeniia)". In *Antropologiia goroda: Materialy konferentsii molodykh uchenykh. Moscow, 4–6 December 2013*, 116–125. Moscow: IEA RAN.

Ponomareva, E.Ya. 2015. "Dramaturgiia konflikta v erevanskoi ulichnoi kul'ture". In *Lavrovskii sbornik: Materialy XXXVIII u XXXIX Sredneaziatsko-Kavkazskikh chtenii 2014–2015 g.g.: Etnologiia, istoriia, arkheologiia, kul'turologiia*, 472–476, St Petersburg.

Raleigh, D.J. 2006. *Russia's Sputnik Generation: Soviet Baby Boomers Talk about Their Lives, Indiana–Michigan Series in Russian and East European Studies*. Bloomington: Indiana University Press.

Razinkin, V. 1995. *Vory v zakone i prestupnie klany*. Moscow: Kriminologicheskaia Assotsiatsiia.

Rodgers, D. 2006. "The state as a gang: conceptualizing the governmentality of violence in contemporary Nicaragua". *Critique of Anthropology*, 26 (3): 315–330.

Sánchez-Jankowski, M. 1991. *Islands in the Street: Gangs and American Urban Society*. Berkeley: University of California Press.

Slade, G. 2013. *Reorganizing Crime: Mafia and Anti-Mafia in Post-Soviet Georgia*. 1st edition. ed, *Clarendon studies in Criminology*. Oxford: Oxford University Press.

Sokolov, V. 2004. "From guns to briefcases: The evolution of Russian organized crime". *World Policy Journal*, 21 (1):68–74.

Stephenson, S. 2008. "Searching for home. Street youth and organized crime in Russia". In *Globalizing the Streets. Cross- cultural Perspectives on Youth, Social Control, and Empowerment*, edited by D. Brotherton and M. Flynn, 78–92. New York: Columbia University Press.

Stephenson, S. 2012. "The violent practices of youth territorial groups in Moscow". *Europe-Asia Studies*, 64 (1): 69–90.

Stephenson, S. 2015. *Gangs of Russia: From the Streets to the Corridors of Power*. Ithaca: Cornell University Press.

Sutherland, E.H. and Cressey, D.R. 1970. *Criminology*. Philadelphia: Lippincott.

Suttles, G.D. 1968. *The Social Order of the Slum. Ethnicity and Territory in the Inner City*. Chicago: University of Chicago Press.

Taylor, B.D. 2011. *State Building in Putin's Russia: Policing and Coercion after Communism.* Cambridge: Cambridge University Press.

Tsipursky, G.V. 2009. "'Obshchestva', 'shtaby', 'kluby'. Gorodskoe molodezhnoe khuliganstvo v Sovetskom Soiuse 'ottepel'nykh' let." In *Molodezhnye ulichnye gruppirovki: vvedenie v problematiku*, edited by D.V. Gromov, 73–93. Moscow: IEA RAN.

Varese, F. 2001. *The Russian Mafia: Private Protection in a New Market Economy.* Oxford: Oxford University Press.

Venkatesh, S.A. 2000. *American Project: The Rise and Fall of a Modern Ghetto.* Cambridge,MA: Harvard University Press.

Volkov, V. 2002. *Violent Entrepreneurs: The Use of Force in the Making of Russian Capitalism.* Ithaca, NY: Cornell University Press.

Whyte, W.F. 1993. *Street Corner Society: The Social Structure of an Italian Slum.* Vol. 4th, Chicago: University of Chicago Press.

Yusupova, M. 2015. "Masculinity, criminality, and Russian men". *Sextures*, 3 (3): 46–61.

Zakharova, E. 2015. "The Tbilisi 'street' as a legal and political phenomenon in Georgia". In *State and Legal Practice in the Caucasus: Anthropological Perspectives on Law and Politics*, edited by S. Voell and I. Kaliszewska, 69–82. London: Routledge.

Zakharova, Ye. Yu. 2010. "Tbilisskaia ulitsa kak sreda muzhskoi sotsializatsii". *Laboratorium. Zhurnal Sotsialnykh Issledovanii* (1): 182–204.

Zakharova, Ye. Yu. 2012. "Tbilisskaia ulitsa kak iavleniie pravovoi i politicheskoi zhisni Gruzii". In *Obshchestvo kak ob'ekt i sub'ekt vlasti. Ocherki politicheskoi antropologii Kavkaza.*, edited by Yu. Yu. Karpov, 111–130. St Petersburg: MAE RAN.

6 Illegal enterprises and the city

When territorial control is an issue of urban governance. Lessons from Medellín, Colombia

Laure Leibler

Introduction

> The families complied with the order [of armed groups] and began fleeing. While on the move, they called their relatives, looking for a place to stay that Sunday night. On Monday, the forced displacement was undeniable. The police, the army and officials of Medellín's city hall arrived. The paradox is that instead of restraining people from fleeing and assuming control of the territory, they ended up loading people's belongings onto trucks.
>
> (*Redaccion Semana*, 2013)

This anecdote, reported in a Colombian investigative magazine in 2013, refers to an instance of massive intra-urban displacement that took place in the 13th district of the city. The report underlines two issues there: The fact that people can be forced to leave their home and belongings due to imminent threats by illegal actors, a phenomenon called forced displacement, in the second largest city of Colombia that is now promoted as "half a miracle" (Fukuyama and Colby, 2011) for its decrease of urban violence, and the fact that local civil servants and the army helped people fleeing, questioning the ability of state governance to provide safety. This event raises the question of "who has control in Medellín?" (Isaza, 2015). Both the existence of intra-urban forced displacement and the acknowledgement by officials and the media of such a phenomenon and their subsequent reactions (whether it is to try to mitigate the impacts and the loss of the people forced to flee or to criticise such an action) are interesting to study from a geographical perspective. In fact, Medellín is a relevant study case of the role played by illegal groups at the local scale and in an urban setting, and as such raises the more general question of local governance when the state does not have the monopoly of violence.

It questions the concomitance of legal and extralegal forms of governance (Varese, 2010) in a given area. By looking precisely at the neighbourhood as being this interface between two distinctive forces of power (one legal, one criminal), the evidence-based analysis of this chapter aims to raise conceptual issues on urban governance. When entrepreneurial criminal enterprises exercise power over space and people, how does it impact the way a city is controlled and administrated by local public authorities? Looking at the relationship between the illegal actors of violence and the city through observation, testimonies, interviews and official reports collected through three years of field work in Medellín, this chapter intends to untangle some aspects of this issue. Beyond the case of Medellín, it is a call for a territorial approach to study the local actions of illegal enterprises in an urban context, in order to raise awareness on how territorial control is an issue for urban governance. The first part of this chapter presents the case of Medellín in the light of a conceptual framework on organised crime and extralegal governance. The second part will focus on the shift to a more geographical approach through the idea of territorial control. The last part will present the main aspects of territorial control as exercised by illegal groups, taking mainly the case of the first and second districts of Medellín. The conclusion underlines the Medellín paradox: By acknowledging the existence of a concomitant territorial control and tackling its effects, the local administration can reinforce its governance and display innovative politics.

Medellín, a tale of two cities

The city of Medellín, Colombia, is the second largest in the country. More than 2.5 million inhabitants live and work there and move around its streets. On the one hand, Medellín is a major Colombian city, a developed industrial and financial center, with a ten per cent unemployment rate in 2015, 140 cultural events, 360 superior education programs, an 80 per cent rate of access to primary school and a decrease in homicide rates from 52/100,000 inhabitants in 2012 to 20/100,000 (Medellín Como Vamos, 2016). It is nowadays considered an innovative city and one that has won many international prizes (Andrews, 2016) for urban policies, good governance and innovative public transport systems (Musset, 2014). For more than a decade, Medellín City Hall has been promoting inclusive development by investing massively in the working-class neighbourhoods that used to have the highest homicide rates. For instance, a cable-car system linked to the metro network was inaugurated in 2004 to connect the Popular and Santa Cruz boroughs (the first and second districts) to the center. Those two areas located in the Northeast of the city were also the scene of many social and urban transformations through massive investment to improve the quality of public spaces, mobility, education, access to new technologies, cultural projects and living conditions (Leibler and Musset, 2009; Leibler and Brand, 2012).

On the other hand, Medellín has faced the presence of illegal violent groups since the 1980s, especially criminal enterprises linked to drug trafficking. According to an official report by the City Hall, there are nine illegal organisations linked to drug trafficking who coordinate 75 gangs,

> a situation that leads to territorial control exercised by these groups and hence, the occurrence of the crime of forced displacement … that can be a consequence of the disputes (between groups) or a strategy of depopulation

> and repopulation of the territories with the aim to reinforce the presence of collaborators in different places.
>
> (Alcaldia de Medellín, 2015, p. 28)

Since 2002, 67,650 people have been forcibly displaced in Medellín by illegal groups, according to this same report. This number is based only on the number of people who have declared to the authorities that they have been forced to leave their home, neighbourhood and often belongings. For the authorities, this intra-urban forced displacement is a consequence and a symptom of strategies of control over illegal economies. This phenomenon occurs both in places where groups have an armed dispute over the territory and in places with the hegemonic presence of one criminal organisation. The existence of forced displacement within a city cannot be understood without tackling the issue of territorial control and the presence of illegal actors. As I will explain later, it is both a consequence and a means to reinforce territorial control for illegal armed enterprises.

The phenomenon of intra-urban forced displacement, its existence even, questions the nature of illegal actors in Medellín. Indeed, if the illegal enterprises forcibly and often violently displace people, if they have the means and the latitude to do so, is it only as entrepreneurial criminal enterprises, "configurations that serve economic functions in the sense that they are geared toward generating material benefits" (Von Lampe, 2016a, p. 22)? Are they structures that have political purposes and as such could be considered as non-state armed groups? Are they hybrid criminal organisations (Passas, 2003, pp. 22–23) with both economic and political ambitions? This is and has been a debate amongst scholars, local officials and victims' advocates and NGO's in Medellín, since the beginning of armed conflict. This is the point where *the political approach* comes into the picture. One aspect of the intellectual debate on the issue is whether those groups can be qualified as political or not. This argument is ongoing. Some intellectuals think they are linked to the political armed conflict that Colombia has known since the mid-1960s, while officials prefer to say they are common delinquents with no political aspirations. This may seem like a minor detail, but the possibility of illegal actors entering rehabilitation programs, being considered as child soldiers or receiving aid for being victims of internal conflicts, depends on the political categorisation of the illegal armed groups. Until 2003, intra-urban forced displacement was not legally recognised as such. Therefore, the people who underwent intra-urban displacement had to fight to receive help and the success of their petitions depended on the status – political or not – of those who had forced them to leave (see Atehortua, 2010; and also Ramirez, in Dowdney, 2005).

Some sociological accounts have sought to make precise diagnoses as to who these illicit actors are and have considered violence in Medellín within its historical context (Duncan, 2014; Jaramillo in Giraldo, 2011; Salazar, 1991). These studies have shown the complexity and diversity of illegal armed groups there. As difficult as it is to sum up some of their findings, it is necessary to keep in mind that the city of Medellín has known various periods of intense violence due to the presence of different illegal groups. Going back to the 1980s, the infamous

"Medellín Cartel" was responsible for a spike in the homicide rate because of a conflict between the state and this illegal drug ring led by Pablo Escobar. The cartel was actually both a vertical and horizontal organisation, since it had different local groups compete at the neighbourhood level by assigning different missions to each of them (Martin, 2013, pp. 135–145). After Pablo Escobar died, many of those small criminal groups tried to maintain their positions in their neighbourhoods. At the end of the 1980s and the beginning of the 1990s, numerous neighbourhoods witnessed the formation of urban militias, originally trained by urban guerrillas (Medina Franco, 2006, pp. 43–45). They absorbed the latter's ideology as they learned strategic combat in urban settings. They assigned to themselves the mission of pacifying their neighbourhoods and bringing security to working-class areas where small groups of traffickers were entrenched (Medina Franco, 2006). After a local disarmament and rehabilitation program was adopted, militias laid down their arms in 1994. This process was political. Subsequently, the local gangs grew in strength again and an attempt to federate them was initiated by groups linked to the paramilitary groups, which had a nationwide presence (Jaramillo, 2011, in Giraldo Ramirez, 2011, p. 91).

In 2003, many illegal paramilitary actors entered a process of disarmament and also a reinsertion program. For a while, all illegal actors answered to one man (sentenced both for paramilitary activities and drug trafficking), which led the press to talk of "Don Bernabilidad", a play on words combining Don Berna, the boss's nickname, and *gobernabilidad*, or governance. "Don Berna's governance" coincided with a reduction in homicide rates in Medellín (Avila Martinez, 2010, p. 18). And nowadays? According to the investigation done by Ana Maria Jaramillo, it would seem that the illegal actors are hybrids between entrepreneurial criminal structures and illegal armed groups (Jaramillo, 2011, pp. 92), marked by the fluidity of allegiances and strategies of associations between groups. If we considered their official denomination by Colombian authorities as delinquent organisations associated with drug trafficking, there is no political motive to the territorial control they have exercised. But the inhabitants I interviewed often stay vague on the characterisation of these groups. Many have noticed the permanence of the same people involved in the same activities in the neighbourhood. When I asked people that have been displaced who forced them to leave, they were not keen on answering, but when asked if they knew the person or people who made them leave, they would identify them as neighbours, reminding us of the strongly embedded local nature of those groups. Studies show the permanence of some practices of "extra-legal governance" (as defined by Varese, 2011) within specific places in this particularly complex context. Some practices such as beatings, killings and displacement have been taking place in some neighbourhoods for more than 20 years (*El Tiempo*, 2016, 13 December, 23 November). This is why I chose to focus on the local dimension in this chapter. These criminal organisations, though not transnational, are "ever mutating interlocking networks of locally based serious criminality" (Hobbs, 1998, p. 419). In the two districts that I have studied, one group especially has managed to create a strong hegemony (*El Colombiano*, 2015) as an illegal enterprise dedicated to illegal trafficking (local drugs markets, arms trafficking and prostitution, mainly), while imposing territorial control. By looking at the spatial expression of the territorial control of the entrepreneurial criminal groups in Medellín, we might shed some light on the relations between urban governance and illegal enterprises.

Towards a definition of territorial control as an evidence based concept

The difficulty of characterising the illegal actors in Medellín, the debates it generates, may be linked to the issue of territorial control. Is exercising territorial control necessarily a political act, as it is a form of governance? "In this sense organised crime is not just criminal business, it is criminal government" (Hill, 2006, p. 9).The state is supposed to have territorial control, especially because it is the entity having the monopoly of legitimate violence (Weber, 1965), the means to have the ability to impose its rule. Weber adds, moreover, that the state is the only entity that provides the "right to violence". It is also the only entity to have the ability to delegate – as well as, privatise – or legitimise the use of violence. Therefore, there can be other actors wielding violent force in a territory with the consent of the state. Every place administered and ruled by private entities with the agreement of the state has the ability and the latitude to exercise territorial control. In fact, cities know concomitant legal territorial controls (e.g. all the public places managed by companies or private entities such as malls, or gated communities). Legal territorial control is supposed to serve the best interests of the inhabitants and benefit the group of the territory. The main issue arises when this territorial control takes place outside the law, in particular when it is exercised by illegal groups. The first problematic given by territorial control exercised by illegal armed groups is the potential for arbitrary violence. But the second one is that this territorial control becomes an important part of the criminal activity and actions of the illegal armed group. The question of an alternative power through and over space exercised by actors that are not legal is raised by the literature on organised crime, since mafia groups, an "industry which produces, promotes and sells private protection" (Gambetta, 1993, p. 1), have the possibility of exercising territorial control (Gayraud, 2008). As such, the territorial actions of illegal actors are a challenge to legitimate authority. But this philosophical and political debate puts aside a more pragmatic analysis as to how legal and illegal practices of territorial control interact. How can two groups (or more) enforce non-exclusive territorial control of a given area? This could potentially occur through shared, complementary or competitive territorial control.

Power is, according to its basic definition, the ability and latitude to do something. Territorial control is the ability and latitude to define and shape a given area. To bring some light to this issue, identifying the main manifestations of territorial control could offer a pragmatic theoretical definition. If an entity – a public or private structured group – has the ability and latitude to a) mark its presence in a given space, b) establish rules and normative usages in the area, c) impose its rules by assuming law and order capacities – meaning a police/investigative force and an ability to pass judgment and carry out sentences, d) be paid to provide such services thanks to a tax and e) define the limits of the area (who may go through, stay, live, have an economic activity in the area), then this structured entity has control over a given territory. Those elements can be considered as the five pillars of territorial control. Taken together, they are the very definition of territorial control.

Territorial control of illegal enterprises in Medellín

Marking their physical presence in a given area

The illegal actors occupy the streets, especially corners and certain strategic points, and demand access to the rooftops in the north-eastern part of the city. According to a local leader, "They are better organised than the State, they even have patrols" (interview with a local leader of the 1st district, 2012). The police also have 16 patrols in the area. Both illegal groups and the State share the streets and the territory. Day and night, both entities organise patrols and surveillance. I have observed in some strategic places the co-presence of the legal and illegal personnel in charge of dissuasion and surveillance. The difference is that while the police and army carry their weapons openly, the guns of illegal actors are not visible. The presence of the illegal actors can also be witnessed through tags and graffiti, whereas the state marks its presence with flags, schools, social services or public transportation. They do not need to show signs of power, because the community knows who they are. Nor is there necessarily a need for tattoos or distinctive outfits as in the case of the Maras in San Salvador (Poveda, 2008). In this sense, the internal structure of the group is closer to a criminal enterprise than to a gang. When the group consolidates its presence and offers "protective services" (Bedoya, 2010, pp. 73–79) it needs less visible symbols of its power. One informant told me the story of how the elderly woman, who owns the small food shop around the corner from his house, intervened to prevent the murder of a man only by telling "them" not to do so. Because she was the sister of one of the founders (retired) of the local group, "she is well respected you know" (interview with 26 years old man, 2012). The social network of the neighbourhood is intertwined with the criminal networks:

> Crime networks are defined by the illicit entrepreneurial activities of the individuals in the network. Those individuals may simply be entrepreneurs who serve as nodal points around which network participants perform their tasks. They may be a relatively stable group of core network members who bring others into the network as their skills, resources or talents are needed. Participants in crime networks may not regard themselves as being members of a criminal group, and may not be regarded as being a criminal group by outsiders.
>
> (Potter and Willingham, no date, p. 2)

The close relationship between the members of illegal groups and the neighbourhoods makes it easier for them to establish their control. The family kinship and friendships, the small town mentality and the gossiping make it easier to spread rumours. As seen in the second district in Medellín, the long-lasting involvement of the same actors limits the use of violence to exemplary measures. According to Gayraud, "generalised fear makes it possible to limit and avoid the use of violence. In his meditation on power, Thomas Hobbes perfectly summed up the situation: "Reputation of power is power, because it draweth with it the adherence of those that need protection"" (Gayraud, 2008, p. 206). By making sure everyone knows the rules, the illegal actors have the power to actually control the place. Gossip, whispers and unverified yet credible stories are key instruments for achieving territorial control. Once again, the power of illegal actors is well established in this area and their threats are inscribed in a tradition of violence. Using information and managing communication also means promoting a certain lifestyle and training new recruits in order to ensure lasting control over the territory.

Imposing their rule on those who live in or use the space

Medellín is not a no-man's land. It is one of the most important cities in Colombia. But in the territories marked by the presence of illegal enterprises, another code is also in force to rule the place and control urban practices. A 26-year-old informant states:

> The rules of the neighbourhood are: (1) Family matters must be resolved behind closed doors except if it comes to murder. In this case, you are forced to leave or be killed. (2) Don't smoke weed where kids can see you. This gives you "la pela" [a beating] or forced displacement. (3) Don't speak. Blabbing is forbidden. Otherwise, here comes "la pela". It's omertà. Whatever you saw or didn't see, do not tell anyone. Silence. (4) Respect the hierarchy. If they are members of the group, do not look at them, or cross them in any way. You ought to behave well otherwise you will immediately get "la pela". (5) It is not tolerated to steal or beat your mother. (6) Rape… There are many cases of uncles abusing their nieces. That means death. The guys respect religion and good people. They respect the discreet girl that stays home and is not the neighbourhood bitch. (7) If they see you hanging around in the Galera sector, when war time comes, you are going to be a suspect. If they see you talk to the police, you are a dead man. (8) If someone owes money, and the guy doesn't have the means to pay you back, they take stuff from his house to pay you with. If the debt is too high, they just kill the guy. It is the community itself that sees them as the authority. "You pay us and we will make them pay you". When there is a rumor that something is going on, they complain to the old man. The guys show up and talk to the people involved. And then decide if they give him la pela or if he has to leave. I also noticed that when there is someone well off, they make him leave out of jealousy. (9) They make you pay the extortion price. Either you pay or your house is robbed or they make you go. (10) Don't mess around with the group leaders' women. (11) Don't you dare sell marijuana on the side. (12) Don't have a weapon unless you

> belong to the group. My own personal motto is: behave well, not too smart, not too stupid. What we have nowadays are not gangs but entrepreneurs.
>
> (Interview with a young adult from Popular, 2012)

The rules and regulations established by the illegal actors often relate to social or economic aspects of a neighbourhood life. There are no rules about intra-familial or gender-related violence, for instance, as long as it does not bring attention by public authorities to the neighbourhood or jeopardise social cohesion. Most of the rules directly favor the preservation of the illegal group, starting with the code of silence. A 17 year old told me in confidence that he could not buy his marijuana from his regular supplier anymore, since there was a rumour that now everyone had to buy from the local group otherwise they would receive a beating (Interview with a teenager in the Popular neighbourhood, first district, 2012). This is a measure aimed at protecting a market against competitors. When I asked if he would comply, he told me he would not take any chances. Getting caught carried too high a price. The gang used the same logic at a movie theatre that does not allow customers to bring their own food, creating the conditions of a monopoly for one of their main sources of income, drug trafficking. Illegal enterprises use territorial control for the same purpose as any legitimate economic actor would do: For their own benefit.

Assuming law and order capacities

The question of assuming law and order capacities follows directly from the previous point and refers to the ability to enforce the rules that apply to the area. The norm must be upheld. In practice, this means that the actor has the ability and legitimacy to investigate, judge and impose punishment. It has the ability to both define the sanction for disregarding a rule and carry out such a sanction. This requires legitimacy, a degree of coercion and the will to regulate living practices within the given space. This might be the most interesting and yet controversial aspect of territorial control when the actor is illegal. It has everything to do with governance, urban or otherwise. As Klaus Von Lampe explains:

> Illegal governance, just like legal governance, has an element of coercion [...]. Illegal governance provides benefits for subordinates by reducing uncertainty [...]. Illegal government implies that there is a concentration of power, an illegal monopoly of violence [...]. Inherent in illegal governance crimes is that they tend to acquire some degree of legitimacy over time. This means that subordinates accept illegal governance crimes as justified and useful in the furtherance of individual and common interests.
>
> (Von Lampe, 2016b, p. 76)

In the testimony quoted above, one can see that for each violation of the code, there is a sanction. The more structured the group and the more complete its hegemony, the less arbitrarily it behaves to those who follow its rules and the less violence is involved. In Medellín, I studied a neighbourhood controlled by the same groups for more than a decade, and where a threat was as efficient as a punishment. The threats were credible, since they were issued in the context of well-known acts of violence. A teacher working in a school in the northeast area remembers:

> For speaking the wrong way to one of them, the punishment is "la table" (being hit with a night stand). The other day, they gave "table" to a sixty-eight-year-old gentleman. He always left for work at four in the morning with his small radio against his ear. They killed him the next day. So that he should die in pain … Another one who had stolen a tape from a shop, they killed in broad daylight in the bike lane while the INDER (the city sport administration) was in the street and there were kids around. About four years ago, they raped a couple of high-school students who were lesbians, they were ripped to shreds and they had to leave.
>
> (interview with a high-school coordinator in the first district, 2012)

The rules are absolutely illegal and there is a high level of arbitrariness and discretionary power. Indeed, many studies of Medellín's violence report the existence of a climate of fear (Villa Martinez *et al.* 2003). The fact that established groups need not resort to actual violence to enforce their rule may be one of the factors responsible for the impressive drop in the number of homicides. The punishment, when it is carried out, is exemplary. Whether it is a beating, torture or a physical injury, the illegal actors make sure the whole neighbourhood they control knows about it. Homicide, the ultimate punishment, is rarely used when the group enjoys uncontested hegemony. More control means less need to kill.

A former paramilitary explained to me the way they investigated and decided on the punishment:

> If someone did something against the rule, like, say, rob a place, we would investigate. We would ask him to pay for the crime. If he didn't have the money, we would go to his place. If he kept on doing bad things, and the warnings didn't help, we would give him a beating. If he still didn't comply, he would have to leave the area. And if he refused to leave? Ah! He would eventually turn up dead. What else can you do with such a "specimen"?.
>
> (interview with a former paramilitary member, 2012)

Although the paramilitaries' original political agenda may have included the elimination of traffickers, today's illegal actors have adopted the former's practices. Some members of the dominant group I studied had also been members of the paramilitaries at some point, though they mainly dedicated themselves to drug and arms trafficking, illegal gambling and prostitution rings. This former paramilitary member told me that you were not allowed to kill or rob without proper authorisation. Indeed, some rules apply to the members of the criminal group itself. The high school coordinator confirms:

> When it is one of them that has done something wrong, they make him leave. Before that, they give him "tabla" in the back street behind the school.

> Whatever the problem, they give you "tabla." They used to open the sewers and leave the guy in there for twenty-four hours but they no longer do that.
> (interview with a high school coordinator in the first district, 2012)

The illegal entrepreneurs also serve as mediators and are often called upon to solve minor conflicts between neighbors. The system is arbitrary, violent and unfair, and yet it plays a major role in local governance. Another local leader once told me the story of two neighbours, one of whom owed back rent to the other. The mere intervention of the local lieutenant saying, "Either you resolve this or else ..." was enough to sort out the issue (Interview with a leader of the second district, 2011). The same applies to car accidents or party walls, for instance. And people do support this system, particularly because if they sought redress through legal channels they would waste more time, and the process would not be as efficient as that offered by the group. This kind of power is certainly a factor that can draw some people to this line of work. They definitely do not choose to join an illegal organisation for the pay or the long hours of work. It is, however, unlikely to be their main motivation. A former head of security in the local administrations explained off the record that:

> The legitimacy is gained through the resolution of minor conflicts. (…) the illegal groups handle a quick, effective justice. Those people solve small conflicts (debts, etc.). They are often asked to intervene by the people themselves. To have a friend or a family member in the illegal group helps when it comes to solving problems that would otherwise need a long bureaucratic and inefficient process.
> (interview with former official in charge of security in Medellín's administration, 2012)

Illegal groups have taken upon themselves the role of mediators, because they have inherited the practices of the paramilitaries, whose aim was to rule, and the resolution of neighbourhood conflicts was part of the plan. They fill a void and it works to their advantage, so why not continue? It is a kind of power that may be considered as opportunistic.

Being paid to provide protection services

Maintaining an armed force to ensure safety and keep order is not without cost and requires logistics. The population of the territory must contribute to its upkeep in cash, goods or time, for the system to last and the territory to be regulated and organised. That is why the inhabitants cannot be separated from the entities that ensure the territorial control of an area. The former both contribute (more or less willingly) to and benefit from the territorial control. The benefit might be minimal (such as being alive or able to stay in the area) but it cannot be ignored. If no one pays, there is no way for a given group to establish or maintain territorial control. On the other hand, if one individual pays, everyone will have to pay. In Medellín, racketeering is common (Gimenez, 2010). It can be estimated at hundreds of thousands of dollars per year since, for instance, in the neighbourhoods I studied, every household had to pay a tithe each week. The illegal actors also shake down the buses, taxis and bars; shops pay a weekly fee to ensure protection and services (Morales, 2010). But it is necessary to keep in mind that this a mere drop in the ocean compared to the sums that local drug trafficking can generate in a year. The main reason to keep exercising territorial control is to protect the drug and arms market. Nevertheless, by having people paying for such "services", the illegal actors force the inhabitants to acknowledge their power and their role. Beyond the monetary value, the racketeering is the ultimate way to impose a recognition of their power. The illegal actors gained legitimacy when they manage to have people pay for their "services" (Bedoya, 2010).

Defining the territory

Defining the territory is a key aspect of territorial control for an entity. Who can come in? Who can stay? Who must leave? It is by controlling these factors that the identity of an area is defined. You must have the ability to organise mobility within a space, as well as open it up or close it off. These choices are based on social, economic, cultural or political reasons, but serve the interests both of the inhabitants and of the entity that has control over the area. For instance, not granting a given population access to some areas can be strategic to maintaining the monopoly of the entity or the security of the place. Defining a territory therefore means, on the one hand, excluding, and on the other hand, creating an identity. This process is already controversial when carried out by a State, and it is even more so when illegal actors have the ability to impose their will. Once again, the question of approval and legitimacy must be kept in mind. In Medellín, especially in the Northeast boroughs, there are still some "invisible boundaries" that affect everyday life, especially for teenagers and young people. The issue of denied access is even more acute when it comes to intra-urban forced displacement. A middle aged woman who used to live in the first district testifies in an interview:

> Twenty years ago, the situation in Granizal started to worsen. They started racketeering households [*pedir vacuna*]. We were in the middle of gangs because our house was located just below the church. We didn't think of moving because the people that belonged to the gang were the neighbors' kids, people we had known our whole life and with whom we grew up. (…) Then they started threatening people to take over their houses. They forced them to leave so they could be there and sell drugs and everything. They didn't allow people the possibility of renting the place after leaving. In our backyard, there often were shootings. We were really scared. And then one day, a poster was displayed in the street saying that we had to leave. We talked to a sibling who was living in another neighbourhood. In a week we organised everything and left, on a morning of February 2000. It will be twelve years this month.
>
> (interview with a woman who was displaced, 2012)

As previously explained, this type of punishment is much like banishment used to be. But it is more than that, since it is part of the ability and capacity to redefine urban space. Forced displacement is an illegal group's ultimate power. Not only can it decide who is allowed to live in the area, but it can also take over displaced victims' houses and give them to people it considers more favourable to it. Only a couple of illegal actors have so far been brought to justice for forced displacement. It is an extremely difficult crime to establish and study, and practically an invisible phenomenon (Jaramillo, 2011). In term of governance, it is also the most problematic issue. It is impossible to understand intra-urban forced displacement, the fact that some people are forced to flee and leave the neighbourhood but choose to stay within the limits of the metropolitan area, without analyzing the system of territorial control that is in place. People are forced to leave because some illegal actors can make them leave. They have the power and latitude to do so. Displacement is both a consequence of territorial control exercised by illegal actors and an illustration of the fifth pillar, the capacity for an entity to decide who is allowed to be in the area.

In Medellín, in the same neighbourhoods where the local administration has invested in urban planning, social programs and public transportation, there is evidence of territorial control exercised by illegal actors. The violence and arbitrariness of those practices contrast with the visibility of the State administration. Both legal and illegal territorial control is seen in the same area. Those neighbourhoods are a shared space of territorial control.

Conclusion: Medellín's paradox of governance

To conclude, let's go back to the anecdote of people helped by the army to flee their home mentioned at the beginning of this chapter and the subsequent question raised by the journalist: "Who has control in Medellín?" By recognising the de facto existence of a competitive territorial control, and by taking measures to tackle this issue, Medellín's administration has proven to be innovative and efficient. The fact that the army and civil servants helped people to leave their homes was a pragmatic response to the inevitable loss of all their belongings. Though it may seem to those who reported the story the evidence of weakness or a failed State governance, it really shows the capacity of Medellín City Hall to adapt, to the best of its abilities, to the situation. Whereas many countries have never recognised intra-urban forced displacement though it is present (e.g. El Salvador), Medellín's administration has found ways to attend to the citizens affected by the alternative territorial control. The administration has waived local property taxes for displaced people, dedicated a responsive unit to attend emergencies and it helps victims in the process of recognition. Unlike San Salvador, Medellín's City Hall has tackled this issue with innovative measures, although it still has to find new ways to improve its governance. What may at first appear as loss of control and failed governance might actually be the basis for rethinking urban governance and proof that territorial control can be multiple. Illegal territorial control redefines urban space. It impacts the urban economy by raising the cost of goods and services for ordinary citizens. It redefines people's mobility and daily practices. It also has an impact on land values. The State is forced to adjust to this situation, just as it does when dealing with private and legitimate instances of territorial control. Medellín is particularly interesting, because the local authorities fight the illegal actors and try to limit their territorial control, while acknowledging their presence and consequently admitting the existence of dual territorial control. The city firmly denounces illegal groups, and I have seen no indication that it might give covert support to any of them. By accepting the need to address the issue, facing it and allowing researchers to study it, the city has actually proved that it maintains high standards of governance. The next step would be to look for efficient ways to limit the violence induced by the exercise of territorial control by illegal enterprises. As shown in this chapter, the issue is not so much why territorial control is a matter of urban governance but how we, as researchers, public officials, policy makers and inhabitants, can face the paradox of a shared territorial control.

References

Alcaldia de Medellín. Desplazamiento Forzado y Desplazamiento Forzado Intraurbano: Contexto y dinámica en Medellín durante el 2014, Medellín, mayo de 2015.

Andrews, J., 2016. Medellín wins World City Prize. *Cities Today*, 18th March, https://cities-today.com/Medellín-wins-world-city-prize/.

Angarita Cañas P. E., Gallo, H. and Jiménez Zuluaga, B. I., 2008. *Dinámicas de Guerra y Construcción de Paz: estudio interdisciplinario del con icto armado en la comuna 13 de Medellín*. IPC. Medellín: Universidad de Antioquia, Corporación Región, Universidad de Medellín.

Atehortua-Arredondo, C. L. 2010. , Política pública y desplazamiento forzado. La realidad de la aplicación del sistema de atención, *Estud. Socio-Juríd* [online]. 12 (1): 173–198.

Ávila Martínez, A. F. 2010. *Grupos armados ilegales, violencia urbana y mafias coercitivas. Gobernabilidad y crisis democráticas*, San José, C. R.: FLACSO.

Bedoya, J. 2010. *La protección violenta en Colombia, El caso de Medellín desde los años noventa*, IPC, Medellín, Colombia.

Dowdney, L. 2005. *Nem Guerra Nem Paz: Comparaçoes Internacionais de Crianças e Jovens em Violencia Armada Organizada*, Rio de Janeiro: 7Letras.

Duncan, G. 2014. *Más que plata o plomo. El poder político del narcotráfico en Colombia y México*, Madrid: Editorial Debate.

Fukuyama, F., Colby S. 2011. Half a miracle, *Foreign Policy*, 25 April, http://foreignpolicy.com/2011/04/25/half-a-miracle/.

Gambetta, D. 1993. *The Sicilian Mafia: The Business of Private Protection*, Harvard: Harvard University Press.

Gayraud, J.-F., 2008. *Le Monde des Mafias, Géopolitique du Crime Organisé*, Paris: Odile Jacob.

Gimenez Morales, G. 2010. Botín de guerra en Medellín supera los 700 millones de dólares, El Colombiano, 7 November.

Hill, P. 2006. *The Japanese Mafia Yakuza, Law, and the State*, Oxford: Oxford University Press.

Hobbs, D. 1998. Going down to the glocal: the local context of organised crime, *The Howard Journal*, 37 (4): 407–422.

Isaza, G. 2015. Quien manda en las comunas 1 y 2 ? *El Colombiano*, 23 September.

Jaramillo Arbelaez, A. M., 2011. Acerca de los estudios sobre conflicto armado y violencia urbana en Medellín: 1985–2009, in: Ramirez, J. G. (ed.) *Economía Criminal en Antioquia: el Narcotráfico*, Medellín: Universidad EAFIT y Colciencias.

Jaramillo Arbelaez, A. M., 2011. *La Huella Invisible de la Guerra. Desplazamiento Forzado en la Comuna 13*, Buenos Aires: Aguilar.

Leibler, L., Brand, P., 2012. "Movilidad e inclusión social: la experiencia desde la periferia de Medellín y el primer Metrocable", *Bulletin de l'Institut français d'études andines,* 41 (3): 363–387.

Leibler, L., Musset, A., 2010. ¿Un Transporte hacia la Justicia Espacial? El caso del Metrocable de Medellín. *Scripta Nova. Revista Electrónica de Geografía y Ciencias Sociales*. [En línea]. Barcelona: Universidad de Barcelona, 1 de agosto de 2010, vol. XIV, nº 331 (48).

Martin, G. 2013. *Medellín Tragedia y resurrección Mafias, ciudad y Estado*, Medellín: La Carreta Editores.

Medellín Como Vamos, 2016. Informe calidad de vida de Medellín 2012–2015, June, http://www.Medellíncomovamos.org/la-ciudad-2/.

Medina Franco, G. 2006. *Una Historia de las Milicias de Medellín*, Medellín: IPC, Instituto Popular de Capacitación.

Morales, J. G. 2010. Hay extorsiones hasta de 500 pesos, *El Colombiano*, 7 November.

Musset, A. 2014. Mort à la ville innovante, inclusive et equitable, *Divergences*, https://divergences2.divergences.be/spip.php?article992.

Passas, N. 2003. Cross-border crime and the interface between legal and illegal actors *Security Journal*, 16 (1): 19–38.

Potter, G. and Willingham A. (no date). Deviant places, deviant networks: an ethnographic understanding of underground criminality in rural Kentucky, http://justicestudies.eku.edu/sites/justicestudies.eku.edu/files/deviant_places.pdf.

Poveda, C. (Director). (2008). *La Vida Loca* [Motion picture]. France: Ad Vitam.

Redaccion El Tiempo. 2016. Combos siguen con poder armado en laderas de Medellín, *El Tiempo*, 13 December. http://www.eltiempo.com/colombia/Medellín/balance-de-derechos-humanos-personeria-de-Medellín-35109.

Redaccion El Tiempo. 2016. Hasta por música a alto volumen desplazan en los barrios de Medellín, *El Tiempo*, 23 November. http://www.eltiempo.com/archivo/documento/CMS-16756803.

Redaccion Semana. 2013. ¿ Quién tiene el control en Medellín ? *Revista Semana*, 11 May, http://www.semana.com/nacion/articulo/quien-tiene-control-Medellín/342945-3.

Salazar, A. 1991. *No nacimos pa' semilla: la cultura de las bandas juveniles de Medellín*, Bogota: CINEP.

Varese, F. 2010. What is organized crime?, in Varese, F. (ed), *Organized Crime: Critical Concepts in Criminology*, London: Routledge. Varese, F. 2011. *Mafias on the Move.* Princeton, NJ: Princeton University Press.

Villa Martinez, M. I., Sanchez, L. A. and Jaramillo Arbelaez, A. M. 2003. *Rostros del Miedo. Una Investigación Sobre los Miedos Sociales Urbanos*, Medellín: Corporacion Region.

Von Lampe, K. 2016a. The ties that bind: A taxonomy of associational criminal structures, in Antonopoulos, G.A. (ed.) *Illegal Entrepreneurship, Organized Crime and Social Control: Essays in Honour of Professor Dick Hobbs*, New York: Springer International publishing, pp. 19–33.

Von Lampe, K. 2016b. *Organized Crime: Analyzing Illegal Activities, Criminal Structures and Extra-Legal Governance*, New York: Sage.

Weber, M. 1965. *Politics as a Vocation*. Philadelphia: Fortress Press.

7 Mobs, *sucanchiuostru*, anti-communists

Global and local actors in the Sack of Palermo

Vincenzo Scalia

Introduction

The term "Sack of Palermo" (*Sacco di Palermo*) refers to the massive transformation Palermo underwent between the 1950s and 1970s, and the legacy which continues to negatively affect the city. Between 1951 and 1991, 175,000 blocks of flats were built in Palermo (Lima, 2000). The *Conca d'Oro* (Golden Shell), the fertile citrus plain surrounding the city, was engulfed with 300 million m^3 of concrete, four m^3 per inhabitant (Gucciardo, 2002). This disproportionate development negatively affected not only the local territory, but also the local society. The Sack of Palermo marred any other chance of economic development. The consumption of territory destroyed agriculture, led to the decline of industry, and it choked trade and financial activities. First, because most of the economic resources were conveyed into the construction sectors, relevant investments into trade, industry and services were thus neglected. Second, because the massive looting of the territory did not leave room to develop such amenities as a central business district, industrial estates or bio-technological parks. Its consequence was a patronage oriented economic policy (Chubb, 1983), led by the Christian Democrat Party (DC), which based its consent on the control of public expenditure conveyed to Sicily from the central government.

The Sack of Palermo resulted in the decay of the ancient city, which had also suffered significant bombing during the Second World War. The political and economic choice to develop the semi-rural areas of the Conca d'Oro marched hand in glove with the decision to abandon the historical and monumental area of the city, with its once thriving crafts and marketing activities progressively decaying, and most of the population was forced to move to newly-built council flats, swelling the ranks of a new, wider *lumpenproletariat.* Developers thought it desirable to ruin the ancient city, in order to justify at some point the demolition of the old buildings, as well as of the urban maze, whose development dated back to the Arabs (827–1069), and turn the city centre into a modern business district. This part of the plan, fortunately, was not successful, although the refurbishment of the ancient city has only occurred recently. Finally, the Sack of Palermo allowed the notorious criminal organisation *Cosa Nostra* to rise further as a prominent political and economic local actor, moulding the transformation of the city according to its own interests.

This chapter explores the global and local factors underpinning the processes that made the Sack possible. It will show how the interaction between local and global elements developed the network of political and economic alliances that led to the victory of the *Sackers* and to the marginalisation of the *Opponents*. Local elements are the most prominent social and economic actors of 1950s Palermo: by using an ideal type, we can argue that noblemen absentee landlords, professional bourgeoisie, local administrators, *sucanchiostru* (that is, the clerical petty bourgeoisie who migrated to Palermo from the rest of Sicily)[1] and members of the underclass rank among the Sackers; whereas the entrepreneurial bourgeoisie, intellectuals, the working class are in the ranks of their opponents. The Sicilian Cosa Nostra is the connecting element among the Sackers, as its network of relations spanning across the social spectrum of Palermo allows the criminal organisation to wield a hegemonic role within those who advocated the massive development of the construction sector.

Global elements appeared on the stage in the 1940s, as far as the political context is concerned. Italy had a strong working class movement, whose influence had spread also in the South and in Sicily. To prevent an advance of the left, both landlords and Mafiosi had created a political alliance whose aim was, at the beginning, the independence of Sicily (Minna, 1971). The concession of special autonomy to Sicily in 1946 by the Italian government oriented the centre and conservative political forces, which will later be the backbone of the Sackers, towards the support of Christian Democrats. Moreover, many Mafiosi had strong connections with the Allied forces, whom they had helped to land in 1943, obtaining their appointment as local administrators soon after the liberation of the island (Gaja, 1990; Pantaleone, 1970). Despite the conservative-Mafiosi bloc's activism and connections, the left-wing *Blocco del Popolo* (People's Bloc) managed to win the first regional election of 1947. The massacre of Portella della Ginestra followed (Santino, 2000), a killing of 11 peasants gathered on the mountainside to celebrate the electoral victory on May Day. The victory of the left-wing coalition was regarded by the political forces connected to the Mafiosi and absentee landlord interests as a threat to the economic and social configuration of late 1940s Sicily (Gaja, 1990; Santino, 2003). It was later found out, after the US State department declassified the files about the massacre, that a commando of Mafiosi, American Military Service and Italian Secret Services were the perpetrators of the mass killings (Casarrubea, 2001). The anti-Communist role the Mafia played alongside conservative forces, as well as its connection with its overseas "friends", were to secure Cosa Nostra not only a prominent role in the legal domain, but also a pivotal position in international drug trafficking since 1957 (Santino, 1994; Stancanelli, 2016).

Theoretical and methodological aspects

This chapter will draw on two main criminological interpretations of organised crime: the first is the *paradigm of complexity*, an analytical approach developed by Umberto Santino (2016). According to Santino, in order to achieve an in-depth analysis of organised crime, we must consider the interaction between economics, politics, culture and society. All these four elements play their own part in shaping the dynamics of criminal organisation, as well as help us understand their interaction with the "legal world". In my view, it is important, though, to outline the prominent role that relations of production play between these four elements. Organised crime is neither an anomaly of modern society, opposed to the birth of modern State and capitalist economy (Gambetta, 1992), nor a legacy of the pre-modern age (Paoli, 2000), but, rather, a prominent actor in the social transformation of some areas, such as Sicily. Criminal organisations, as Ruggiero (1996) points out, account for an important part of capitalist economies in three ways: first, they provide the market with those illegal goods and services which cannot be purchased legally; second, their organisation reflects the division of labour of legal enterprises; and third, the profits of illegal activities, such as drug trafficking, are invested in the legal economy, thus making organised crime an important economic actor. This is the second theoretical standpoint of this work. Ruggiero provides an important theoretical lens, to the extent that he paves the way for an analysis of organised crime which shows how the transformation of illegal actors are specular to those of legal economics, politics and society (Hall, 2013; Hudson, 2014).

Capital, organisation, identity and consent turn organised crime, in this case the Sicilian Cosa Nostra, into a crucial actor in contemporary Palermo. This chapter will show how the interaction between the "legal" and the "illegal" parts of society can take place within the common interests of profits and power, such as those ones the mafia shared with the Palermo bourgeoisie, so as to engender a "Mafioso bourgeoisie" (Mineo, 1953). In particular, it will be emphasised how such local peculiarities as the articulations of Palermo society (such as the massive housing demand by the *sucanchioustru*), the political context of 1950s, the post-war economic context set the framework for the Sack of Palermo. The outcome is the osmosis between legality and illegality. The legal and illegal spheres of economy and politics, such as drug trafficking, money laundering, the construction sector, professionals, local governments and criminal organisations, moved in the same direction and blended together into a peculiar form of capitalist economy and society. A social polarisation and economic deprivation was the outcome in the long term, as the globalisation following the fall of the Berlin Wall reduced the political importance of the mafia, as well as affecting the routes of illegal economies. The Sicilian Cosa Nostra could not enjoy anymore the political protection due to its active anti-Communist role (http://legislature.camera.it/_bicamerali/nochiosco.asp?pagina=/_bicamerali/antimafia/home.htm). Moreover, the repression strategies enacted since 1980s by the Central government have resulted in a change in the role played by Cosa Nostra in the local context (Scalia, 2016). Despite these changes, Palermo has not recovered yet from the consequences of the Sack, as its metropolitan area is characterised by a high unemployment rate, and emigration is still endemic (www.tuttitalia.it/sicilia/81-palermo/statistiche/censimenti-popolazione/).

This chapter will rely on the use of qualitative methodology, as it will draw on such sources as the judicial files of the big Anti-Mafia trial of 1986 (AA. VV., 1990), as well as on the dossier of the Anti-Mafia Committees of the Italian

Parliament (http://legislature.camera.it/_bicamerali/nochiosco.asp?pagina=/_bicamerali/antimafia/home.htm), and a host of secondary sources.

The Mafia and Palermo: a local peculiarity

Different authors have analysed the dynamics of organised crime. Most of them have focused on the structure of criminal organisations (Block, 1980), their businesses (Gambetta, 1992), their relation with legal economy and politics (Ruggiero, 1996; Sciarrone, 2011) and the movements of organised crime outside their "traditional areas" of settlement (Varese, 2011). Some of these interpretations supply important tools to understand and explain criminal organisations. Among these scholars, though, very few have considered the importance of space articulation as a key factor in the development of criminal organisations, except for those who single out culture as a key element of the mafia (Paoli, 2000; Hall, 2013; Hudson, 2014). In the case of the Sicilian mafia, the relationship between territory and organised crime development is a peculiar one, which enhances understanding of such phenomena as the Sack of Palermo. Moreover, since the definition of organised crime is very general, it tends to blur the picture (Levi, 1994); therefore, an analysis focused on local, spatial aspects could provide the necessary tools to demonstrate how every criminal organisation has its own peculiarities, which interact differently with global or over-local elements. Although these peculiarities have often been either neglected or dismissed as superficial (Albini *et al.*, 1997), I believe they need to be considered to achieve a more in-depth understanding of organised crime. This outcome can be achieved by focusing on the internal social dynamics affecting Sicilian society.

The first aspect to be considered in relation to local peculiarities concerns the relationship between Cosa Nostra and the Sicilian ruling class: it would have been hard for the criminal organisation to develop as a prominent social actor without the support of local landlords, entrepreneurs and politicians (Renda, 2000). The second aspect relates to the relationships within Sicilian society: Anton Blok (1971) describes the Mafioso as mediators between the local, latifundia-based society and the global, finance and politics-based society. This analysis can be an important starting point if we accept both the existence of a Mafia organisation and the connection between the development of Cosa Nostra and the capitalist transformation of Sicily.

Cosa Nostra developed as an informal power within the large estates of Sicily (Renda, 2000) managing the capitalist transformation of the Sicilian economy: the administration of the latifundia by the recruitment of cheap labour, the control of agricultural production, salt and sulphur, and the securing of safety through its para-military control of the territory (Santino, 2000) number among the main activities of the Sicilian criminal organisation. Despite its rural origin, Cosa Nostra would move to gain the control of the capital city of Sicily, turning some specific local peculiarities to its own advantage.

Firstly, Palermo had a very articulated urban structure: the city was surrounded by the Conca d'Oro, whose citrus groves grew in large landed estates which were owned by noblemen and absentee landlords (Lupo, 2011) and were administered by the Mafioso, who either rented them or were hired to grant the security of the estate. As a consequence of this Cosa Nostra grew to be the main political and economic actor in the Palermo suburbs, developing that network of *violence industry* (Franchetti, 1876) around which the *middle-class mobs* became a powerful power syndicate (Block, 1980), engaged both in the maintenance of public order and in the production and commercialisation of citrus crops.

Every *borgata*, or suburban borough of the city, had its own *cosca*, or mafia family. The hierarchical organisation of the *cosche* ensured Cosa Nostra the political and military control of the territory, as the Mafioso were the *de facto* leaders and administrators of the local units in which they were based. Two networks of relationships developed in the territory. The vertical ones concerned the mafia connections with the local landlords, politicians and entrepreneurs. Cosa Nostra grew to have an hegemonic position not only because of the use of violence, but especially because the Mafiosi became part of a power network (Lupo, 1993; http://legislature.camera.it/_bicamerali/nochiosco.asp?pagina=/_bicamerali/antimafia/home.htm) wherein all the actors involved had mutual advantage: the Mafiosi had their political and economic hegemony, whereas entrepreneurs were satisfied with massive production at a cheap price, and the local politicians were spared the efforts of maintaining public order, as well as enjoying the Mafioso support during the elections. The second network is the horizontal one: the mafia members were usually born and brought up in the *borgata* in which their *cosca* was located. It was by this token possible for them to develop those family, kinship and friendly relationship known as *strong ties* (Granovetter, 1983), which ensured them a firm grasp of the territory, through the manipulation of such typical Sicilian institutions and values as family, friendship and honour. This double network became a crucial resource for the Sack of Palermo, as it enabled the Mafioso to deploy their ties both in the political domain, either when choosing their own candidates or when conveying the votes of the *borgata* they ruled to a party, and in the economic sphere.

Second, the close ties within the city helped them develop close relationships with the enterprise syndicates of the urban districts of Palermo, such as smugglers, receivers and robbers (Santino and La Fiura, 1989). The protagonists of the Sack of Palermo are *gabbelloti* (administrators) of the latifundia such as Michele Greco, illegal traffickers such as the La Barbera brothers, as well as many other criminal actors. The outcome of these connections, facilitated by the territorial proximity, was the hybridisation of criminal organisational models, which resulted into the creation of a peculiar criminal organisation. Cosa Nostra became thus an actor engaged both in legal and in illegal trafficking, combining politics with economy, through the manipulation of family, friendship and honours.

Unlike the Neapolitan *camorra*, which developed mainly as an organisation regulating the illegal and informal trafficking in sixteenth century Naples (Sales, 1987), and the Calabrian *ndrangheta* (Ciconte, 1992; Violante, 1993), which was originally a family-based organisation of territorial self-defence, Cosa Nostra is a hybrid organisation, both because it encompasses a wide range of activities and because of its combination of legal and illegal activities. We are therefore facing a *local* element in the development of organised crime, which is not a uniform phenomenon.

Third, Palermo was the main trading location of western Sicily, where all the products of the land were bought and sold. It was by this token possible both for the rural and for the suburban and urban Mafioso to establish *horizontal networks* between the same criminal actors, and *vertical networks* with legal economic actors. The para-military organisation of Cosa Nostra, as well as its network of close-knit relations within the territory, provided a crucial tool to gain hegemony in economic relationships. Once again, we are facing a double articulation of networks out of which Cosa Nostra could draw advantage, as it was possible both to engage in illegal activities, such as cattle smuggling, and to force the other legal actors to accept the informal "mediation" provided by the Mafiosi in the trade of agricultural products and lands, as well as to develop favourable relationships with the landlords. This aspect proved to be crucial when the land estates had to be commercialised to trigger the development of the construction sector.

Finally, Palermo has been for centuries the political terminal of Sicily. Most noblemen, who were the absentee rural landlords whose latifundia were administered by the Mafiosi, resided there. Moreover, such institutions as the Bank of Sicily, as well as, from 1947, the Sicilian Parliament, were based in Palermo. It was therefore possible for Cosa Nostra to reinforce its strong connections with the local elite, who formally owned the land they administered and managed. It was within these widely-articulated networks that the conditions for the Sack of Palermo developed.

After the Second World War, the noblemen had turned into a class of passive rentiers who had wasted most of their financial possessions in leisure activities (Cancila, 1986). They needed to sell their lands to pay their debts. Their Mafiosi administrators wanted to boost urban development in order to increase their power and wealth. Their aims matched the expectations both of the professional bourgeoisie and of construction entrepreneurs, who cherished the possibility of massive profits. It was this convergence of interests between such economic and social actors which triggered the Sack of Palermo.

Politics also played an important role. In 1946 the Italian government granted Sicily a "special status" autonomy, following the growth of the nationalist movement in the previous three years (Di Lello, 1997; Minna, 1971). Autonomy provided Sicily with its own Parliament, a regional bureaucracy and autonomous legal status. Sicilian politicians took the chance of regional autonomy to launch a patronage-oriented policy, aimed at building a mass consent (Santino, 1994). The mass hiring of petty bourgeois clerks as local government bureaucrats, the financial support to enterprises owned by businessmen who were sympathetic to the government majority, a massive program of modernising public works (motorways, dykes, council flats) through an unconventional use of public expenditure, were the backbone of the "Reconstruction" policies. The structure of Palermo's population massively changed in those years, by making the clerical petty bourgeoisie, or *sucanchiuostru* (ink suckers, as the old Palermo people called them) a central element of the local social landscape (Santino and La Fiura, 1989). Mass patronage was possible because of the massive resources the Italian government pumped into Sicily, in order to quench the growth of the peasant movement, which had been fighting for the redistribution of the land, and to prevent a leftward shift of Sicilian electors which could have changed the whole political orientation of Italy in the Cold War context (Casarrubea, 2001).

Ideology of the Sack of Palermo

The Sack of Palermo drew its ideological and practical legitimisation from three elements. The first one was the reconstruction that was necessary to do away with the consequences of the Second World War (such as housing shortage – average housing density was three persons per room at that time; Cannarozzo, 2000) and to grant a flat to every family. The second element was that of "Progress", that is both the economic development and the adoption of modern architectural criteria, such as building high rise tower blocks and the massive private use of cars. A flat, a car and a job were regarded more as a status symbol than as means to run an ordinary life. The third element concerned the necessity to provide jobs to the mass of unemployed people whose living conditions had worsened as a consequence of the war. The definition of "ideological" refers to the existence of different ways to approach the post-war problems of Palermo: as far as the "reconstruction" is concerned, the term itself suggests that the ancient city was to be reconstructed, because of the massive wartime bombing. All the master plans approved by the Palermo administration, from 1947 to 1959, focused on urban development in the large land estates surrounding the city. The ancient part of the town was regarded like a huge debris to be removed, in order to leave areas for new urban redevelopment (Gimdalchà, 1982).

High rise and high density building prevailed, leaving marginal space for public utilities, as well to the protection of both the environmental and the monumental peculiarities of the Conca d'Oro. This rigid, single-faceted idea of progress ruled out any other possibility of economic development. Until 1951, one quarter of the Palermo population was employed in manufacturing (Cancila, 1986). The city had a reputation for its harbour and its shipyard, and an International Trade Fair, the *Fiera del Mediterraneo*, had been created in 1946. The safeguard of both the territory and the monuments, combined with the boosting of manufacturing and trade activities, could have been a chance for both the economic development and the urban regeneration of Palermo, as well as for its modernisation. First, construction entrepreneurs envisaged an immediate chance of making massive profits through urban development; second, an enhancement of the construction sector matched different needs, as the landlords could pay their debts by selling the land, the Mafiosi could increase their economic power, as well as their control of the territory; third, a stagnant economy, based on construction and bureaucracy, could provide the politicians who ruled Palermo with the chance to boost a patronage-oriented policy, as mass unemployment forced the Palermo underclass to find the protection of politicians, whereas the *sucanchiuostru* were hired on the basis of their political affiliation to the ruling parties (Cristantino, 1987). In Northern Italy, urban development combined with a massive development of manufacturing industry, finance and services. The Palermo economy, from the 1950s onwards, was oriented towards a massive exploitation of estates for construction combined with public expenditure and illegal trafficking. The creation of a passive *sponge city*, depending on bureaucracy, patronage and illegal economy, served the purpose not only of discouraging independent entrepreneurship, but also the reproduction of economic, political and cultural subjugation to organised crime, which, at the end of the day, left the social balance of power and status intact, and avoided any political shift to the left within Palermitan society.

Cosa Nostra was a crucial actor of this transformation: first, by providing its services to the construction market, such as regulating the competition between constructors, ensuring private protection, and directing the construction-related market (tiles, concrete, etc.). Second, by giving outspoken support to the ruling centre right's coalitions: either legally, that is, by providing votes, or illegally, by intimidating or killing their political opponents. Finally, Cosa Nostra laundered its profits in the construction sector, as well as employing people from the lower classes in illegal activities, thus ensuring an income to thousands of families and reducing social tensions (Fiandaca, Costantino, 1992). The Sack of Palermo shows how the mafia was not an external element in the socioeconomic dynamics of the city, but rather a driving force of the radical transformation of its social and urban fabric. The interests of Cosa Nostra matched the aims of an important section of local politicians, entrepreneurs and noblemen, creating an osmosis wherein the legal and illegal blur.

The practice of the Sack of Palermo

Reconstruction, progress and employment inspired the building of the first of the city's council flats in 1950s. The new dwelling places were built in estates which were—five to six km away from the city centre, on estates belonging to small landlords, (Cannarozzo, 2000). It became in this way possible for the city council to win over public opinion, by claiming they were tackling and solving the housing problems of the city. The Opposition-related public opinion, such as the newspaper *L'Ora* and some politicians opposed to the political majority in the City Council, noticed that the consequence of this choice was that the City Administration had to provide the newly built areas with such facilities as roads, heating, gas, light, water and sewers, which passed through the middle of those estates belonging to the noblemen and administered by the Mafiosi (http://legislature.camera.it/_bicamerali/nochiosco.asp?pagina=/_bicamerali/antimafia/home.htm). The price of the land suddenly soared, making those areas valuable for urban development. The *Banco di Sicilia* (Bank of Sicily, one of the oldest banks in Italy) funded both the developers and the *sucanchioustru* who searched for a favourable mortgage. The city council declared the targeted areas as developable, by approving several *varianti* (changes) to the 1947 Reconstruction Master Plan, which tried to contain, to a certain extent, the engulfing of the Conca d'Oro, as it focused, mainly, on the housing needs of the inhabitants whose dwelling places had been damaged by the war bombings.

As the pressure towards a boost in the building of private apartments increased, the aim to provide homeless and poor people with public housing was gradually overshadowed. The Master Plans of 1956 and 1959, drafted by the most prominent architects of Palermo (Inzerillo, 1980; Lima, 2000), endorsed the trend towards unrestrained private building, focused on the construction of high density (360 inhabitants per hectare) tower blocks, the demolition of some historical villas and boroughs, marginalisation of productive activities, massive reduction of agricultural lands and small spaces for public facilities and green areas. The expected result was the growth of the city to a population of 900,000 inhabitants. Consider that in the 1950s the city had around 500,000 inhabitants, and today it accounts for 650,000 residents.

Because of this, many baroque and historic "liberty" villas were demolished to make way for modern blocks of flats, while the ancient areas of the city kept decaying. The degradation of the historical part of Palermo, the only European city still keeping the ruins of the Second World War, justified the building of 15,000 new public housings on the outskirts of the city, thus triggering the vicious circle of further massive building (Chubb, 1983), according to the mechanism described previously. The final aim was to demolish the most ancient parts so as to promote the building of a modern business district, a project which was fortunately unaccomplished because of the mid-1970s economic crises.

The construction boom started in late 1950s, with more than 4,320 building licences released from 1957 to 1963 (http://legislature.camera.it/_bicamerali/nochiosco.asp?pagina=/_bicamerali/antimafia/home.htm). As high rise building prevailed, this high number of licences resulted in the construction of several flats. It would not be possible both to describe and to analyse the Sack of Palermo without considering the leading role the Mafia played within its dynamics. Cosa Nostra performed multifaceted tasks, which enhanced its role as a local actor and increased its wealth and power.

First, the *cosche* imposed the *guardiania*, or the "surveillance" of the building sites, extorting a price for the protection they allegedly offered. The *guardiania* was not the supply of a private protection service. Its meaning is symbolic, and it reaches beyond the real need to prevent trouble on the building sites. Construction entrepreneurs were either *advised* to accept the private protection service, or forced to request it after an attack to their building sites, consisting of a theft, a broken crane or an accident to some of the workers. When a developer accepted the *guardiania*, he recognised the command of the Mafia over the area in which he was working. Stories of accidents, robberies and killings were accurately circulated, so that it was the entrepreneur himself who searched for the *capomafia* of the area and requested his protection (http://archiviopiolatorre.camera.it/l-impegno-parlamentare-nazionale). The construction sector did not oppose the presence of the Mafia, because to do so would have required an adequate military organisation, or, at least, an intervention by the State (the Italian State formally recognised the existence of organised crime only in 1992). The control of the territory by the men of honour was regarded positively to the extent that it regulated competition for the estates and reduced the risks of crime (Santino, 2016).

Second, the Mafioso were themselves prominent construction entrepreneurs, either directly or as partners of other businessmen, as such cases as the La Barbera brothers and Moncada illustrate. There were two ways for Cosa Nostra to infiltrate the construction sector. The first one, more straightforward, consisted of operating as a legal construction entrepreneur (Santino and La Fiura, 1989). In this case, the Mafiosi took advantage both of their reputation and of the lack of an effective anti-Mafia legislation, which would not be passed until 1982. The second way was related to money laundering. In this case, entrepreneurs could use the gains of illegal activities as capital to employ in the construction market. These monies could be a "loan" from a Mafioso, the share of a partnership or the entire capital of a mob actor which were invested on behalf of a society run by a fake owner. Between 1957 and 1963, 90 per cent of the 4,000 construction licences released by the City of Palermo belonged to a very small number of people (4!) (Pantaleone, 1970). In any case, the construction market, as well as the Palermo economy, looked favourably upon capital investment operated by the Mafioso, as it provided fresh resources to be employed also in other economic sectors, such as trade and finance.

Third, the Mafia regulated the construction-related market, as they "suggested" to developers where they bought tiles, concrete, cranes and other materials, as well as suggesting, in some cases, the names of professionals to be employed in the planning and building stage. It thus became possible both to keep the prices of materials under control and to regulate competition, by favouring all of those companies who put themselves under the patronising influence of the Mafia. The companies that refused this approach were excluded from business, either because no entrepreneurs worked with them or due to threats. As Rocco Sciarrone (2011) points out, there is a range of relationships between Mafiosi and economic actors: the *victims* are the ones who do not accept the mafia rules, the *colluded* are those who legitimise the power of the crime syndicates and, finally, the Mafiosi themselves act as entrepreneurs. During the Sack of Palermo, most of the entrepreneurs ranked among the two latter typologies.

Finally, Cosa Nostra regulated the labour market in a broader sense: only those workers who accepted flexible working hours and were not members of trade unions could be hired in the construction sector. Their recruitment was filtered by the patronage network: either workers were resident in the *borgata* wherein urban development took place, and thus tied to the Mafiosi by obligation and gratitude, or they were friends and relatives of those *reliable* workers already hired. In both cases, the outcome was a peaceful and cheap working process, with no strikes and reduced labour prices. Moreover, the Mafiosi enhanced their role as mediators: they were the crucial knot of this legal-illegal network, as they could ask politicians to change the master plans in exchange for votes, or they could ensure constructors further land or estates in exchange for flats, and ask for loans to the banks in exchange for laundering and investing money, as well as lending money to entrepreneurs or becoming their partners, so that illegal money was laundered.

The *grey area* between legal and illegal worlds (Sciarrone, 2013) was quite explicit during the Sack of Palermo, and this connection between the legal and illegal world grew rapidly without any fear of judicial repression. The reason for this is twofold. On the one hand, there are judicial reasons behind it, because the crime of Mafioso association was not enforced and prosecuted until 1982, by the Rognoni-La Torre Act, which implied a change in article 416 of the Italian penal law. The law defined "criminal organisation" as a group of three or more persons who associate permanently to engage in illegal activities using violence. It was because of this change that Mafia bosses, particularly those belonging to the prominent side of the *Corleonesi*, such as Luciano Liggio, Totò Riina and Pippo Calò were tried in 1986 and sentenced in 1992. During the years of the Sack of Palermo, when these judicial opportunities did not exist, most of the Mafiosi carried on with their business, and it was easy for politicians, professionals, bureaucrats and ordinary citizens to claim that the Mafia did not exist, and justify the relationship with the members of criminal networks. On the other hand, it was not possible to prosecute either for illegal or criminal behaviour people who enjoyed the consent of a vast section of the population, as well as being mutually tied by a web of obligations, gratitude, partnerships and social status. Those who opposed the hegemonic dynamics were either marginalised or forced to leave the city, before being threatened or even killed (Pantaleone, 1970; Stancanelli, 2016.). Moreover, the social bloc who carried out the Sack of Palermo could enjoy the advantages of the international political context, wherein all those legal and illegal actors and practices which used the shield of anti-Communism, were tolerated and appreciated.

Cosa Nostra gained its hegemony in Palermo society, as its members both provided an occupation to unemployed and dispossessed people, and ensured co-operation in the construction market, giving a chance to all the professionals and entrepreneurs who abided by its rules. Politicians gained the consent of large strata of the Palermo population, as they were the official promoters of the construction-centred development (Chubb, 1983). Many lower-class people were employed in the construction sector, many others became shop assistants in the new areas or worked as housemaids for the residents of the new flats, or they found jobs in the low ranks of public sector thanks to the mediation both of politicians and of Mafiosi.

For more than 20 years Palermo appeared to be a booming city: new buildings, new jobs, new shops and plenty of cars made most people believe that the city had been modernised, neglecting the decay of the ancient city, the decline of manufacturing industry, mass emigration and the lack of basic amenities, such as schools and public parks. The urbanised area, for example, grew from six square kilometres in 1951 to 65 square kilometres in 1971. The mainstream Palermitan public opinion denied the existence of a criminal organisation, either by calling the mafia wars "residual pre-modern vendetta", or, as the Bishop Ernesto Ruffini did, by calling it "an invention of the communist propaganda" (Cannarozzo, 2000).

The Sack of Palermo is the outcome of a contamination between the legal and illegal economy and politics. The border between legality and illegality is quite blurred: all the Mafioso-led enterprises were legal, and the master plan had been approved by the City Council, and conversely politicians, entrepreneurs and professionals knew they were working with a criminal organisation, but consented to launder money and were actively engaged in promoting patronage-oriented policies, as well as in blocking the enforcement of an Anti-Mafia law by the Italian Parliament. A widespread consent, based on "progress" and "employment", ensured the necessary impunity which allowed this multifaceted alliance of noblemen, professionals, developers, bankers, bureaucrats, politicians, Mafiosi, *sucanchiuostru* and underclass to hegemonise the social and political spectrums of Palermo.

The crisis of the Mafioso hegemony started in early 1980s and reached its peak 15 years later, for various reasons. First, because of the reaction of the Italian government after the so called *delitti eccellenti* (excellent homicides), such as the killing of prominent politicians, judges, police officers and journalists like Michele Reina, Piersanti Mattarella, Pio La Torre, Cesare Terranova, Pippo Fava and Emanuele Basile. The crime of mafia was enforced by the 416 bis law in 1982 (Rognoni-La Torre Act), whose approval by the Italian Parliament was triggered by the reaction of civil society to the ruthless mafia homicides of those years. (La Spina, 2005). Second, the repressive policies were helped by an inner war (Deaglio, 1993) between the *Corleonesi* group and the so-called *perdenti* (losers). Some prominent members of the latter faction, such as Tommaso Buscetta and Totuccio Contorno, became supergrasses, helping judicial enquiries against the mafia, the main outcome of which was the 1986–1987 trial of 474 alleged Cosa Nostra members. In 1992, the Italian Supreme Court confirmed the validity of the sentences, thus making a breakthrough move: for the first time, after 132 years of its existence, the Italian state declared that organised crime existed. Third, the fall of the Berlin wall deprived Cosa Nostra of that political protection, both national and international, that the criminal organisation had enjoyed because of the Cold War (Violante, cit.). On the one hand, the change of the political scenario triggered a violent reaction by Mafiosi, as the 1992–1993 attacks prove (Santino, 2016). In 1992, Giovanni Falcone and Paolo Borsellino, the two most famous and qualified anti-mafia prosecutors, were killed in bomb attacks that also killed their guards and, in the case of Falcone, his wife. In 1993, bombs exploded in Milan, Florence and Rome, damaging such famous monuments and galleries as the Uffizi. On the other hand, it became possible both for police forces and magistrates to prosecute, arrest and sentence more and more mafia members. Fourth, after 1989, new criminal actors emerged, both in Italy and abroad (Varese, 2011), exploiting the new opportunities provided both by the opening of Eastern European borders and by globalisation. Such new actors as the Calabrian 'Ndrangheta and the Russian Soln'cevo appear to have undermined the monopoly of Cosa Nostra in the drug sector (http://direzioneinvestigativaantimafia.interno.gov.it/semestrali/sem/2016/1sem2016.pdf). Finally, the expansion of the global markets re-shapes the forms and the contents of criminal activities, thus making the line between legal and illegal activities more and more indistinct.

Currently, Palermo is facing a deep social and economic crisis, due both to the transformation of criminal organisations, which reduces the amount of illegal money

(DIA, 2014), and to the past exploitation of the territory. All the areas have been exploited during the Sack. Nowadays there is not much room left to build a central business district, a bio-technological park, or a container terminal in the harbour. International competition makes things even more difficult for Palermo. The public expenditure cuts make it difficult to support a new massive public sector development, so that also the *sucanchiuostru* feel unsafe. Maybe this is the new beginning …

Conclusions

This chapter used the *paradigm of complexity* and the *dirty economies* approach to analyse the case of the Sack of Palermo under a criminological lens. We saw how organised crime is neither an external actor of social dynamics, nor the product of some anomaly. The Sicilian mafia could gain a hegemonic position within Palermo society because it had been for two centuries a prominent economic and political actor, building a network of relationships with politicians, entrepreneurs and ordinary citizens, gaining consent both through the manipulation of the most important Sicilian values, and through the satisfaction of such basic needs as employment and housing. Cosa Nostra managed to exploit both the local peculiarities of Palermo, such as the administrative role of the city and the presence of latifundia, and the global opportunity of becoming part of the anti-Communist alliance. The Mafiosi hegemony was hardly thwarted by the Palermo leading classes, who found in the mediation of organised crime an opportunity to make profits, as well as to gain prominent positions in politics and society. The underclass and the clerical petty bourgeoisie of the *sucanchiuostru* actively supported this alliance, to the extent they could draw advantage from the patronage policies, as well as from the range of legal and illegal activities which were either promoted or controlled by organised crime.

The Sack of Palermo is a relevant case for social science, because of its multifaceted implications. First, because it proves that the borders between legality and illegality are never that clear. Second, it shows how important gaining consent is for criminal organisations. Third, the Sack of Palermo proves there is not a unique model to explain the dynamics of organised crime, but rather that the combination between local and global peculiarities can provide scholars with a wide-ranging analytical focus. Finally, in an increasingly globalised world, this combination is far from declining, because the social peculiarities of a local context remain an element to consider, as every territory faces changes differently. The dialectic between local and global, combined with that between legal and illegal, remain crucial analytical elements to understand organised crime, in particular in a post-Fordist society (Ash, 1994; Scalia, 2016), wherein delocalisation draws advantage from the local peculiarities of a territory.

Note

1 *Sucanchiuostru* (inksucker) refers to the habits clerk had, before ballpoint pens became popular, to suck the remaining ink of a cartridge to use it.

References

Albini, J.L., Rogers, R.E., Shabalin, V., Kutushev, V., Moiseev, V. and Anderson, J. 1997. Russian organized crime: Its history, structure and function, in Ryan, P.J., Rush, G.E., *Understanding Organized Crime: A Reader*, pp. 81–132, Thousand Oaks, California: Sage.

Ash, A. ed. 1994. *Postfordism. A Reader*, London: Routledge and Kegan Paul.

Block, A. 1980. *East Side, West Side. Organizing Crime in New York City, 1930–1950*, New York City: Transaction Publisher.

Blok, A. 1971. *La Mafia in un Villaggio Siciliano*, Turin: Einaudi.

Cancila, O. 1986. *Palermo*, Bari: Laterza.

Cannarozzo, T. 2000. Palermo: mezzo secolo di trasformazioni, in *Archivio Regionale di Studi Urbani*, pp. 173–211, 67: 1, Milan: Franco Angeli.

Casarrubea, G. 2001. *Salvatore Giuliano. Morte di un capobanda e dei suoi luogotenenti*, Milan: Franco Angeli.

Chubb, J. 1983. *Patronage, Power and Poverty in Southern Italy. A Tale of Two Cities*, Cambridge: Cambridge University Press.

Ciconte, E. 1992. *'Ndrangheta*, Bari: Laterza.

Cristantino, A. 1987. *La Città Spugna*, Palermo: Edizioni CSDGI.

Deaglio, E. 1993. *Raccolto Rosso*, Milan: Feltrinelli.

Di Lello, G. 1997. Il Separatismo Siciliano, in *Annali della Storia d'Italia*, vol XVII, pp. 544–568, Turin: Einaudi.

Fiandaca, G., Costantino, S. 1992. *La Mafia, Le Mafie*, Bari: Laterza. Franchetti, L. 1876. *Indagine sulla Sicilia*, Vallecchi: Firenze.

Gaja, F. 1990. *l'Esercito della Lupara*, Milan: Maquis.

Gambetta, D. 1992. *La Mafia Siciliana. Un'Industria della Protezione Privata*, Turin: Einaudi.

Gimdalchà, I. 1982. *Progetto Kalhesa*, Padua: Marsilio.

Granovetter, M. 1983. The strength of weak ties: a network theory revisited, *Sociological Theory*, 1: 201–223.

Gucciardo, G. 2002. Abusivismo: il margine dell'illegalità. In Fofi, G., Leogrande, A. (ed.), *Nel sud, senza bussola*, Naples: L'Ancora del Mediterraneo, pp. 37–64.

Hall, T. 2013. Geographies of the illicit: globalisation and organised crime. *Progress in Human Geography*, 37: 3, 366–385.

Hudson, R. 2014. Thinking through the relationships between legal and illegal activities and economies: Spaces, flows and pathways. *Journal of Economic Geography*. 2014; 14: 775–795.

Inzerillo, S.M. 1980. *Società e Urbanistica a Palermo, 1945–1980*, Palermo: Flaccovio.

La Spina, A. 2005. *Mafia, Legalità Debole, Sviluppo del Mezzogiorno*, Bologna: Il Mulino.

Levi, M. 1994. Violent Crime in Maguire, M., Morgan, R., Reiner, R., *The Oxford Handbook of Criminology*, pp. 295–334, Oxford: Oxford University Press.

Lima, A.I. 2000. *Palermo*, Palermo: Flaccovio.

Lupo, S. 1993. *Storia della Mafia*, Rome: Donzelli.

Lupo, S. 2011. *Il Tenebroso Sodalizio*, Rome: XL.

Mineo, M. 1953. *Scritti sulla Sicilia*, Palermo: Flaccovio.

Minna, R. 1971. *Storia del Separatismo Siciliano*, Rome: Editori Riuniti.

Pantaleone, M. 1970. *Antimafia: Occasione Mancata*, Turin: Einaudi.

Paoli, L. 2000. *Fratelli di Sangue*, Bologna: Il Mulino.

Renda, F. 2000. *Storia della Sicilia*, Palermo: Sellerio.

Ruggiero, V. 1996. *Economie sporche*, Turin: Bollati Boringhieri.
Sales, I. 1987. *La Camorra, Le Camorre*, Rome: Editori Riuniti.
Santino, U. 1994. *L'Alleanza e il Compromesso*, Soveria Mannelli: Rubbettino.
Santino, U. 2000. *Storia del movimento antimafia. Dalla lotta di classe All'impegno civile*, Rome: Editori Riuniti.
Santino, U. 2003. *Portella della Ginestra. Una Strage per il centrismo*, Rome: Donzelli.
Santino, U. 2016. *Dalla Mafia alle Mafie* (III ed.), Rubbettino: Soveria Mannelli.
Santino, U. 2016. *Mafia and Antimafia*, London: IBS Tauris.
Santino, U. and La Fiura, G. 1989. *L'Impresa Mafiosa*, Milano: Franco Angeli.
Scalia, V. 2016. *Crime, Networks and Power. The Structural Transformation of the Sicilian Cosa Nostra*, Basingstoke: Palgrave.
Sciarrone, R. 2011. *Mafie Vecchie, Mafie Nuove*, Rome: Donzelli.
Sciarrone, R. 2013. *Alleanze nell'ombra*, Rome: Donzelli.
Stancanelli, B. 2016. *La Città Marcia*, Padua: Marsilio.
Varese, F. 2011. *Mafie in Movimento*, Turin: Einaudi.
Violante, L. 1993. *I Corleonesi*, Rome: Editori Riuniti.

Internet Sites

Archivio Pio La Torre http://archiviopiolatorre.camera.it/l-impegno-parlamentare-nazionale
Commissione Parlamentare Antimafia: http://legislature.camera.it/_bicamerali/nochiosco.asp?pagina=/_bicamerali/antimafia/home.htm
Direzione Investigativa Antimafia: http://direzioneinvestigativaantimafia.interno.gov.it/semestrali/sem/2016/1sem2016.pdf
Instituto Centrale di Statistica http://www.tuttitalia.it/sicilia/81-palermo/statistiche/popolazione-andamento-demografico/

8 Filling governance and development vacuums

A role for development actors or criminal groups?

Sasha Jesperson

Introduction

Particularly in fragile and conflict-affected states, on the surface, organised crime can have a stabilising influence if it provides governance structures, economic opportunities, a form of security and even mediation and justice that the state may not be able to. While this can be beneficial in the short term, in the longer term it reinforces structures and systems that can undermine democracy, good governance and promote structural violence and corruption. There is also a danger of reinforcing alternative governance structures and patronage networks that not only compete with traditional structures, but also the formal state.

While generally viewed in a negative light, the governance and development vacuums that allow criminal groups to fill these spaces provide a new entry point to address organised crime. It has already become clear that the standard law enforcement responses are antiquated and inadequate for addressing increasingly complex drivers of and impacts from organised crime – and that these responses can either push crime elsewhere or, at worst, exacerbate it (Felbab-Brown 2010; 2013a; Jesperson 2016). In response, an increasing role for development actors has been posited, resulting in a comprehensive approach.[1] This is often framed as a multifaceted response that addresses 'all the complex reasons that populations turn to illegality, including law enforcement deficiencies and physical insecurity, poor rule of law, suppression of human rights, economic poverty and social marginalisation' (Felbab-Brown, 2013a).

In practice, this frequently becomes a set of tools that can be applied to address criminality. Rarely are responses based on a political economy analysis, which means they do not critically engage with how organised crime manifests. This is a missed opportunity, as a key contribution from development actors is the ability to tackle the factors that make a country conducive to organised crime, rather than just responding to criminal activity once it is present. Yet there is limited evidence of what should be done and no critical review of planned or implemented approaches.

This chapter seeks to rectify this. It outlines the shift in approach from a predominantly law enforcement or security focus to become more comprehensive through the inclusion of development tools. Then focusing in on governance, the chapter unpacks the importance of governance from a peacebuilding of development perspective, how organised crime groups fill governance vacuums by engaging in strategic or political strategies and to what effect, before assessing what this means for the response.

The chapter examines the role of criminal groups in fragile and conflict-affected states, where governance vacuums are the most pronounced. Organised crime is approached from an interventionist perspective, considering the aims of peacebuilding and development actors. While the findings point to entry points to transform criminal agendas, this would require further, more specific and detailed analysis. Theoretically, the chapter draws on a critical peacebuilding perspective; it stems from the assumption that current peacebuilding approaches are inherently flawed and need to be fundamentally rethought. This allows a much more radical consideration of how to respond to organised crime than policymakers and practitioners can engage in. In that vein, the governance potential of criminal groups is discussed, along with the possibility that development actors could work with rather than against them to further peacebuilding and good governance agendas. The chapter begins by reviewing the increasing involvement of development actors in the response to organised crime, followed by a discussion of the impact organised crime has on development, and in particular governance. The chapter then assesses whether there is scope to work 'with' criminal groups rather than against them.

A shift in approach

Traditionally, organised crime has been understood as a security problem, to be addressed through law enforcement strategies. For example, the 1961 Single Convention on Narcotic Drugs emphasised law enforcement strategies 'at the cost of alternative methods from the medical, educational and development fields' (Carrier and Klantschnig, 2012: 4). The US initiated 'war on drugs' added a further security dimension to drug control, and several Latin American countries have adopted legislation allowing planes suspected of drug trafficking to be shot down (Cawley, 2014). Rather than eradicating organised crime, however, these strategies have merely pushed criminal groups into more sophisticated strategies or alternative methods for moving their products to market.[2]

In response, there has been greater recognition of the need for comprehensive approaches. This began at the 1998 UN General Assembly special session on drug control, which acknowledged that rather than eradicating the drugs trade, 'illicit cultivation of the opium poppy, the coca bush and the cannabis plant continues at alarming levels' (UN General Assembly, 1998: 17). In response, the meeting advocated for a balanced approach that included alternative development strategies to prevent and eliminate cultivation of illicit crops, rural development measures, economic growth and sustainable development (UN General Assembly, 1998).

Alongside the recognition of the need for a balanced approach, the development impact of organised crime has also been acknowledged. On a micro level, many individuals will earn an income from criminal activity, particularly when there are few other opportunities. At the macro level, organised crime also undermines the state economy, as it can 'undermine competition and investment, hollow out production capacity and fuel inflation, fatally weakening state revenues' (Cockayne and Lupel, 2009: 153). These factors also overlap with the security threat as countries that host criminal networks 'risk becoming shell-states: sovereign in name but hollowed out from the inside by criminals in collusion with corrupt officials in the government and security services. This not only jeopardises their survival, it poses a serious threat to regional security because of the transnational nature of the crimes' (UNODC, 2008: 1).

The recognition of both the security and development impact of organised crime has resulted in comprehensive approaches that engage with both security and development aspects. And yet, while the focus on organised crime has expanded beyond the security sector, it continues to confound the development community. While some governments' development agencies are engaging in debates around the issue, progress consistently flounders when it comes to translating those discussions into actions. As a result, few development actors have actually moved towards adapting their approach, even though organised crime directly touches upon multiple areas where they are concerned and puts the achievement of programming goals at risk.

Some advances have been made. USAID has produced a programming guide on drug trafficking in Africa (USAID, 2013). DfID has commissioned research on what development programming can offer initiatives to address organised crime, resulting in the report, *Getting Smart and Scaling Up: Responding to the Impact of Organised Crime on Governance in Developing Countries* (Kavanagh, 2013). Yet, there has been limited engagement in practice. One development professional noted that it has taken a long time to acknowledge the relationship between security and development, and development actors are still not there, organised crime is another step beyond: 'we're where we were 10 years ago with human security'.[3]

More recently, DfID has been working with the Global Initiative against Transnational Organised Crime to produce a toolkit for a multifaceted approach to organised crime that includes a political economy analysis alongside a market and power analysis, followed by prioritisation by measuring harm and identifying entry points and then a response that focuses on isolating criminal markets, addressing impunity and mitigating harm and building resilience, which is being piloted in several countries (see GI-TOC, 2016). This approach begins to engage in the wider factors that facilitate organised crime, but it continues to respond to crime once it occurs – although it does acknowledge that 'investments in accountable governance that do not explicitly target criminal markets may close the space for criminal markets to operate and gain influence over the long term' (GI-TOC, 2016: 32).

The World Development Report 2011 (World Bank, 2011) has been widely cited for recognising that fragile and conflict-affected states can become breeding grounds for organised crime because of the governance vacuums that exist. While current development responses engage with aspects of this, such as providing alternative opportunities for individuals that may be recruited by organised crime networks, criminal activity is not something that can be pulled out and addressed in isolation from other issues, particularly governance, especially as criminal groups increasingly have strategic as well as economic aims (Cockayne, 2016). A deeper analysis is required to tackle the nexus between weak governance and organised crime.

As the response and analysis is being led by practitioners, the shift in approach is confined to what is considered appropriate by government agencies, which often lacks imagination and remains limited by institutional barriers. This points to a need for scholarly thinking to challenge assumptions on development approaches to organised crime and consider potentially radical alternatives.

A waning monopoly on governance and development

Although the current populist wave challenges the prominence of democratic governance, Bastian and Luckham (2003: 1) point out that recent history has been 'an era when political systems based on liberal democracy and economic models promoting global capitalism enjoy almost unchallenged hegemony'. Accordingly, governance has been the priority of peacebuilding missions in conflict-affected states.

The end of the Cold War, and the subsequent withdrawal of US and Soviet Union support from a number of countries resulted in weak or failed states that were prone to conflict and instability because of inadequate state structures, including 'poorly guarded borders, weak law enforcement, incipient taxation, underdeveloped financial systems' (Kostovicova and Bojicic-Dzelovic, 2009). This period of instability and persistent conflict ushered in a period of intervention mandated by the UN Security Council, which was no longer constrained by Soviet Union and US vetoes. These interventions quickly evolved to focus on state-building – the construction of legitimate and effective state institutions. The aim was to create institutions to manage the political and economic reforms required to transition from conflict to peace (Paris 2004). 'Rebuilding institutions in collapsed states means organising government departments and public agencies to discharge their functions both efficiently and democratically' (Ottaway, 2002: 1004).

Although the international community has become far less interventionist since this early post-Cold War period, the establishment of democratic states remains the goal of many international actors, particularly development agencies. Governance programmes have become the core focus of many development agencies. Commitment to governance was reaffirmed at the 2005 World Summit and again by Heads of State and Government in 2010 (UN Task Team, 2012). Since then governance has been included in the Sustainable Development Goals through Goal 16 – peace, justice and strong institutions – as 'without peace, stability, human rights and effective governance, based on the rule of law – we cannot hope for sustainable development' (UNDP, 2015). The World Development Report 2011 emphasised that 'strengthening legitimate institutions and governance to provide citizen security, justice and jobs is crucial to break cycles of violence' (World Bank, 2011: 2).

Traditionally, a state has been understood as a hierarchical, centralised organisation that holds a monopoly on legitimate force over a defined territory.[4] However, it has come to refer to much more than that – states are expected to act in the public interest, and a range of international laws have been developed to entrench that, extending to economic, social and cultural rights. States must ensure rule of law and accountability, being responsive to the needs of society. This is the basis of the social contract as defined by Rousseau whereby individuals surrender some of their freedoms to the state in order for their interests and rights to be protected. In reality, this often becomes procedural – 'that is periodic free and fair multiparty elections that allow citizens to choose and discipline their rulers' (Fukuyama, 2014: 24). But good procedures do not automatically equate to substantive results.

In many 'democratic' countries, leaders have sought, sometimes successfully to extend term limits to maintain power. In recent years, Presidents in Burkina Faso, Burundi, Benin, Democratic Republic of Congo and Rwanda have all aimed to 'dispense with or circumvent' term limits (Dulani, 2015). Fukuyama (2014) sets up Denmark as the goal of state accountability – prosperous, democratic, secure, well-governed, with low levels of corruption. He then acknowledges that state-building seeks to turn the likes of Afghanistan, Somalia, Libya and Haiti into this, with no idea how (Fukuyama, 2014).

The process of instituting good governance has been fraught with difficulties, and many states, including those buoyed by the promise of the Arab Spring, have gone backwards rather than forwards. In part, this arises because political institutions take a long time to consolidate, and this approach assumes that international actors can take a shortcut to a Weberian state, even though most states have taken decades to develop effective and legitimate institutions (Ottaway, 2002; Paris and Sisk, 2007).

The challenge however, is that in the interim, and particularly when governance reforms make things worse, a governance vacuum is created. This creates the ideal conditions for conflict, as there is no monopoly on legitimate use of violence. However, it also creates the ideal conditions for criminal groups to gain traction. The added danger of criminal groups active in fragile and conflict-affected states is that the priority of international actors seeking to reinstate stability is reducing violence and creating the conditions for governance reforms rather than addressing crime. But by not engaging with criminal agendas immediately, the grip of criminal groups is only strengthened.

A legitimate actor?

There is an assumption that because criminal groups are primarily driven by economic motives, they are not focused on rule of law or accountability – particularly as their business model is premised on subverting rule of law. However, conventional governance structures and institutions may be equally averse to rule of law and accountability. As Bastian and Luckham (2003: 2–3) point out, 'even democratic institutions and elected governments … may or may not open spaces for democratic politics; they may or may not be responsive to the political demands of the poor, women and minorities; they may or may not facilitate the management of conflict'. In many instances, criminal networks have played a more effective role than states.

The OECD (2010) argues that legitimacy arises out of the distinction between rule by consent and rule by coercion. As the dominance of criminal groups is based on factors other than democratic elections, such as economic power and the threat of violence, this suggests that their rule is by coercion. While they may work in the interests of communities where they are based, this is to the extent that it serves their own criminal interests. However, the OECD (2010: 7) also concedes that 'a political order, institution or actor is legitimate to the extent that people regard it as satisfactory and believe that no available alternative would be vastly superior'.

In many instances, criminal networks need legitimacy to maintain their operations. They need the complicity, or at least the acquiescence of the communities where they base their operations to minimise disruption by law enforcement. This can be achieved in many ways including through violence. But it is much more effective if it is not forced. After the war in Bosnia, criminal actors that had defended Sarajevo were viewed as heroes, which gave them a level of legitimacy and untouchability (Andreas, 2010). A Bosnian NGO said this arose as 'the only real defence in the first six months [of the war], it was organised crime groups … we had people who were like, still criminals, but half heroes, and local political circles wouldn't dare to touch them'.[5] By protecting civilians, organised crime groups are viewed positively. This legitimacy allows criminal networks to fill the governance vacuum outlined above.

In the Western Balkans more broadly, criminal groups also filled the vacuum created by the transition from the Communist former Yugoslavia to open markets. 'Suddenly people who have been guaranteed security from the cradle to the grave are forced to negotiate an unfamiliar jungle of inflation, unemployment, loss of pension rights and the like. At such junctures, those personal networks from the Communist period become very important' (Glenny, 2008: 74). In this context, organised crime networks were able to take over the patronage networks of the Communist era, providing support that the state was no longer able to provide.

The post-conflict period in particular provides a governance and development vacuum that criminal actors can fill. 'Organised crime can offer survival strategies or even sustainable livelihoods, creating a ladder of opportunity and upward mobility for communities with few other economic prospects' (Cockayne and Lupel, 2009: 153). There are many examples of criminal networks providing services and opportunities including livelihoods, social mobility, social services, security and protection that undermine the legitimacy of the state. The Yakuza provided humanitarian assistance after the Kobe earthquake; criminal groups in Colombia that control the cocaine trade provide minimum wage and social security services; Haitian gangs provide medical services (Cockayne and Lupel, 2009; Cockayne, 2016).

The services provided by organised crime groups are not limited to economic opportunities. In Pakistan, even though violent crime and terrorism was on the rise, a perception study found that people felt safer than they had previously, but at the same time police were perceived as corrupt and predatory, indicating that security was being provided by alternative actors (GI-TOC, 2016). In Brazil's favelas and Jamaica's garrison towns, the security void was filled by criminal groups (Kavanagh, 2013). These factors ensure that criminal groups have legitimacy and support from the communities in which they operate, challenging the dominance of the state.

While these examples point to criminal networks taking on state-like functions, increasingly the state and criminal groups are not so distinct. Moses Naim (see, for example, Naim, 2012) has written extensively on the aims of criminal groups to 'capture' states, where they ultimately end up controlling state bodies, politicians, judges, police forces or territory in order to fulfil their objectives. Miklaucic and Naim (2013) propose that state capture exists as a spectrum depending on the degree of criminalisation. This is well articulated by Cockayne and Lupel (2009) who distinguish between predatory, parasitic and symbiotic groups, referring to ever increasing linkages. Miklaucic and Naim's (2013) own spectrum covers criminal penetration, where agents within the state are advancing criminal interests; criminal capture, where agents become so powerful they can't be challenged; and criminal sovereignty, where criminality becomes institutionalised. Liberia under Charles Taylor's rule is considered to fit within this category. Grzymala-Busse (2008) argues that strategies differ depending on the level of distribution – whether supporters are rewarded or not, and compatibility with competition, particularly democratic competition.

Ultimately, with state capture, the legitimacy of criminal groups becomes less important. By exercising control over elements of the state, the disruption of criminal activity through official channels becomes impossible, which means the group no longer requires the support of the communities within which it operates. Groups may continue to support these communities, particularly if they have other strategic objectives, however their rule is likely to become more coercive and violent. Although some level of popular support would dissuade social movements formed in opposition to criminal groups.

In some instances, rather than criminal actors filling governance vacuums, they are becoming a resource for politicians and officials. This is often evident in state procurement processes and allows large sums to be diverted away from legitimate channels and into the hands of corrupt public officials and criminal groups (Briscoe and Kalkman, 2016). For example, in Afghanistan, organised crime groups exploit mining contracts, allowing government actors to profit, while in Colombia law enforcement and public authorities are complicit in illegal gold mining (Noorani, 2015; Masse and Camargo, 2012; Reitano and Hunter, 2016). In using criminal groups to divert resources however, the state effectively hands power over to criminal groups. This predatory behaviour has often been met with discontent. For example, many civilians protested about defective governance after the complicity (and subsequent lack of response) to the disappearance of 43 trainee teachers in Mexico, and in several Latin American countries, including Brazil, protestors have called for military rule over corrupt democracy (Briscoe and Kalkman, 2016). Corrupt states only deepen the vacuum in governance, providing an opening for criminal groups to strengthen their legitimacy by playing all sides.

To what effect?

Particularly in fragile and conflict-affected states organised crime can be a stabilising factor when it provides governance, services, opportunities and security that the state in unable or unwilling to provide. It meets the needs of communities in those places in which its operations are based. While beneficial in the short term, the long term impact may be destabilising, further endangering state-building.

Crime undermines governance

In conflict-affected states, governments are only beginning to regain control over the economy, security forces and rule of law when conflict ends. With incomes that dwarf official revenues, criminal groups have the potential to undermine state capacity to control security threats by leveraging government officials. The OECD estimates that drug trafficking profits alone are around $US125 billion, giving organised crime groups significant economic power in contrast to governments emerging from conflict (van Veen, 2013).

In Guinea Bissau, drug trafficking organisations offered government officials US$700,000–$1 million to protect drugs brought into the country and facilitate onward transportation (Shaw, Kemp and Boutellis, 2013). This is difficult to resist and it gives criminal groups significant political and military power. As a result, Government policies are going to be formulated to protect the interests of criminal groups rather than the needs of citizens. This undermines the state's capability to deliver public goods. The influence of criminal groups in Guinea Bissau was so powerful that it became widely known as a narco-state (see, for example, Shaw and Reitano, 2013).

Undermines international assistance

Once criminal activity takes hold, it becomes difficult for international actors to achieve their goals in conflict-affected countries. In Iraq, criminal groups and their ties with political leaders undermined the international intervention and post-conflict reconstruction by supporting insurgency, terrorism and sectarianism, weakening governance and heightening economic problems (Williams, 2011). The potential for international assistance to be undermined is particularly pertinent when organised crime is supported through corruption, as state institutions will participate in criminal activity directly or not stop criminal groups from doing so.

Corrupt institutions can also serve as a conduit to siphon off international assistance. It is estimated that 30 per cent of aid is siphoned off by corrupt and criminal actors, the majority of which happens in post-conflict states (ICAR, 2011). For instance, the US military estimates that US$360 million of US government spending has ended up in the hands of the Taliban and criminal groups (Riechmann and Lardner, 2011).

Crime trap[6]

Once crime becomes entrenched in a post-conflict state, there is a risk of becoming locked in a crime trap. Criminal activity creates 'shell states', hollowed out by criminals that corrupt officials and security services (UNODC, 2008). The criminal economy becomes the primary revenue source, which perverts local economies. The underside of this is that people are discouraged from finding legitimate jobs or starting up new businesses – criminal activity provides more lucrative opportunities and will seek to undermine new enterprises.

Criminal activity also affects official revenue streams by undermining competition and investment; it hollows out production capacity and fuels inflation, further weakening state revenues (Cockayne and Lupel, 2009). This limits the rebuilding of a functioning state and economy, making it even more difficult to address criminal activity.

The development challenges posed by organised crime are also more pronounced in post-conflict states. The World Bank estimates that organised crime has a similar impact on development as violent conflict – both result in 20 per cent less development performance (GI-TOC, 2013). These factors ensure that states become reliant on criminal revenue and lose the capacity to respond to and address criminal activity. For citizens, the result is a reduction in social spending as fewer resources are available. With the risk that criminal activity poses to governance, it also limits the beginnings of democracy.

The risk of a crime trap was particularly pertinent to the UK's involvement in Afghanistan. When the UK government prepared to drawdown, the cross-party report documented that 'poppy cultivation is soaring to record levels and there is no sign that the Government of Afghanistan has the will or the means to tackle the problem' (UK HoC, 2014). The report also recorded concern 'that this will continue to fund organised crime and undermine the development of democratic government and governance' (UK HoC, 2014). With few other revenue sources, this poses the risk of dependence on the illicit drug trade.

Return to conflict

The destabilising effect of the criminalised peace on governance and the risk of becoming locked in a crime trap can result in a return to or creation of violent conflict. This was highlighted by Mali's transition from what was considered a development success to violent conflict. During a visit to the country in 2010, UNDP director Helen Clark commended the country on its progress towards the Millennium Development Goals and democratic governance (UNDP, 2010). While the transition from fragile state to democracy was considered a success, external actors did not acknowledge the role of drug trafficking in supporting the government. This created an environment of impunity where traffickers became bolder, increasing their activities and area of operation (Shaw, 2012).

Links between the state and criminal actors contributed to the destabilisation of the country and violent conflict. The state's reluctance to curb revenues from drug trafficking and deal with the groups involved was a key factor in the growth of Al Qaeda in the Mahgreb (AQIM) and the conflict in northern Mali (Lacher, 2012). Even when discussions have turned to rebuilding Mali's institutions and democratic elections, the involvement of organised crime remained a blind spot for all actors (Reitano and Shaw, 2013).

Even without a return to conflict, criminal activity can result in high levels of violence. Clashes between criminals and authorities in Latin America have the intensity of urban conflict (Felbab-Brown, 2013b). Similarly, in Karachi criminal violence has been compared to low-intensity warfare, with some regarding it as a microcosm of civil war as thousands are killed each year (Felbab-Brown, 2013b). For citizens in countries affected by criminalised violence, the impact is similar to armed conflict. This indicates that responses to organised crime need to be built into post-conflict programming much earlier.

An entry point for responses?

The impact of organised crime groups in fragile and conflict-affected states paints a bleak picture of a cycle that continues to undermine governance with destabilising effects. Although the dynamics between criminals and the state differ in all of these examples, Reitano and Hunter (2016: 7) argue that in all cases 'organised crime perpetuates poverty and inequality, while threatening economic growth, and by extension, democracy itself'. However, a deeper analysis of how organised crime manifests itself suggests that the situation is more nuanced, and it actually provides entry points for more constructive responses.

The discussion above refers to organised crime networks as though they are a monolithic entity (Figure 8.1). However, much analysis of organised crime acknowledges their flexibility and adaptability, using entrepreneurial tools to remain agile, dynamic and ahead of law enforcement (Goodman, 2011). Rather than traditional, hierarchical mafia-type organised crime groups, organised crime has become much more fluid and networked, with individuals moving in and out as required. For many groups, minimising risk has also become a priority, resulting in a shift from large shipments of high risk commodities, such as cocaine, to smaller, more frequent shipments of less risky, even licit commodities, such as alcohol or cigarettes, with much less specialisation than previously (Edwards and Jeffray, 2015). This suggests a linear shift however, from traditional mafia to modern, business like criminals, which is not the case. This is the case for many, profit driven networks, but a diversity of organisational types exists.

In the context of fragile and conflict-affected states, a spectrum can be identified from strategic and highly organised groups to those that are maximising opportunities. The strategic and highly organised end of the spectrum has been dominated by foreign cartels taking advantage of fragile states. For example, after international law enforcement intercepted vessels transporting cocaine across the Atlantic in the early 2000s, Colombian cartels sought to identify transit hubs on the West African coast, identifying Guinea Bissau as a weak spot ripe for state capture (Jesperson, 2017). But it is not only foreign organised crime groups that occupy this end of the spectrum.

In West Africa, and indeed globally, Nigerian organised crime has become notorious for its sophistication, organisation and ruthlessness. As with Colombian cartels in Guinea Bissau, which managed to get President Vieira onside during his 2005–2009 term, as well as senior military officers, Nigerian organised crime has also been linked to the political system, which is renowned for fraud, embezzlement and illicit violence (O'Regan and Thompson, 2013; Ellis, 2016). Because the groups are closely linked to the state apparatus, they already have a level of impunity, so tend to avoid the cover of conflict for the transit of illicit goods. Instead they tend to maintain their dominance through coercion and violence as they are hostile to any effort to control their behaviour (Williams, 2001: 183). Stedman (1997) considers them 'greedy spoilers' as their 'goals expand or contract based on calculations of costs and risks'.

Responding to these groups through anything other than similarly coercive approaches such as law enforcement is likely to be ineffectual. Although a range of development strategies can be applied to prevent individuals from being recruited into their activities. While these groups take advantage of state structures, they are rarely in competition with the state and do not fill governance vacuums. Rather they rely on a strong, corruptible state to facilitate their activities, resulting in a symbiotic relationship.

For the purposes of this analysis, the other end of the spectrum is more interesting. These are groups that do take advantage of governance vacuums. Rather than the strategic or coercive approach of the Colombian or Nigerian organised crime networks, these groups tend to be opportunistic, often responding to the lack of services, opportunities and security provided by the state as a result of conflict or fragility. Many of these groups are not particularly sophisticated or business-like. Based on her research in Nepal, Felbab-Brown found that:

> The criminal groups tend to be mostly small, territorially limited organisations, and their operations are not highly complex. They have nowhere near the level of sophistication and organisational complexity of the criminal groups operating in India's or Pakistan's slums, for example. The level of violence the Nepali criminal groups perpetrate in support of their profit-seeking activities is also fairly limited when compared with criminal organisations in other parts of the world, such as Colombia or Mexico. Nor do they yet systematically deliver "public" goods to local populations to cultivate support independent of the state, as other criminal groups – from India to Japan, Italy, and Colombia – have learned to do.
>
> (Felbab-Brown, 2013: 57c–8)

As these groups develop to take on service delivery functions, there is an opportunity and a danger. Cockayne (2016: 25) argues that strategic criminal organisations compete with the state 'not just to be the individual's protector, but to be the source of the rules and discretion by which that individual is ultimately governed'.

This is usually done through violence and corruption resulting in either state capture as witnessed with the Colombian and Nigerian cartels or a war-like situation with high levels of violence as witnessed in Mexico, where the 2011 death toll was higher than battle deaths in Afghanistan, Iraq and Sudan (HSRP, 2013).

This shift is outlined in the figure below. Although there is not a clear distinction between the two categories, there is a consistent shift from the opportunistic, ad hoc side of the spectrum towards the strategic, sophisticated end. This is rarely reversed. The shift begins as groups become more organised, usually marked by their engagement in service provision, as they start to fill governance vacuums rather than just taking advantage of them. This then places the group in competition with the state, and depending on the state's strength and openness to capture, will result in an increased amount of violence and coercion on the part of the criminal group.

This paints a bleak picture – a pathway to increased sophistication and coercion. However, a nuanced analysis of groups like those outlined by Felbab-Brown may identify potential avenues for transformation before they slide down the spectrum to become more violent and organised. A growing body of literature is beginning to engage with the need to embrace alternative, and perhaps at times, less palatable forms of governance. Based on their research on state formation in the territory of Somalia, Leonard and Samantar (2011: 559) call for a rethink of state-building approaches, arguing that 'it frequently is better to allow for bottom-up, organic, disjointed negotiation of indigenous governance solutions (even though they probably will not conform to Western ideas of liberal democracy) than for the international system to impose top-down answers'. For criminal groups that begin to engage in service provision and have a legitimate governance function, there is scope to 'catch' them before they become extremely violent and coercive.

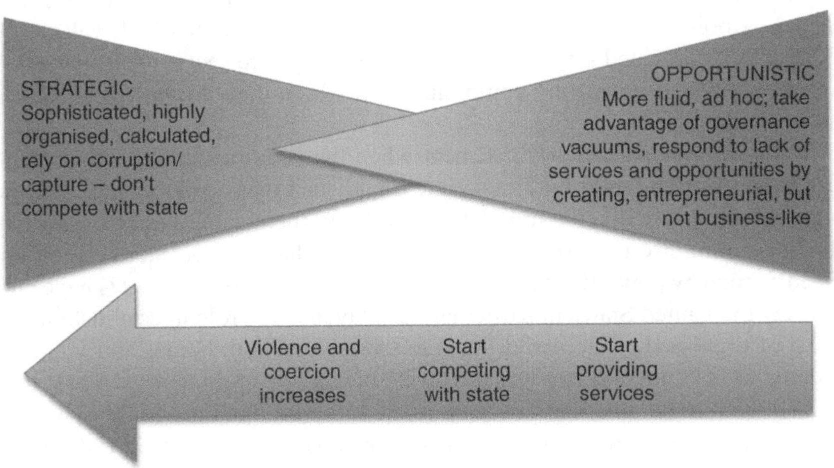

Figure 8.1 Shifting models of organised crime networks.

In many contexts criminality is not a malicious attempt to subvert law and order, but arises because legitimate opportunities do not exist or the way business operates generally is not in line with the law. This is particularly the case where the line between the formal and informal economy is not clear cut. Andreas (2004) and Pugh, Cooper and Goodhand (2004) have all warned against a firm distinction between legal and illegal and call instead for a deeper and more complex understanding. This discussion is drawn out in more detail elsewhere in this volume (see introduction, also Hall, 2013; Hudson, 2014).

Greed may be a key driver, but that is not so different from early state formation. Fukuyama (2014: 25) highlights that 'at one stage in human history all governments could be described as patrimonial, limited access or extractive'. However, they have evolved towards legitimate, accountable and democratic institutions. Writing about mafia-type organisations, Skaperdas (2001: 164) points out that they are 'more similar in their structure and economic impact to pre-modern forms of predatory states'. This suggests that they could evolve in a similar way to states, becoming legitimate economic actors.

There are of course risks in boosting the legitimacy of criminal groups, as it may entrench traditional structures, such as patronage networks, and without inbuilt accountability mechanisms, they may be open to manipulation by the powerful. However, many formally recognised states are not immune to this either. In their examination of Somalian piracy, Shortland and Varese (2015: 2, 15) outline the role of criminal groups in providing 'protection against extortion, protection against theft and police harassment, protection in relation to informally obtained credit and the retrieval of loans, and the settlement of a variety of social disputes', which establishes 'a general framework of legal and extra-legal governance that puts gangs, mafias, insurgencies and states on the same continuum'. This framework disregards systems of accountability that have been developed over time to keep the state in check.

While this may not be the most palatable governance system, Easton (1965: 21) considers a political system to be 'those institutions through which values are authoritatively allocated for a society'. If these groups are seen as legitimate and thus empowered to govern by communities in which they are based, is there a basis to challenge it?

This question is particularly pertinent when the activities that groups engage in are legal. A 2015 report by Transcrime established that many organised crime groups in Europe are diversifying their portfolio to include legitimate businesses in order to minimise risk. However, commodities that are considered illicit are defined as such by powerful states. Hobbs and Antonopoulos (2013: 27) have outlined how the United States in particular has played a key role in establishing the context of organised crime and using it to 'stereotype both heroes and villains'. Similarly, the US government was the driver behind the criminalisation of drugs, initiating the various international drug-related treaties that opened the space for the large profits that encouraged organised criminal involvement in trafficking. However, in many countries debates are now raging to make a number of drugs from cannabis to cocaine legal, or at least decriminalised.

While often attributed to personal greed, the aims of some criminal groups may be more benevolent than the state. Sociologists and anthropologists, such as Berry (1993) and Marie (1997) have identified that wealth generation in some African countries is often driven by a desire to meet social obligations and purchase status. In some cases, of course, greed will be the overarching driver, but these examples suggest that there are entry points to transform these groups into more legitimate governance actors.

Any attempt to transform criminal actors would need to draw on a rigorous political economy analysis of how the groups functions, its relationships with the state, communities and other stakeholders, and the broader context within which they are operating in order to identify any factors that may inhibit or strengthen transformation. This kind of approach is not new. Although difficult, mediation between groups with criminal agendas has taken place, as well as negotiation between these groups and the state (Cockayne, 2013). Gang truces, initially in El Salvador and subsequently replicated in Mexico and Honduras, resulted in gangs agreeing to reduce crime and violence in exchange for promises of jobs, rehabilitation and other support (Cockayne, 2013). In Brazil and Haiti, community violence reduction programmes have aimed to bring gang members into civic life through community programmes (Cockayne, 2013). These processes have all had their difficulties, including ensuring mediators are respected on all sides and sustaining economic transformation, but they highlight that it is possible to transform criminal activity, even that which is overtly violent.

Alongside existing strategies that seek to counter organised crime once it is already entrenched, this approach is more preventative, engaging with groups before they become too violent or coercive. Although it would be resource intensive initially in order to undertake analysis and programming, it would have a long-term benefit.

A role for development actors

As discussed earlier, law enforcement responses to organised crime are inadequate and the need for a comprehensive approach has been widely acknowledged. Although development actors have become increasingly involved, their reluctance to engage with organised crime has resulted in a pragmatic response that often takes a lead from law enforcement. Even the toolbox being developed by DfID and the Global Initiative against Transnational Organised Crime is primarily reactive, responding to organised crime once criminal activity is underway.

Development actors have a much deeper experience that can contribute to this response (see Jesperson, 2015 for a comprehensive review on the role of development actors). Programming that engages with governance vacuums and provides services and opportunities to the population can be important. However, care needs to be taken in applying development tools to organised crime. Midgely *et al.* (2014) have highlighted how development doesn't necessarily eradicate organised crime, but just like law enforcement strategies can change its nature. Similarly, critical development literature has identified how improved development can actually create opportunities for organised crime, particularly through enhanced infrastructure, transport etc. (see, for example, Hastings, 2009).

Even with these challenges, development actors have an advantage in responding to organised crime. There is an emphasis on understanding the context and nuance of a given situation and tailoring a response appropriately. This is what is needed for organised crime. Engaging with non-state actors has been one of the challenges of liberal peacebuilding models that has underpinned the involvement of development actors in fragile and conflict-affected states. However, in many areas of post-conflict reconstruction, such as security and justice sectors, donors have had to engage with plural orders (see Denney, 2013 and 2014 on security sector reform in Sierra Leone for example). Rather than just learning from law enforcement to develop their approach, these are the lessons with which development actors should be engaging, considering how their governance programmes can transform crime rather than eradicate it once it is already entrenched.

Conclusion

This chapter has only scratched the surface of what is a complex issue. Although the focus here has been on fragile and conflict-affected states, the challenges and the differences between criminal groups exist in other contexts also. Cockayne (2016: 26) argues that 'the reduction of state social services and trade and financial market liberalisation has reduced the role of the state in meeting the needs of citizens, potentially generating an unmet demand for government, creating space for alternative providers'. Particularly as the informal economy grows in the developed world, there is increased scope for actors that straddle the blurred division between licit and illicit economies to provide services to their communities and to become seen as more legitimate than the state. These groups are not necessarily 'bad', as they are merely maximising opportunities. These groups, in contrast to much more organised crime networks, provide an opportunity to bring their activities more fully into the licit, formal economy, and establish a formal governance role that works in tandem with the state, not in opposition to it. However, this would require renewed faith in formal governance structures, something that is waning everywhere.

Much research on organised crime has emerged from disciplinary silos that focus on different elements of the problem, whether criminology, political science or others. By focusing on fragile and conflict-affected states, this chapter has aimed to bring a state-building lens to the problem of addressing organised crime. With an overwhelming focus on governance, it opens alternative avenues to respond, which although not palatable, may be more sustainable and cost-effective in the long-term.

Notes

1 A number of agencies, such as the UK's Department for International Development (DfID), US Agency for International Development (USAID) and the German Gesellschaft

für Internationale Zusammenarbeit (GIZ) have taken this on board and designed initiatives that respond to organised crime.

2 This has been most comprehensively documented in relation to the 'balloon effect' and the cocaine trade, where law enforcement strategies have resulted in new transit routes (see for example Villar and Cottle 2011).

3 Interview, USAID, New York, 27 March 2013.

4 This is the foundation of public international law, based on the theories of Thomas Hobbes and Max Weber.

5 Interview with representative of an international NGO, Sarajevo, 7 October 2011.

6 The Crime Trap concept has been developed by James Cockayne, see for example Cockayne (2014).

References

Andreas, Peter (2004). 'The clandestine political economy of war and peace in Bosnia', *International Studies Quarterly* 48(1): 29–51.

Andreas, Peter (2010). 'The Longest Siege: Humanitarians and profiteers in the battle for Sarajevo', in Wolfgang Benedek, Christopher Daase, Voijin Dimitrijevic and Petrus van Duyne (eds), *Transnational Terrorism, Organised Crime and Peace-Building: Human Security in the Western Balkans*. Basingstoke, New York: Palgrave Macmillan.

Bastian, Sunil and Robin Luckham (2003). 'Introduction: Can democracy be designed?', in Sunil Bastian and Robin Luckham (eds) *Can Democracy be Designed? The Politics of Institutional Choice in Conflict-Torn Societies*, London and New York: Zed Books.

Berry, Sara (1993). *No Condition is Permanent: The Social Dynamics of Agrarian Change in Sub-Saharan Africa*. Madison, WI: University of Wisconsin Press.

Briscoe, Ivan and Pamela Kalkman (2016). *The New Criminal Powers: The Spread of Illicit Links to Politics Across the World and How it Can be Tackled*. The Hague: Clingendael Institute.

Carrier, Neil and Gernot Klantschnig (2012). *Africa and the War on Drugs*. London: New York: Zed Books.

Cawley, Marguerite (2014). 'Honduras approves drug plane shoot-down law, Bolivia set to follow', available at http://www.insightcrime.org/news-briefs/honduras-approves-drug-plane-shoot-down-law-bolivia-set-to-follow.

Cockayne, James (2013). 'Strengthening mediation to deal with criminal agendas', *Oslo Forum Papers No. 2*. Geneva: Centre for Humanitarian Dialogue.

Cockayne, James (2014). 'Breaking the crime trap: Factoring crime into development policy', *IPI Global Observatory*, 13 February 2014, http://theglobalobservatory.org/analysis/678-breaking-the-crime-trap-factoring-crime-into-development-policy.html.

Cockayne, James (2016). *Hidden Power: The Strategic Logic of Organised Crime*. London: Hurst.

Cockayne, James and Adam Lupel (2009). 'Conclusion: From iron fist to invisible hand – peace operations, organised crime and intelligent international law enforcement', *International Peacekeeping*, 16(1): 151–168.

Denney, Lisa (2013). 'Overcoming the state/non-state divide: An end-user approach to security and justice'. *International Peacekeeping*, Special Issue on Security Sector Reform, 21(2): 251–268.

Denney, Lisa (2014). 'Liberal chiefs or illiberal development? The challenge of engaging chiefs in DFID's security sector reform in Sierra Leone'. *Development Policy Review* 31(1): 5–25.

Dulani, Boniface (2015). 'African publics strongly support term limits, resist leaders' efforts to extend their tenure', *Afrobarometer Dispatch No.* 30, available at http://afrobarometer.org/sites/default/files/publications/Dispatches/abr6dispatchno30.pdf.

Easton, David (1965). *A Systems Analysis of Political Life*. New York: John Wiley & Sons.

Edwards, Charlie and Calum Jeffray (2015). *On Tap: The Illicit Trade in Tobacco, Alcohol and Pharmaceuticals*. London: Royal United Services Institute.

Ellis, Stephen (2016). *This Present Darkness: A History of Nigerian Organised Crime*. London: Hurst.

Felbab-Brown, Vanda (2010). 'The design and resourcing of supply-side counternarcotics policies', available at http://www.brookings.edu/research/testimony/2010/04/14-drug-funding-felbabbrown.

Felbab-Brown, Vanda (2013a). 'A state-building approach to the drug trade problem', available at: http://www.brookings.edu/research/opinions/2013/07/18-state-building-drug-trade-problem-felbabbrown.

Felbab-Brown, Vanda (2013b). 'Crime-war battlefields', *Survival: Global Politics and Strategy,* 55 (3): 147–166.

Felbab-Brown, Vanda (2013c). 'A Case Study of Nepal', in Camino Kavanagh (ed), *Getting Smart and Shaping Up: Responding to the Impact of Drug Trafficking in Developing Countries*. New York: NYU Center on International Cooperation.

Fukuyama, Francis (2014). *Political Order and Political Decay: From the Industrial Revolution to the Globalisation of Democracy*. London: Profile Books.

Glenny, Misha (2008). *McMafia: A Journey through the Global Criminal Underworld*. New York: Alfred A. Knopf.

Global Initiative against Transnational Organised Crime (GI-TOC) (2013). Global Initiative against Transnational Organised Crime Launch Event, New York, June 2013.

Global Initiative against Transnational Organised Crime (GI-TOC) (2016). *Development Responses to Organised Crime: An Analysis and Programme Framework.* Geneva: Global Initiative against Transnational Organised Crime.

Goodman, Marc (2011). 'What business can learn from organized crime', *Harvard Business Review*, available at https://hbr.org/2011/11/what-business-can-learn-from-organized-crime.

Grzymala-Busse, Anna (2008). 'Beyond clientelism: Incumbent state capture and state formation', *Comparative Political Studies,* 41(4–5): 638–673.

Hall, Tim (2013). 'Geographies of the illicit: Globalisation and organised crime', *Progress in Human Geography*, 37(3): 366–385.

Hastings, Justin (2009). 'Geographies of state failure and sophistication of maritime piracy hijackings', *Political Geography,* 28(4): 213–223.

Hobbs, Dick and Georgios Antonopoulos (2013) 'Endemic to the species: Ordering the "other" via organised crime', *Global Crime* 14(1): 27–51.

Hudson, Ray (2014). 'Thinking through the relationship between legal and illegal activities and economics: Spaces, flows and pathways', *Journal of Economic Geography*, 14(4): 775–795.

Human Security Report Project (HSRP) (2013). *Human Security Report 2013: The Decline in Global Violence: Evidence, Explanation, and Contestation*. Vancouver: Human Security Press.

International Centre for Asset Recovery (ICAR) (2013). *Development Assistance, Asset Recovery and Money Laundering: Making the Connection*. Basel: Basel Institute on Governance.

Jesperson, Sasha (2015). 'Development engagement with organised crime: A necessary shift or further securitisation?' *Conflict, Security and Development,* 15(1), 23–50.

Jesperson, Sasha (2016). *Rethinking the Security-Development Nexus: Organised crime in post-conflict states.* London: Routledge.

Jesperson, Sasha (2017). 'Kept at bay: Political–criminal alliances in Sierra Leone', in Felia Allum and Stan Gilmour (eds), *Handbook on Organised Crime, Politics and Governance.* London: Edward Elgar.

Kavanagh, Camino (2013). *Getting Smart and Scaling Up: Responding to the Impact of Organized Crime on Governance in Developing Countries.* New York: NYU Centre on International Cooperation.

Kostovicova, Denisa and Vesna Bojicic-Dzelilovic (2009). 'Introduction: Persistent state weakness in the global age', in Denisa Kostovicova and Vesna Bojicic-Dzelilovic (eds), *Persistent State Weakness in the Global Age.* London: Ashgate.

Lacher, Wolfgang (2012). 'Organised crime and conflict in the Sahel-Sahara region', *The Carnegie Papers.* Washington DC: Carnegie Endowment for International Peace.

Leonard D.K. and M.S. Samantar (2011). 'What does the Somali experience teach us about the social contract and the state?' *Development and Change,* 42(2): 559–584.

Marie, Alain (ed.) (1997). *L'Afrique des individus.* Paris: Editions Karthala.

Massé, Frederic and Johanna Camargo (2012). *Actores Armados Ilegales y Sector Extractivo en Colombia* [Illegal Armed Actors and Extractive Industries in Colombia]. Bogota: CIT pax- Colombia and Observatorio Internacional.

Midgely, Tim, Ivan Briscoe and Daniel Bertoli (2014). *Identifying Approaches and Measuring Impacts of Programmes focused on Transnational Organised Crime.* London: Saferworld.

Miklaucic, Michael and Moises Naim (2013). 'The criminal state', in Jacqueline Brewer, Michael Miklaucic and James G. Stavridis (eds), *Convergence: Illicit Networks and National Security in the Age of Globalisation.* Washington DC: National Defense University Press.

Naim, Moises (2012). 'Mafia states: Organised crime takes office', *Foreign Affairs,* 91(3): 100–111.

Noorani, Javed (2015). *Afghanistan's Emerging Mining Oligarchy,* United States Institute of Peace, https://www.usip.org/sites/default/files/SR358-Afghanistan-s-Emerging-Mining-Oligarchy.pdf.

OECD (2010). *The State's Legitimacy in Fragile Situations: Unpacking Complexity,* OECD, Paris.

O'Regan, David and Peter Thompson (2013). 'Advancing stability and reconciliation in Guinea-Bissau: Lessons from Africa's first narco-state', *ACSS Special Report No.* 2. Washington DC: Africa Centre for Strategic Studies.

Ottaway, Marina (2002). 'Rebuilding state institutions in failed states', *Development and Change,* 33(5): 1001–1023.

Paris, Roland (2004). 'Still an inscrutable concept', *Security Dialogue,* 35(3): 370–372.

Paris, Roland and Timothy Sisk (2007). 'Managing contradictions: The inherent dilemmas of postwar state-building'. *Research Partnership on Postwar State-building.* New York: International Peace Academy.

Pugh, Michael, Neil Cooper and Jonathan Goodhand (2004). *War Economies in a Regional Context: Challenges of Transformation.* Boulder, London: Lynne Reinner.

Reitano, Tuesday and Marcena Hunter (2016). *Protecting Politics: Deterring the Influence of Organised Crime on Public Service Delivery.* Strasbourg: International IDEA.

Reitano, Tuesday and Mark Shaw (2013). 'Check your blind spot: Confronting criminal spoilers in the Sahel', *Policy Brief No.* 39. Pretoria: Institute of Security Studies.

Riechmann, Deb and Richard Lardner (2011) 'Afghan Taliban, criminals siphon US funds', available at http://www.sfgate.com/world/article/Afghan-Taliban-criminals-siphon-U-S-funds-2335014.php.

Shaw, Mark (2012). 'Leadership required: Drug trafficking and the crisis of statehood in West Africa', *Policy Brief No.* 37. Pretoria: Institute of Security Studies.

Shaw, Mark and Tuesday Reitano (2013). *The Evolution of Organised Crime in Africa.* Pretoria: Institute for Security Studies.

Shaw, Mark, Walter Kemp and Arthur Boutellis (2013). *The Elephant in the Room: How Can Peace Operations Deal with Organised Crime?* New York, International Peace Institute.

Shortland, Anja and Federico Varese (2015). 'State-building, informal governance and organised crime: The case of Somali piracy', *Political Studies*, 2015: 1–21.

Skaperdas, Stergios (2001). 'The political economy of organised crime: Providing protection when the state does not', *Economic Governance*, 2: 173–202.

Stedman, Stephen (1997). 'Spoiler problems in peace processes', *International Security,* 22(2): 5–53.

UK House of Commons Defence Committee (UK HoC). 2014 *Afghanistan: Fifteenth Report of the Session 2013–14*, HC994. London: The Stationery Office.

UN General Assembly (1998). *Measures to Enhance International Cooperation to Counter the World Drug Problem.* New York, UN.

UN System Task Team on the Post-2015 UN Development Agenda (2012). Governance and Development Thematic Think Piece. New York: UN.

UNDP (2010) 'Helen Clark concludes Mali visit', available at http://www.undp.org/content/rba/en/home/presscenter/articles/2010/05/04/helen-clark-concludes-mali-visit.

UNDP (2015). 'Sustainable development goal 16', Sustainable Development knowledge platform, available at https://sustainabledevelopment.un.org/sdg16.

UNODC (2008). *Drug Trafficking as a Security Threat in West Africa.* Vienna, UNODC.

US Agency for International Development (USAID) (2013). *The Development Response to Drug Trafficking in Africa: A Programming Guide.* Washington DC, USAID.

Van Veen, Erwin (2013). 'Organised crime is a development challenge', Being tough is not enough: Curbing transnational organised crime, International Expert Conference, Friedrich Ebert Stiftung, 28 February–1 March 2013.

Villar, Oliver, and Drew Cottle (2011). *Cocaine, Death Squads, and the War on Terror: US Imperialism and Class Struggle in Colombia.* New York: Monthly Review Press.

Williams, Phil (2001). 'Transnational organized crime, illicit markets, and money laundering', in P. J. Simmons and Chantel Ouderen (eds), *Challenges in International Governance.* Washington: Carnegie Endowment.

Williams, Phil (2011) 'Organized crime and corruption in Iraq', in James Cockayne and Adam Lupel (eds) *Peace Operations and Organised Crime: Enemies or Allies?* New York: Routledge.

World Bank (2011). *World Development Report: Conflict, Security, and Development.* Washington DC, World Bank.

9 Planning for marijuana

Development, governance and regional political economy

Michael Polson

Planning the future: Development, timber and marijuana

In a series of court decisions and legislative acts between 1965 and 1971, California came to require that every county and municipality produce a General Plan. The plan is intended to guide every decision about a county's spatial development (e.g. placement of roads, expansions of housing, disposition of natural resources). All land use regulations—the primary governmental power of localities—must operate according to this plan, making it a foundational document in the governance of California's 39 million residents and the 6th largest economy in the world. The state's supreme court labeled the General Plan a 'constitution for all future development' (*O'Loane v. Roark* 1965; cited in Hall 1976), suggesting that the plan's purpose was not only to project a vision of the locality's future, but to constitute itself in the present, to define the contours of its political body. Despite planners' hopes for a de-politicized, technocratic consensus about a locality's constitution and future, general planning is not without controversy—especially given the mandate for localities to undergo a General Plan Update (GPU) every ten years.

Humboldt County last agreed on a complete General Plan 33 years ago. The document's delay is symbolically telling—the county, having missed three GPU deadlines, has been unable to define itself or its future for decades. For counties with extractive economies, like Humboldt's timber economy, the General Plan's mandate to account for conservation, environmental justice and the regularization of nebulous land markets makes it controversial. This is especially so in Humboldt, where a robust environmental movement has developed over the past several decades. Faced with divergent visions of the relation between nature, labor, capital and government, it was no wonder the county struggled with a General Plan. As of this writing, an updated General Plan languishes. Yet the plan is ceaselessly in formation through hearings, workshops, drafts, lawsuits, administrative reports, op-eds, advocacy briefs and informal communications—a contentious future forming in the present.

Though excluded from the General Plan,[1] marijuana, Humboldt's other major natural resource beside timber, has figured centrally, if opaquely, into county development and governance. Marijuana has been a form of shadow development underlying Humboldt's formal developmental process—an unwritten plan undergirding the General Plan. This chapter explores marijuana's pivotal role in defining Humboldt's extraction and post-extraction developmental regimes.[2] It does so by tracing marijuana's transformation from a prohibited substance to its new articulation as an object of civil regulation and formal development. This chapter argues that prohibition barred marijuana from formal county development, but nevertheless became critical to the political-economic maintenance of a timber-based developmental regime, particularly during timber's socioeconomically and ecologically treacherous decline. After timber's definitive crisis in 2007, marijuana became the central object around which post-extractive political-economic factions organized in their aim to articulate compelling visions for a now-uncertain future. Two visions predominated—one based on smart growth environmentalism and the other on the growth of rents and unproductive consumption. Timber, *rentier* capital and smart growth developmental visions related to marijuana in different ways. This chapter will argue that the demarcation of illegality from legality is a crucial element in defining all three of these developmental forms. Correlatively, development not only affects its formal, named objects, but (under)develops that which it defines itself against—the illegal.[3]

The chapter, which is based upon 19 months of fieldwork and numerous interviews of variously positioned informants across the legal/illegal spectrum, first situates this study within examinations of extraction-based regional political economies,[4] attending to the uneven development of governing capacities in these regions. Then it traces the growth of Humboldt's timber developmental regime, its articulation with marijuana prohibition, and, following timber's industrial decline, the struggle that emerged among environmentalists and *rentier* capitalists to guide the development of marijuana and the county's broader political economy.

Regional political economy, the il/legal and developmental regimes

Humboldt County, which is nearly the size of Connecticut, or half the size of Slovenia, might be considered a region unto itself, but it is also a part of a broader region called the North Coast and the informally named Emerald Triangle, so named for the density of marijuana growing since the 1970s. The region is an appropriate level of analysis for two reasons. First, in the face of ongoing federal prohibition, marijuana policy has devolved to the local and regional level. In California, municipal and county governments have been charged with policy development since voter approval of medical marijuana in 1996, largely because of an inability to pass regulations at the state level. Marijuana policies in California have thus been unevenly invented and adopted by local governments. This uneven development calls for an examination of why liberalizing policies advance in some places but not others.[5] This chapter grounds the analysis of the abstract processes of prohibition and liberalization within the regional dynamics that give them shape, thus following Heyman and Campbell (2009)'s entreaty to root the study of abstract processes in an analysis of particular arrangements of regional spaces and networks (see also Gidwani 2008; Watts 2004).[6] Second, a regional frame enables an analysis of the everyday relations and spaces that structure marijuana. This is critical because prohibition banished marijuana from a formal, regulated and overt spatiality—relegating marijuana to an infra-spatiality that covertly shapes regional political, social and economic life. Liberalization—and the re-entry of marijuana into formal social realms—marks a return to an overt spatiality and enables a fuller understanding of marijuana's long-standing relation to regional economic development.

The region has been looked to as a critical unit of analysis because of its rearticulated role in global capitalism (Agnew 2000; Heyman and Campbell 2009; Hudson 2007; Narotzky and Smith 2006; Piore and Sabel 1984; Scott and Storper 2003; Smith 1990). Analysis is incomplete, as this volume suggests, to the degree it accounts only for the legal and formal aspects of society. This chapter argues that the demarcation of the *line* between legality and illegality is an integral aspect of a region's development. On the one hand, the il/legal line (Nordstrom 2007) designates who and what is *included* and *excluded* from development (Ghertner 2015). On the other hand, development regimes often substantively *depend* upon criminal(ized) actors and illicit traffic across legal and illegal bounds for their maintenance, particularly when an illegal economic activity is lucrative or politically stabilizing (Smart 2001), as marijuana has been. Illegality can thus define both the limits to and substance of development. Scholars have explored this relationship between illegality and development across agrarian (Campbell 2015; Linebaugh 1976; Schneider and Schneider 1976; Thompson 1975), urban (Dawdy 2008; Mullings 2003; Robotham 2003; Smart 2001; Weinstein 2008) and extractive (Campbell 2015; Coronil 1997; Tsing 2005; Watts 2004) developmental regimes. These studies indicate the necessity of understanding il/legality in terms of the dominant regional mode of value production and its related socio-spatial organization.

The relation between law, governance and development in extractive economies, like Humboldt's, has been theorized in terms of the 'resource curse' (Bunker 1985; Ross 1999; Sachs and Warner 1995), which proposes that the presence of resources lends itself to underdevelopment by authoritarian and often violent governmental regimes. Though the causal relation between resources and governmental form has been roundly criticized (see Brunnschweiler and Bulte 2008; Robinson *et al.* 2006; Watts 2004), the theory does provide several key insights. When extractive industry predominates, it lends itself to the development of certain governmental capacities. Namely, it tends to maximize the rights of property owners and extractionists, which often means minimizing civil-regulatory capacities of government, such as land regulation, environmental review and infrastructural development beyond what is necessary to facilitate extraction. Relatedly, extraction regimes tend to minimize expenditures on laboring populations, like public health, welfare and housing programs. Extractionists are compelled to minimize payments to the state for the reproduction of labor because, especially in the case of timber, extraction depends upon seasonal and cyclic labor (see Wilk 2014) and value production depends less on labor input and more upon the expropriation of nature's use value (Coronil 1997).

The underdevelopment of government's capacities to reproduce labor has important implications for the relation of extraction regimes to law and illegality.

First, government officials can become dependent upon extraction-based rents and non-responsive to other constituencies, which can lead to graft, corruption and, short of that, the crafting of governance and law around the interests of extractive industry (DiJohn 2002; Le Billon 2001). Second, because government can lack capacities to reproduce and govern laboring populations, other mechanisms of social governance must be improvised, particularly during economic downswings when the connection of labor to capital is tenuous and government has little means of maintaining social peace. In the absence of other governing modalities, law enforcement and prohibition function as means to govern populations through the illegalized market. This minimal, disciplinary engagement of the government with laboring populations might appear to be a type of dominance without hegemony (Guha 1998) but, as Richard Widick (2009) illuminates in the case of Humboldt's timber economy, this rendering ignores extra-state governing modalities that have sutured together labor and timber capital in Humboldt, namely one based on a yeoman/frontier ethos of self-reliance, private property and freedom from government.

In this respect, liberalization of marijuana policy represents not only a legal shift, but a shift in governance, institutional arrangements and local commonsense. As mentioned above, liberalization became integral to two post-timber developmental visions, one centered around landed capital and the other around environmentalist smart growth. While these visions have differences, they share three general characteristics. First, they were impacted by the emergence of a formerly criminalized population—marijuana producers and market actors—into civic life. Second, the civic integration of marijuana implied a process through which knowledge about and meanings of marijuana were consolidated, made public and organized in ways that constituted marijuana's new 'social life' (Appadurai 1988). Third, because the exact form of marijuana's organization was in contention, it became a site of anticipatory and speculative practices (see Campbell 2015; Ghertner 2015) that attempted to predict and precipitate marijuana's future social form in the present (e.g. positions in regulatory debates, business investments, claims differentiating legitimate/deserving and illegitimate/undeserving market and political actors). Amidst these general dynamics, the precise elaboration of marijuana's liberalization was and is dependent upon the regional political-economic forces analyzed below. Through studies like this we gain insight into how abstract processes like prohibition and liberalization become material, the role of il/legality in developmental schema, and, in a momentous period of reform and retrenchment of a century of marijuana prohibition, an analytic approach to how and why this process occurs in some places and times but not others.

Timber, marijuana prohibition and the crisis of extractive developmentalism

Since Jedidiah Smith ventured into Humboldt in 1828, searching for gold and a port to export California's natural resources, the region has been ensnared in developmental projects (Raphael 2007 [1974]). Though gold was scarce, timber quickly became a valued resource. To develop it, colonizers had to regularize property and resource claims—and to delegitimize competing claims from indigenous people. The law—and the racist, vigilante violence it justified against local tribes—was critical to guiding Humboldt's early economic development.[7]

The power to criminalize secured and maintained timber's developmental grasp on Humboldt for the county's first 150 years. In the 1870s and 1880s, amidst a growing resentment of Chinese laborers by labor organizations, nuisance laws helped to construct Chinese residents as criminal aliens (Pfaelzer 2007: 121–166), leading to the expulsion of the county's entire Chinese population in 1885. This racialized criminalization forestalled demands for better working conditions and an end to endemic land fraud, thus securing timber-dominated governance for a generation (Cornford 1987). Labor activists were criminalized and expelled from the county in the early twentieth century, culminating in local government decisively siding with timber by opening machine gunfire upon striking workers and torching unpermitted shantytowns in 1935 (Cornford 1987). Efforts by back-to-the-land migrants in the 1970s to challenge predominant land use patterns predicated by timber were met with civil enforcement against improper land use and structures (Anders 1990; McCubbrey 2007), an action that often snowballed into criminalization of marijuana growers and smokers. Indeed, the criminalization of marijuana became central to the buttressing of the timber industry beginning in the 1980s. Episodically, criminalization displaced internal contradictions of timber capitalism and neutralized threats to its continued extractive operation.

Criminalization also helped constitute what was to be developed. The criminal outsider acted as a foil against which proper citizenship was measured (e.g. no racial intermixing, no radical organizing, no challenging cultural norms). More importantly, criminalization was an important basis of establishing a timber-centered paternalism. While the welfare state increasingly took the role of paternal caretaker from 1900 to the 1930s nationally, in Humboldt timber corporations acted as paternal figure—the caretaker of labor camps, builder of roads, funder of limited civil services like sanitation (Cornford 1987). Amidst the underdevelopment of government's capacity to reproduce laboring populations (and the stalled development of unions to articulate labor's collective aspirations), a decentralized social ethos of individual freedom predominated, cutting across capital and labor, both of which were ostensibly at liberty to pursue their interests. This independence ideal was the basis for a socially-*dependent* type of corporate[8] paternalism. Labor and capital were a family that cared for each other beyond state mandates—an ethos that articulated with mythicized ideals of the frontier, the distant state and the rugged yeoman so instrumental to the region's colonization (Widick 2009). Corporate paternalism implied that timber corporations would care for the economy, land and labor. Criminals—Native Americans, Chinese workers, labor activists, hippies—were not only illegal but they were also familial interlopers—outsiders who threatened the social, moral and economic order. As long as industry, workers and the land were cared for—and the values of private property and self-reliance upheld—this paternalism would ostensibly hold in perpetuity, bringing prosperity to all sheltered under timber's wing. In this way, illegality in

Humboldt mirrors broader constructions of the criminal as an interloping, alien 'other' against which respectable society was defined (Hobbs and Antonopolous 2013) and through which a governable laboring population was produced (see Schneider 2009), thus affirming a paternalistic understanding between corporations and the community (Hönke 2012; Solecki 1996).

Timber's paternalistic care, however, would decline along with its industrial strength.

Humboldt timber peaked in 1955 (Morgan *et al.* 2004), when a major flood struck followed by a second major flood in 1964 (both caused by the destruction of water-absorbing forests from the county's hills). The state legislature became concerned that timberlands—and the rural economies built around them—would disappear in the face of more lucrative land uses. In 1972 and 1976 California passed legislation to exempt forestlands from these land market pressures, enabling an industrial boom in the 1970s until 1979 when national interest rate hikes sent timber into a tailspin. The price of timber dropped 48 per cent over four years and California production nearly halved (Morgan *et al.* 2004).

In the 1980s, corporate paternalism disintegrated in the timber industry and across the industrial US (Harris 1997; also Doukas 2003; Nash 1989; Pappas 1989). A deregulated financial industry accelerated mergers and acquisitions, which intensified industrial consolidation, the de-localization of ownership, and placed pressure on the timber industry to produce shareholder profits and, when needed, liquidate holdings (i.e. entire forests; Harris 1997). As corporations clear-cut across Humboldt, the notion that they were responsible land stewards appeared increasingly flimsy. As for labor, in 1960 timber accounted for 31 per cent of total jobs. By 1982, it was down by half (16.5 per cent) and by 2001 it was a shadow of its former presence—5.8 per cent of total county employment (Farnsworth 1996; Roa 2007).

As corporate paternalism in Humboldt and elsewhere dissolved, politicians became concerned with the morally-endangered American family (Lasch 1991), a concern that fueled the expansion of drug prohibition nationally—and in Humboldt in 1982, where President Reagan initiated some of the first, most significant and longest-lasting marijuana eradication campaigns in the domestic US. As with previous forms of criminalization, marijuana prohibition served to strengthen the weakening grip of timber on the region's political economy—especially because it provided a means to confront a rising regional environmental movement, which posed the most significant challenge to timber's dominance since the labor unrest of the 1930s.

In the late 1960s and early 1970s southern Humboldt County was one of many destinations of the approximately one million (Jacobs 1996) countercultural back-to-the-land migrants (Anders 1990) who settled in the rural US and Canada. Moving into cheap, timber-denuded hills, these migrants were involved in environmental reclamation and rejuvenation. At first this was a self-contained project as back-to-the-landers built utopian, insular communities, but soon they were pulled into local and regional politics as code enforcement targeted their alternative, unpermitted structures, multi-family residences and dissonant way of life

(Anderson 1990). A contained environmentalism and defensive battles with local government soon evolved into major efforts to reclaim watersheds, protect old growth forests, reintroduce salmon, establish parks and innovate permacultural agrarian and homestead techniques. By the late 1980s, these efforts had grown into the basis of a region-wide effort to combat the timber industry, stop the intensified clear-cutting of the county's forests, and organize a radical environmental movement (Coleman 2005).

Back-to-the-landers not only germinated the region's environmental movement, they also cultivated marijuana (Raphael 1985). What was once a hobby plant for personal consumption or extra cash, soon became a primary means of support at a time when back-to-the-land settlements across the country were fading (Edgington 2008). Marijuana funds were critical in funding community ventures—schools, roads, firehouses, health centers—and provided an important base of support, in terms of both people and cash, for the environmental movement. As Humboldt became a net exporter and the price of domestic 'kind bud' jumped in the late 1970s and early 1980s, the bonds between marijuana and environmentalism strengthened. In 1983, however, state and federal governments initiated major eradication campaigns that increased risks and severed the connection between growers and environmentalists. Many had to choose between money and political ideals, leading many growers to go underground, invent secret codes, insulate their communities and distance themselves from governmental attentions and political action (McCubbrey 2007), a shift that led many countercultural informants to rue the growth of the marijuana market. Though some continued to funnel cash to environmental organizations, intensified criminalization of growers dampened marijuana-growing activists' public engagement.

As the rewards of marijuana increased, several informants attested, countercultural growers increasingly assumed the politically-stunted ethos of private property—rugged individualism, aversion to government—that characterized Humboldt's cultural history (Widick 2009). Prohibition also transformed countercultural communities into inward-facing, defensive, privatized enclaves, which were internally vibrant but averse to external engagement for fear of being discovered (McCubbrey 2007). Coalescing with efforts by timber corporations and county government officials to stymie the advances of environmentalists (Harris 1997), prohibition protected timber extraction by hobbling the base of its regional opposition.[9]

Intensified prohibition also had a fundamental effect on timber workers. Risk-inflated prices created a lucrative market for economically struggling timber workers and their communities as layoffs occurred. Because capital investment and technological incorporation were discouraged by the omnipresent threat of seizure, marijuana production had low barriers to entry and required large amounts of labor. As a state policy, prohibition might be seen as a shadow job creator or redistributive program in an era characterized by the retraction of the welfare state (Polson forthcoming). Indeed, one might envision marijuana prohibition as a shadow economic stimulus program, which inflates prices and creates markets through which to redistribute large amounts of cash that would not otherwise exist, but only does so on terms that incite antipathy toward the state, which is configured as prohibitive, rather than generative. This antipathy resonated among Humboldt's timber workers and back-to-the-land migrants, both of whom distrusted government, albeit for differing reasons.

Ironically, prohibition—and the marijuana economy it spawned—structured a nascent political solidarity between, in the terms of one informant, 'hippies' (back-to-the-landers, environmentalists, marijuana growers) and 'rednecks' (timber workers and ranchers, unemployed rural residents, homesteaders). Marijuana growing became an interactive field through which the long-standing divide between 'locals' and 'newcomers' dissolved as people shared horticultural techniques, filled bulk orders and protected local codes of secrecy. Judy Bari, a key forest activist, believed solidarity among workers and environmentalists was an explosive combination that could topple timber's developmental regime (Coleman 2005). Though prohibition fostered this nascent solidarity, it prevented it from materializing publicly by severing private-criminal lives from public-activist action. Marijuana prohibition politically secured the timber industry even as it laid off workers, clear-cut forests and eroded any semblance of paternal care (Polson forthcoming).

The years between 1999 and 2007 marked a turning point for timber. In 1999, the county was party to the historic Headwaters deal, a pact between environmentalists and timber corporations that signaled the shift of the county from timber partisan to mediator between timber and environmentalists. By 2007, the county was fighting *against* the timber industry when it opposed the bankruptcy debt restructuring plan of Pacific Lumber Company, one of the most controversial clear-cutting timber corporations. Between 2007 and 2008 the gross value of timber declined by 25 per cent (Humboldt County 2010), part of a statewide trend that saw gross timber production decline by 50 per cent between 2000 and 2012 (McIver *et al.* 2015). Timber waned and the county's entire political economy was upended—transformations that had significant implications for marijuana's role in public life.

The struggle over marijuana's development

Following timber's implosion, the question arose: what developmental schema would replace timber and what coalition of forces would fight to realize it? Two answers emerged. The first came from the vestiges of timber's political economy and was comprised of three major actors—rural landowners, developers and government and law enforcement officials. This *rentier* bloc had matured under timber. A kind of scaffolding to timber extraction, they assured timber's easy acquisition and transfer of land, infrastructural support, regulatory facilitation and control of active and unemployed laborers. Timber was the productive engine upon which these rent-based actors depended—it supported land values, filled tax coffers and instigated private-public infrastructural developments. Without timber, the *rentier* bloc was scaffolding with no structure.

Its inheritance of timber's mantle, then, depended upon the articulation of a convincing developmental schema to guide the county. They advanced a vision characterized by the growth of property values, tourism and low-end service jobs; the policing of the resulting wealth-stratified landscapes; and the minimization of state expenditures on an often-criminalized laboring population. The growth of property values was the economic core of this vision yet, in the late 2000s, amidst the mortgage crisis, property value growth was hardly assured. Regardless, this bloc attempted to manufacture a power transfer from timber. This transfer did not go as planned—not least because of the rise of an oppositional smart growth developmental bloc.

This second developmental bloc had emerged from the environmentalist movement of the 1980s and 1990s, developing numerous organizational forms that anchored it in county life, thus setting the stage for the occupation of governmental positions in the 2000s. They promoted a 'smart growth' developmental vision based upon the development of dense urban spaces, a vibrant civil society, preservation of nature and rural spaces and transformation of police from a repressive force centered on fighting crime to a civil-regulatory force focused on facilitating orderly commerce and social life (see Foucault 2007). This vision economically hinged upon localism, artisanal cottage production and sustainable resource management, yet, as with the *rentier* bloc, none of these sectors clearly anchored economic development in ways that timber had. As a result, this vision largely remained marginal, best suited to the liberal university town of Arcata and the small lifestyle tourism and telecommuting populations in what was otherwise a remote county nearly six hours from San Francisco and Portland.

In 2007, marijuana production was considered to be largely a nuisance issue in urban areas and a topic only spoken of in whispers in the county's rural areas. In this marijuana-producing county, marijuana production had been largely unaffected by the emergence of medical marijuana since 1996, which had liberalized distribution and consumption but relegated production to the shadows. Many localities were loath to regulate production for fear of being accused of violating federal law. By 2010, however, the county's shadow economy had burst into the limelight. The Obama administration signaled a greater lenience to medical marijuana and a statewide ballot held out a realistic possibility of full legalization. Suddenly, marijuana production appeared not as a criminal act or nuisance, but as a potential avenue for building a new developmental pathway for the county.

In what follows I argue that both developmental blocs converged on an acceptance of marijuana as a central aspect of development, but that each bloc sought to integrate marijuana in differing ways into county political economy. The *rentier* developmental bloc ambivalently related to marijuana—it was dependent upon marijuana as a value-producing land use but also dependent upon prohibition to realize lucrative land values (see Polson 2013). The smart growth developmental bloc forthrightly sought to formally develop marijuana, configuring its unrealized potential—and its adverse environmental effects—as a problem to be addressed through regulatory interventions to incite formal economic development (see Li 2007).

Timber's scaffolding: The rentier developmental bloc and ambivalence over marijuana

Rural Landowners: In 2007, Pacific Lumber Company, owned by the multinational Maxxam Corporation, declared bankruptcy and sought to restructure its debt by converting its lands from timber to residential zoning. This conversion, utilized many times before, was a key basis of the political union between timber and rural landowners (and speculators, realtors and financiers). Land could be stripped of timber and when its utility (and value, based upon timber) expired, the lands could be transformed into residential lots. Overnight, the value of depleted lands would multiply (see Polson 2013). Maxxam's release and conversion of lands signified a major transfer of economic—and thus political—power from timber to landowners.

The conversion, however, was deemed not in accordance with the county's General Plan and was rejected, thereby foiling what might have been a smooth transition from a timber-based economy to an economy based upon rural residential development. Rural landowners responded by forming several property rights organizations, which vehemently fought the regulatory changes, sought to install friendly officials in key offices, and to remove the liberal Community Services Director, who had advanced the restriction on conversions (Burns 2013). The director was in charge of overseeing the General Plan Update, which could either enable or disable the conversion process. With timber no longer a lucrative land use and conversions no longer able to produce a windfall of wealth, rural landowners had to find another land use from which to gather rents. Marijuana was one such land use (Polson 2013). Yet the rents that owners realized on marijuana were dependent upon the price inflation caused by prohibition. Under prohibition, the wholesale price of marijuana was high, resulting in significant wealth for growers and a large rent distribution to owners. As marijuana's distribution system developed under the state's medical system, the price to producers declined precipitously (by anywhere from 55–85 per cent depending on a person's capacity to command prices). A more complex and competitive commodity chain demanded a redistribution of marijuana's wealth away from producers and, by extension, landowners. Landowners were placed in the odd position of both supporting marijuana production as well as the price supports of prohibition. Thus, when marijuana regulation entered public debate, landowners ambivalently regarded the process.

Commercial Developers: Humboldt's urban areas were centers for the processing and transport of timber but as milling declined, land developers looked for new capital investments. Developers were particularly interested in Eureka, the seat of county government and the county's most populous city. Relying on significant funds from the state, they envisioned Eureka's waterfront as a redevelopment and tourism zone, which would bring a certain kind of growth to the city and county. A monthly arts-walk, a farmers' market, a renovated public square and a focus on improvement of blighted buildings, often through historic restoration funds, were characteristic of this effort, making the area eminently consumable for the county's gentry and moneyed tourists (Cahill 2012). This higher-end consumption zone was distinct from the rest of the city, which was structured around low-end consumption for meagerly-paid service workers. In this vision, Eureka was informally zoned into areas of investment and disinvestment. This spatial organization represented a *rentier* model of wealth production and produced stratification between owning classes and those that serviced them.

This development model, however, foundered. For instance, one key proponent of the redevelopment of a polluted railroad yard on Eureka's waterfront was rebuffed in his attempts to circumvent environmental review (Faulk 2006) by environmentally-minded organizations, officials and residents. (Notably, this person, one of the counties richest persons, had entered into commercial development and finance after having made his fortune in timber processing.) Developers were also supportive of efforts to widen a major highway connecting the county to the San Francisco Bay Area (Walters 2014). This effort also failed when environmentalists objected that the project would require the removal of old-growth redwood trees. One of the aims of widening the highway was to enable the opening of the county to larger trucks, which would supply big box stores (St. George 2011), like Walmart. But even the effort to bring Walmart to Eureka failed in the late 1999, when local activists objected to the stultifying effects it would have on surrounding commerce and wages (Hodgson 2011). Like rural landowners, commercial developers also lost out in the county's decision to prohibit timberland conversions to residential uses—major housing developments were stymied. Finally, in 2011 developers received a *coup de grace* when California eliminated funding for all of the state's county-based redevelopment offices (Cahill 2012). Commercial developers found themselves struggling to articulate a convincing economic vision, leaving an economic vacuum into which marijuana distributors walked. In 2010, Eureka, a city known not only as a focal point of commercial development projects but also for its staunch opposition to and heavy policing of marijuana, tepidly agreed to permit marijuana dispensaries within city limits, a development unimaginable just a few years prior.

Government and Law Enforcement: As suggested, anti-marijuana law enforcement was key to the maintenance of timber's developmental regime. Prohibition served to control a cyclical and declining workforce, buttress the dominance of timber capital, and was indicative of the underdevelopment of the government's civil capacities to reproduce labor. Under timber, law enforcement was one of the few developed capacities of county governance and this capacity mushroomed in the 1980s and 1990s with numerous grants and funds for marijuana eradication. It is perhaps no surprise that as timber lost its grip on county governance, law enforcement itself went into crisis. The realignment began in the late 1990s with two signal moments. There was a large public backlash against county law enforcement after pictures surfaced of officers swabbing the eyes of environmentalist protestors with pepper spray (Ganga 1997). The second moment was a staged standoff by medical marijuana activists, who challenged the Sheriff and District Attorney (DA) to arrest a marijuana patient for growing medicine. The county did not take the bait and publicly acknowledged marijuana's limited medical allowance. These two events were followed in short order by the arrest and charging of a former county sheriff with misappropriation of funds, placing its credibility in question (North Coast Journal 1998).

The disarray of law enforcement led to the 2002 election of a reformist District Attorney and the defeat of a sheriff who refused to return confiscated medical marijuana to a patient (Gurnon 2003). The DA vowed to clarify medical marijuana rules for law enforcement (Gurnon 2003). The DA also broke with the county's longstanding defense of the timber industry by filing a lawsuit against Pacific Lumber Company for fraudulent environmental impact reports. The DA survived the backlash and then took to reforming the police themselves (Easthouse 2004). He prosecuted two police officers for a shooting and a police chief in a local municipality in addition to reconstructing the priorities and personnel of his prosecutorial team (Burns 2010). By 2010, the DA was an active proponent of marijuana regulation and promoted the repurposing of police from anti-marijuana enforcement to civil regulators of marijuana, ready to double as farm inspectors if the county approved such regulations (Blue Ribbon Commission on Marijuana Policy 2015). The DA was joined in this advocacy by a newly-elected sheriff, whose popularity rose when he endorsed regulation of medical marijuana production. Once in office, he was instrumental in eliminating the department's Marijuana Enforcement Unit, a measure that was complemented by the state government's de-funding of the Humboldt Bay Drug Task Force and the Campaign Against Marijuana Planting, which had been flying eradication missions over Humboldt for nearly 30 years (Burns 2012). The prohibition system, fostered under timber's wing, was crumbling and a new form of law enforcement was emerging.

The DA reforms were effective at the county level but had little control over municipal police forces. Since at least the 1935 massacre of striking workers, Eureka was seen to be the control center of timber's power (Cornford 1987). Since 1960 and the slow deflation of the industry, the city's population had been in decline and poverty rates in the 2000s hovered 50 per cent above state averages. With Highway 101 cutting through town, it was a hub for meth and heroin commerce, a large homeless population and the highest crime rate in Humboldt. It had a violent crime rate approximately 90 per cent higher than that of California and, in 2007, it was over twice the national rate. (Sims 2014). Eureka recorded frequent police shootings—one every 19 months (Males 2014)—little surprise for a county that had the second highest police shooting rate in California (Males 2014) and the highest arrest rate of any county in California (Houston 2016a). Relations between an aggressive police force and the community were fraught in a city that had been modeled on zoned development and disinvestment, as described above. When a woman with mental health issues was shot by Eureka's Special Weapons and Tactics (SWAT) team in 2006 (one of three residents shot that year), the Humboldt DA charged Eureka's police chief and a lieutenant with manslaughter following a large public outcry (Burns 2010). Though the case failed, it ousted Eureka's police chief from office and led to the appointment of a reformist police chief, who banned the city's SWAT team, established designated areas for homeless camps and implemented a problem-oriented policing unit to identify and address issues in the community, officer training around mental health and domestic violence issues and a citizen's academy to improve community-police relations (Burns 2011c).

This new style of community policing posed a challenge to the mode of spatial control envisioned by developers, which divided the city into a waterfront zone of anti-blight, quality-of-life policing (Cahill 2012) and the rest of Eureka, which was treated with much more repressive and violent policing (see Burns 2011c; Heraldo 2011; Sims 2006). The stratified policing that prevailed in Eureka mirrored the economic stratification implicit to developers' vision: high-end consumption zones for the county's landowning gentry and tourists and low-end consumption zones and heavy policing for the city's service sector and floating population. The reformist police chief thus posed a predicament for Eureka's city council. The council had a supermajority of former law enforcement officials and advocates in 2011 but was also pro-developer. The council was compelled to project support for the police chief, but the chief's actions challenged the accepted program of redevelopment, blight elimination and punitive control of laboring and floating populations. Begrudgingly, they accepted the chief's reforms just as they accepted the process of permitting medical marijuana dispensaries in Eureka.

In sum, the three vestigial pillars of timber's developmental regime—rural landowners, commercial developers and law enforcement-intensive government—were disoriented (if not defeated) by the early 2010s. Their efforts to transfer political-economic power from timber to a new *rentier* economy failed. A re-vision was needed and it was at this time that marijuana regulation and development appeared possible. The *rentier* bloc, however, regarded marijuana ambivalently—partly because it had matured in a system based on prohibition and partly because it depended upon prohibition for the maintenance of its institutional and economic power. In the face of potential legalization and with a growing acknowledgment of marijuana's fundamental economic importance to the county, the *rentier* bloc accepted the need to regard marijuana production as a long-neglected sector in need of development. But they did not take the lead in these efforts.

Smart growth development and the rise of environmentalism

A second bloc of smart-growth environmentalists also converged upon marijuana as a fix for their inability to formulate a countywide vision of development. This bloc had succeeded in reforming timber-dominated environmental review processes, preserving a large amount of county acreage, promoting sustainable forestry, cleaning up Humboldt Bay and making important inroads with county officials. In addition to the DA, who had sued and confronted the county's timber industry, a key ally was the Community Services Director, appointed in 1997 amidst a wave of environmental reforms. He directed the building, planning offices, economic development and natural resources agencies—a powerful position insofar as it oversaw the spatial and economic development of county lands and natural resources at a time when the spatial, economic and environmental order was rapidly shifting. (The director notably guided the General Plan Update process, mentioned above.) He utilized this power to attempt to clarify shadowy rural land markets, halt timber-to-residential conversions, strengthen conservation programs and promote smart growth efforts to make the county's urban areas more dense, navigable and environmentally sound (Burns 2011b). The director found an important ally in the 2008 election of Supervisor Mark Lovelace, an environmental advocate in Humboldt, who gained notoriety for his role in the 2007 Pacific Lumber bankruptcy case. Lovelace was also a proponent of smart growth. He supported and proposed measures such as low-income housing developments, broadband internet expansion and park creation, and established two organizations to promote environmentally-sound economic development in Humboldt (Houston 2016b). Indicative of a post-extraction trend within county government, these officials represented the ascension of environmental discourses and activists to county prominence. They offered an alternative to timber and opposed the ambitions of the floundering *rentier* bloc—big box stores, rural residential expansion, redevelopment contracts with large developers and so on.

Though the smart growth bloc focused on a reformulation of county governance, it had a limited economic plan, hoping that telecommuters, artisanal local producers and sustainable resource management would carry the economy (for example, see SmartVoter.org 2012). In 2010, this bloc (along with the recently elected Sheriff) took the lead in endorsing efforts to regulate—and economically develop—marijuana. Indicative of this trend, Supervisor Lovelace had initially viewed marijuana as a nuisance issue and found political support among irritated homeowners hoping to stop indoor urban marijuana growing. Two years later, he was a guiding force in crafting Humboldt's regulatory response to a monumental meeting of marijuana growers to discuss the industry's future (see Brady 2012), the first semi-public meeting of its kind in recent memory. At its most basic, pro-environment smart growth advocates lacked an economic motor, while marijuana producers lacked a regulatory framework to protect their communities and livelihoods if and when marijuana became legal. The political-economic alliance was the basis of a renewed smart growth bloc that advanced marijuana regulation at the county level.

Lovelace's partnership with producers was symbolically significant for three reasons, all of which revolve around the geographic, social and political divisions between Northern Humboldt (NoHum) and Southern Humboldt (SoHum). First, marijuana production largely began in SoHum, home of a back-to-the-land intelligentsia, which viewed county government, located in NoHum, as a distant and invasive force (manifested in code enforcement, marijuana raids and pro-timber politicians) (see Anders 1990). The cooperation of SoHum marijuana producers with NoHum government officials was significant in garnering a North-South alliance to propose marijuana development. Second, as a NoHum environmentalist, Lovelace's version of environmentalism valued state preservation of rural lands, whereas SoHum environmentalists generally advocated a working conservation, administered by local communities (often in opposition to the state). Although not all marijuana growers were environmentalists, the most vocal regulatory advocates expressed environmental concerns and nearly all advocates employed a (nebulous) discourse of 'sustainability.' This North-South alliance, then, was significant in consolidating a consensus around a general value of environmental care. Third, the working unity of regulation-averse SoHum growers with NoHum regulation-oriented officials was significant in consolidating a full-county commodity chain, spanning production in the county's rural south and distribution and consumption in the denser markets of the north.

In debates over marijuana's regulation, numerous ideas were advanced, ranging from the formation of an environmentally-friendly, boutique, tourist-driven marijuana sector comprised of homesteads and cottage industries to a vertically-integrated county industry, replete with trademark protections, certification processes and inter-jurisdictional marijuana supply arrangements. Running through these ideas were two major themes. First, the emerging industry would be 'local,' meaning that it would seek to protect Humboldt's marijuana from consolidation by outside economic forces—a theme that dovetailed with Humboldt's familial self-understanding. Second, marijuana would be 'sustainable,' meaning that it would forefront care for community, labor, ecology and economic livelihood—thus replacing timber as a purveyor of care and instilling environmental consciousness in the industry from its outset.

Though the process of formulating marijuana regulations surfaced many divisions among advocates, growers and officials, from a distance it was an apex of smart growth development. Born of the environmental movement, this bloc had at its fingertips a budding industry that it sought to develop according to concepts of sustainability, environmental care and an economy based on the development of human capacities through the expansion of regulatory governance. It challenged the extractive relationship of industry to nature; sought to create an economy that relied upon human labor rather than extraction, consumption or the extraction of rent; and aimed to reform a system of policing based upon criminalizing repression of laboring populations. As discussed below, however, this bloc's claim to hegemony was stifled by the resurgence of federal prohibitionism. Its designs on Humboldt's future were curtailed as the county readjusted to a new political-legal environment.

Even this smart growth developmentalism depended upon new criminalizing categories—undocumented workers, polluting producers, unregulated market actors and so on. In this way, throughout the developmental blocs described illegality remains integral to the process of development, thus pointing to the importance of licitness—what is permissible if not sanctioned or legal—discussed in this collection's introduction (see also Galemba 2013). Following this work and Heyman (2013), this chapter has attempted to expand beyond emic notions of what is licit and illicit to highlight how these categories exist in relation to dominant modes of production and governance. Through this we might sustain comparative, broad analyses amidst the uneven development of prohibition and liberalization among regions, nationally and globally. Though this analysis may not produce its own 'general plan,' in the terms of this chapter's introduction, it does provide tools to conceptualize how developmental plans are made through legality, criminality and licitness.

Back to the future: Prohibition, property and the new regulation

In late 2011, the US Attorney of the Northern District sent a letter to Eureka's city manager assuring him that regulating marijuana would violate federal law and regulators may be held civilly or criminally responsible for its abrogation. The letter halted Eureka's marijuana dispensary permitting process. By mid-2012, Arcata and Humboldt County governments followed suit (Burns 2011a). A chill descended upon California's marijuana industry, which found itself caught in a several-year federal offensive targeting the medical marijuana industry.

The power to regulate marijuana reverted from civil to criminal law. The pro-regulation DA and Sheriff became de facto regulators, utilizing discretionary powers to enforce and prosecute according to their priorities. These priorities centered around those who harm the environment, violate land use codes or employ undocumented laborers (Suzelle 2014), but the ability of the DA and Sheriff to dictate these priorities was compromised by their involvement with federally led multi-agency efforts to pursue cases that aligned with different priorities (Burns 2012).

The failure of marijuana regulation was a significant blow to smart growth development. Supervisor Lovelace found himself the lone environmental smart growth advocate on the county board when two new supervisors were elected, both who were supported by a key county developer and the county's primary property rights and rural landowner organization (St. George 2012). This new board dissolved the Community Services Department, thereby eliminating the director's position—and his influence over land use, conservation policy and natural resources (Tam 2012). The General Plan to this day remains in contention.

A resurgent prohibition favored the *rentier* bloc's developmental vision. The two new property rightist supervisors were pivotal in appointing a controversial property rightist rural landowner to a position on the county's planning commission (Burns 2017). In Eureka, a Walmart was approved to open (Hodgson 2011) and the city council began planning for a new development vision for its waterfront (Burns 2015) after it fired its reformist police chief. Soon, the interim police chief (a veteran of the force since 1957) returned to raiding homeless encampments (Cejnar 2012). A furor erupted when a conditional offer was made to replace the interim police chief with one of the officers involved in a 2006 police shooting of a woman with mental issues (Poor 2013). Though this officer was not hired, only months after a new chief took office, community-police relations were once again inflamed when a hard-of-hearing 22 year old man with a BB gun was fatally shot by officers (Iovino 2017), thus jeopardizing the shift to community policing and the governance shift it implied.

Marijuana went underground again. Multiple dispensaries closed and those remaining retreated to quasi-formal shadows. Producers, some of whom had been starring in reality television shows a few years prior, returned to the illegal market or left the sector altogether (Mozingo 2012). Marijuana advocacy organizations, which had arisen in response to the county's call to regulate marijuana, dissolved. Reinstituted prohibition dovetailed with a trend toward outdoor growing, leading to a boom in land prices and a windfall to rural landowners who leased or transacted lands (Smith 2016).

Marijuana's development did not halt, then, it just articulated with illegality under a resurgent federal prohibition. In the absence of formal regulation, the primary regulatory force upon producers was profit, the need to pay rents for land being used illegally, and, correlatively, maximum extraction from the land. Conjuring timber's ghost, marijuana increasingly looked like a new extractive industry, evidenced by an uptick in illegal deforestation (Butsic and Brenner 2016; Zuckerman 2013). The reformulated *rentier* bloc is now well positioned to capitalize upon a newly legalized marijuana. Whether this has the same implications for the underdevelopment of civil governing capacities, devastation of nature and unequal distribution of wealth remains to be seen.

Although the *rentier* bloc advanced at the county level, environmentally minded producers reconnoitered at the state level through an environmentally informed growers' association. Their advocacy paid off in 2015 when they helped craft medical marijuana legislation preventing vertical consolidation of the marijuana industry, protecting the market position of small producers and implementing significant environmental protections (Harkinson 2015). For places like Humboldt, it remains to be seen whether an industry can emerge that bucks the history of minimalist, extractive governance that has presided for so long. Such a shift would not only sweep away the residue of prohibition—it would deeply challenge the relation of capital to nature, labor and governance. The road to this future, however, remains undeveloped.

Notes

1 Even when marijuana was medicalized and county government attempted to allow marijuana as a land use, it was always under a 'special' or 'conditional' permission. Thus, marijuana was always an exception to the General Plan and land use regulations, requiring case-by-case exceptions to be made in what was otherwise a landscape exclusive of marijuana.

2 Pempel (1999; also see Wylde 2014) defines developmental regimes as an agglomeration of relationships among social, economic and governmental actors, institutions and public policies. Ghertner (2015) and Campbell (2015) highlight the importance of everyday practices, discourses, imaginaries and artifacts in constituting these regimes.

3 At its most basic level, this chapter builds upon work done on the relation of illegalization to political economy (Chambliss 1975; Greenberg 1981; Hall *et al.* 1978; Linebaugh 1976; Thompson 1975), a relation that attempted to understand the relationship between economic modes of production and political-legal forms. This literature was prematurely dismissed in simplistic characterizations of structuralist concepts of base, superstructure and determination, a dismissal that lost much of what was valuable about Marxian historical political economy—namely the ability to grasp the complex interrelationships between value production, institutional arrangements, law and that which lies beyond formal economies.

4 Throughout this chapter I refer to 'regional political economy' although my unit of study is at the county and municipal levels.

5 Even the federal marijuana prohibition of 1937 was the culmination of multiple regional projects, such as efforts to contain and police demobilized farmworkers in Southern

California, manage US-Mexican relations along the Texas border and maintain Jim Crow segregation through the targeting of jazz clubs in northern US cities (Sloman 1979).

6 This is not to dismiss the interrelatedness of scales (Smith 1990; Swyndegouw 1997), but rather to highlight how scaled processes, like prohibition or statewide policy reform, materialize through particular political-economic dynamics.

7 For instance, settler-colonists could petition for the removal of Native Americans from any lands they desired—a petition received and granted without the testimony of Native Americans who were barred from testifying in court. Once consigned to penury and vagrancy they could be arrested and put up for auction. According to the new laws bounding land and its movable property, if they 'stole' cattle to ameliorate their impoverishment, they would not only be met with legal sanctions but often roving massacres by legally-inspired colonists. The question of whether Native Americans could be subjected to settler-colonial law, namely the Major Crimes Act of 1885, was settled by a case from Humboldt (*US v Kagama*)—a decision that allows for the subjection of Native Americans to federal criminal law even as it denies them the host of rights guaranteed to citizens.

8 Corporate in the double sense of forming a singular, though differentiated, social body as well as a paternalism guided by timber corporations.

9 The depth of this forced fissure between environmentalists and marijuana growers emerged after 2008 when marijuana growers in one watershed initiated a countywide debate over the environmental effects of marijuana growing. Not only had several informants felt the pressure of a choice between politics and economics but some felt they could not even discuss the environmental impacts of their marijuana growing on their own watersheds.

References

Agnew, J. 2000. From the political economy of regions to regional political economy. *Progress in Human Geography*, 24(1): 101–110.

Anders, J. 1990. *Beyond Counterculture: The Community of Mateel*. Pullman, WA: Washington State University Press.

Anderson, M.S. 1990. *Whatever Happened to the Hippies?* Eureka, CA: Miles & Miles.

Appadurai, A. (1988). *The Social Life Of Things: Commodities In Cultural Perspective*. Cambridge: Cambridge University Press.

Blue Ribbon Commission on Marijuana Policy. 2015. Policy Perspective: An Interview with Paul Gallegos. *Safeandsmartpolicy.org*. Accessed February 26, 2017 at: https://www.safeandsmartpolicy.org/wp-content/uploads/2015/04/Policy-Perspective-Gallegos.pdf.

Brady, E. (2013). *Humboldt: Life on America's Marijuana Frontier*. New York: Grand Central Publishing.

Brunnschweiler, C.N. and Bulte, E.H. 2008. The resource curse revisited and revised: A tale of paradoxes and red herrings. *Journal of Environmental Economics and Management*, 55(3): 248–264.

Bunker S.G. 1985. *Underdeveloping the Amazon: Extraction, Unequal Exchange, and the Failure of the Modern State*. Chicago: University of Chicago Press.

Burns, R. 2010. DA Trials. *North Coast Journal*. May 27. Accessed February 26, 2017 at: http://www.northcoastjournal.com/humboldt/da-trials/Content?oid=2131062.

Burns, R. 2011a. The marijuana shuffle. *Northcoastjournal.org*. October 4. Accessed February 26, 2017 at: http://www.northcoastjournal.com/NewsBlog/archives/2011/10/04/the-marijuana-shuffle-updated.

Burns, R. 2011b. Why do people hate Kirk Girard? *North Coast Journal*. November 3. Accessed February 26, 2017 at: http://www.northcoastjournal.com/humboldt/why-do-people-hate-kirk-girard/Content?oid=2132649.

Burns, R. 2011c. Why was Garr fired? *North Coast Journal.* June 30. Accessed February 26, 2017 at: http://www.northcoastjournal.com/humboldt/why-was-garr-fired/Content?oid=2132251.

Burns, R. 2012. Downey calls for backup. *North Coast Journal.* July 26. Accessed February 26, 2017 at: http://www.northcoastjournal.com/humboldt/downey-calls-for-backup/Content?oid=2166911.

Burns, R. 2013. HumCPR rising. *The North Coast Journal.* March 28. Accessed February 26, 2017 at: http://www.northcoastjournal.com/humboldt/humcpr-rising/Content?oid=2194355.

Burns, R. 2015. Eureka launching ambitious waterfront development project. *Lost Coast Outpost.* April 23. Accessed February 26, 2017 at: https://lostcoastoutpost.com/2015/apr/23/eureka-launching-ambitious-waterfront-development/.

Burns, R. 2017. Controversial county planning commissioner Lee Ulansey up for reappointment Tuesday. *Lost Coast Outpost.* January 16. Accessed February 26, 2017 at: https://lostcoastoutpost.com/2017/jan/16/controversial-county-planning-commissioner-lee-ula/.

Butsic, V. and Brenner, J.C. 2016. Cannabis (Cannabis sativa or C. indica) agriculture and the environment: A systematic, spatially-explicit survey and potential impacts. *Environmental Research Letters*, 11(4): 044023.

Cahill, J.F. 2012. The death of redevelopment? *North Coast Journal.* March 29. Accessed February 27, 2017 at: http://www.northcoastjournal.com/humboldt/the-death-of-redevelopment/Content?oid=2133061.

Campbell, J.M. 2015. *Conjuring Property: Speculation and Environmental Futures in the Brazilian Amazon*. Seattle: University of Washington Press.

Cejnar, J. 2012. Greenbelt sweeps highlight ongoing cycles; eureka police find drugs, criminals, families at homeless campsites. *Eureka Times-Standard.* April 23. Accessed February 27, 2017 at: http://www.times-standard.com/article/ZZ/20120423/NEWS/120429442.

Chambliss, W.J. 1975. Toward a political economy of crime. *Theory and Society*, 2(1): 149–170.

Chiodelli, F. Hall, T. Hudson, R. and Moroni, S. Grey governance and development of cities and regions: the variable relationship between (il)legal and (il)licit. *Corrupt Places.* Chiodelli, F., Hall, T., and Hudson, R., Eds. London: Routledge.

Coleman, K. 2005. *The Secret Wars of Judy Bari: A Car Bomb, the Fight for the Redwoods, and the End of Earth First!* San Francisco: Encounter Books.

Cornford, D.A. 1987. *Workers and Dissent in the Redwood Empire*. Philadelphia: Temple University Press.

Coronil, F. 1997. *The Magical State: Nature, Money, and Modernity in Venezuela*. Chicago: University of Chicago Press.

Dawdy, S.L. 2008. *Building the Devil's Empire: French Colonial New Orleans*. Chicago: University of Chicago Press.

DiJohn, J. 2002. Mineral resource abundance and violent political conflict: A critical assessment of the rentier state model. Crisis States Programme, Development Research Centre.

Doukas, D. (2003). *Worked Over: The Corporate Sabotage of an American Community.* Ithaca: Cornell University Press.

Easthouse, K. 2004. Just another day. *North Coast Journal.* February 19. Accessed February 27, 2017 at: http://www.northcoastjournal.com/021904/cover0219.html.

Edgington, R.H. 2008. "Be receptive to the good earth": Health, nature, and labor in countercultural back-to-the-land settlements. *Agricultural History*, 82(3): 279–308.

Farnsworth, K.F. 1996. *Gyppo Logging in Humboldt County: A Boom–Bust Cycle on the California Forest Frontier.* MA Thesis, Humboldt State University, Geography.

Faulk, J. 2006. Two in the eye of the storm. *Eureka Times Standard.* November 3. Accessed February 27, 2017 at: http://www.times-standard.com/general-news/20061103/two-in-the-eye-of-the-storm.

Foucault, M. 2007. *Security, Territory, Population: Lectures at the Collège de France, 1977–78.* New York: Palgrave.

Galemba, R. 2013. Illegality and invisibility at the margins and borders. *POLAR: Political and Legal Anthropology Review*, 36(2): 274–285.

Ganga, M. 1997. Police sued over use of pepper spray on protestors. *Los Angeles Times.* October 31. Accessed February 27, 2017 at: http://articles.latimes.com/1997/oct/31/news/mn-48656.

Ghertner, D.A. 2015. *Rule by Aesthetics: World-Class City Making in Delhi.* New York: Oxford University Press.

Gidwani, V. 2008. *Capital, Interrupted.* Minneapolis: University of Minnesota Press.

Greenberg, D.F. 1981. *Crime & Capitalism.* Palo Alto: Mayfield Publishing Company.

Guha, R. 1998. *Dominance without Hegemony: History and Power in Colonial India.* Oxford: Oxford University Press.

Gurnon, E. 2003. Humboldt hard lines soften. *Los Angeles Times.* January 6. Accessed February 27, 2017 at: http://articles.latimes.com/2003/jan/06/local/me-gallegos6.

Hall, C. 1976. The right of control over the city plan. Local planner versus the state legislature and the court. *Pepperdine Law Review*, 3(3): S106–S135.

Hall, S., Critcher C., Jefferson, T., Clarke, J., and Robers, B. 1978. *Policing the Crisis: Mugging, the State, and Law and Order.* London: Macmillan Palgrave.

Harkinson, J. 2015. New California laws are a big deal for people who care where their pot comes from. *Mother Jones.* September 16. Accessed February 27, 2017 at: http://www.motherjones.com/politics/2015/09/california-medical-marijuana-bill-pot-smokers-environment.

Harris, D. 1997. *The Last Stand.* Berkeley: University of California Press.

Heraldo. 2011. Archive for the 'Garr Nielsen' Category. *Humboldt Herald.* Accessed February 27, 2017 at: https://humboldtherald.wordpress.com/category/garr-nielsen/.

Heyman, J. 2013. The study of illegality and legality: Which way forward? *POLAR: Political and Legal Anthropology Review*, 36(2): 304–307.

Heyman, J. and Campbell, H. 2009. The anthropology of global flows: A critical reading of Appadurai's disjuncture and difference in the global cultural economy. *Anthropological Theory*, 9(2): 131–148.

Hobbs, D. and Antonopoulos, G.A. 2013. 'Endemic to the species': Ordering the 'other' via organised crime. *Global Crime* 14(1): 27–51.

Hodgson, J. 2011. Touchdown Wal-Mart. *North Coast Journal.* December 15. Accessed February 27, 2017 at: http://www.northcoastjournal.com/humboldt/touchdown-wal-mart/Content?oid=2132782.

Hönke, J. 2012. Multinationals and security governance in the community: Participation, discipline and indirect rule. *Journal of Intervention and State Building*, 6(1): 89–105.

Houston, W. 2016a. Humboldt County: Highest arrest rate in state. *Eureka Times-Standard.* February 22. Accessed Feburary 27, 2017 at: http://www.times-standard.com/article/NJ/20160222/NEWS/160229970.

Houston, W. 2016b. Mark Lovelace looks back on eight years in office. *Eureka Times Standard.* December 16. Accessed February 27, 2017 at: http://www.times-standard.com/article/NJ/20161216/NEWS/161219855.

Hudson, R. 2007. Regions and regional uneven development forever? Some reflective comments upon theory and practice. *Regional Studies*, 41(9): 1149–1160.

Humboldt County 2010. Forest resources: Assessor/planning presentation. *Humboldt County General Plan Update*. March 11.

Iovino, N. 2017. Eureka settles police shooting lawsuit. *North Coast Journal*. January 5. Accessed February 27, 2017 at: http://www.northcoastjournal.com/humboldt/eureka-settles-police-shooting-lawsuit/Content?oid=4266626.

Jacobs, J. 1996. The North American back-to-the-land movement. *Community Development Journal*, 31(3): 241–249.

Lasch, C. 1991. *The True and Only Heaven: Progress and Its Critics*. New York: Norton.

Le Billon, P. (2001). The political ecology of war: Natural resources and armed conflicts. *Political geography*, 20(5), 561–584.

Li, T. 2007. *The Will to Improve*. Durham: Duke University Press.

Linebaugh, P. 1976. Karl Marx, the theft of wood, and working class composition: A contribution to the current debate. *Crime and Social Justice*, 40(1): 5–16.

McCubbrey, J.P. 2007. *Impacts of Illicit-drug Policy on Community Cohesion: A Case Study of the Campaign Against Marijuana Planting in Southern Humboldt County, California*. Doctoral dissertation, Western Institute for Social Research.

McIver, C., Meek, J., Scudder, M., Sorenson, C., Morgan, T. and Christensen, G. 2015. California's forest products industry and timber harvest, 2012. United States Department of Agriculture.

Males, M. 2014. Killing by law enforcement in California: It's not what you think. *Center on Juvenile and Criminal Justice*. Accessed February 27, 2017 at: http://www.cjcj.org/news/8533.

Morgan, T., Keegan, C., Dillon, T., Chase, A., Fried, J. and Weber, M. 2004. California's forest products industry: A descriptive analysis. Portland: USDA.

Mozingo, J. 2012. Medical pot returning to underground. *Chicago Tribune*. September 6. Accessed February 27, 2017 at: http://www.chicagotribune.com/lifestyles/health/la-me-pot-delivery-20120907-story.html.

Mullings, L. 2003. Losing Ground. *Souls*, 5:1–21.

Narotzky, S. and Smith, G.A. 2006. *Immediate Struggles: People, Power, and Place in Rural Spain*. Berkeley: University of California Press.

Nash, J.C. 1989. *From Tank Town to High Tech: The Clash of Community and Industrial Cycles*. Albany: SUNY Press.

Nordstron, C. 2007. *Global Outlaws: Crime, Money, and Power in the Contemporary World*. Berkeley: University of California Press.

North Coast Journal. 1998. Upfront: Renner Conviction 'Just'. July. Accessed February 27, 2017 at: http://www.northcoastjournal.com/july98/7-98.upfront.html#RENNER%20CONVICTION%20%27JUST%27.

Pappas, G. 1989. *The Magic City: Unemployment in a Working-Class Community*. Ithaca: Cornell University Press.

Pempel, T.J. 1999. The developmental regime in a changing world economy. *The Developmental State*. Woo-Cummings M, Ed. Ithaca: Cornell University Press. 137–181.

Pfaelzer, J. 2007. *Driven out: The Forgotten War against Chinese Americans*. New York: Random House.

Piore, M.J. and Sabel, C.F. 1984. *The Second Industrial Divide: Possibilities for Prosperity*. New York: Basic Books.

Polson, M. 2013. Land and law in marijuana country: Clean capital, dirty money, and the drug war's *rentier* nexus. *Illegal Anthropology*. Special Issue of *PoLAR: Political and Legal Anthropology Review*, 36(2): 215–230.

Polson, M. (forthcoming). Marketing marijuana: Prohibition, medicalisation and the commodity. *Fraud, Crime and Corruption in a Neoliberal Era.* Carrier, J. Ed. Berghahn Books.

Poor, K. 2013. Former EPD Sergeant given conditional offer for chief post; Johnson involved in Cheri Lynn Moore shooting. *Eureka Times-Standard.* July 4. Accessed February 27, 2017 at: http://www.times-standard.com/article/zz/20130704/NEWS/130709595.

Raphael, R. 1985. *Cash Crop: An American Dream.* Mendocino, CA: Ridge Times Press.

Raphael, R. 2007 [1974]. *An Everyday History of Somewhere.* Mendocino: Bored Feet Press.

Roa, M. 2007. *Redwood Ed: A Guide to the Coast Redwoods for Learners and Teachers.* Sacramento: Stewards of the Coast and Redwoods.

Robinson, J.A., Torvik, R. and Verdier, T. 2006. Political foundations of the resource curse. *Journal of Development Economics*, 79(2): 447–468.

Robotham, D. 2003. How Kingston was wounded. *Wounded Cities: Destruction and Reconstruction in a Globalized World.* Schneider, J. and Susser, I., Eds. New York: Berg. 111–128.

Ross, M. 1999. The political economy of the resource curse. *World Politics*, 51(2): 297–322.

Sachs, J. and Warner, A. 1995. *Natural Resource Abundance and Economic Growth.* Institute for International Development.

Schneider, J. 2009. Abstinence and power: The place of prohibition in American history. *Empirical Futures.* Baca, G., Khan, A., and Palmié, S. Eds. Chapel Hill: University of North Carolina.

Schneider, J. and Schneider, P.T. 1976. *Culture and Political Economy in Western Sicily.* New York: Academic Press.

Scott, A.J. and Storper, M. 2003. Regions, Globalization, Development. *Regional Studies*, 41(S1): S191–S205.

Sims, H. 2006. Scenes from a shooting. *North Coast Journal.* April 27. Accessed February 27. 2017 at: http://www.northcoastjournal.com/042706/cover0427.html.

Sims, H. 2014. No, it's not just you: Crime in Humboldt County is getting much worse. *Lost Coast Outpost.* November 18. Accessed February 27. 2017 at: https://lostcoastoutpost.com/2014/nov/18/no-its-not-just-you-crime-humboldt-county-getting/.

Sloman, L. 1979. *Reefer Madness: The History of Marijuana in America.* Indianapolis: Bobbs-Merrill.

Smart, A. 2001. Unruly places: Urban governance and the persistence of illegality in Hong Kong's urban squatter areas. *American Anthropologist*, 103(1): 30–44.

Smartvoter.org. 2012. Full biography of Mark Lovelace. Accessed February 27, 2017 at: http://www.smartvoter.org/2012/06/05/ca/hm/vote/lovelace_m/bio.html.

Smith, N. 1990. *Uneven Development.* Oxford: Basil Blackwell.

Smith, P. 2016. A marijuana land rush is underway in northern California. *Alternet.* June 4. Accessed February 27, 2017 at: http://www.alternet.org/drugs/marijuana-land-rush-northern-california.

Solecki, W. 1996. Paternalism, pollution, and protest in a company town. *Political Geography*, 15(1): 5–20.

St. George, Z. 2011. *North Coast Journal of Politics, People, and Art.* June 2. Accessed February 27. 2017 at: http://www.northcoastjournal.com/humboldt/tight-squeeze/Content?oid=2132159.

St. George, Z. 2012. District Soup. *North Coast Journal.* May 10. Accessed February 27. 2017 at: http://www.northcoastjournal.com/humboldt/district-soup/Content?oid=2133199.

Suzelle. 2014. Humboldt County district attorney Paul Gallegos on environmental impacts of large marijuana grows. *KMUD.org.* March 2. Accessed February 27, 2017 at: http://www.kmud.org/programs-mainmenu-11/talk-shows-mainmenu-143/civil-liberties-hour/item/3057-humboldt-county-district-attorney-paul-gallegos-on-environmental-impacts-of-large-marijuana-grows.html.

Swyngedouw, E. 1997. Neither global nor local: Glocalization and the politics of scale. *Spaces of Globalization: Reasserting the Power of the Local.* Cox, K., Ed. New York: Guilford. 137–166.

Tam, D. 2012. Girard resigns as director of community development services; taking new job in Santa Clara. *Eureka Times-Standard.* May 8. Accessed February 27, 2017 at: http://www.times-standard.com/article/ZZ/20120508/NEWS/120509323.

Thompson, E.P. 1975. *Whigs and Hunters.* London: Penguin.

Tsing, A.L. 2005. *Friction: An Ethnography of Global Connection.* Princeton, NJ: Princeton University Press.

Walters, H. 2014. Not exactly curtains for Richardson Grove. *Northcoastjournal.com.* December 5. Accessed February 27, 2017 at: http://www.northcoastjournal.com/NewsBlog/archives/2014/12/05/not-exactly-curtains-for-richardson-grove-widening.

Watts, M. 2004. Resource curse? Governmentality, oil and power in the Niger Delta, Nigeria. *Geopolitics*, 9(1): 50–80.

Weinstein, L. 2008. Mumbai's development mafias: Globalization, organized crime and land development. *International Journal of Urban and Regional Research*, 32(1): 22–39.

Widick, R. 2009. *Trouble in the Forest: California's Redwood Timber Wars.* Minneapolis: University of Minnesota Press.

Wilk, R. 2014. Poverty and excess in binge economies. *Economic Anthropology*, 1(1): 66–79.

Wylde, C. 2014. The developmental state is dead, long live the developmental regime! Interpreting Néstor Kirchner's Argentina 2003–2007. *Journal of International Relations and Development*, 17(2): 191–219.

Zuckerman, S. 2013. Is pot-growing bad for the environment? *The Nation.* October 31. Accessed February 27, 2017 at: https://www.thenation.com/article/pot-growing-bad-environment/.

10 Embedding illegality, or when the illegal becomes licit

Planning cases and urban transformations in Rome

Barbara Pizzo and Edoardo Altavilla

Introduction

The spreading of illicit behaviours is increasingly emphasised within political and public debate worldwide. Similarly, the issue of informality is getting attention because of its controversial overlapping with illegality. As far as human settlements are concerned, in all the three cases – illegality, illicitness and informality – planning is often seen as the field where many of those behaviours are displayed; or also as one possible causal origin. Politically, these behaviours and practices may have a twofold interpretation: they can be considered either as the distortion of a good or acceptable system (for example, the current regulative system in a given place) or as the manifestation of its malfunction, inefficiency and also injustice.

For the sake of clarity, we assume here a simple definition of illegality, considering illegal to be what is 'not allowed by the law', or what is done 'against the established rules', so that a penalty, a sanction or a punishment is expected. However, we recognise that the concept of illicitness cannot be constrained within a strict legalistic interpretation, since it has more ethical, moral, cultural and customary roots and implications, and is subject also to circumstantial justifications. Hence, by illicit, we mean something that is considered as unacceptable in terms of the dominant social perception and custom and practice in a specific time/space context. With regards to informality, this concept is even more slippery, since it can be conceptualised as opposed to the formality of the law, or of the rules, but also as sets of spontaneous arrangements, which go beyond the idea that some rule is needed, particularly if pre-defined. Needless to say, informal arrangements can be either illegal or perfectly legal, and all the possible combinations with licitness/illicitness apply.

Our thesis is that, apart from deliberate illegality, addressed to fraud or criminality, there can be different, even conflicting implications in spontaneous, self-organising forms of action 'outside of the boundaries of the established rules' – that nonetheless means illegal. Framed by different values, some behaviours are socially perceived as illegal *and yet* licit, highlighting the controversies of certain norms and rules. In this sense, what is illegal can be interpreted as insurgent or subversive, and as a tool for recognition of unrecognised rights. But this is not always the case, and the examples we present here will show how at least the effective, material impacts of those behaviours, although motivated by different intentions, can be everything but insurgent or progressive: on the contrary, they are useful for maintaining the status quo in socioeconomic relationships, and through them, in the economic and political power system.

Consequently, our aim here is to critically inquire into informal and illegal behaviours considered as licit in their relationships with the urban space. We address the issue by discussing some examples from Rome in order to demonstrate how these behaviours, which can have different origins, justifications and orientations, might be functional within certain systems, instead of being subversive of given institutional assets and current market logics. The reason why some of them are tolerated while others are not depends on the socioeconomic and political role they, often unintentionally, play. In fact, the illicit has been recognised as 'genetically entwined' with the licit, and together they work as "'normal" operations of contemporary capitalism, integral to the workings of the capitalist economy rather than a marginal and unusual anomaly' (Hudson 2014, p. 775).

Following a long-lasting research path seeking to disentangle the conditions under which urban transformations in Rome are shaped (Pizzo and Di Salvo 2015, Moini and Pizzo 2017), the focus here is on the particular socioeconomic, cultural and political environment which 'permits' different kinds of formally illegal 'auto-organisation' to be tolerated, if not accepted. In other words, we are interested in exploring the shift from illegality into licitness, while considering its causes, meanings and implications.

This chapter proceeds as follows: first, we frame the issue in disciplinary terms; then we present three cases from Rome as examples, providing evidence for our arguments. The evidence we present resulted from a combination of fieldwork (including surveys, interviews and workshops), and secondary sources, that we collected during various research activities. After that, we discuss the cases in the light of some theoretical questions, related to political geography and to state theory. Finally, we present our interpretive hypothesis and conclusions.

Framing the issue

As already stated, the concept of illegality is relatively straightforward to define, as it is anything 'outside the law'. By contrast, the concepts of illicitness and informality are more slippery, and more subject to temporal, spatial and cultural variations. We recognised two main perspectives that seemed useful for framing the Italian case: one comes from institutional research; the other from geography (political and economic geography in particular). Mapping the various contributions of these two literatures, one finds that the latter is mostly dedicated to the 'Global South'. Illegality and illicitness (sometimes confused, or used as synonyms) are considered mostly in their relationship with corruption (Hagedorn 2007), while informality, even when it leads to forms of illegality, is often part of an alternative economy and development discourse, focused on different sorts of 'survival strategies' – of the poorest or of the weakest (women often playing a fundamental role), or of particular groups which, deliberately or not, act at the margins of or (seemingly) outside the market (for example, Fernandez-Kelly and García 1989; Portes *et al.* 1989; Beneria and Feldman 1992; Chant 1991; Fernandez-Kelly and Shefner 2006).

In abstract terms, it is difficult to define the difference between different types of illegality (the one related to corruption, and the one related to extreme need). What permits us to define that difference, which can be perceived as a fundamental divide, is the slight move from legality/illegality towards licitness/illicitness, since (in Italy as in most Western countries) this second dyad goes beyond the formal rule and problematises its content (motivations and circumstances) and its value system (fighting for life is more important than breaking a rule).

In the Italian administrative culture, illegal and illicit behaviour is a well-known – and researched – phenomenon. Behaviours and formal rules constitute the two critical variables of institutional research. The bulk of the study of institutional performance is how (if at all) the two can influence one another (Putnam *et al.* 1994). These concepts are usually treated with respect to the phenomena of corruption of public powers involving illegal groups (Hagedorn, 2007) that seek to influence (or better seize) public spending. Therefore, the very notions of informality, illicitness and illegality are observed against a whole set of formal laws and regulations that define what is acceptable (and accountable) and what is not. However, it has been acknowledged that those concepts and their opposites do not exist as strict dichotomies, but rather in a reciprocal relationship, while in practice they are 'genetically entwined' (Hudson, 2014, p. 775).

Nevertheless, informality, illicitness and illegality suffer from a poor systematic operationalisation. As a consequence, those concepts have rarely been deployed in empirical studies in ways that reveal their *systemic* nature (see Hudson, ibid.).[1] The predominantly abstract and theoretical direction within the literature reflects the fact that studies of the illegal and informal stem from the field of state theory (Heyman, 1999).

From the examples provided by the literature, one can argue that in contexts where institutional consolidation is non-organic and patchy (for example, where different government levels and their respective regulations do not always overlap consistently, and also intersect with a number of norms and rules with different origins, as for example, in India), the formal/informal, legal/illegal dichotomies tend to merge into one another more than in contexts of solid institutional systems. At the same time, it is this merging of notions, which corresponds to a broader range of practices, which probably explains why we find a more in-depth investigation on illegality and informality in the 'Global South literature' (Fernández-Kelly and Shefner, 2006; Portes *et al.* 1989), which describes how the two can work as self-reinforcing ingredients in structure/agency interplay; especially in the plan, project or policy implementation phase. As public institutional robustness (and longevity) decrease, governments can choose to rely in some ways on the informal sector. All the more so when it comes to legalising former illegal situations, a contingency that constantly occurs in planning.

Though focused on a specific case, Rao (2013) shows how tapping the 'social capital' of informal and illegal realities is often an effective way for governments to work around legal formalism. Moreover, she states that the negotiation needed to implement a plan in the Global South is a tool for 'outcome achievement' (ibid.), because of the practical limits of rational urban planning in developing countries. Urban planning in Rome reveals interesting similarities. With a focus on planning we assume that legal/illegal–licit/illicit relationships are not just 'genetically entwined', but even necessary for the implementation of a development plan – which 'depends on the making of unlawful buildings and illicit artifacts', (Rao 2013, p. 771) – and that the ambiguities in between those notions help realising the 'desired outcome' (Rao 2013, p. 770). In this sense, we can say that informality, illicitness and even illegality are often instrumental / functional to a certain plan or system. In this chapter we problematise the idea of different geographies of illegality, illicitness and informality and, more precisely, we argue that the North/South divide, as expressed in the literature, is not helpful. The examples we choose will contribute in clarifying this point.

Three cases from Rome as examples

1 The phenomenon of 'self-made' housing in Rome: between informality and illegality

In bare quantitative terms, more than 50 per cent of the existing buildings in Rome are somehow illegal (Pizzo & Di Salvo, 2015),[2] although with different degrees of illegality. Minor changes in the building structure include, for example, the addition of one room, through closing what was formerly a balcony or a loggia, to the extension of the number of storeys. These two cases are widespread within the historical city centre where, in 2015, the police of the 1st Borough (that covers the historical city centre) received 10,000 notifications of alleged illegal transformations (Mari and Savelli, 2016). Major urban transformations refer to entirely self-made (illegal) housing neighbourhoods (Cellamare 2013, see also S.M.U.R. 2014). We focus here on the last case.

Scholars (see, for two quite different perspectives, Insolera 1962 and Clementi and Perego, 1983) recognised different 'waves' in the developing of this phenomenon in Rome. A first phase, which started immediately after the Second World War but went on until the mid-1960s, has two main features: (a) most of the self-made housing has been built outside of the land use plan but, since that plan (dated 1931) did not cover the whole municipal territory of Rome, cannot be considered properly as illegal; (b) self-made housing interventions that seemingly responded to a much shared claim to urgently provide shelter for people who, after WWII and during the very rapid urbanisation process which characterised the 1950s and 1960s, arrived in great numbers in Rome from neighbouring regions as well as from the Mezzogiorno, a process that the state was unable to manage. This phase was generally considered as primarily need-oriented. Most of the housing was of rather poor quality, built rapidly and just for necessity. Most scholars agree on this interpretation.

In contrast, the following phases have a more contentious character. On the one hand, self-made housing continued to be justified by the lack of housing in Rome, particularly of public housing and low-income private housing. This condition was examined by many scholars (Ferrarotti, 1970, 1974, 1981; Berlinguer and Della Seta, 1976; Martinelli, 1986) as well as in more popular media, becoming the object of a stream of novels and films (notably the work of Pasolini). But, on the other hand, it increasingly turned into forms of speculation and rent-seeking, which interested the middle,[3] but also the lower, social classes. Self-made housing started to increase in numbers, and to be intended for more than one family, opening up the opportunity to (illegally) sublet spare rooms. To own a house, whatever house it might be, started to represent a form of investment and also of income for an increasingly larger proportion of the population in Rome.

Clearly this phenomenon has had huge impacts across the city. The illegal settlements deriving from the first wave of self-made housing entered into the master plan [Piano Regolatore Generale] of 1965 in order to be legalised. They were named 'F1' zones and numbered 44. In the following waves, 73 other illegal settlements have been included in local planning tools, and designated in 1983 as 'O' zones. The legalising mechanism involved a post-payment of the development fees, or infrastructure charges, plus a fine. Subsequently, another 71 or 80 settlements (both figures appear in official sources) have been identified and named 'Toponimi' in the master plan of 2008 (see: http://www.urbanistica.comune.roma.it/toponimi-stato.html).

After the issue of unmanaged land-use, which severely undermined the environmental qualities of the well-known *Campagna Romana* [Roman countryside], another highly debated topic is the impact on public expenditure. To provide public infrastructure and facilities to even the most distant and isolated illegal neighbourhoods constitutes an enormous cost, which still weighs on the finances of the city. These interventions became more systematic and very onerous after each amnesty (declared at the national level), when the public administration found itself obliged to provide infrastructures, to which the ex-illegal owners also (partially) contributed through taxes and fines.

What is more difficult to explain is how and why public facilities (such as water, light, gas, telephone lines, which were provided by public companies, and also public buses, and so on), were present in many illegal settlements even before the amnesties. Whilst we cannot explore this in depth here, there are two main explanations, which can be traced back to the 'double nature' of the phenomenon. Despite being strictly intertwined, we propose to define the first one as 'self-driven', the second one as 'other-driven'. The former is more complex, since it includes the political power of the inhabitants of these settlements, particularly in some years (the 1970s and mid-1980s), and the voice they were able to raise while associated (Coppola, 2008, 2013), but in addition types of micro-network relationships, also related to forms of corruption, which permitted a number of illegal inhabitants to obtain an address (albeit provisional), and so a connection to the public technical infrastructures. What happened then, in such cases, is that more than one family connected to each service drop, and paid fees to the family which obtained the original connection. The latter is more contentious, since it has to do with the role that these illegal settlements played in the development of Rome. Italo Insolera (1962) introduced the idea of 'bridgeheads' as a key-concept for understanding a fundamental mechanism of urban development in Rome. From the end of the nineteenth century, he recognised that 'strategic' settlements have been located far away in the rural landscape, seemingly without any logic. For many years, they consisted mainly of public interventions (public housing). What Insolera explained is that in this way it was the public who paid all the infrastructure costs to serve the new settlements, while all the lands in between those settlements and the city centre, which were privately owned, mostly by big land owners who also acted as real-estate investors, increased their value (see Scalia in this volume for a similar process in the case of Palermo). Ad hoc land use regulations, which recurred frequently as variations of the master plan, did the rest. The occurrence of public infrastructure and facilities in formerly illegal settlements can be explained by this same mechanism. We can argue, together with other scholars (Della Seta, 1988; Tocci, 2015), that the illegal settlements had a key – not marginal – role in urban development. Through the role they played in the increase of land value for the benefit of the big land-owners, they contributed to shifting the costs of infrastructure and facilities, which should have been paid by private investors, on to public shoulders, and so contributed to concentrating the advantages in the hands of private interests. Moreover, this phenomenon contributed to the spreading of a culture of illegality.

An entire and complex black economy grew up from these illegal behaviours. Surprisingly enough, the issue does not emerge as a main subject of economic analysis. At the same time, it is clear that against the public costs it produced, this phenomenon generated (and still generates) private advantages and wealth. In a city where land and real estate rent is a primary component of the local economy, this phenomenon can have two antithetical interpretations. From one point of view, it can be interpreted as the sign of the predominance of private property and private interest. From a different point of view, it can be (as in fact often is) perceived from the inhabitants as a form of (re)distribution, implemented through a behaviour which is just formally defined as illegal (the houses have been built against the provisions of the land use plans), but that was overall perceived as licit (Pizzo and Di Salvo 2015). In this sense, the meaning of the word licit emerges as something that is illegal, but justified by the simple fact that what was established by law was wrong. Licit in this case is the illegal perceived as right, right against the law. The moral sense of what is right largely overcomes what is formally defined as right by the law, which became increasingly contentious. The huge number of cases of self-made housing is clear and incontrovertible evidence of the latter interpretation. The repeated amnesties for the infringements of building and planning regulations, enacted at different government levels, contributed to reinforce the conviction of the licitness of the illegal.

It is obviously impossible to believe that none of the different institutions involved was aware of what was happening: from the municipality, which formally assigned a name to streets in formally non-existent neighbourhoods, and acknowledged them as the official domicile of a huge amount of people, to the public companies providing facilities and services, water, electricity, telephone lines and so on, acting in a similar way. To comprehend this process, one has to understand who actually benefitted from it. Firstly, it was not an opportunity for all, as it is sometimes presented. In order to get benefit, you must own a parcel of land, you must have the money to build (at least to cover the costs of building materials), and you must be inclined or open to acting illegally. Previous research (Pizzo and Di Salvo, 2015) demonstrated how illegal neighbourhoods did not have an overall positive impact on the housing market (for example, producing a decrease of housing prices or acting as a form of price control, as social housing in some other European countries succeeded in doing). On the contrary, they represented a fundamental component for realising and increasing rent gaps, which just partially benefitted the 'small' transgressors, and much more traditional and well-established landowners and real estate investors – this means that illegal neighbourhoods were also a fundamental component of the accumulation strategy pursued by the main local economic actors. Moreover, actual tolerance of illegal neighbourhoods contributed to the consolidation of political consensus among the middle and lower classes in the immense suburbs of Rome. More precisely, political elites in Rome established and preserved their power through what has been called 'a double strategy', a main economic-political strategy which involved the few big real-estate owners and investors on one side, and a seemingly minor, but broadly diffuse sort of laissez-faire strategy, which tied small owners of unauthorised buildings to local politicians and the system they represent (Pizzo and Di Salvo, 2015).

2 The case of the 'Consorzi di autorecupero' [self-recovery consortia] and the question of the 'Toponimi' in the master plan of Rome of 2008

This example can be considered as a particular case of the broader phenomenon of illegality that characterises the development of Rome over the years. We treat it separately because we want to explore the relationships between illegality and illicitness that a new planning approach reveals.

The master plan of the city of Rome approved in 2008 contains specific norms addressed to the legalisation of the more recent illegal neighbourhoods, which continued to emerge over time.[4] The plan identifies two main illegal situations: first, the already legalised, or formerly illegal neighbourhoods called 'O' zones, which are the object of planning norms oriented to urban rehabilitation; second, the more recent cases of self-made housing, often too sparse to become a neighbourhood of their own, and too distant from other neighbourhoods to be considered as their offshoots. These latter settlements have been called 'Toponimi'. The master plan defined and preliminarily bounded 71 or 80 (see above) *Toponimi*, which covered around 1,900 hectares, included 90,000 inhabitants, and established a new legalising mechanism. The legalisation procedure that followed the previous amnesties produced unsatisfactory results. The public costs that they generated were too high, and the public works actually realised were less, quantitatively and qualitatively, than expected (something that could be assumed as a basic demonstration of the overall unsustainability of this kind of growth).

Moreover, *Toponimi* were very dispersed. This led to demands for a number of small public interventions which proved more expensive (particularly in terms of infrastructure provision) and difficult to manage. These are among the main reasons that brought the Municipality to approach the issue in a different way, through specific norms defined within the same master plan.

According to those norms, the inhabitants of each *Toponimo* were required to join and constitute a consortium, called *consorzio di autorecupero* [self-recovery consortium], conceived as a way for the inhabitants to effectively manage the redevelopment of the former illegal settlements with a certain autonomy. In fact, they were expected to submit proposals for the public works to be realised to enhance their settlement, and also establishing priorities, which the Municipality would assess in terms of coherence with overall planning objectives. This solution seemingly lightened the duty of the municipality, while promoting citizens' participation. In fact, compared with previous experiences, in the O zones the rehabilitation plans were defined by the public; while in the case of *Toponimi* the consortia are in charge of specifying the land use plan and of its implementation[5].

One of the contentious features of this approach is that, since many *Toponimi* are in extreme need of public infrastructures and space for public services, the consortia can involve other land parcels in order to realise infrastructure provision. This is why their boundaries have been just 'preliminarily' defined within the master plan. The Municipality 'refunds' the private landowners who concede their parcels for public infrastructures and services with building rights (Cellamare 2016a). In this way, and contrarily to what was initially declared by the local government regarding the containment of urban sprawl, the *Toponimi* are expected to grow, both in surface area and in population. What happened is that the consortia soon started to use this 'window of opportunity' as a way of obtaining a quantity of building rights and to increase land rent, and the primary objective of the operation (legalising illegal neighbourhoods and providing them with the public facilities and services) was soon overshadowed. However, this mechanism did not work as intended, and the new definition of the boundaries of *Toponimi*, which included new land parcels, created rent gaps that were exploited by private interests. Furthermore, the attribution of new building rights did not correspond to the payment of the fees and fines, so that by 2015 investigative journalists revealed a hole of millions of euros in the consortia's coffers (Di Pasquale, 2012). Furthermore, the amount of money that they are (at least potentially) able to manage is not perceived as public money belonging to the Municipality. They were perceived by the consortia as their own money, to be used for their own purposes.

So, a second controversial feature emerges, regarding the alleged participatory process, and the form and meaning that it actually assumed. The mechanism hinged upon a willingness to contribute to a common project through the direct involvement of the inhabitants of each *Toponimo*. What actually happened is rather different. During the meetings within each consortium private interests strongly prevailed against any public or collective interest, while the consortia assumed a more coherent position when negotiating with the Municipality, becoming (or being presented and largely perceived) as a strong political power.

An argument emerged, particularly during the election campaign of 2008, which maintained that that money within consortia coffers was potentially available, if the negotiations with the Municipality concerning the approval of their plans and the authorisation of the related expenditure had a positive outcome, to be used to relaunch the local economy. This fundamental misunderstanding, by the owners of illegal housing, of the fees and fines perceived as private funds instead of public money generated a sort of short-circuit between private involvement and project implementation. In fact, soon after the legalisation mechanism has been defined, the private interests involved in the consortia interpreted the mechanism and the consortia themselves not as a tool for legalising their settlements, but primarily as a window of opportunity for obtaining extra building rights and the related economic benefits, which became the very object of negotiations with the Municipality.

Nevertheless, what has actually happened up to now is rather insignificant, in terms of material implementation of infrastructures, except for the political meaning that these consortia have assumed over time. In fact, the consortia progressively assumed such a high political weight that they were able to influence the vote locally. In this case, the main point is the inconsistency between the behaviour of the actors involved in the construction of the illegal settlements, and their claiming 'rights' (whose licitness or illicitness is quite contentious), against the Municipality of Rome, the same public institution whose rules and norms they previously completely ignored.

3 The case of the informal, self-organised secondary housing market in a social (public) housing neighbourhood in Rome (Tor Bella Monaca)[6]

As with many social housing neighbourhoods, Tor Bella Monaca was developed as a unitary plan and architectural project quite isolated from the rest of the city. The neighbourhood was designed to host 30,000 inhabitants and was realised in less than three years at the beginning of the 1980s, an extraordinarily quick development for Rome. Since the buildings were completed a two-sided process has emerged. From one side, the apartments were assigned by the Municipality of Rome[7] on the basis of an official list of right holders (from a range of disadvantaged situations); on the other side, they started to be illegally occupied by social movements such as the *movimento per il diritto alla casa* [right to housing movement]. This happened because the assignment procedure was judged as too long (and not completely transparent, nor just) and the need of people too pressing. It may have also occurred due to a lack of control and management capacity by the public institutions involved. This means that, from the very beginning of the story of this neighbourhood, what was (is) legal was strongly contested, and so legality and illegality, licitness and illicitness went on together in a way that is now very complicated to disentangle.

In order to better frame the problems of living in such a neighbourhood, and possibly to contribute in shaping some solutions, recent researches (see, for example, Cellamare 2016a) tried to better understand a few phenomena that have emerged there. The first is that, alongside the official list of right holders, there were ‘unofficial’ lists of people waiting to get into a social housing apartment. These unofficial lists could be managed by different people/organisations, at different levels: from the same people who initially started their political activity within the *movimento per il diritto alla casa*, which means that they act at the urban/metropolitan scale, moving families from one social neighbourhood to the other, if the possibility occurs; to single apartment blocks organisations, which tend to give priority to their own relatives or to people they know personally.

The second phenomenon was the emergence of an informal, illegal market, where it became increasingly ‘normal’ (licit) for right holders or even illegal tenants to ‘sell’ their house (for a similar case in Nairobi, see Amis, 1984). Since the houses are public, and they cannot be sold officially, what is sold is the priority to get into an apartment, in the face of official and even unofficial lists. The sum varies from less than 5,000 euros to more than 20,000 euros, a not insignificant sum for those for whom this housing was primarily built. This payment is often justified by the residents as a form of compensation for the maintenance of the apartment, which was expected to be the duty of the two public owners (the municipality and the agency for public housing): a duty which was almost completely unfulfilled, so that many tenants started to maintain and sometimes also to develop the apartments themselves.[8] A side effect of this illegal market is that, from their own point of view, public institutions are somehow legitimised in not doing any maintenance of the buildings, since many apartments are illegally occupied, and many legal occupants do not pay the rent.

This relationship between the public institutions in charge of social housing and the tenants contributes to increasingly confounding what is legitimate and what is illegitimate. As already mentioned, in this case a strong political content characterises illegal behaviours. At the same time, a few features of this self-organisation suggest dangerous similarities with the mafia organisation, including the references to a sort of subsidiary – if not alternative – welfare system, that emerge from many interviews with local inhabitants and associations. Interestingly, ATER is perfectly aware of all the aspects and implications embedded within this case that are common to many other public housing neighbourhoods, and it is currently looking for solutions that would take advantage of local resources and capacities, which are numerous (Pizzo and Montillo 2016), but within a legalisation process.

The reasons why these behaviours are often perceived as licit and get justified reside (also) in the risk that one is keen to run, which is taken as a sign of extreme need, and this turns illegality into licitness, significantly resembling one of the core arguments of Global South literature on informal/illegal economies being perceived as licit.

Reflecting on illicit practices: Different points of view and possible interpretations

There are several possible points of view from which the above examples may be interpreted, showing how the concepts of illegal, illicit, informal can be variously framed. In our view, among the more problematic – and therefore intellectually stimulating – perspectives, two main lines of inquiry emerge. One is related to what we called a geography of the illicit; the other is related to state/market relationships, and to state theory. After having discussed these possible interpretations, we will introduce our main interpretive hypothesis, which concerns the city as our main object of inquiry.

Different geographies of the illicit?

Through reviewing the existing literature, one cannot help but notice that it treats and tries to illuminate the various nuances of informality, illicitness and illegality related to cities and to urban planning, largely through cases from the Global South. In our opinion, this North/South divide (involuntarily) suggests a sort of implicit understanding that not 'under some conditions', but 'in some parts of the world' illegality emerges a) as a necessity, so that it can be tolerated or even accepted, and/or b) as insurgent practices (Sandercock, 1995, 1998, 1999; Roy, 2009a, 2009b; Meth 2013; Miraftab 2015). We problematise this point of view, recognising the significance of specific conditions, which may occur in many places, since they are the outcome of each specific socioeconomic and political system. Stated differently, we may assert that since illegality and illicitness are defined according to the definition of their opposite concept – what is illicit or illegal depends on the definition of what is licit or legal – illicit or illegal behaviours emerge within each specific context.

Nevertheless, some similarities can be recognised between cases. The examples from Rome demonstrate that the relationship between legal and illegal (in real estate development and the housing market in particular) is a sort of structural one. Interestingly, for a quite different context, that of India, Rao (2013) showed how informality and even illegality are deeply intertwined with legality, and necessary for the implementation of the formal /legal urban market. Looking back to earlier studies, an in-depth analysis of these mechanisms in Latin America was provided by Edwards (1982), while interesting analogies can be found in the case of Nairobi reported by Amis (1984); and Gilbert (1983) examining the role of 'self-help housing' in the constitution of a whole illegal housing market and its relationship with the legal one, in 'less developed countries'. This convergence allows us to attempt some theoretical generalisation.

We noted that illegality might emerge 'simply' as a necessity, as the only way for certain people in certain places to try to survive. In particular, all the three cases we presented can be interpreted as autonomous solutions to problems to which the state is unable to give timely and adequate answers. But they represent a solution to just *some* people. This kind of opportunity could be taken only by the people who had a certain economic capacity, but also by those ready and able to break the law. Illegal arrangements, then, can contribute to increasing senses of insecurity and marginalisation (Rao 2013, p. 761).

In other instances, illegality is considered licit for its insurgent meaning, as a tool for fighting against a certain system – the same system that defines what is legal and what is not, and generates the conditions of illegality to emerge. Significantly, the examples presented here showed that none of those practices succeeded in actually changing the system. On the contrary, a number of rather simple, bounded malfunctioning of public institutions (which are potentially a precise and defined object of political contest) are not reckoned, due to the muddle of illegal behaviours and unachieved responsibilities of the different actors involved. In fact, as the case of Tor Bella Monaca in particular shows, the unworthy behaviour of public bodies became somehow 'justifiable' in the light of a diffuse illegality that generated forms of short-circuits which led to a fundamental paralysis, so that it seems that *really* nothing can change.

Not least, both of the above mentioned interpretations consider the current system as a given – the people 'obligated' to find their own way and place through recourse to illegal or illicit behaviour, as unavoidable by-products of a generally functioning system, which is not necessarily the case. On the contrary, these practices turn out to feed that same system they presume to overcome or to contrast. All this considered, we could sustain that the practices we examined can hardly be considered as insurgent: on the contrary, as far as we understood, they end up in reinforcing, burdening further a system, which is fundamentally unequal and unjust.

Which state (theory)?

Undoubtedly, at first glance the three examples seem to support the idea of a failure on the part of the state. It was the state which was unable to provide housing and failed in its control-power over the territory, being unable to have its laws and rules respected. So, is the state the system we are talking about? With a different perspective, one can argue that it is the market which is not working properly (for its own agents and mechanisms), so much that it needs, and determines, illegality (Fernandez-Kelly and García 1989 in/and Portes *et al.* 1989; Beneria and Feldman 1992; Chant 1991; Fernandez-Kelly and Shefner 2006, Rao 2013; Hudson 2014). In this view, the state is involved in as far as it is able, or not, to enforce its regulatory power, a power that is increasingly subjected to external global forces. From a different starting point, we can say that each state, through its rules and regulations, can shape a different landscape of legality (and so of illegality). In this sense, the state can be considered as a co-cause of illegality (albeit indirect or even involuntary). Furthermore, states are said to apply a 'discursive selectivity' (Hudson 2014, p. 790) in tackling the issue of illegality. Under the lens of the globalised (neoliberal) economy, the strict relationship between licit and illicit, legal and illegal results not as an exception, but rather as the rule (Hagedorn 2007). In that perspective, the state still plays (and is expected to play) a fundamental role that, among the various forms it can acquire, includes different levels of acceptance or tolerance for the multiplicity of features that illegality and illicitness can assume.

So what became central is *why* the state applies this 'discursive selectivity'? For the interest of whom? Which is the state we are talking about? The cases we presented showed that the state is not unitary and independent, or the homogeneous and rational Weberian entity acting with direction and purpose, nor the totalities that it claims to be (Heyman 1999). Moreover, and particularly if we recognise the substantial multiplicity of states as state-spaces within a given national territory (Brenner, 2004), we also need to emphasise legality and illegality, formality and informality in their constant process of social and political construction and negotiation (see Rao, 2013). These dyads are historically and geographically determined, *and* politically constructed.

Interpretive hypothesis: The city as the space of negotiation of licit and illicit

All this considered, we might say that the particular system we are referring to is the city, and the capitalist city in particular, as the place for capital to reproduce itself (Lefebvre 1968, 1974; Harvey 1974, 1978, 1985; Harvey and Chatterjee 1974; Jessop 1983; Krätke, 2014). We might define the city as the space in which these relationships and interactions (between legality/illegality, formality/informality) are continuously redefined and shaped. Moreover, this means that the city is always produced through actions and behaviour that are licit and illicit, formal and informal and also legal and illegal. In this sense, we might also say that the city can be conceptualised as the space where these divides (between legal and illegal, etc.) are continuously negotiated (although tacitly); and that the result of these negotiations shapes a 'particular' city. In the case of Rome – which has a specific form of capitalism (Toscano 2002; Pagnotta 2009; Violante and Annunziata 2011), and where a particular urban regime has been recognised (d'Albergo and Moini 2015) – it emerges that informal, illicit and even illegal behaviours have been and still are structural components of the development model that the city pursued – with intentional goals, but also through spontaneous, involuntary behaviours and actions. This considered, the city results as the outcome and the expression of power relationships (hegemonic relationships, in Gramscian terms) where the political and economic elites predominate or prevail. Within the city, the state emerges not as a unitary, fully rational agent, and its power (the power it represents) does not necessarily derive from a rational, explicit fight among different actors and powers; on the contrary, it can derive from daily contrasts and 'tacit negotiations' between groups or individuals with different needs and goals, where the interaction of elements of structure *and* agency must be scrutinised. In any case, the city results as the outcome of conflict and antagonism, so *necessarily* the expression of hegemonic power. The state *states* what is legal and so establishes also what is not, according to a range of criteria, which include ethics and tradition/habit/custom, but is keen to tolerate some illegality, and specifically those forms of illegality which are more 'acceptable' (according to some groups), and mostly those that 'turn out' to be functional to preserve a certain system (the capitalist city). Nonetheless, we use the expression 'turn out' deliberately, to convey the idea that they may not be the result of a fully rational project. However, a long list of cases reported in the literature, as well as the examples we considered here, demonstrate that informality, but also illegality and illicitness as 'unwanted' outcomes, are not contrasted; on the contrary they are 'assumed' and 'used': a (perverse) sign of the 'intelligence of institutions'?

Conclusions

Our exploration, particularly through the empirical evidence from the examples provided, shows fundamental societal, economic and spatial impacts of illegality and illicitness. We followed two main lines of inquiry, which also emerge from the literature: one related to what can be called 'a geography of the illicit', the other to state theory. Our analysis convinced us that different geographies of illegality and illicitness exist, and are worth considering, but we recognise also that there are some shared features, and a similar logic, which associate countries of the Global North and of the Global South, and that, more than the 'places' where illegality or illicitness materialises, what counts are the 'conditions' under which they emerge. Thus the city becomes the outcome and the expression of hegemonic relationships in which the political and economic elites prevail, where what is illicit is stated, and what is informal, illicit or illegal is tolerated and exploited.

We follow Antonio Gramsci (1958, 1975) in framing the issue of the illegality and illicitness within state theory, and we consider the illicit, which exists just in mutual relation with the licit, as continuously redefined, according to the dominant (hegemonic) economic and political power. While illegality is often considered as a sign of state failure, and the helplessness of the state in preventing (or at least limiting) illegal behaviour is often strongly emphasised, its opaque relationships with the market are often undervalued. Illegal behaviours often represent not an alternative system, as the conceptualisation of illegal as insurgent argues. Rather they evolve as strictly intertwined with the system they pretend to overcome, interacting with it (even if unintentionally), creating conditions of benefits for the very few, which are not more just, but unjust in a different way, as even more hidden and opaque. From our examples, we derive that whereas 'illicit actors' perform important governance and development functions in some circumstances, more often they are unable to become developmentally progressive. They can have important material impacts, but these impacts are mostly useful for maintaining the status quo in socio-economic relationships, and through them, in the sphere of economic and political power.

Notes

1 Gregson and Crang (2016) have argued that this is mostly due to a disciplinary divide (geography and planning dealing with the legitimate – the legal and licit), and anthropology and criminology dealing with the illegitimate (the illegal and illicit).
2 This percentage demonstrates the 'intermediate' position of Rome in the geography of illegality concerning space and planning, between Global North and Global South, where the percentage can be much higher.
3 The middle classes we are referring to here are those employed in the tertiary sector, and into the public administration.
4 The illegal settlements we are considering here are those that resulted as still illegal at the mid of the 1990s.
5 In order to realise the works, through the fees and fines related to legalisation, they have to open a specific bank account instead of paying those sums to the municipality. This means that they can more directly manage the whole process. Nevertheless, these sums enter in a targeted budget, and the expenses have to be approved by the municipality

while approving the plans. The consortia are expected to realise the public works (primary infrastructure first) using that budget, and their implementation is a necessary precondition of any other transformation.

6 This discussion is based largely on the outcomes of fieldwork, including ethnographic approaches (reported in Cellamare 2016b), and a number of interviews conducted in the last two to three years with inhabitants, students of the local high-school, representatives of local associations, civil servants and representative of ATER, the public institution which owns and is in charge of maintain some of the public housing.

7 Despite public houses at Tor Bella Monaca belonging to the Municipality *and* to ATER (formerly IACP – Agency for public housing), it is just the municipality who is in charge of updating the lists of beneficiaries and assigning the houses.

8 As regards the illegal payments, it is interesting that public attention is usually concentrated on the people who ask for the money and not on the ones who pay. We could wonder if there is a substantial difference, and in what it consists, between other forms of corruption and that of getting advantage over others in obtaining accommodation through illegally paying a sum in order to enter public housing outside of the official allocation process.

References

Amis, P. 1984. Squatters or tenants? The commercialization of unauthorized housing in Nairobi. *World Development*, 12, pp. 87–96.

Beneria, L. and Feldman, S. (Eds). 1992. *Unequal Burden: Economic Crises, Persistent Poverty, and Women's Work*. Boulder, CO: Westview Press.

Berlinguer, G. and Della Seta, P. 1976. *Borgate di Roma*. Roma: Editori Riuniti.

Brenner, N. 2004. Urban governance and the production of new state spaces in Western Europe, 1960–2000. *Review of International Political Economy*, 11(3), 447–488.

Cellamare, C. (ed.) 2013. Roma, "Città fai-da-te"/Rome, "Self-Made Urbanism". *Urbanistica Tre*, 2.

Cellamare, C. (ed.) 2016a. *Fuori raccordo. Abitare l'altra Roma*. Roma: Donzelli.

Cellamare, C. (ed.) 2016b. Praticare l'interdisciplinarietà. Abitare a Tor Bella Monaca [Practicing interdisciplinarity. Living in Tor Bella Monaca]. *Territorio*, 78, pp. 26–92.

Chant, S. 1991. *Women and Survival in Mexican Cities: Perspectives on Gender, Labour Markets and Low-Income Households*. Manchester: Manchester University Press.

Clementi, A. and Perego, F. 1983. *La metropoli "spontanea"*. Bari: Dedalo.

Coppola, A. 2008. Le borgate romane tra '45 e '89. Esclusione sociale, movimenti urbani e poteri locali. In: Cremaschi M. (ed.). *Tracce di quartiere. Il legame sociale nella città che cambia*. Milano: Franco Angeli

Coppola, A. 2013. Vetero-liberismo di borgata. Urbanistica e attivazione degli abitanti nella 'Città da ristrutturare'. Il caso delle borgate Morena e Centroni. In: Centro per la Riforma dello Stato & Altramente – Scuola per tutti (ed.) *Le forme della periferia*. Roma: Rapporto finale di ricerca.

d'Albergo, E. and Moini, G. 2015. *Il regime dell'urbe. Politica, economia e potere a Roma*. Roma: Carocci.

Della Seta, P. 1988. *I suoli di Roma. Uso e abuso del territorio nei cento anni della capitale*. Roma: Editori Riuniti.

Di Pasquale C. 2012. April 29. I consorziati. Report. [Video file]. Retrieved from: http://www.report.rai.it/dl/Report/puntata/ContentItem-d6f864b8-ba06-43c3-b82d-e1b4a33e3efb.html.

Edwards, M. 1982. Cities of tenants: Renting among the urban poor in Latin America. In: Gilbert A. G. , Hardoy, J.E. and Ramirez, R. (eds.). *Urbanization in Contemporary Latin America*. New York: John Wiley & Sons, pp. 129–158.

Ferrarotti, F. 1970. *Roma da capitale a periferia*. Roma-Bari: Laterza.

Ferrarotti, F. 1974. *Vite di baraccati*. Napoli: Liguori.

Ferrarotti, F. 1981. *Vite di periferia*. Milano: Mondadori.

Fernandez-Kelly, P. and García, A. 1989. Informalization at the core: Hispanic women, homework, and the advanced capitalist state. In: Portes, A., Castells, M. and Benton, L. (Eds). *The Informal Economy: Studies in Advanced and Less Developed Countries*. Baltimore: Johns Hopkins University Press, pp. 247–264.

Fernandez-Kelly, P. and Shefner, J. (Eds.) 2006. *Out of the Shadows: Political Action and the Informal Economy in Latin America*. University Park, PA: Pennsylvania State University Press.

Fondazione Centro per la Riforma dello Stato. 2013. *Le forme della periferia*. (Final report). La periferia metropolitana come bene comune [Available at: http://www.centroriformastato.it/le-forme-della-periferia/].

Gilbert, A.G. 1983. The Tenants of self-help housing: Choice and constraint in the housing markets of less developed countries. *Development and Change*, 12, 449–477.

Gramsci, A. 1958. *Scritti giovanili*. 1914–1918. Torino: Einaudi.

Gramsci, A. 1975. *Quaderni dal Carcere*. 1929–1935. Torino: Einaudi.

Gregson, N., and Crang, M. 2016. Illicit economies: Customary illegality, moral economies and circulation. *Transactions of the Institute of British Geographers*, pp. 1–14 [doi: 10.1111/tran.12158].

Hagedorn, J.M. (Ed.) 2007. *Gangs in the global city: Alternatives to traditional criminology*. Urbana and Chicago: University of Illinois Press.

Harvey, D. 1985. *The Urbanization of the Capital: Studies in the History and Theory of Capitalist Urbanization*. Baltimore, MD: John Hopkins University Press.

Harvey, D. 1974. Class monopoly rent, finance, capital and urban revolution. *Regional Studies*, 8, (3–4), pp. 239–255.

Harvey, D. 1978. The urban process under capitalism. A framework for analysis. *International Journal of Urban and Regional Research*, 2(1–4), pp. 101–131.

Harvey, D. and Chatterjee, L. 1974. Absolute rent and structuring of space by governmental and financial institutions. *Antipode*, 6 (1), pp. 22–36.

Heyman, J.M. 1999. *States and Illegal Practices*. Oxford: Berg.

Hudson, R. 2014. Thinking through the relationships between legal and illegal activities and economies: Spaces, flows and pathways. *Journal of Economic Geography*, 14 (4), pp. 775–95.

Insolera, I. 1962. *Roma Moderna. Un secolo di Storia Urbanistica 1870–1970*. Torino: Einaudi [New edition revised: 2011 / English translation forthcoming].

Jessop, B. 1983. Accumulation strategies, state forms, and hegemonic projects. *Kapitalistate*, 10, pp. 89–111.

Krätke, S. (2014). Cities in contemporary capitalism. *International Journal of Urban and Regional Research*, *38*(5), 1660–1677.

Lefebvre, H. 1968. *Le droit à la ville*. Paris: Anthropos.

Lefebvre, H. 1974. *La production de l'espace*. Paris: Anthropos.

Mari, L. and Savelli F. 2016, October 21. Mansarde, ville e balconi: su Roma le mani dell'abusivismo edilizio. La Repubblica. Retrieved from: http://roma.repubblica.it/cronaca/2016/10/21/news/roma_abusi_edilizi-150311924/.

Meth, P. 2013. Unsettling insurgency. *Dialogues in Urban and Regional Planning*, 5, 70.

Miraftab, F. 2015. Situating radical planning in the Global South. *Readings in Planning Theory*, 480.Martinelli, F. (1986). *Roma nuova: borgate spontanee e insediamenti pubblici. Dalla marginalità alla domanda dei servizi.* Milano: Franco Angeli.

Moini, G. and Pizzo, B. 2017. Riding roughshod over people. Reading politics, economy and civil society in metropolization. A case study in Rome. In: T. Reilly (Ed.). *The Governance of Local Communities. Global Perspectives and Challenges*. New York: Nova Publ.

Pagnotta, M.G. 2009. *Roma industriale. Tra dopoguerra e miracolo economico*. Roma: Editori Riuniti.

Pizzo, B. and Di Salvo, G. 2015. Il nodo della rendita immobiliare. In: E. D'Albergo and G. Moini (Eds.). *Il regime dell'Urbe. Politica, economia e potere a Roma.* Roma: Carocci Ed.

Pizzo, B. and Montillo, F. 2016. Riscoprire progettualità e risorse latenti. In: Cellamare, C. *Praticare l'interdisciplinarietà. Abitare a Tor Bella Monaca.* Practicing interdisciplinarity. Living in Tor Bella Monaca. *Territorio*, 78, 85–92.

Portes, A., Castells, M. and Benton, L. (Eds.) 1989. *The Informal Economy: Studies in Advanced and Less Developed Countries*. Baltimore: Johns Hopkins University Press.

Putnam, R.D., Leonardi, R. and Nanetti, R.Y. 1994. *Making Democracy Work: Civic Traditions in Modern Italy*. Princeton University Press.

Rao, U. 2013. Tolerated encroachment: Resettlement policies and the negotiation of the licit/illicit divide in an Indian metropolis. *Cultural Anthropology*, 28(4), 760–779, American Anthropological Association.

Roy, A. 2009a. Strangely familiar: Planning and the worlds of insurgence and informality. *Planning Theory*, 8(1): 7–11.

Roy, A. 2009b. Why India cannot plan its cities: Informality, insurgence and the idiom of urbanization. *Planning Theory*, 8(1): 76–87.

Sandercock, L. 1995. Making the invisible visible: New historiographies for planning. *Planning Theory*, 13: 10–33.

Sandercock, L. 1998. Introduction: Framing insurgent historiographies for planning. In: Sandercock, L. (ed.). *Making the Invisible Visible: A Multicultural Planning History.* Berkeley: University of California Press, 1–33.

Sandercock, L. 1999. Introduction: Translations: from insurgent planning practices to radical planning discourses. *Plurimondi*, 1(2): 37–46.

S.M.U.R. – Self Made Urbanism Rome - Cellamare, C. (ed.) 2014. *Roma, città autoprodotta*. Roma: Manifestolibri.

Tocci, W. (2015). Non si piange su una città coloniale Note sulla politica romana. Available at: http://waltertocci.blogspot.it/2015/05/non-si-piange-su-una-citta-coloniale.html

Toscano, P. 2002. *Le origini del capitalismo industriale nel Lazio. Imprese e imprenditori a Roma dall'Unità alla Seconda Guerra Mondiale.* Cassino: Edizioni dell'Università degli Studi di Cassino

Transparency International Reports and Datasheets, available online at: http://www.transparency.org/cpi2014.

United Nations. 1987. The relationship between tenure legalization and housing improvement: Evidence from Mexico City. *Development and Change*, 18, 463–481.

USPR – Ufficio Speciale del Piano Regolatore, Comune di Roma. 1981. *Il recupero degli insediamenti abusivi*. USPR Documenti 1.

Violante, A. and Annunziata, S. 2011. *Rome-Model: Rising and Fall of an Hybrid Neo-liberal Paradigm in Southern Europe*, Paper presented at RC21 Conference, Amsterdam. Available at: http://www.rc21.org/conferences/amsterdam2011/edocs/Session%204/RT4-1-Violante.pdf.

11 Building legitimacy through the spatial aesthetics of the illicit

Non-state urban actors in post-3.11 Japan

Margrete Bjone Engelien, John Edom and Hannah Wood

Introduction: Rebuilding after disaster

This chapter examines how shared understandings of the licit and the illicit are built and rebuilt in Ishinomaki, Japan in the aftermath of the Great Tōhoku Earthquake and Tsunami of 11 March 2011 (hereafter referred to as 3.11). A city traumatised by disaster is a fragile environment, both in its capacity to provide for the basic material needs of its citizens, and as a stable, meaningful social space. This fragility opens space for – indeed necessitates – the emergence of actors that are able to move quickly to propose and enact processes for rebuilding the city within this provision gap. The role of such processes of urban reconfiguration are brought to the fore in the case of Ishinomaki.[1]

Ishinomaki is a small but sprawling coastal city in the Miyagi prefecture, located 42 kilometres northeast of Sendai, with a population of approximately 145,000. It suffered catastrophic damage and loss of life on 3.11 as one of the cities individually worst affected by the earthquake and tsunami, the epicentre of which was around 75 kilometres to its east off the Tōhoku coastline. 3,264 citizens lost their lives, while 452 remain missing, 50,758 people were displaced and 7,298 households required temporary housing provision. In total, 73 square kilometres of Ishinomaki Municipality were flooded, accounting for 30 percent of the city's densely built areas, and 56,701 buildings were destroyed or damaged (Ishinomaki municipal government figures, January 2016). Leng (2015) notes that 3.11 was the most expensive natural disaster on record, with overall costs surpassing US$210 – 300bn. The required scale of the post-3.11 clear-up, its visibility on a national and international scale, the financial resources directed towards it, and the delay in state remobilisation, opened a space for diverse non-state actors to become involved and define goals for reconstruction in Ishinomaki.

The community building organisation Ishinomaki 2.0 was instigated in May 2011, two months after the disaster. Ishinomaki 2.0 presents itself as a collaborative platform for the digital age, to which its name alludes; a non-hierarchical network made up of around ten core members, over half of whom are designers, architects, information technology professionals, entrepreneurs and other 'creatives' from around Japan. The remainder are local staff of non-profit organisations or self-employed people. Ishinomaki 2.0's representative director, Gota Matsumura, is a native of the city, and has a background in non-profit work.

According to figures provided by Ishinomaki 2.0, the scale of the damage in Ishinomaki attracted up to 280,000 volunteers – many working within non-state organisations – to assist in the clear-up effort during the year following the disaster alone. Debris was removed and basic infrastructure restored to working order relatively quickly, providing the opportunity for Ishinomaki 2.0 to begin to consolidate a vision for recovery and opening a space within which to redefine the city at an early juncture. The organisation was also brought on board by the municipal government to assist in reconstruction and urban planning.

Post-3.11 Ishinomaki provides a case study through which to examine how claims for legitimacy to act in the public interest are articulated through spatially inscribed notions of the licit and the illicit in Japan. Through a focus on the aesthetic characteristics of various reconstruction strategies, this chapter examines how transformations in urban space impact upon shared understandings of the licit and the illicit. It is argued that by remaking the city, and through the employment of spatial strategies that are positioned in relation to socially and spatially inscribed understandings of the licit and the illicit, the actors concerned also derive legitimacy to set an agenda for the city's future.

Following the theoretical framework set out by the editors in the introduction to this volume, we understand the licit and illicit to pertain to the acceptability and thus legitimacy of a particular act according to dominant social perceptions, customs and practices within a specific context. By extension, we understand definitions of licit and illicit to contain the potential for slippage between shared understandings of what constitutes acceptable and legitimate action across various interpretational frames of reference, what Appadurai (1990) calls 'ideoscapes'. As such, we argue that certain acts have projective potential that may test boundaries and activate grey zones, particularly when differently situated frameworks for legitimacy are brought to bear on a localised issue, as is the case when the rebuilding of a city in the aftermath of a natural disaster becomes a locus of local, regional, national and international attention and action. Indeed, it is argued that a devastating event such as 3.11 in itself produces fundamental shifts in how legitimacy is framed in the place affected by it. As will be elaborated, this projective potential attains particular force in the forum of the Japanese urban environment where various socially and legally defined discourses relating to legitimacy intersect.

However, in reference to the theoretical framework laid out in the introduction, while it may be the case in other contexts that illicit or illegal acts can be considered 'good' in view of their positive consequences, actions which, within certain perspectives, are legal, legitimate and licit must be critiqued when the result is the production of exclusionary outcomes: a negative consequence of acts that are considered licit. In order to construct this critique, we consider it relevant to focus on how legitimacy is built in relation to shifting notions of what constitutes licit and illicit, and changing categorisations of what is legal and illegal, in a specific context. This approach illuminates how certain actions have the potential to reframe what counts as licit and illicit through an aesthetic, spatial and social reconfiguration of the urban environment, as shall be argued in this case.

We find it instructive to situate these aesthetic and social processes within a broader Japanese social imaginary. We draw upon socially inscribed understandings of licit and illicit and trace how these concepts are understood in reference to shared urban space in Japan through the spatio-linguistic conceptual pair of *omote* and *ura* – translated as 'front' – or 'face' – and 'back', respectively. *Omote* and *ura* codify the licit and the illicit as spatial and aesthetic constructs and, vice versa, specific spaces and aesthetic qualities as licit or illicit. This approach provides a means to trace the correspondences between socially inscribed understandings of the licit and illicit as they intersect and overlap in Japanese urban space, and the question of the public interest in Japan that has historically been closely related to city planning through official and legally defined constructs.

The chapter will open with a discussion of the socio-spatial constructs of *omote* and *ura*, as concepts that inscribe notions of the licit and illicit in Japanese urban space, and of aesthetics as a means to theorise the relationship between the spatial construction of licit and illicit and the production of a community of shared values. The case of post-3.11 Ishinomaki shall then be examined. The emergence of Ishinomaki 2.0 as a legitimate urban actor is situated within the historical development of Japanese civil society, in particular as a response to natural disasters and other events that have impacted upon Japanese urban space, marking a trajectory whereby legislative moves to loosen state control and the assertive intervention of non-state actors have produced competing claims for legitimacy to define the public interest and resultant shifts in how the licit and illicit are framed within Japanese society. The chapter will close with a discussion around the broader implications of spatial strategies that negotiate shifting understandings of licit and illicit in order to legitimate claims to act in the public interest, and the impact that this has had in Ishinomaki.

Omote and *ura*

The spatio-social constructs of *omote* and *ura* demonstrate how notions of the licit and the illicit are produced both discursively and spatially in a Japanese context. These concepts have not received a great deal of attention, particularly within Western scholarship, but are discussed by Bachnik (1992), Bollonow (1963), Doi (1973, 1986), Johnson (1980), Kanazawa (2002), Till *et al.* (2011) and Tuan (1977). Doi (1973: 258) argues that the concepts of *omote* and *ura* represent a two-fold structure of consciousness that, though a universal human trait, is 'cultivated to an unusual extent in Japan so that it has become a definite pattern of living'.

Doi notes that in everyday linguistic and conscious use the two concepts occupy complementary ends of a sliding scale, the ability to shift appropriately between one and the other in a given context being a key aspect of personal integrity within Japanese society. For example, matters of *omote* (*omote no hanashi*) are what one does to impress those toward whom one is guarded, while matters of *ura* (*ura-no hanashi*) are the secrets that one will disclose only to those closest to him (ibid: 259). Kanazawa (2002) notes that these dialectical constructs are rooted in a social territorialisation of the city and a wider set of notions related to the public's experience of urban space. *Omote* is associated with attractiveness, busy, clean, modern and well-controlled areas, and encompasses typical typologies of bank, shop or government office that exhibit an open, outward looking face to the street, an urban imaginary that reflects Meiji restoration ideals and guides the layout of urban form through official planning authorities. Conversely, *ura* is associated with the shaded and hidden from view, complex urban typologies that characterise the back street: dark alleys, love hotels and, perhaps unsurprisingly, areas associated with illegal and illicit activity such as gambling, prostitution and criminality [e.g.: see Figure 11.1]. The paired concepts are used widely as prefixes to describe various aspects of the urban landscape, linking spatial typologies – for example *omote-dori*, the busy street, versus *ura-kaido*, the lonely alley – with socially inscribed positive and negative connotations (Doi 1973).

What is clear from Doi and Kanazawa's analysis is that the ascription of positive and negative values is ambiguous, requiring flexibility in its application by the individual depending on context. In this sense, while there is a correspondence between usages of each term in spatial and social contexts, the spatial use entails a greater degree of disambiguation in order to ensure intelligibility among the different actors that inhabit that space[2]. The regime of shared value inscribed within the Japanese urban environment and understood with reference to the concepts of *omote* and *ura*, thus, appear as more or less stable, even within a context of urban catastrophe. Indeed, it is argued that the spatialisation of these concepts becomes more visible in such a context. However, radical processes of destruction and reconstruction in an urban environment necessarily produce shifts in the ascription of value to specific spaces and built objects. In post-3.11 Ishinomaki, the destruction of a large proportion of the built urban fabric has increased the visibility of *ura*, in that previously hidden unadorned backs of buildings and complex narrow alleys have been exposed [e.g.: see Figure 11.2]. The removal of the

Figure 11.1 A shaded alleyway leading to inner courtyard in Higashimatsushima, a suburb of Ishinomaki.

Photo: H. Wood (2015).

Figure 11.2 An abandoned department store at the main intersection in the historic centre of Ishinomaki, the built gradient from public to a private exposed by the destruction of neighbouring buildings.

Photo H. Wood (2015).

omote face reveals the balance that is required in the pair: without *omote, ura* is no longer hidden and the illicit tends to become licit by the mere effect of visibility. Given that *omote* and *ura* refer both to urban objects with visible aesthetic and spatial qualities and to common values that frame understandings of licit and illicit, this spatial and conceptual rebalancing illustrates how interventions within the urban environment can produce shifts in shared value.

In examining how the licit and illicit are constructed spatially within Ishinomaki, we draw upon Rancière's theorisation of aesthetics (2000, 2006, 2010, 2011), which describes a framework of shared meaning from within which different forms of art derive recognition and significance, but in a broader sense, refers to what he calls the 'distribution of the sensible'. Rancière's theorisation of aesthetics pertains to what can be perceived in the world, its particular forms, and how these forms produce a community as a critical mode of articulation for distributing value and assigning positions among its constituents: it designates the community's members and, by extension, those who are excluded. Aesthetics produces shared understandings about what is do-able and say-able within a community and institutes a sense of the values that are shared by its members, thus providing a framework for identifying the licit and the illicit, and defining legitimacy to act in the community's interest. Rancière's conceptualisation of aesthetics may thus be deployed productively in the analysis of urban aesthetics and spatial design interventions: the means by which a community is produced through the distribution of the sensible within an urban environment. Aesthetic qualities, in this sense, are a means to identify shifts in the way the public interest is articulated and understood in an urban context, how this in turn delineates a regime of licit and illicit acts and, in doing so, produces and defines a community.

We suggest that the Japanese urban environment can be thus be seen as a repository of objects of shared value where spatial and aesthetic reconfiguration may provide the means to redistribute the values of the community. As Rancière notes:

> Statements or forms of expression undoubtedly depend on historically constituted systems of possibilities that determine forms of visibility or criteria of evaluation, but this does not mean that we jump from one system to another in such a way that the possibility of the new system coincides with the impossibility of the former system ... At a given point in time, several regimes coexist and intermingle in the works themselves.
>
> (2006: 50)

A focus on *omote* and *ura* provides a means to identify aesthetic and spatial interventions that reconfigure more or less durable associations between object and value. This is an active aesthetics which makes and remakes the city; one which displays and markets an internationally legible public 'face' and produces a shared set of political principles and values through its visual and material properties. The actors involved in the production of this urban aesthetic – whether present in the city or at a distance – are therefore also 'produced' as communities based on shared understandings of – and adherence to – the values implied by it. These actors form overlapping groupings and networks of action beyond direct government oversight, and which are not only delocalised but also operate across potentially contradictory frameworks of social legitimacy and prohibitive discourses. An already complex conception of the licit and the illicit as sites of disjuncture is further blurred by their insertion into ingrained hierarchical political structures present in Japanese society that have historically provided a relatively durable framework for public understandings of the licit and illicit, as well as the nebulous realm of globally networked digital media where shifts in legitimacy may be amplified and multiplied exponentially.

Furthermore, the site of disjuncture that characterises the aftermath of 3.11 in Ishinomaki coincides with a state of shock caused by the physical destruction of the built environment and a consequent removal of familiar aesthetic coordinates through which value was previously distributed. The role of 3.11 in reconfiguring the city, exposing its hidden *ura* spaces, has had the converse effect of foregrounding the work of polishing that has been invested in the street-face since the disaster. This *omote* face is produced, shared by, and thereby provides legitimacy for, a new community in the process of being produced itself, and a subsequent impetus for ongoing renewal of the city. Within this context, it is suggested that aesthetic strategies may operate as a *re*-distribution of the sensible, in so far as the margins for manoeuvre within these consecutive fields of meaning are far broader than would be the case under 'normal', well-defined urban conditions and frameworks of legitimacy. The 3.11 disaster provides a 'test' for this redistribution of the sensible, directly impacting the way legitimacy is articulated locally in the specific urban context of post-3.11 Ishinomaki. In this sense, it is clear that the specific geography and history of Ishinomaki impact upon how the licit and the illicit are understood locally, and begin to reveal the ways in which these categories are negotiated within space.

The case of Ishinomaki 2.0

The emergence of Ishinomaki 2.0 as an urban actor, and its claim to legitimacy to define a trajectory of recovery for the city, must be situated within a context of historical shifts in the relationship between the Japanese state and civil society, and competing claims to define the public interest in relation to urban space. The historical development of Japanese civil society, particularly in relation to urban planning and disaster response, has received attention from, among others, Haddad (2007), Hein and Pelletier (2006), Kawato *et al.* (2012), Pekkanen (2000, 2002, 2004), Pharr and Schwartz (2003), Sorensen (2002, 2006, 2007, 2009), Sorensen and Funck (2007) and Yamamoto (1999). Our understanding of civil society, which may be a problematic concept to transpose directly from its historically Western root, follows Leng (2015) who proposes 'a more inclusive framework for civil society in Japan that embraces a large number of social groups, organisations and movements as long as they meet minimal requirements of dual autonomy, have the potential for collective action, are non-usurpatory and are voluntary in nature.' This definition of Japanese civil society thus encompasses a range of voluntary groups: non-profit foundations, charities, non-profit organisations (NPOs) and non-governmental organisations (NGOs), including Ishinomaki 2.0.

Independent civil society was historically suppressed by the Japanese state which, in the interests of maintaining its own legitimacy to define the public interest, tended to frame such movements as acting upon selfish interests or in an anti-Japanese manner (Sorensen 2007). Traditionally, the Japanese government has thus been seen as the sole guardian of the public interest, a trend that can be traced to the etymological root of both 'government' and 'public' as *ko*, a conflation encouraged during the Meiji Restoration of 1868 onwards and which led to Japan being a 'public-equals-official' society (Yoshida 1998). Political power was unambiguously centralised and the Japanese state retained bureaucratic control over all aspects of decision making in relation to city planning – defined as the provision of basic infrastructure to facilitate economic growth for the public good – through the Home Ministry (*Naimu-shō*) (Sorensen 2007). Sorensen (2006, 2007) provides a detailed account of key developments in administrative processes of city planning that have led to changes in the relationship between the state and civil society, and traces consequent shifts in the ways that legitimacy to define the public interest is perceived and articulated within Japanese society.

Despite the emergence of civilian protest movements in the 1960s and 1970s in reaction to a series of environmental disasters triggered by largely unregulated post-war industrial development, a normative interpretation of civilian subservience vis-a-vis the authority of the Japanese state has persisted, even while a series of planning laws were introduced which allowed greater public engagement in urban development (Sorensen 2007). However, one significant outcome of the environmental protests was the *machizukuri* movement, a model for citizen-led initiatives focussed on local shared spaces, comprising small neighbourhood groups that would take decisions on matters concerning the community and liaise with local planning authorities to deliver improvements (ibid). The emergence of *machizukuri* – a compound verb derived from *machi* – community or neighbourhood – and *tsukuru* – to build – owes a good deal to 'American' ideals of community that have entered Japanese society as a corollary of civil society models adapted from other contexts (Bosman 2007). The *machizukuri* phenomenon is now so widespread and the term so flexibly applied that it is used to describe 'community building' practices as diverse as 'Government-sponsored road construction, citizen-led monitoring of municipal governance, the erection of apartment buildings by private developers, and even karaoke parties' (Watanabe 2006: 128).

The ambiguity of *machizukuri* enables groups engaged in 'community building', however broad the scope of activities to which the term can be applied, to influence and enact decisions relating to the urban environment and the public interest, and has been easily appropriated by hybrid organisational structures incorporating private and corporate interests, international humanitarian organisations and local Non-Profit Organisations (NPOs). The loose definition and organisational make-up of *machizukuri* groups is particularly visible in times of crisis, where the 'shock' generated by urban trauma temporarily disables central government, generating a novel platform that admits non-state actors through shifting frameworks of legality and the public interest. Activities oriented toward transformations in the urban environment, formerly considered illicit and classified as illegal activity due to a history of non-state groups' legal prohibition in Japan, may now be performed within a socially licit *machizukuri* framework. Indeed, *machizukuri* activities appear to derive even greater social legitimacy from the legal ambiguity entailed by the shift from illicit/illegal to licit/legal: there is a sense in which such activities retain an imperative of local necessity and informality against a persistent general tendency to entrust responsibility for matters pertaining to the public interest and shared living spaces to the Japanese state.

The most recent and important shift toward increased manoeuvrability for non-state actors in Japan was the introduction of the NPO Law of 1998. The law can be seen as the reaction of a government made to appear ineffective by the spontaneous response of citizen-led organisations in the aftermath of the 1995 Hanshin Awaji earthquake (Makoto 2003) and undermined by a series of corruption scandals that emerged during the 'zero growth period' following the 1990 Bubble Collapse. The 1998 Law sanctions the status of NPOs, the emergence of whom as an influential force in Japanese society coincided with an implicit critique of the state's effectiveness and the possibility of an alternative mode of formulating and enacting the public interest (Pekkanen 2002). The full effect of this legal reform was felt in the aftermath of 3.11 in Ishinomaki and neighbouring cities, as a series of further legislative adjustments and exceptions were introduced to facilitate NPOs in providing a swift response and allowing 499,300 volunteers to be registered and participate in the relief effort (Leng 2015; Avenell 2012). The NPO response to 3.11 was framed in an overwhelmingly positive light by the Japanese media, in contrast to the response of the state which was reported widely as being dogged by bureaucracy and delays (Leng 2015, Samuels 2013). The 3.11 disaster thus provided one of the first large-scale opportunities for civil society groups in Japan to engage in the urban landscape as legitimate actors and offered unprecedented possibilities for non-state actors to define and advance alternative spatial strategies relatively unchecked by official oversight. However, the influx of volunteers also brought its own logistical difficulties, with many lacking the appropriate registration, a place to stay or experience of volunteer work. Avenell (2012) also highlights the risk that this facilitated mobilisation had of rendering invisible or excluding other types of involvement, critical voices from within and critical oversight from without, a concern that is shared by the authors and will be elaborated below.

Ishinomaki 2.0 presents itself as a grassroots community building organisation that provides a specific response to the disaster's impact on the city. However, the disaster is also framed as an opportunity to address underlying issues that affected Ishinomaki pre-3.11: economic stagnation, an aging population, an inability to retain or attract younger residents and a consequent progressive depopulation of the city. Equally, Ishinomaki 2.0 articulates a desire to renew in terms of less tangible pre-3.11 negatives: lack of community, the 'closed-off nature' of the city, entrenched interests and conservative business structures. The organisation's mission statement is framed in opposition to these perceived failings as a desire to make the 'most interesting town in the world'; a place for people to express themselves freely, accommodating of diverse values, welcoming towards outsiders, not bound by conventional wisdom, creative, exciting and open (University of Michigan Center for Japanese Studies, 2015). As such, this regime of alternative shared values can be understood as evoking a newly defined register of licit, positive and desirable *omote* qualities in opposition to negative *ura* qualities associated with the city's past.

Events to projects to independent organisations

The post-3.11 socioeconomic context, characterised by a subtraction of the physical city and a subsequent influx of human and financial resources, in combination with the acquired freedom for non-state actors to set local development goals, has generated a number of aesthetic commonalities that are reflected in Ishinomaki 2.0's 'events to projects to independent organisations' model of activism: a focus on small scale temporary interventions [e.g.: see Figure 11.3] that are later developed into larger scale, more permanent projects run by subsidiary organisations, other Japanese NPOs and international NGOs, or as businesses, all as part of the emergent spatial aesthetics of the Ishinomaki 2.0 network. These interventions are characterised by explicit informality or degrees of ephemerality, creative, innovative and experimental solutions that depart visibly from traditional or official models, an emphasis on 'do-it-yourself' or 'doing more with less', implied phasing – whether ultimately implemented or not – and the deployment of the disaster as a sympathetic device through the extraction of material fragments of urban trauma from their context to be repositioned as marketable products. These

Figure 11.3 A weekend play event for local children, temporarily occupying streets usually reserved for traffic.

Photo: M. Bjone Engelien (2015).

qualities can be read in a broad range of architectural and other design interventions, and are sustained as core features throughout the transformation of a provisional and potentially illicit *ura* aesthetic into an *omote*, legitimate and durable urban fixture. Each of the independent community projects concurrently operates among other punctual interventions that, through Ishinomaki 2.0 as the 'mothership' (University of Michigan Center for Japanese Studies, 2016), are consolidated into a form of urban master plan and the creation of a coherent city brand.

As a network, Ishinomaki 2.0 is not easily delineated, and shares close ties with numerous other NPOs working in the city and other areas, local businesses, multi-national corporations such as Apple, Yahoo and the US furniture manufacturer Herman Miller, as well as playing a role in planning processes within the municipal government. This diffuse character is reflected in Irori, Ishinomaki 2.0's shared work-space headquarters, a converted parking garage on the high street of Ishinomaki's historic centre, designed by architect Ashizawa Keiji and furnished by the 'do- it-yourself' furniture manufacturer Ishinomaki Laboratory. The office has become a meeting place for the many incomers that have moved to Ishinomaki since the disaster, and it is thus difficult to identify whether those working there are directly involved with the organisation or not. The building also provides a highly visible demonstration of the values the organisation promotes, through the conversion of an *ura* typology into an *omote* symbol of openness, creativity and the drive to build something out of nothing [see Figure 11.4].

Another highly visible, yet small-scale and aesthetically informal spatial intervention in the city is the furniture of Ishinomaki Laboratory, one of Ishinomaki 2.0's independent organisations. Ishinomaki Laboratory was initiated shortly after 3.11 as a workshop for residents to build furniture to replace objects lost during the disaster, with tools and materials donated by the US furniture manufacturer Herman Miller. Ishinomaki Laboratory was incorporated as a for-profit business in 2013 and now manufacturers and distributes a range of furniture initially designed to meet immediate need following 3.11. The Ishinomaki bench, for example [see Figure 11.5], was produced in order to provide seating for an outdoor Friday cinema in a vacant lot, with films projected onto an exposed party wall. As a representative of Ishinomaki 2.0 explains: 'If this had been organised by government or big NGO, this wouldn't have been allowed, because [there was] a big collapsing building not so far from where we were having this event. But we had some volunteers who were standing around that area so that people wouldn't go into that area. This was shortly after the disaster, so we needed to have some event where people can gather and kids can smile' (University of Michigan Center

Figure 11.4 Irori, Ishinomaki 2.0's shared work-space headquarters.

Photo: J. Edom (2015).

Figure 11.5 Ishinomaki Laboratory benches on Nakaze Island, Ishinomaki.

Photo: J. Edom (2015).

for Japanese Studies, 2015). Legitimacy to act in the public interest through a creative, community oriented, but potentially illicit intervention is thus invoked in opposition to the expected actions of the bureaucratic state or a more formalised non-state entity.

The furniture itself explicitly references the *ura* aesthetic qualities of the unpolished, hand-made and make-shift in objects that would usually remain hidden inside the house, in an enclosed yard or used for occupation of space in a back-street, temporarily extending the private and hidden spaces of the domestic realm outside. The furniture's distribution throughout Ishinomaki, prominent use for specific public events, placement in the fronts of shops on the main street, and marketing and distribution as a branded item both in Japan and internationally, illustrates the conversion of this *ura* aesthetic into a desirable *omote* quality that occupies a visible position in the city's public spaces and beyond. However, it is argued that illicit, undesirable and *ura* conditions that characterised the aftermath of 3.11, and which the furniture was initially produced to ameliorate, continue to define the everyday experience of many of the disaster's victims. The experience of victimhood – and the disaster itself – is thus deployed as an aesthetic quality and converted by a specific grouping of actors into a product that demonstrates a positive *omote*, sympathetic and consumable image. The furniture is marketed as being emblematic of the city's urban, social and economic renewal, but offers few tangible benefits to victims of the disaster among the broader population.

Ishinomaki Real Estate

A further example of an 'event to project to independent organisation' is Ishinomaki 2.0 Real Estate, a project initiated in order to secure accommodation in the city for volunteers. During the initial clean-up operation, vacant accommodation in the upper rooms of businesses and re-purposed offices was used to house volunteers in dormitory style conditions. However, as this stage was completed, accommodation for new residents who wished to initiate or contribute to ongoing renewal projects became a key focus. Ishinomaki 2.0 frames the need for innovative housing solutions against what is described as an obstructive government policy of prioritising accommodation for displaced residents, requiring the introduction of 'the concept of AirBnB' (University of Michigan Center for Japanese Studies, 2015) as creative, networked and flexible, but potentially unsanctioned and illicit, alternative means to secure space in the city. Ishinomaki 2.0 Real Estate provides a formalised business structure to negotiate rental agreements with property owners, and renovate apartments 'DIY style' into unconventional living arrangements such as shared housing.

Collective forms of habitation are increasing in popularity among the younger generation in Japan, though this has not traditionally been desirable, particularly outside of the major metropolitan centres and with the older generation (Hildner 2013). The accommodation offered for rent by Ishinomaki 2.0 Real Estate is thus designed to appeal to a specific demographic, and due to the relatively small-scale potential of the operation, demand, and subdivision to achieve collectivity, entail that rents up to six times the amount projected by the property owner may be generated (University of Michigan Center for Japanese Studies 2015). In her study on post-3.11 Ishinomaki, Klein (2016) discusses how young newcomers are often motivated to relocate to the city as a reaction to Japan's 'post-growth' structural labour market insecurity, in search of opportunities to engage in networked leisure and work-based activities associated with better qualities of life as an alternative to more conventional forms of tenured company employment. The benefit of attracting young people to move to the city is made very explicit by Ishinomaki 2.0: 'These young people who come to the city, they are pretty cool, so when they start living in these places, the place itself becomes cool' (University of Michigan Center for Japanese Studies, 2015). The visualisation of an unconventional business model through the aesthetic and spatial qualities of the accommodation thus provides a direct means to upgrade the city by attracting a specific social group that encompasses and therefore amplifies those values. The values promoted in this aesthetic vision for the future, as well as a reaction to perceived negative aspects of the city pre-3.11, provide a visible break with a broader set of negative connotations associated with the corruption, bureaucracy and strict hierarchy of the 'official' system revealed by the political crises of the 1990s and the Hanshin Awaji Earthquake. Within this formula, the 'community' becomes the legitimate figure for defining the public interest, tracing a continuity with the *machizukuri* movement, as well as resonating with familiar Western discourses of grassroots activism and community engagement. However, an aesthetics of urban space that is designed and marketed to attract a specific 'value' of population, destined to inhabit the city and form its community, also necessarily excludes others.

The exclusionary aesthetics of licit and illicit

Ishinomaki 2.0 occupies a particularly visible position, not only within Ishinomaki itself but among the diverse initiatives and organisations involved in processes of reconstruction in the broader context of the Tōhoku region, and is often cited as providing an exemplary model for grassroots urban recovery.[3] A key reason for this wide recognition is the emphasis that Ishinomaki 2.0 places upon communication. The organisation maintains a strong social media presence, distributes graphically sophisticated publicity and reporting materials, often in English in addition to Japanese, develops signature products and organises a wide range of initiatives designed to attract attention across a range of scales. These include activities for young people in the area, a radio station to broadcast local stories, efforts to attract investment from individuals in other parts of Japan and collaboration from international non-government organisations and multinational corporations. This intensive communication is part of an aesthetic strategy that signals transparency and capability, an extremely visible distribution of the sensible that sets the parameters for recovery in the city and coalesces and legitimises a community of shared values. This community is thus not confined to Ishinomaki as a geographically delimited entity, even while the physical urban environment of the city provides its focal point. As Klein (2016) notes, many of Ishinomaki 2.0's events are designed primarily to attract participants in Tokyo and are announced to local residents at short notice or not at all.

Non-state organisations and civil society groups can be seen as an effective means to gather broad coalitions around a specific issue, involving diverse actors and facilitating collaboration between multiple fields of expertise, across different regions or even national territories. However, when this non-geographically constrained organisational potential is applied to a specifically local issue, in this case the future vision for the urban and economic development of a small provincial city in the aftermath of a disaster, the priorities of the existing residents – no longer a central or even necessary driving force for the movement – risk being marginalised.

The example of Ishinomaki can be read within globalised cultural and aesthetic shifts in the articulation of 'community', the role of civil society and the increasing agency of the private sector to define urban development. In Japan this coincides with a progressive – though relatively recent – 'opening up' to international actors and resources, propelled in part by severe instances of urban trauma. 3.11 has increased the visibility of Ishinomaki, both domestically and internationally, as the object of a range of discourses relating to recovery and renewal, widely distributed sympathy and broad networks of aesthetic and financial resources, as well as impacting upon the ways that city spaces are used and what kinds of social practices are considered licit or otherwise. Ishinomaki's aesthetic and social rebuilding processes are recognisable as part of a current trend of creative 'community' movements whose emergence has been well documented in many urban areas around the world, highlighting concerns about their exclusionary outcomes.

Urban interventions that are spatially and aesthetically differentiated from 'official,' bureaucratic forms and processes, and derive logic from the broader social contexts within which they appear, may build legitimacy for the actors that deploy them among a broad public in Japan and further afield. International observers may recognise in these aesthetics a globally legitimised urban planning tool, and further evidence of the healthy development of a Japanese civil society towards a participatory model which can actively engage in local communities. For observing actors from across the wider field of Japan's broader political and economic spheres, this development may be interpreted as a demonstration of innovative social practices supporting new economic models for the revival of a city hereto in decline. For local residents – even those that do not benefit directly – it may be interpreted as resistance to conventional and demonstratively ineffective models of governance through the creation of an active community that holds its fate in its own hands. While dissenting views on some aspects of the implementation of this form of urban recovery are present, the severity of the disaster provides an imperative that is hard to argue against: something must be done, even if the results are not entirely positive. This is thus an aesthetics that is subject to interpretive slippage and a multiplication of creative energy through ambiguity.

However, the elaboration of an aesthetics of 'public-equals-unofficial', in a departure from a normative Japanese discourse of 'public-equals-official', may – upon further analysis – be illusory if the Japanese state's active encouragement of a civil society is read as an adaptive consolidation of authority by other means. Indeed, it is worth noting that the activities of the non-state actors described here take place in an urban context where state or official mechanisms operate in parallel. Large scale infrastructural investment in housing, sea defences and relocation of entire villages throughout the affected Tōhoku region provide evidence of the government's efforts to be visibly active, even while the effectiveness, scope and timescale of these interventions are the subject of ongoing debate within Japanese society and continue to be enacted through opaque commissioning processes. The main effect of the ambiguity entailed by an apparent shift in legitimacy to define the public interest – from government to non-state actors – seems to be the impact on those sections of Ishinomaki's population whose interests as a public are no longer clearly represented or taken into consideration: to an extent, both government and non-state groups expunge responsibility by sustaining the false binary that appears to separate them.[4]

While the deployment of an aesthetic of shared value as a means to build a community in relation to a specific urban space, and legitimise unconventional spatial strategies, may produce measurably positive local outcomes for a city recovering from disaster, it is argued that in Ishinomaki it also generates – whether intentionally or otherwise – a form of exclusion relatively free from official oversight or accountability.

Evocations of 'community' become shorthand for a regime of values that define what the community *is*, and conversely, what it is not. Sandercock (1997: 190–1), suggests that such evocations often rely on historically constituted models that define community 'uncritically as the sole repository of virtue—of meaningful social relationships, of human scale, of wholesome (non-market) values—vis-a-vis the (oppressive) state or the (rapacious) market.' Bosman (2007: 318) suggests that definitions of 'community' that relate to historically derived discourses imply that 'it is linked with 'truths' rather than politics and regulation—hence it becomes an effective means of harnessing the population and normalising conduct.' Indeed, appeals to a specific conception of community that emphasises collective sacrifice and consensus were mobilised explicitly by various levels of the Japanese government in the aftermath of 3.11 (Samuels, 2013).

In the case of Ishinomaki 2.0, the push toward a specific social and economic future at times appears to supersede or make invisible the visions of former or current inhabitants who may be de-legitimised as stakeholders deserving a voice in the reconstruction of the city, their concerns dismissed as representative of the old conservative order. The choice offered to the older generation or former residents who remain in emergency accommodation is to participate positively – or at least uncritically – in a movement that is presented as forward thinking and open to all, or to remain on the sidelines. Many residents displaced after 3.11, having lost their homes and businesses, lack the means to secure accommodation and work that would allow them to return to Ishinomaki from emergency 'temporary' housing complexes rapidly deteriorating five years on from the disaster. Their complaints about poor living conditions expressed during community meetings may easily be dismissed as conservative unwillingness to become involved in the community and contribute positively to renewal, selfishness or even laziness (Gota Matsumura, co-founder and representative director of Ishinomaki 2.0, personal communication, 16 October 2015). Indeed, given that shifts in spatially inscribed understandings of licit and illicit are inscribed in Japanese urban form as *omote* and *ura*, impacting upon how legitimacy to define the public interest is articulated, and community created, they may be difficult for former residents to register and resist, or – conversely – to align with by engaging in activities that would allow them access to that community as it is now defined.

The physical transformation of urban space and redistribution of the sensible through the development of an aesthetic that makes collectively tangible a set of shared associated values thus has a tendency to characterise a specific regime of others that fall outside this new framework for the licit: in effect, these others are redefined as illicit. In this case, an aesthetic re-framing of the licit and the illicit as ambiguous aspects of the urban environment, also serves to naturalise a situation in which former residents of the city disenfranchised by 3.11 are no longer included in the community, their concerns re-cast as illicit against the new aesthetic of the licit.

The approach employed here privileges the ways in which the licit and the illicit are produced spatially, rather than taking the effects of illicit activity on a specific space as a starting point. It is argued that instances of urban upheaval – which may include, but are not limited to, natural disasters – and the processes of reordering that take place in the effort to return to or establish new shared aesthetic and spatial coordinates, may provide further productive cases for analysis of the role of illicit in the governance and development of cities.

Conclusion

Instances of urban trauma, such as the devastation wrought by a natural disaster, reveal the solid and implicit as fragile and mutable, and may expose to view the spatially inscribed foundation for understandings of the licit and the illicit in a specific context. The physical destruction of Ishinomaki on 3.11 opened a space from which the state has largely withdrawn, offering the space – physical and legislative – for non-state actors to intervene. As has been discussed, these actors have been afforded the legitimacy to redefine certain areas of the city both physically and socially through the use of urban space for specific activities, the encouragement of new populations to appropriate the city and the greater influence of these actors in 'official' planning and decision-making processes.

The foregrounding of 'informal' spatial interventions that refer to an *ura*, informal, non-official, temporary, and improvised aesthetic, and then undergo a transformative processes of formalisation, gaining visibility and permanence, before finally becoming legitimate *omote* urban interventions that are situated visibly as part of a broader occupation of urban space, can be seen as an aesthetic mode that redistributes the sensible. This potentially illicit aesthetic, in the shift between *ura* and *omote*, derives intelligibility and legitimacy, becoming licit, through a reconfiguration of urban space as an imperative of the post-disaster context, through broader shifts in the way these concepts – and actions associated with them – are articulated in Japanese society, and through the deployment of an aesthetic that is identifiable within an international arena of grassroots community building and humanitarian action. The post-disaster context has fundamentally altered how the city is inhabited and understood. In a sense, the rebuilt urban environment concretises a set of 'truths' about the new community that are as solid and indisputable as the objects that evidence them, but these must be problematised when they result in instances of exclusion.

Notes

1 The research outlined in this paper is based on fieldwork conducted by the authors in Ishinomaki and the wider Tōhoku region during September and October 2015. Field research was largely qualitative, with data collection based on personal photographic records, surveying and mapping of the city's urban fabric and its uses, informal interviews, textual analysis of a large but non-exhaustive collection of printed communication material retrieved from a number of key actors in Ishinomaki, including Japanese NPOs, international and domestic NGOs and the local government planning department, online resources such as websites and recordings of lectures, archival research in Sendai and personal observation. As a reflection of the primary means of communication employed by the internationally oriented organisations under discussion, close attention was also paid to a number of online resources (cited in the bibliography).

2 Klein (2016) in her discussion on the alternative lifestyles being enacted in post-3.11 Ishinomaki notes the emphasis on collapsing conventional Japanese ideals of a strict separation between work and leisure, for a more 'relaxed' nomadic attitude to work. Though we are not able to expand on it here, this trend would appear to have consequences for how attitudes towards public and private activities are shaped and, thus, the meanings associated with urban space and its reconfiguration.

3 For example, 'Editorial: Give priority to putting disaster victims' lives back in order', *The Mainichi*, 09 March 2016; *The Lonely Planet* (2012) 'Tōhoku and Northern Honshu, Supplementary chapter', Lonely Planet Publications.

4 Though we are unable to develop the idea here, this dynamic may also be read as a variation on a state of exception (after Agamben, 2005), whereby a crisis provides the state with an opportunity, rather than consolidating power directly, to divest itself of responsibility through its symbolic delegation.

References

Agamben, G. 2005. *State of Exception*. Chicago: University of Chicago Press.

Appadurai, A. 1990. Disjuncture and difference in the global cultural economy. *Theory, Culture, Society*, 7 (2): 295–310.

Avenell, S. 2012. From Kobe to Tōhoku: The potential and the peril of a volunteer infrastructure. In Kingston, J. (ed.) *Natural Disaster and Nuclear crisis in Japan: response and recovery after Japan's 3/11*. London: Routledge, pp. 53–77.

Bachnik, J.M. 1992. The two "faces" of self and society in Japan. *Ethos*, 20 (1): 3–32.

Bollonow, O.F. 1963. *Human Space*, trans. Shuttleworth. C. 2011. London: Hyphen Press.

Bosman, C. 2007. Building community places—Machizukuri—neoliberalism, suburbanisation and 'Americanisation'. *International Planning Studies*, 12 (4): 309–325.

Doi, T. 1973. Omote and ura: Concepts derived from the Japanese two-fold structure of consciousness. *Journal of Nervous and Mental Disease*, 157 (4): 258–261.

Doi, T. 1986. *The Anatomy of Self: The Individual Versus Society*. Tokyo: Kodansha International.

Haddad, M.A. 2007. *Politics and Volunteering in Japan: A Global Perspective*. New York: Cambridge University Press.

Hein, C. and Pelletier, P. eds. 2006. *Cities, Autonomy, and Decentralization in Japan*. London: Routledge.

Hildner, C. 2013. *Future Living: Collective Housing in Japan*. Basel: Birkhauser Verlag AG.

Johnson, C. 1980. Omote (explicit) and ura (implicit): Translating Japanese political terms. *The Journal of Japanese Studies*, 6 (1): 89–115.

Kanazawa, S. 2002. Cognition of front and back in urban space and the correlation with urban structure: Downtown area of a Japanese City, Saga. *Journal of Asian Architecture and Building Engineering*, 1 (2): 201–208.

Kawato, Y., Pekkanen, R. and Yutaka, T. 2012. Civil society and the triple disasters: Revealed strengths and weaknesses. In Kingston, J. (ed.) *Natural Disaster and Nuclear Crisis in Japan: Response and Recovery after Japan's 3/11*. London: Routledge.

Klein, S. 2016. Reinventing Ishinomaki, reinventing Japan? Creative networks, alternative lifestyles and the search for quality of life in post-growth Japan. *Japanese Studies*, 36 (1): 39–60.

Leng, R. 2015. Japan's civil society from Kobe to Tōhoku: Impact of policy changes on government-NGO relationship and effectiveness of post-disaster relief. *Electronic Journal of Contemporary Japanese Studies*, 15 (1) (accessed at: http://www.japanesestudies.org.uk/ejcjs/vol15/iss1/index.html 07/12/2016).

Makoto, I. 2003. The voluntary response to the Hanshin Awaji Earthquake: A trigger for the development of the voluntary and non-profit sector in Japan. In Osborne, S. (ed.) *The Voluntary and Non-Profit Sector in Japan: The Challenge of Change*, London: Routledge, pp. 40–50.

Pekkanen, R. 2000. Japan's new politics: The case of the NPO law. *Journal of Japanese Studies*, 26 (1): 111–143.

Pekkanen, R. 2002. The politics of regulating the non-profit sector. In Osborne, S. (ed.) *The Voluntary and Non-Profit Sector in Japan: The Challenge of Change*. London: Routledge, pp. 53–75.

Pekkanen, R. 2004. Japan: Social capital without advocacy. In Alagappa, M. (ed.) *Civil Society and Political Change in Asia: Expanding and Contracting Democratic Space*. Stanford, CA: Stanford University Press, pp. 223–255.

Pekkanen, R. and Simon, K. 2002. The legal framework for voluntary and non-profit activity. In Osborne, S. (ed.) *The Voluntary and Non-Profit Sector in Japan: The Challenge of Change*. London: Routledge, pp. 76–101.

Pharr, S. and Schwartz, F. 2003. *The State of Civil Society in Japan*. Cambridge: Cambridge University Press.

Rancière, J. 2000. What aesthetics can mean. In Osborne, P. (ed.) *From an Aesthetic Point of View: Philosophy, Art and the Senses*. London: The Serpent's Tail, pp. 13–33.

Rancière, J. 2006. *The Politics of Aesthetics: The Distribution of the Sensible*, trans. from French by Rockhill, G. London: Continuum.

Rancière, J. 2010. *Dissensus: On Politics and Aesthetics*, trans. from French by Corcoran, S. London: Bloomsbury.

Rancière, J. 2011. The thinking of dissensus: Politics and aesthetics. In Bowman, P. and Stamp, R. (eds.) *Reading Rancière*, London: Continuum, pp. 1–17.

Samuels, R.J. 2013. *3.11: Disaster and Change in Japan*. Ithaca: Cornell University Press.

Sandercock, L. 1997. *Towards Cosmopolis: Planning for Multicultural Cities*. Hoboken: John Wiley.

Sorensen, A. 2002. *The Making of Urban Japan, Cities and Planning from Edo to the Twenty-First Century*. London: Routledge.
Sorensen, A. 2006. Centralization, urban planning governance, and citizen participation in Japan. In Hein, C. and Pelletier, P. (eds.) *Cities, Autonomy, and Decentralization in Japan*, London, New York: Routledge, pp. 101–127.
Sorensen, A. 2007. Changing governance of shared spaces: Machizukuri as institutional innovation. In Sorensen, A. and Funck, C. (eds.) *Living Cities in Japan: Citizens' Movements, Machizukuri and Local Environments*, London: Routledge.
Sorensen, A. and Funck, C. eds. 2007. *Living Cities in Japan: Citizens' Movements, Machizukuri and Local Environments*. London: Routledge.
Till, J., Awan, N. and Schneider, T. 2011. *Spatial Agency: Other Ways of Doing Architecture*. London: Routledge.
Tuan. Y. 1977. *Space and Place: The Perspective of Experience*. Minneapolis: University of Minnesota Press.
Yamamoto, T. (ed.) 1999. *Deciding the Public Good: Governance and Civil Society in Japan*. Tokyo: Japan Centre for International Exchange.
Yoshida, S. 1998. Rethinking the public interest in Japan. In Yamamoto, T. (ed.) *Deciding the Public Good: Governance and Civil Society in Japan*. Washington: Brookings Institution, pp. 140–145.
Watanabe, S.J. 2006. Machizukuri in Japan. In C. Hein and P. Pelletier (eds.) *Cities, Autonomy and Decentralization in Japan*. London: Routledge, pp. 128–138.

Other resources

Anonymous. 2016. Editorial: Give priority to putting disaster victims' lives back in order. *The Mainichi*, 09 March 2016 (accessed at: http://mainichi.jp/english/articles/20160309/p2a/00m/0na/012000c, 05/12/2016).
'*Creating the Most Interesting Town in the World*,' video of lecture by Matsumura, G., 22 October 2015, published by University of Michigan Centre for Japanese Studies, (accessed at https://www.youtube.com/watch?v=c2xm8jEZEK8, 22/08/2016).
Ishinomaki City, Japan: A Case Study of Community Revitalization in the Post-Industrial Era, video of lecture by Iwai, S. and Matsuzaki, B., 28 January 2016, published by University of Michigan Centre for Japanese Studies, (accessed at: https://www.youtube.com/watch?v=WbSBXgJXdI4, 22/08/2016).
Lonely Planet, 2012. *Tōhoku and Northern Honshu, Supplementary chapter*, Lonely Planet Publications, (accessed at: http://www.lonelyplanet.com/blog/2012/11/20/free-download-lonely-planets-new-northern-honshu-tohoku-chapter/, 05/12/2016).

12 The corruption of politics or the politics of corruption? Reconsidering the role of organised crime in the geo-politics of corruption

Sue Penna and Martin O'Brien

Introduction

> Too often in the policy debate, however, corruption has been seen as a generic problem. Its deeper origins, the ways it is embedded in political and economic processes, and its role as a symptom of diverse and problematical relationships between wealth and power, public and private interests, and state and society, are acknowledged but only poorly understood in depth.
>
> (Johnson, 2005: 14)

Corruption is a slippery subject to research. The activities that might be considered corrupt are many and varied, and frequently clandestine, making definition and measurement imprecise, and rendering the subject matter elusive as an object of study (Johnston, 2005; Fletcher and Herrmann, 2016; Jancsics and Jávor, 2012). Notwithstanding such difficulties, corruption became established as an international social and economic problem nearly two decades ago, leading to the United Nations Convention Against Corruption (UNCAC) in 2003. The UNCAC marked a significant attempt to develop a 'global regulatory regime' (Getz, 2006) that could tackle corruption: it is the first legally binding international instrument, and a protocol to the United Nations Convention Against Transnational Organised Crime (2000).

Reflecting concerns about the relationships between corruption, organised crime, money-laundering, the financing of terrorist activity, and sustainable development in developing or transitional States (UNODC, 2004: 5), the UNCAC is a far-reaching instrument, dealing with forms of corruption that had not been covered by earlier conventions. It obliges signatory States to implement a wide and detailed range of anti-corruption measures that aim to promote prevention, criminalisation and law enforcement, international cooperation, asset recovery, technical assistance and information exchange, and mechanisms for the implementation of these measures. Getz (2006: 256) characterises the anti-corruption regime that develops as a prohibition regime, criminalising illicit and informal economic transactions that are on the edge of legality, by utilising both 'soft' (quasi-legal international instruments containing statements of principles, norms, standards, aimed at changing behaviours), and 'hard' law (legal instruments carrying obligation). The concerns laid out in the UNCAC specify the harms wrought upon political and economic development. Corruption and bribery – with the emphasis primarily on bribery – are said to fuel poverty, impede economic development, and produce negative consequences for individual citizens and populations, from not being able to afford to pay bribes to send a child to school, or have a crime investigated, to the awarding of contracts for sub-standard construction projects, such as bridges that then collapse. These moral and practical problems lead the UNCAC (2004: 2) to express concern 'about the seriousness of problems and threats posed by corruption to the stability and security of societies, undermining the institutions and values of democracy, ethical values and justice and jeopardizing sustainable development and the rule of law'. Johnson (2005: 1) points out that corruption here is seen as consisting essentially of bribery, varying only in degree across societies, and reform as the process of making developing societies more like the West.

The extensive, albeit fragmented, literature on corruption points to the different manifestations of corruption in different parts of the world, raising many problems for scholars. Not only is much of the activity hidden from view, but where research has been carried out, it is by researchers from different disciplines, with different agendas, making comparison between regions difficult: for example, different forms and practices of corruption have been presented in statistical indexes, different cultural perceptions of business practices have been noted, and different power relationships in different economies and places have been analysed (c.f., Findlay, 2008; Getz and Volkema, 2001; Graycar and Monahan, 2015). In this chapter our analysis has been derived from consideration of four conceptual models.

First is the concept of 'syndromes' of corruption developed by Johnston (2005), which proposes that the factors that influence corruption – understood as the way people pursue, use, and exchange wealth and power – within any society, reflect stages of economic and political development. Johnston identifies four ideal-typical corruption syndromes that he argues are shaped by a), the degree of democratic and economic participation within a society and b), the stability of institutions guaranteeing political rights, civil liberties, and the rule of law. Johnson's inclusion of corruption within advanced as well as developing societies highlights the fact that corruption can, and does, occur within affluent, established, liberal democracies, and that the forms of corruption found in these societies, together with their dominant conceptions of reform, have done much 'to shape the difficulties and opportunities facing developing societies' (Johnson, 2005: 3). This observation alerts us to the relationship between developed and developing countries, which we consider later in this chapter. Locating corruption in the long-term development processes and political-economic dynamics of a particular society also emphasises the specificity of context and location.

Second, while Johnson's work method has a developmental and processual focus, Graycar and Monaghan's (2015) classification of corruption events – by type, activity, sector, and place (TASP) – provides an analytical model that recognises corruption in mature democracies as 'bribery, extortion, misappropriation, self-dealing, conflict of interest, abuse of discretion, patronage, nepotism, cronyism, trading in influence, and "pay to play"'(Graycar and Monaham, 2015: 587). This was particularly useful in identifying and analysing forms of corruption in New Jersey, where later we consider Johnson's view of 'Influence Market' corruption, the type of corruption associated with mature democracies, involving '… efforts on the part of private interests to rent access and influence within well-institutionalised policy processes, often through political figures acting as middlemen' (Johnston, 2005: 3). Graycar and Monahan (ibid.) draw attention to how this might be achieved: 'Some potential *activities* are appointing personnel, buying things (procurement), delivering programs or services, making things, controlling activities, and administering.' The model also indicates where the activities are likely to occur, naming '… main government and industry sectors, such as construction, health, tax administration, customs and immigration, welfare systems, and agriculture, among others.' They further specify that places can be geographical localities such as countries, regions and workplaces.

Third is the importance of social networks to the events Greycar and Monahan highlight. Social network analysis has provided criminologists with new insights about the social connections that link sets of actors (Coles, 2001). Investigators will usually look for two kinds of patterns: one is the collections of actors who are closely linked to one another; the other is the social positions of sets of actors who are linked in the network (Freeman, 2006). Of interest is the activities of key individuals, what determines their participation in a network, and how network connections endure and reform. Network analysis has been used fruitfully by many working in the field of crime, such as Arias (2006) in his examination of the ongoing problems of crime and corruption in Rio de Janeiro, where NGO representatives and government officials have often forged deals with criminal networks, and Fröhlich's (2003) study of environmental crime which identified numerous networks, with those of the highest sophistication consisting of corrupt game wardens, customs officers, wildlife officers, and transnational networks of purchasers, couriers, and wholesalers. From these and other studies, we see that networks offer a flexibility that enables them to tap into opportunities and adapt effectively to potential risk and changing circumstances.

Last, is the importance of 'opportunity factors' in an analysis of corruption events. This concept is highlighted in criminology by those working within a field known as 'Routine Activity Theory', where there is a focus on the situations in which crimes occur, emphasising that opportunities to commit crime are often found in the usual rhythms of everyday life. For a crime to occur, three factors need to come together in an environment. First there must be a motivated offender, an individual who is not only capable of a committing criminal activity, but is willing to do so. Secondly, there must be a suitable target, a person or object that is seen by the offender as vulnerable or particularly attractive. Thirdly, there must be a lack of a 'guardian', a person or factor that prevents the opportunity from being seized by the offender. Thus, the factors that render a particular target attractive are situational and crime specific. In this view, crime can be committed by anyone that has the opportunity, and understanding changing 'crime-potential contexts' involves understanding criminal opportunities as processes, influenced by factors such as friendship networks, socioeconomic conditions and how cooperation between offenders is enacted (Kirby and Penna, 2010).

Together, these four frameworks point us to a focus on the relationships between actors in different societies, both in terms of the opportunities within their environment to engage in corrupt practices, and in terms of the wider political-economy of corruption. We begin by detailing understandings held by policy-making and operational agencies of the role of organised crime in corruption processes, before examining how corrupt relationships in New Jersey and the City of London are managed, reproduced, and facilitated. We aim to show that the anti-corruption discourse that has become globally established through the UNCAC ascribes a disproportionate importance to organised crime in processes and practices of corruption, and ignores factors which allow its continued participation in such relations – that is, where actions may be corrupt but licit. We highlight this point by focusing on corruption in affluent, developed societies.

The global institutionalisation of anti-corruption discourse: Organised crime as agents of corruption

The UNCAC heralds what Sampson (2010) has described as the global institutionalisation of anti-corruption discourse and anti-corruption practice. This narrative of corruption and anti-corruption positions the grand corruption found in many developing countries as the major problem facing anti-corruption agencies and initiatives. As Hofmann (2009: 8) notes, 'On the political level the fight against corruption and impunity is a precondition to strengthen governance and limit the influence of organised crime on democratic structures'. This is because the use of national resource wealth or other national financial assets that have been appropriated for the private use of Heads of State, senior government officials, and their families and friends, often in autocratic regimes that abuse human rights, has been of particular concern. The role of organised crime groups as agents in the maintenance of such regimes has formed much of the subject matter of research into corruption. According to the UNODC this can occur in a number of ways: organised crime can '... compromise legitimate economies and directly impact public processes by "buying" elections through corruption', and '... can permeate government agencies and institutions, fuelling corruption, infiltrating business and politics, and hindering economic and social development. And it is undermining governance and democracy by empowering those who operate outside the law'.[1]

One example is Latin America, where in Colombia and Peru relatively recent democratic government structures have been undermined by powerful drug cartels. These non-state actors have a detrimental effect on the ability of states 'to govern and fulfil the basic principles of modern statehood: the control of territory, the security of its citizens, a well-functioning judicial system and the monopoly on the legitimate use of force' (Hofmann, 2009: 2). Here their geographic position as producers of cocaine, with transportation links that allow for insertion into a global drugs market, intersects with weak democratic structures and the extensive use of violence and corruption. In poverty-stricken regions with high levels of inequality, a flourishing drugs trade enables organised crime's exertion of power over state and civil society alike (Thoumi, 2003: Hofmann, 2009). In Central Asia, conditions of poverty, widespread unemployment, and weak central power also create conditions for the development of a state-crime nexus, mediated by the legacy of the Soviet Union. Marat (2006: 13) points out that since the 1980s organised crime has developed throughout the post-Soviet area, including its satellite East European states. In Central Asia, weak central power and lack of economic infrastructure and skills have left a vacuum which has been filled by drugs trafficking. There are several major trafficking routes through the region, including a 'maze of trails through the mountains and across "green borders" to avoid detection' (UNODC, 2008: 6). In Central Asia, as in other post-Soviet regions, criminal networks have been able to make use of liberalised border regimes more quickly and efficiently than governments. Unlike Latin America, though, the relationships between criminal networks, organised crime, and the state displays degrees of cooperation, rather than violent conflict, with corruption oiling the wheels of this cooperation.

It is not only in countries with weak governance structures that organised crime and corruption pose problems however. The United Nations Interregional Crime and Justice Research Institute (UNICRI) notes that 'Organized crime adopts all forms of corruption to infiltrate political, economic and social levels all over the world'[2] How these forms of corruption are utilised and manifested depends on various factors, including historic and social and economic differences in different societies, as noted in research on corruption within the European Union carried out by the Center for the Study of Democracy (CSD, 2010). Different forms and levels of corruption are identified, across different sectors and involving different actors (see pp. 13–14). What is noteworthy is the extent of various corruptions. The CSD considers political corruption to be 'organised crime's most powerful tool' (ibid.: 14), detailing how corrupt practices affect all public institutions in some countries, including the judiciary and law enforcement agencies such as the police and customs, while in other countries:

> … politicians, magistrates, and white-collar criminals form closed corruption networks that are not systematic in nature. White-collar crime at the middle level of government bureaucrats is common (at various degrees of intensity) to almost all member states. In countries with low level of corruption, the cases are sporadic. The most wide-spread and systematic forms of corruption targeted by organised crime is associated with the low-ranking employees of police and public administration. Organised crime also targets tax administrations, financial regulators and any other regulatory body that might impact criminal activities, but in a less systematic and significant way.
>
> (ibid.: 13)

EUROPOL at various times has identified the most threatening manifestations of corruption by organised crime groups as that directed at high-level targets within the public sector in the EU and low-level representatives of law enforcement or the judiciary (Europol, OCTA, 2006; 2008), as well as the way that the criminal activities of organised crime groups are linked to the use of legal business structures. What is clear from these reports is that established criminal networks and widespread corruption are decisive facilitating factors for the operations of organised crime, and international drug trafficking in particular (Europol OCTA 2009: 19; 34).

At the policy level, then, there is a focus on organised crime as an agent of corruption in both developing and transitional countries. However, in examining the relationships between organised criminality and corrupt actors in New Jersey and the City of London, we aim to show that rather than being understood as an agent of corruption, organised crime is better understood as a symptom of established corruption environments. We turn next to these relationships.

New Jersey: Embedded political corruption and the management and maintenance of organised crime

> To an outsider, it looks like crime and political corruption are the fabric from which the Garden State's government is woven.
>
> (Ingle and McClure, 2008: 2)

William Chambliss' ground-breaking study ([1978] 1988) of crime and corruption in Seattle found a set of networks that involved several actors from both the illegal and legal worlds, from low-level drug dealers and pimps through to law-enforcement agencies, bankers, people in commerce, and politicians. It was through these networks that relationships between the supply of, and demand for, various illegal goods and services, political favours, and corrupt practices were managed and maintained, and opportunities seized and realised. This same pattern can be observed in New Jersey, a state in the northeast of the United States, described as having had an organised crime presence since the early twentieth century. For a relatively small state, it is densely populated, and has 'a large government machinery' for its size State (Ingle and McClure, 2008: 4–5), a factor that becomes important in understanding the widespread corruption found here. Its geographical position, together with rackets characteristic of the entertainment industry – gambling, prostitution, and speakeasies, for example – made it a pleasant place for the relaxation of members of different organised crime families from neighbouring cities, and avoided the turf wars that had plagued other urban areas, according to Ingle and McClure (2008). In this milieu, gangsters rubbed shoulders with politicians and administrators of the political machinery of the State, a machinery already steeped in corruption. Details of this corruption abound in accounts by investigative journalists (c.f., Ingle and McClure, 2008), official investigations (c.f., Stern, 2008), and court reports. What emerges from these accounts is an embedded culture of corruption, involving conflicts of interest, bribery, rackets, and frauds. We turn to an illustration of these forms of corruption before detailing the role of organised crime.

The prohibition on using public office for private gain seems almost non-existent in New Jersey. Not only do 'politicians of all stripes kowtow to special interests while seeing how many relatives they can pack on the payroll' (Ingle and McClure, 2008: 7) but the practice is widespread through the city administration and beyond, a large administration consisting of 566 municipal governments and 616 school districts, and 'more school superintendents than the states of Maryland, Virginia, and Delaware combined' (Ingle and McClure, 2008: 4. See also Schwartz, 2014).

For example, in the higher education system, we have the case of the University of Medicine and Dentistry of New Jersey (UMDNJ), which, as the *New York Times* put it in 2006, came 'to symbolize the corruption and cronyism that so many people reflexively associate with the Garden State'. In 2005 the board of UMDNJ was given a choice by the US Attorney: it could be taken over by an appointed federal guardian or face indictment for a $4.9 million Medicare fraud. The fraud investigation revealed numerous corrupt practices and led to 'at least a hundred' further investigations (Ingle and McClure, 2008: 11: Stern, 2008: 5) which included: false accounting and widespread 'financial mismanagement' including many instances of fraud and bribery; operating an illegal laboratory; political patronage in grading students; and what the US Attorney described as 'one of most brazen examples of public corruption he had ever prosecuted', which led to prison sentences for a former Dean of the School of Osteopathic Medicine, who was convicted of bribing a State Senator who was then chairman of the Budget and Appropriations Committee, and who took a $35,000-a-year 'no-show' job at the institution.

This case should be understood as part of a practice of creating 'no show' jobs. The hiring of staff took place within a system created by the Human Resources (HR) department that assigned numbers 1, 2 and 3, to job applicants. These numbers designated the density and breadth of an applicant's political connections. Number 1 indicated an applicant was well-connected to a political patron, and HR would seek to place such an applicant, regardless of their qualifications, creating 'bogus jobs' when necessary, a practice which on indictment saw such posts classified as a bribe (Ingle and McClure, 2008: 9–12). This, as well as other specific instances of misconduct, was not confined to UMDNJ. Schwartz's (2014) study of the case of UMDNJ found that these practices had precedent at other Universities (Schwartz, 2014: 9 *et passim*). The State of New Jersey Commission of Investigation claimed that:

> The State Commission of Investigation's own broader inquiry into the operations and administration of public higher education in New Jersey has revealed an entire system vulnerable to problematic governance, serious shortcomings in oversight, accountability and transparency and outright violations of the public trust.
>
> (2007: 1)

Similarly, Ingle and McClure (2008: 277) found that the practice of 'jobs for favours' was widespread across public organisations, as was the placing of family and friends, such that 'putting the faithful into jobs regardless of qualifications or whether the job is needed' marked an accepted and embedded form of corruption across the state government agencies. These instances of illegal but licit practices are readily apparent in the environment in which UMDNJ existed. Large bureaucracies create opportunities for hiring family, and those owed a favour, with further opportunities for developing projects to reward lawyers, engineers and others who had made financial contributions to political campaigns and expected some benefit in return. These contributions are seen as an investment, 'one that gives a much better return than any bank' (Ingle and McClure, 2008: 266–267). Schwartz (2014: 8 *et passim*) draws attention to the tensions existing between a progressive political culture in New Jersey upholding values of good governance, and a long and 'deeply entrenched' tradition of 'machine politics', this latter permeating the governance of the state via its 566 municipalities, providing multiple opportunities for corruption. The political system displays numerous levels of governance and actors but, since the turn of the twentieth century, has been 'ruled by bosses who carve up the state like medieval fiefdoms' (Ingle and McClure, 2008: 71).

The 'bosses' are unelected Party bosses, a person who controls a unit of a political party and who provides chosen candidates with money to run a campaign. Crucially, because they are unelected, party bosses do not have to make financial disclosures. Those who donate hefty amounts to campaigns expect to be rewarded and often this is by way of being awarded public contracts. This situation is described as a 'corruption tax', for not only are contracts awarded for contributions received but, in a similar way to the creation of bogus jobs, unnecessary contracts are given out, usually with negotiated prices inflated. Additionally, in return for contributions, laws and regulations are manipulated to the advantage of the donors. For party bosses, 'for favour' jobs build up power bases for politicians who employ supporters whose loyalty is secured through the pay and pensions offered in these jobs, helping to create political fiefdoms. Ingle and McClure (2008: 72) cite one news investigator as claiming that 'This souped-up version of nineteenth century politics has left New Jersey as the last state that relies heavily on party bosses to control elections, re-districting, patronage jobs and much of state, county and local government'. This 'pay to play' system is widespread, and shades into and overlaps with conflicts of interest, such as the case of Govenor McCreevy taking gifts of hospitality from the International Longshoremen union, then under investigation for ties to the Genovese organised crime family. In fact, McGreevey's administration was dogged by scandal, including his chief counsel and chief of staff resigning, as well as the commerce secretary and chief of the state police, because of conflict of interest investigations.

There are numerous and on-going ties between politicians and organised crime families, often through marriage, such as that between Louis Auricchio, a gangster who was convicted in 1994 of aggravated murder, and was the brother-in-law of party boss and former senate president John Lynch. Lynch had been a key backer of Govenor McGreevy who, on being elected, had shut down a two-year enquiry that was on the verge of indicting several conspirators from the legal and organised crime worlds. McGreevy's favours to organised crime extended to paroling gangsters without going through official channels. Ingle and McClure, (2008: 79–82, 222–3, 225, 241, *et passim*) recount example after example of the links between organised crime families and politicians, and the benefits conferred and received through these links, with these benefits being particularly visible in the criminal justice system, where, again, there are many instances of organised crime figures, particularly important figures in crime families, being paroled after serving the minimal sentence for eligibility, especially when Governors appointed mob-connected friends to chair parole boards (ibid.: 243–9). It is rumoured that 'paroles were for sale at a cost of $10,000' (ibid.: 247). Within the prison system in the 1970s these ties were apparent also. Ingle and McClure (ibid.) report a case of a county corrections officer who was convicted of official misconduct and imprisoned, for helping a mob connected prisoner 'come and go' so that he could meet women and eat pizza, and was subsequently re-employed (aged 72) by the State on his release, despite admitting to knowing senior people in organised crime.

The relationships and links between organised crime and political actors are frequently mediated by union officials. During elections, unions deliver votes to candidates who will return the favour by way of legislation favourable to their interests (Jacobs, 2014; Ingle and McClure, 2008). In the casino industry, which according to Walker and Calcagno (2013) is linked to political corruption in the United States, organised crime used labour unions as a means of gaining a stake in the city once gaming was legalised in 1996 (Ingle and McClure, 2008: 252–3). The influence on (and penetration of) labour unions by organised crime has been extensively researched and documented (see Jacobs, 2014) and is explained in part, as Lee and Chelius (1989: 536) claim, by 'the extensive legal protections they enjoy'.

The examples provided here are illustrative of innumerable others, forming part of a systemic corruption of the political system, a political architecture enmeshed in rackets and frauds involving waste facilities, dental plans, land, finance, sports, media and film, education, criminal justice, and more, across the State. 'Pay-to-play', bribery, and conflicts of interest can be everywhere observed. In 1996, Anechiarico and Jacobs (xiii) wrote that 'As this book goes to press, it seems that practically the entire city government of Newark, New Jersey, is under indictment or investigation'. By 2009, Parks was describing prisons as seeming to have 'a revolving door just for state senators. A month after former state senator John Lynch got out of jail for taking kickbacks, former state senator Wayne Bryant was yesterday sentenced to four years in prison for taking a no-show job'. More recently, Grossman and Dawsey (2015) reported senator Bob Menendez's indictment by a federal grand jury for accepting bribes in return for favours.

Although we have chosen to discuss the opportunities for, and relationships of, corruption using New Jersey as an example, it would be a mistake to view this corruption as the outcome of a somewhat archaic 'machine politics' or atypical in some way. Rather, New Jersey can be seen as a microcosm of corrupt relations embedded in the political culture of the United States. Ingle and McClure's (2008: 219) comment that New Jersey is 'a state filled with crooked officials on the take ...' echoes the title of the earlier study conducted by William J. Chambliss *On The Take: From Petty Crooks to Presidents*. Having noted that in previous decades officials from the White House, National Security Council, Congress, State governors and mayors, police officers, and trade unions had not only condoned the presence of organised crime through friendships and business alliances, but been convicted in cases of arms smuggling, perjury, illegal lobbying activities, conflicts of interest, and bribery, Chambliss' (1988: x) study of Seattle examined '... how and why organized crime, politicians, law-enforcement agents, and business people are intimately involved in corruption'. Chambliss concluded that

> organised crime really consists of a coalition of politicians, law-enforcement people, businessmen, union leaders, and (in some ways least important of all) racketeers. Who dominates the coalition varies from city to city and time to time, a point explored by the contributions across this volume. it is a network in which people come and go, dominant offices shift and change, roles vary and fluctuate, but the system goes on and on.
>
> (1988: 9)

The City of London: Embedded corruption and the enabling of organised crime

The UK is not usually considered a place of embedded corruption. Despite (for example) national newspapers involved in the illegal acquisition of confidential information through routine phone tapping, hacking into computers and 'phones, and payments to police officers (c.f. The Leveson Report, 2012), allegations of systematic price fixing in the energy supply (Chazan, 2014) and oil industries (Mason, 2012; Select Committee on Business and Enterprise, 2008), and the falsification of evidence and receipt of bribes by police officers, together with other forms of corrupt practices (Darbyshire, 2015; Newburn, 2015; HMIC, 2015), the illusion of corruption as a matter of a few 'bad apples' persists. However, a close examination of aspects of British institutions demonstrates that far from a 'few bad apples', embedded and systemic corruption serves as a major enabler of criminality, and this is particularly the case in the banking industry located in the City of London. The City of London territory is unique in Britain. It refers to a geographical area of 1,572 km^2 that constitutes an autonomous county within London itself, having been the original town settled by the Romans in the first century AD through to the Middle Ages. It is the heart of the UK's trading and financial services industries, and heart of a network of offshore tax havens, many, if not most of them, shaped around Britain's former empire – Her Majesty's British Overseas Territories and Crown Dependencies – which make up a significant number of the world's tax havens, currently being placed on a 'blacklist' by the European Commission (EUbusiness, 2015; European Commission, 2016). This situation places the City of London as possibly the most important player in the world of financial and corporate secrecy, and among the most notorious global traders of financial services to tax evaders, avoiders, and organised crime. Its position is the 'epicentre' of a web of secrecy and corruption that is the world of international finance (Shaxon, 2012: 14). The status is not random or arbitrary, but derives from the very uniqueness of the City of London as an autonomous financial area with corresponding political autonomy, allowing it to function as a major enabler of organised crime through its money-laundering facilities.

The secrecy afforded enables tax havens which shelter corporate and financial structures that, according to a study of grand corruption and stolen assets carried out by the World Bank, 'form the building blocks of hidden money trails' (van der Does de Willebois, 2011:ix). The report of this study discusses 'the ease with which corrupt actors hide their interests behind a corporate veil and the difficulties investigators face in trying to lift that veil' (ibid.). The work of the Tax Justice Network emphasises that secrecy and corruption go hand-in-hand. Their Financial Secrecy Index (FSI) (Tax Justice Network, 2015) is intended to add to the debate about corruption by showing the connection between what they term the 'demand' and 'supply' relationship. They explain this in relation to grand corruption by stating that:

> In the field of international governance and transparency, the most famous ranking of corruption is Transparency International's Corruption Perceptions Index (CPI). While indexes such as these can be useful, they only tell part of a bigger story. The CPI, for instance, ranks poor countries in Africa and elsewhere – predominantly the victims of an estimated US$1 trillion-odd in annual illicit financial outflows – as the 'most corrupt'. But all these outflows must be received somewhere. So the FSI examines the other side of the coin: those jurisdictions that encourage and facilitate illicit financial flows, by providing an environment of secrecy that allows these outflows – from rich and poor countries alike – to remain hidden, and largely untaxed.[3]

This relationship is what Shaxson details (2012: 3) when considering how oil revenues in African countries disappear in a vast 'web of global corruption secretly connecting the oil industries of former French African colonies with mainstream politics in metropolitan France, via Switzerland, Luxembourg, and other tax havens'. Considering the FSI index upsets dominant narratives of corruption, for 'the most important dirty-money centres' identified 'turn out to be those ranked "cleanest" in more traditional indices' (Tax Justice Network, 2015). London's role as a global hub for illicit finance turns upon its protection of tax havens. As the National Crime Agency states:

> The proceeds of grand corruption committed overseas are laundered through the global financial centres of the world. The UK is one of the most attractive destinations for these funds to pass through and be invested in.
>
> (2016: 29)

The Tax Justice Network, discussing global and regional initiatives to secure transparency in financial and corporate matters, emphasises that:

> The United Kingdom also remains a huge concern. While its own secrecy is moderate, its global network of secrecy jurisdictions – the Crown Dependencies and Overseas Territories – still operate in deep secrecy and have, for instance, not co-operated in creating public registers of beneficial ownership. The UK has failed to address this effectively, though it has the power to do so.
>
> (2015: 2)

The secrecy offered by tax havens ensures that details of banking clients are not released and that there is a low- or zero-level tax rate for people who are non-domiciled. Opening companies in tax havens is legal, with the principal aim of tax avoidance, but the same structures are also used to facilitate tax evasion or to launder the proceeds of crime. Hidden money trails can consist of monies that have been derived through the use of corruption in otherwise legal business transactions, or as the proceeds of criminal activities such as illegally dealing in drugs or arms. The financial services industry based in the City of London thus facilitates a system that makes the UK susceptible to charges of being 'the most corrupt nation in the world' (Carrier, 2016, unpaginated), whose banking institutions form key components of a 'criminal capitalism', which launders drug money through these offshore networks (Saviano cited in ibid.). By 'criminal capitalism' the anti-mafia reporter Roberto Saviano is talking about a space or spaces where money is hidden (tax evasion) or laundered (proceeds of crime). The criminal economy, he claims, is bigger than the legal economy and, in his view, drug trafficking generates more revenue than the oil industry. The point he wishes to emphasise is that 'Mafia and organised crime does not abide by the rule of law – and most financial companies who reside offshore are exactly the same' (cited in Carrier, 2016, unpaginated). As 90 per cent of the owners of capital in London have their headquarters offshore, there are ample opportunities for corruption, for example in the form of investments, many of which are the profits of illegal activity.

London itself offers further opportunities for laundering money. Saviano (in ibid.) points out that foreign criminals use the London housing market to launder billions of pounds. Global Witness, *et al.*, (2015) point out that more than 36,000 properties in London are owned by offshore companies, 38 per cent of them companies registered in the British Virgin Islands. According to Vanbergen (2016) Britain has seen a 600 per cent increase in foreign millionaires buying property in London since 2010, many of whom are hiding stolen money and assets in what is seen internationally as a safe haven, and with some donating to political parties to maintain their safety in the UK. Saviano similarly claims that Russian mafias have contributed to the London housing bubble and inflated prices by investing in property and that one of the practices most commonly used by organised crime is buying and selling property at fake values:

> Let's say a mafia boss buys an apartment in London for £500,000. Using a false name, he opens an offshore bank account, for instance on the Cayman Islands, and deposits the profits of, say, drug trafficking there. After a bit of work – a new kitchen, a paint job – he sells the apartment to the offshore company for £1m. The transaction, in itself apparently perfectly legitimate, has enabled him to show that his money is obtained through legal means. These laundered funds can now be invested.
>
> (2016, unpaginated)

He continues:

> In 2013 a study by the Italian transnational crime research centre Transcrime revealed that Italian mafias have taken over numerous UK businesses: the Sicilian Cosa Nostra has invested in gambling; the Naples Camorra in public building contracts, restaurants, and property development in Scotland; the Calabrian 'Ndrangheta in London property. A number of studies have shown that the City of London is the world capital for laundering the profits of drug trafficking.

Kington (2009) reported that Britain's Gambling Commission had in 2009 suspended the licence of Paradise Bet Ltd., a company that was shut down when its assets were frozen by Italian police as part of their operation to break up the organised crime clan *Parisi*. Francesco Forgione, who was president of the Italian anti-mafia parliamentary commission until 2008, is cited by Kingston as stating that members of the *Secondigliano Alliance*, a group of clans within the Camorra, are suspected of owning shops in London which turn out fake designer goods and also act as hideouts for fugitives and fronts for drug trafficking. Other Mafia clans are similarly investing in London (as well as other cities in the UK), suggesting it is becoming a key location in organised crime's money-laundering operations. These claims are found also in intelligence compiled by the British National Crime Agency, who observe that the UK property market is 'a preferred destination for criminal proceeds'. It is little wonder then that the National Crime Agency (2016) places 'high end money laundering' as one of the top five threats for the year 2016–17. Drawing attention to many ways in which the proceeds of crime and corruption can be laundered in the UK it points out that, 'The full scale of this is unknown, although case studies have shown billions of pounds of illicit money being laundered into and through the UK' (2016: 108).

The networks of actors found in this process are criminals who 'most commonly use intermediaries to disguise and distance themselves from the transaction when paying bribes' (ibid.: 30). Professionals such as solicitors, accountants, estate agents, trust and company service providers, and 'middlemen' facilitate bribery and corruption, as their expertise is crucial to the laundering of illicit funds, involving the 'creation of complex and sophisticated structures that distance the individuals from the money while retaining control of the illicit funds' which require 'the drafting of documentation, dissemination of funds, creation of corporate structures, and in some cases, acting as intermediaries' (National Crime

Agency, 2016: 29; 30; 111). Offenders in this process span the legal and illegal worlds, where members of organised crime groups operate with allies in friendship, social, and employment networks that offer criminal opportunity. Some groups utilise global criminal contacts, while others often have knowledge and experience of the sector deemed most profitable or exploitable, usually through previous employment and contacts (NCA, 2016: 13). For example, in 2009, David Mills, a British lawyer and husband of the then Secretary of State for Culture, Media, and Sport, was found guilty of accepting a £350,000 bribe in return for providing false testimony for Italy's Prime Minister Berlusconi in two corruption trials (see Pierce, 2009).

It appears that the UK's position as a key global financial centre offers a welcoming location for such criminal and clandestine activity, not least because of the lax regulation surrounding the movement of money, for, despite anti-money laundering legislation and anti-bribery legislation, its enforcement is lax (Alexandroni, 2007; van der Does de Willebois, 2011). For example, the Proceeds of Crime Act 2002 obliges anyone who suspects they are witnessing transactions involving the proceeds of crime to submit a Suspicious Activity Report to the National Crime Agency. This is what one UK employee of a bank that had been found in the US to have been complicit in devising a major facilitating tax evasion and money laundering scheme, did in 2008, handing over internal documents to investigators. However, despite the evidence, no action was taken (Burgis, 2016). But the UK is not just failing to act, it can be actively obstructive. A similar outcome met the Serious Fraud Squad investigation, started in 2004, into Britain's Al Yamamah arms-for-oil contract with Saudi Arabia, the biggest export contract in UK history, and a 'government to government' agreement, with BAE Systems (then British Aerospace) as the prime contractor because of the inclusion of 120 Tornado fighter jets, Hawk trainer planes, and other defence equipment made by BAE. As the inquiry unearthed evidence of extensive bribes and corrupt payments in this and other deals, the investigation was closed in 2006 on the orders of the Prime Minister, apparently under pressure from the Saudi Arabian government.

As far as corporations go, hiding profits is becoming easier, rather than harder: Shaxson (2012: ix) points out that in 2011 the UK Government was 'pushing forward with corporate tax reforms to encourage big corporations to shift huge additional profits into overseas tax havens'. Furthermore, in an interview (2016, in Carrier) Saviano discussed the danger of leaving the European Union, which would undermine joint attempts to fight illegal economies. Report after report documents the lack of enforcement activity by the UK, leading Ungoed-Thomas and Boswell (2015, unpaginated) to comment that 'The prime minister needs to show that the UK is as committed to fighting corruption in its own backyard as it is elsewhere in the world'.

Conclusion

The discourse of the global anti-corruption regime positions organised crime as a key agent of political corruption. However, the examples of New Jersey and the

City of London show how difficult it is to see quite who the agents of corruption are. In New Jersey, as in other parts of the United States, there is an abundance of motivated offenders and suitable targets, and a dearth of guardians. It is little wonder that anti-corruption initiatives have been ineffective, for opportunities abound in the bureaucracies of state, and networks of corrupt actors are well placed and practiced at seizing these opportunities. This micro-climate of accepted practices persists despite a raft of anti-corruption and anti-bribery legislation. This 'micro-climate' is enmeshed within a 'macro-climate' which serves to draw attention to the emphasis on corruption in the developing world, as well as the disjuncture between words and deeds.

The United States has perhaps the most widely enforced anti-corruption law in the world, the Foreign Corrupt Practices Act (FCPA), which prohibits American persons and entities from bribing foreign governments. Given that practices now defined as corrupt are not themselves recent, questions posed about why corruption has become the subject of far-reaching policy attention at a particular historical moment (c.f. Williams and Beare, 2003) help to shed light on the macro-climate of corruption environments. Sociologists have long recognised that major policy initiatives emerge through the activity of one or more 'moral entrepreneurs', moral crusaders who seek to promote change through policy programmes. In this case, 'The US exercised moral leadership during two decades, eventually persuading others that the reduction of bribery in international business would not only be mutually beneficial but was morally correct' (Getz, 2006: 256). The context in which concerns over bribery arose were that, following a series of scandals involving American companies, the United States criminalised bribery of foreign officials in 1977 in the FCPA. However, this move coincided with the globalisation of trade, and complaints were soon made about the disadvantages caused to multi- and trans-national companies by the FCPA. The move to regulate the global economy through anti-corruption measures in order to create a 'level-playing field' for American businesses developed at the same time as economic globalisation, and rapid developments in the liberalisation of financial markets, expansion of e-commerce, and off-shore banking (see Williams and Beare, 2003: 90–91, 106) and was thus a critical factor in placing corruption as a global social problem. As Getz and Volkema (2001: 7) stated, 'The growth in international trade over the past few decades has raised concerns about differing business practices that can impede commerce and economic development. One such concern revolves around bribery and corruption. Bribery and corruption are thought by many to be an unavoidable part of international business'. The FCPA and subsequent regulation that criminalised the bribery of foreign officials can be understood as a means for changing the view of corruption as a way of doing business, through the use of the criminal justice system as a vehicle for economic governance (Williams and Beare, 2003; Krastev, 2004). By making the global anti-corruption initiative a Protocol to the Convention on Transnational Organised Crime, the relationship between corruption, organised crime, money-laundering, and the financing of terrorist activity became overlapping concerns.

In trying to regulate a global economy, one avenue has been to focus on changing the commercial practices of legal businesses, and particularly those corporations that are wont to use several forms of corrupt practices such as involving the creation of shell and subsidiary companies, false or inappropriate forms of accounting, and the misuse of various legal vehicles, to avoid sanctions or the full payment of tax. Here, money made in the legal economy is channelled illicitly to different destinations and for different purposes. However, it is not only legal business that has internationalised in the recent past. Transnational organised crime has become an equally (if not more) successful economic actor, comprising many profitable activities. As we have seen, the same vehicles that are used by legal entities are also used by organised crime groups to launder the proceeds of crime, and money that must be laundered mixes with money made in the legal economy, to create significant illicit financial flows. It is difficult, if not impossible, to disentangle these flows.

While there is pressure on governments to close loopholes that allow corporate malpractice, at the same time, illegal monies are referred to as 'the proceeds of crime' whereas the proceeds of corporate crime are not. However, if we treat corporations and organised crime groups alike, as actors in the corruption process, then not only is it difficult to distinguish the proceeds of legal and illegal economic activity within illicit monies flowing around the world, but it becomes clear that their roles within the process are very similar: both make use of the opportunities afforded them, their relationships with actors in the legal world are mutually necessary, and they use the same vehicles to return illicit flows to licit flows – 'the world's tax dodgers, drugs cartels, arms traffickers and other criminals' (Global Witness, 2015) apparently have more in common than is immediately apparent when it comes to corrupt practices. UNICRI's observation[4] that 'Acting as multinational corporations, criminal groups seek profit through the evaluation of countries' risks, benefits and markets analysis' could benefit from noting the similarities in operating in corrupt environments and disposing of illicit funds.

So, on the one hand there is concern with corporate malpractice and complicity in corruption, and on the other, concern that organised crime exploits weak governance regimes in the developing world, contributing to further immiseration of populations. However, the distinction between corporate malpractice and organised crime activity in the corruption process is not as clear-cut as policy and research distinctions might suggest. Examining this distinction leads us to consider the further distinction made between the 'developing' and 'developed' world in accounts of corruption, and analysing these distinctions leads us in turn to argue that both corporate businesses and organised crime function as agents in the corruption process, but are not in themselves agents *of* corruption. That is to say, their role is not the causal factor in processes of corruption. Rather, both exploit the environment for 'doing business', and find in the developed world environments, particularly political environments, that facilitate and protect their practices.

The two examples in this chapter show that these environments indicate different spatial arrangements of corrupt organisation. As noted earlier, the prohibition on using public office for private gain is virtually non-existent in New

Jersey – party bosses are unelected officials who control units of political parties, effectively determining which candidates can run for office. New Jersey resembles a city-state, with contracts, jobs, and other opportunities distributed in return for favours, loyalty, or finance. The politics of corruption in New Jersey is diffuse rather than concentrated. In contrast, in the City of London, a single network controls everything, from who can be voted for to who can vote. The system that controls the geographic area of the City of London is derived from an archaic plutocracy independent of Parliament. There are 25 wards (electoral districts) within this geographic space, and in 21 of them votes are allocated to corporations, not residents. These corporations then appoint the voters. Consequently, the corporate institutions choose the candidates and control the votes. Not only do they decide who will be voted for, but also who will vote for them. To put this in context, at the last census the population stood at 7,325, yet there were 17,000 businesses employing 414,000 workers. Even under the allocation system, corporate votes outnumber citizen votes many times over (Global Research 2016). Thus, the politics of corruption in the City of London is concentrated rather than diffuse. The fact that this is the only part of Britain over which Parliament has no authority is a license for corruption on a scale that has defeated all attempts to tackle it (ibid.).

A situation where corruption becomes normalised, albeit in the different modes operating in New Jersey and the City of London, renders distinctions between licit and illicit deeply problematic. In both cases what defines the domain of social perception, custom, and practice is precisely the entanglement of legal and illegal activities. It is the entanglement that defines how these political economies of corruption function.

Notes

1 https://www.unodc.org/unodc/en/organized-crime/index.html
2 http://www.unicri.it/topics/organized_crime_corruption/
3 http://www.financialsecrecyindex.com/faq/what-has-corruption-to-do-with-cross-border-secrecy
4 http://www.unicri.it/topics/organized_crime_corruption/

References

Alexandroni, S. 2007. London tops the poll. Observations on corruption. *New Statesman*. 4 October. Available at http://www.newstatesman.com/society/2007/10/corruption-london-money-saudi.

Anechiarico, F. and Jacobs, J.B. 1996. *The Pursuit of Absolute Integrity: How Corruption Control Makes Government Ineffective*. University of Chicago Press: Chicago.

Arias, E.D. 2006. *Drugs and Democracy in Rio-de-Janeiro. Trafficking, Social Networks, and Public Security*. Chapel Hill: University of North Carolina Press.

Burgiss, T. 2016. Dark money: London's dirty secret. *Financial Times*. 11 May. Available at https://www.ft.com/content/1d805534-1185-11e6-839f-2922947098f0.

Carrier, D. 2016. Roberto Saviano: London is heart of global financial corruption, *The Guardian online*. 29 May. Available at https://www.theguardian.com/books/2016/may/29/roberto-saviano-london-is-heart-of-global-financial-corruption.

Center for the Study of Democracy. 2010. *Examining the Links between Organized Crime and Corruption*, European Commission.

Chambliss, W.J. [1978] 1988. *From Petty Crooks to Presidents* (2nd ed.), Bloomington and Indianopolis: Indiana University Press.

Chazan, G. 2014. Energy suppliers face prosecution over price fixing, *Financial Times*. August. Available at https://www.ft.com/content/ab44af16-1cbb-11e4-88c3-00144feabdc0.

Coles, N. 2001. It's not what you know—it's who you know that counts: Analysing serious crime groups as social networks. *British Journal of Criminology*. 41: 580– 94.

Darbyshire, N. 2015. The shocking truth about police corruption in Britain. *The Spectator*. 7th March. Available at http://www.spectator.co.uk/2015/03/the-shocking-truth-about-police-corruption-in-britain/.

EUbusiness. 2015. *EU releases world tax havens blacklist*. Available at http://www.eubusiness.com/news-eu/economy-politics.120n.

European Commission. 2016. *Fact Sheet. Questions and Answers on the common EU list of non-cooperative tax jurisdictions*. Brussels. Available at http://europa.eu/rapid/press-release_MEMO-16-2997_en.htm

Europol. 2006. *Organised Crime Threat Assessment* (OCTA). Available at https://www.europol.europa.eu/activities-services/main-reports/octa-2006-eu-organised-crime-threat-assessment.

Europol. 2008. *Organised Crime Threat Assessment* (OCTA). Available at https://www.europol.europa.eu/activities-services/main-reports/octa-2008-eu-organised-crime-threat-assessment.

Europol. 2009. *Organised Crime Threat Assessment* (OCTA). Available at https://www.europol.europa.eu/activities-services/main-reports/europol-review-2009.

Findlay, M. 2008. *Governing through Globalised Crime*. London and New York: Routledge.

Fletcher, C. and Herrmann, D. 2016. *The Internationalisation of Corruption: Scale, Impact and Countermeasures*. London and New York: Routledge.

Freeman, L. 2006. *The Development of Social Network Analysis*. Vancouver: Empirical Press.

Fröhlich, T. 2003. *Organised environmental crime in the EU Member States*. Final Report. Kassel, Germany: Betreuungsgesellschaft für Umweltfragen.

Getz, K.A. 2006. The effectiveness of global prohibition regimes. Corruption and the antibribery convention. *Business & Society*. 45(3): 254–281.

Getz, K.A. and Volkema, R.J. 2001. Culture, perceived corruption, and economics. A model of predictors and outcomes. *Business & Society*. 40 (1): 7–30.

Global Research. 2016. *Money-Laundering and the City of London's 'Crime Scene': Haven of Tax Havens for the Mega-Wealthy*. Available at http://www.globalresearch.ca/money-laundering-and-the-city-of-londons-crime-scene-haven-of-tax-havens-for-the-mega-wealthy/5513335.

Global Witness, Christian Aid, Transparency International UK, and Tax Justice Network. 2015. *The UK's Corruption Problem*. November. Available from Available at https://www.globalwitness.org/en/reports/uks-corruption-problem/.

Graycar, A. and Monaghan, O. 2015. Rich country corruption. *International Journal of Public Administration*. 38(8): 586–595.

Grossman, A. and Dawsey, J. 2015. Justice department indicts Sen. Bob Menendez on corruption charges. *Wall Street Journal*. 1st April, Available at http://www.wsj.com/articles/new-jersey-sen-robert-menendez-indicted-on-corruption-charges-1427900772.

Hofmann, K. 2009. *The Impact of Organized Crime on Democratic Governance – Focus on Latin America and the Caribbean*. FES Briefing Paper 13. Friedrich-Ebert-Stiftung. Berlin.

HMIC. 2015. *Integrity matters. An inspection of arrangements to ensure integrity and to provide the capability to tackle corruption in policing*. London: HMIC.

Ingle, B. and McClure, S. 2008. *The Soprano State. New Jersey's Culture of Corruption*. New York: St Martin's Press.

Jacobs, J.B. 2014. *Is labor union corruption special?* New York University public law and legal theory working papers, Paper 449. School of Law, New York University.

Jancsics, D. and Jávor, I. 2012. Corrupt governmental networks. *International Public Management Journal*. 15(1): 62–99.

Johnston, M. 2005. *Syndromes of Corruption: Wealth, Power, and Democracy*. Cambridge: Cambridge University Press.

Kingston, T. 2009. The British connection: Italian mafia finds UK good for doing business. *The Guardian online*. 27th December. Available at https://www.theguardian.com/world/2009/dec/27/mafia-crime-italy-gangs-camorra.

Kirby, S. and Penna, S. 2010. Policing mobile criminality: Towards a situational crime prevention approach to organised crime, in Bullock, K, Clarke, R.V. and Tilley, N. (Eds). *Situational Prevention of Organised Crimes*. Cullompton: Willan Publishing, pp. 193–212.

Krastev, I. 2004. *Shifting Obsessions. Three Essays on the Politics of Anticorruption*. Budapest – New York: Central European University Press.

Lee, B.A. and Chelius, J. 1989. Government regulation of labor-management corruption: The casino industry experience in New Jersey. *Industrial and Labour Relations Review*. 42(4): 536–548.

Leveson Report. 2012. *An Inquiry into The Culture, Practices and Ethics of the Press. A Report by the The Right Honourable Lord Justice Leveson*, vols 1–4. No. 0780. The Stationary Office: London. Available at http://webarchive.nationalarchives.gov.uk/20140122145147/http://www.official-documents.gov.uk/document/hc1213/hc07/0780/0780.asp.

Marat, E. 2006. *The State-Crime Nexus in Central Asia: State Weakness, Organized Crime, and Corruption in Kyrgyzstan and Tajikistan*. Central Asia-Caucasus Institute & Silk Road Studies Program.

Mason, R. 2012. Oil market will be investigated over price-rigging fears, ministers promise. *The Daily Telegraph*. 13th September. Available at http://www.telegraph.co.uk/news/politics/9541811/Oil-market-will-be-investigated-over-price-rigging-fears-ministers-promise.html.

National Crime Agency. 2016. *National Strategic Assessment of Serious and Organised Crime 2016*. Available online at http://www.nationalcrimeagency.gov.uk/publications/731-national-strategic-assessment-of-serioUs-and-organised-crime-2016/file.

Newburn, T. 2015. *Literature review - Police integrity and corruption*. London: HMIC.

New York Times. 2006. *School for Scandal*, 19 November. Available at http://query.nytimes.com/gst/abstract.html?res=9E07E6DB143EF93AA25752C1A9609C8B63&legacy=true

Parks, B. 2009. Perp walks: Poison ivy in the Garden State. *Wall Street Journal*. Eastern Ed. 25th July. Available at http://www.wsj.com/articles/SB10001424052970204886304574308394035238188.

Pierce, A. 2009. The rise and fall: David Mills jailed for four years over Silvio Berlusconi bribe. 18th Feb. *The Telegraph online*. Available at http://www.telegraph.co.uk/news/

worldnews/europe/italy/4681727/The-rise-and-fall-David-Mills-jailed-for-four-years-over-Silvio-BerlUsconi-bribe.html.

Sampson, S. 2010. The anti-corruption industry: From movement to institution. *Global Crime*. 11(2): 261–278.

Saviano, R. 2016. The real threat to Britain's borders is the flow of dirty money. *The Guardian online*. 23 June. https://www.theguardian.com/commentisfree/2016/jun/23/real-threat-britain-borders-flow-dirty-money-eu.

Schwartz, M.A. 2014. *Trouble in the University: How the Education of Health Care Professionals Became Corrupted*. Leiden: Brill.

Select Committee on Business and Enterprise 2008. *Further supplementary evidence by energywatch. Written Evidence.* Competition Report on the GB Gas and Power Markets. An ENERGYWATCH Discussion Paper. London: House of Commons. Available at http://www.publications.parliament.uk/pa/cm200708/cmselect/cmberr/293/293we36.htm

Shaxson, N. 2012. *Treasure Islands: Tax Havens and the Men Who Stole the World*. Vintage Books: London.

State of New Jersey. Commission of Investigation. 2007. *Vulnerable to Abuse. The Importance of Restoring Accountability, Transparency and Oversight to Public Higher Education Governance*. October. http://www.cnjscl.org/News/SCIhighered report.pdf.

Stern, H. 2008. *End of Monitor Report [Redacted for Public Review] of the Federally-Appointed Monitor for the University of Medicine and Dentistry to Hon. Christopher J. Christie US Attorney for the District of New Jersey*. 3 January. Available at https://dspace.njstatelib.org/xmlui/bitstream/handle/10929/40793/i622008.pdf?sequence=1&isAllowed=y.

Tax Justice Network. 2015. *Press Release*. Available at http://www.taxjustice.net/wp-content/uploads/2013/04/FSI-2015-Presser.pdf.

Thoumi, F. 2003. The numbers' game. Let's all guess the size of the illegal drugs industry! *Crime & Globalisation Paper*. Amsterdam: Transnational Institute. Available at http://www.countthecosts.org/sites/default/files/numbers.pdf.

Ungoed-Thomas, J. and Boswell, J. 2015. Tax havens snub Cameron plea to open up books. *The Sunday Times online*. Available at http://www.thesundaytimes.co.uk/sto/news/uk_news/Society/article1639012.ece.

UNODC (United Nations Office on Drugs and Crime). 2004. *United Nations Convention Against Corruption*. UN:NY, Available at https://www.unodc.org/documents/brUssels/UN_Convention_Against_Corruption.pdf.

UNODC (United Nations Office on Drugs and Crime). 2008. *Illicit Drug Trends in Central Asia*. Republic of Uzbekistan: Regional Office for Central Asia. Available at http://www.unodc.org/documents/regional/central-asia/Illicit%20Drug%20Trends_Central%20Asia-final.pdf.

Vanbergen, G. 2016. Panama Papers barely scratch the surface: Tax havens and money laundering, an appendage of Britain's banking industry, *Global Research*, April 06. Available at http://www.globalresearch.ca/tax-havens-an-appendage-of-britains-banking-indUstry-the-panama-papers-barely-scratch-the-surface-of-uk-complicity/5518866.

van der Does de Willebois, E., Halter, E.M., Harrison, R.A., Won Park, J. and Sharman, J.C. 2011. *The Puppet Masters. How the Corrupt Use Legal Structures to Hide Stolen Assets and What to Do About It*. Washington, DC: The International Bank for Reconstruction and Development/The World Bank.

Walker, D.M. and Calcagne, P.T. (2013) Casinos and political corruption in the US: A Granger causality analysis. *Applied Economics.* 45(34): 4781–4795.

Williams, J.W. and Beare, M.E. 2003. The business of bribery: Globalization, economic liberalization and the 'problem' of corruption, in Beare, M.E. (Ed.). *Critical Reflections on Transnational Organized Crime, Money Laundering and Corruption.* University of Toronto Press, pp. 88–119.

13 Corrupt cities

The illicit in local urban development, the Spanish case

Monica García Quesada and Fernando Jiménez Sánchez

Introduction

Local authorities today carry out many necessary functions and mobilise large financial resources in their communities in Europe. They are, for example, in charge of town-planning and land-use, of issuing building licenses and permits, of purchasing goods and services from private companies, of establishing public-private partnerships, of administering welfare benefits and subsidies, etc. The decentralisation of powers of the last few decades has increased this trend (Wollmann, 2012; Loughlin, 2010). Local authorities are centres of decision-making, economic development and resource mobilisation.

Although academic studies have paid little attention to local corruption (with the exceptions of Andersson, 2008; Erlingsson *et al.*, 2008; Huberts *et al.*, 2008) evidence exists that malfeasance happens in this tier of government. Following the emergence of a high number of cases of local urban corruption in Spain over a decade ago, some research has been dedicated both to describing what has happened in this country and at explaining why. The analyses show that between 1997 and 2007 the number of cases of local urban corruption occurring in Spain increased considerably. They concerned instances where local public representatives – the mayor or councillors – and/or local government officials engaged in illegal practices, most typically the issuing of illegal building permits in exchange for payments (bribery), but also money laundering and influence peddling.

This chapter takes stock of the information and explanations provided in the existing literature on local urban corruption in Spain to examine this phenomenon and to draw lessons. It shows that the Spanish local authorities have been a lucrative and attractive target for corruption, and that certain local authorities have been more prone to corruption than others. The chapter examines the different explanations given as to why corruption has been more prevalent in certain Spanish local authorities than in others. To do so, it follows Mungiu-Pippidi's equation on corruption (Mungiu-Pippidi, 2013), taking each of the elements of this equation to identify and classify the different reasons provided to explain local urban corruption in Spain. Overall, the chapter stresses the need to descend to the subnational level both to describe and to explain corruption. Analyses that focus on corruption at the national level, which are prevalent in the studies of international organisations and think tanks, have not adequately focused on a ubiquitous phenomenon that, however, is not geographically uniform across a country. Attention to local corruption can help to sharpen the existing explanatory approaches concerning the illegal practices not only in this tier of government, but also in others.

The chapter is organised into three main sections plus the conclusion. The following section defines local corruption, discusses how to examine this phenomenon and presents the data on corruption in Spain. Second, the chapter provides an overview of two main views on human action explaining why actors engage in malfeasance. Third, the chapter puts forward an anatomy of the elements that have been considered to be causes for local corruption in Spain. The conclusions bring all these elements together and identify prospective areas of research on the topic.

The illicit in local authorities in Spain

"Abuse of public office for private gain" has been a widely used definition of corruption (Tanzi and Davoodi, 1997). It refers to an inappropriate use of the resources and responsibilities that accompany a public position with the purpose of benefiting private interests. This definition considers corruption to be actions against the norm; it presumes that public office is entrusted to someone not to promote private gain but to promote the public interest. The norm, in this context, encompasses both social norms, customary practices and rules of social acceptability, whose breach constitute illicit acts, and legal norms and formal regulations, whose infringement are illegal acts (see Introduction, this volume). Examining the illicit demands unveiling what social norms have been breached, and has been the focus of certain works examining the local urban development occurring in Spain from 1997 to 2007. The legitimacy of the massive, frenetic and speculation-driven construction growth of the "prodigious decade of urbanism in Spain" (Burriel, 2008) has been questioned (Romero *et al.*, 2012; Schulz-Dornburg, 2012; Fernández Durán, 2006, Selfa, this volume). Alternatively, corruption may refer to illegal practices committed at the local level with the purpose of benefiting private interest: bribing, conspiracy, abuse of office, influence peddling, etc. In the present chapter, we are concerned with this latter type of illegalities, identified as such by the Spanish enforcement forces.

Analysing corruption confronts researchers with difficult tasks because, by nature, corruption takes place most secretly. Given its concealed nature, researchers have needed to develop strategies to measure corruption. At least three different ways exist. Although none of them is completely free from problems of data validity and/or data reliability, they have been widely employed in research examining corruption in Spain and in local urban corruption (for a detailed discussion, Villoria and Jiménez, 2012):

The first way is by employing the rates of prosecution or conviction for misuse of office, as provided by the courts or the police. This method exclusively considers the incidents that enforcement forces have defined as criminal offences. In the Spanish legal framework, such offences are bribery – art. 419 et seq. of the Criminal Code (CC); influence peddling (art. 428 et seq. of the CC); fraud against the administration (art. 436 et seq. of the CC); abusive or unfair management of public funds (art. 432 et seq. of the CC), etc. Following this method, we find that during the period from 1997 to 2006, 676 local authorities (8.3% of the total number) were affected by corruption (Jerez-Darías *et al.*, 2012). As a result, more than 500 mayors were under investigation for cases happening during that period, and while at least 90 have been acquitted, around 90 have been convicted. The corruption cases have most commonly been identified as part of long and complex police and judicial investigations involving several politicians and local administrators. Particularly notable cases have been Operación Malaya, where up to 95 people have been accused in court, including three former mayors, 14 former local councillors and 38 businessmen; the Caso Lanzarote, where, as a result of the investigations, over 100 people, including 11 former mayors, two secretaries, civil servants and private businessmen have been accused of participating in corruption exchanges and bribery linked to the issuing of licenses for the construction of large hotels and residential complexes; the Caso Andratx, where a former mayor and a councillor have been found guilty of bribery and influence peddling; the Caso Pretoria, where a former mayor and an urban development councillor, among others, have been accused of bribery and money laundering (García Quesada *et al.*, 2013).

The main difficulty with this method concerns the existing gaps and inexactitudes in data registry. In Spain there is no specific public registry on corruption crime, and although accounting methods are improving, it is still difficult to have accurate and complete information about the corruption cases identified by the police and brought to court. In addition, given its subterranean nature, the cases identified are most likely only a fraction of all illegal acts that have happened, as not all existing corruption cases have been identified. They are very probably just the tip of the iceberg of a larger number of corruption crimes happening at the local level.

The second method uses the rates and surveys of victimisation as a proxy to quantify corruption. This entails asking citizens anonymously about their own participation in corruption acts. The best known victimisation index is the Global Corruption Barometer published by Transparency International (TI). Respondents, around 1,000 per country, are asked whether they have paid a bribe in the previous 12 months. In Spain, in the six years from 2004 to 2010, between zero to 5% of the respondents admitted to having paid a bribe. Some differences exist as to the sector where bribes are produced, though. According to respondents in Spain in 2009 and 2010, police bribes are about 1% to 2%, bribes in health, tax and judicial education reach 2% to 3%. Bribery in local urban development policy goes up to 3% to 6% – the highest of all sectors. The strength of this strategy is that – provided that respondents are sincere – it allows for accounting for corruption cases that might have never been reported to the enforcement forces. However, one of its main weaknesses is that it only measures one type of corruption crime – bribes – and not other corrupt exchanges that have been also present in the reported cases of urban corruption.

The third way to accounting for corruption in a country is based on corruption perception, either by "experts" or citizens in general. The best-known index of this type is the Corruption Perception Index (CPI) built by the NGO Transparency International (TI). The CPI adds information from a diverse number of sources, including country risk ratings produced by different consulting businesses, surveys, entrepreneurs and executives of national and multinational companies. A higher index reflects a better perception of measures against corruption and, thus, a less corrupted country. This index, however, does not serve to examine local urban corruption because the information is provided as a national index combining different categories and not by sector or government tier.

According to all available data, and despite the methodological difficulties, Spain has presented a significant problem of corruption associated with local urban development. The existence of corruption was not equal everywhere. Data on the local authorities affected by corruption scandals show that, while in some regions up to 57% of local authorities were affected by corruption, in others it affected only just over 1% of municipalities (Jerez Darias *et al.*, 2012). Figure 13.1 shows the cases of corruption that have been identified by police forces and the courts between 2000 and 2011. Local urban corruption has been localised around Madrid and in the Mediterranean coast, places of demographic growth and poles of touristic attraction with a demand for second residencies. The geographical presence of local urban corruption in Spain highlights, as we see further below, how the Spanish building boom and corruption practices have been inextricably linked.

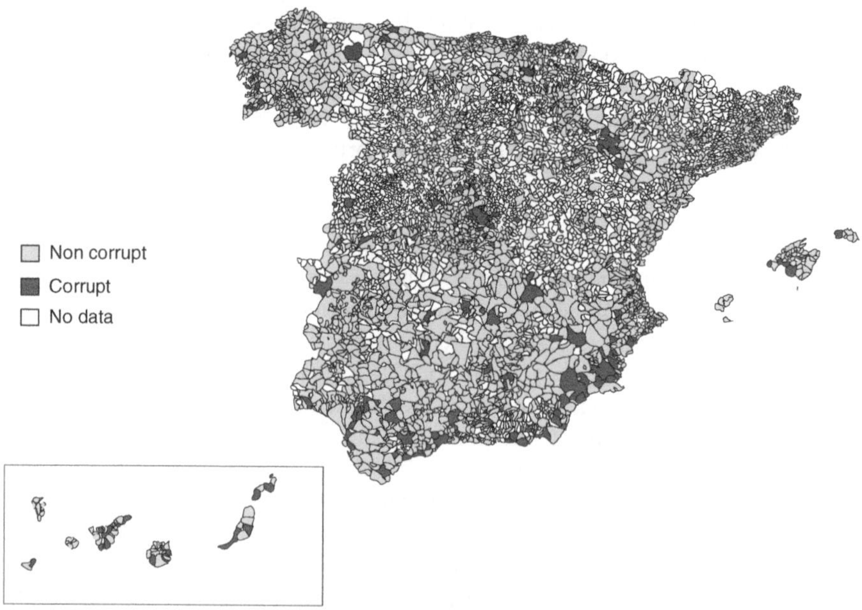

Figure 13.1 Local corruption: Mainland Spain and Balearic Islands.

Source: Authors' elaboration based on González López-Valcárcel *et al.* (2015).

The impact of corruption on social, economic and political life in Spain has been large. Certain estimates point out that the annual cost of corruption in Spain is 40,000 million euros, which includes not only the direct cost of the offences, but also their social consequences – such as loss of potential investment, decrease in the country's productively levels, generation of inequalities, etc. (León *et al.*, 2014). Corruption also accounts for a drop in institutional and social trust which, as attested by the literature, undermines basic principles of a representative democracy, such as accountability, equality and inclusiveness (Torcal, 2014; Jiménez 2016). Indeed, Torcal (2014) shows that, between 2008 and 2012, Spain is among the countries with the largest increase in institutional distrust in Europe. Distrust in Spain rose from 22.9% at the beginning of the period to 51.1% by 2012 for the national parliament, from 53.8% to 77.7% for political parties, from 52.8% to 76.4% for politicians and from 37.1% to 48.4% for the legal system. Torcal presents evidence that this deterioration is caused principally by a critical perception of the unresponsiveness of representative institutions, aggravated by the increasing perception of political corruption. Other factors, such as the economic crisis or the effects of multilevel governance explain to a lesser extent, in his view, the degree of societal distrust. In a similar vein, Villoria *et al.* (2013) have examined how perceptions of administrative as well as political corruption are associated with less satisfaction and lower levels of social and institutional trust. In this sense, if at any point corruption has been evoked as a means to facilitate social exchange and to avoid blockage from inefficient institutions (Leff, 1964), local urban corruption in Spain provides clear evidence that this is not the case.

Causes for local corruption in the literature

A vast literature has developed to identify different factors causing or contributing to corruption acts (for a literature review, see De Graaf, 2007). When addressing why certain actors engage in malfeasance, explanations essentially follow two alternative views on human action: the "logic of consequences" and the "logic of appropriateness". The logic of consequences suggests that all political action, including corrupt behaviour, derives from a rational calculation by actors to maximise preferences. Klitgaard's (1988) equation on corruption is probably the best-known example of this type of explanation, whereby the degree of corruption (C) in any political system is a function of the existence of a monopolistic power (M) enhanced by the possibility to exert that power discretionally (D) and with reduced accountability (A): $C = M + D - A$. This perspective has prevailed since the 1990s and has inspired the work of international organisations in fighting corruption, as they have inspired measures for decreasing political discretion and improving accountability.

Rothstein and Tegnhammar (2006) provide an attenuated version of the rational approach of the logic of consequences, as their explanation stresses that agents are not perfectly rational and fully informed about the world in which they live. In this view, actors are not completely irrational, but they adjust their behaviour based on what they think other agents are going to do. These expectations are generated endogenously by information about what other agents have done in the past (Young 1998). In this sense, actors base their decisions on fragmentary information, they have incomplete models of the process they are engaged in and they may not be especially forward looking.

Other analyses of corruption conceive human action, more or less explicitly, as resulting from a "logic of appropriateness" by which human behaviour is best interpreted as following learnt norms of what is culturally accepted and considered adequate. From this perspective, research has attested how hierarchical cultures focusing on loyalty towards one's social group tend to be more corrupt than more individualist and egalitarian cultures: corruption tends to be higher in cultures that encourage individuals to prioritise loyalty towards one's social group above the individual itself (Rose-Ackerman, 1999; Hofstede, 2001; Schwartz 1999). Others have examined the influence of cultural patterns created by religion and economic systems for the existence of corruption (Sandholtz and Koetzle, 2000). Relatedly, research on local patronage networks has attested that they favour corruption, as they support personal channels and disregard formal rules in order to gain an advantage, such as support and votes in elections or for passing legislation. Patronage networks favour the development of belief systems for allegiance, creating the conditions for the maintenance of illegal practices. Sometimes these networks are of a traditional nature (around local lords or bosses with high influence in the community), or are formed by old-boy connections.

More recently Alina Mundiu-Pippidi (2013) has provided a novel approach to the analysis of corruption by elaborating an equation similar to Klitgaard's. According to her, corruption is the result of two sets of factors: a particular structure of opportunities for actors, which provide the incentives to engage in corruption exchanges, and a set of deterrents and constraints, which limit the actions of actors that would otherwise engage in corruption. Her approach has the virtue of looking at the different elements that facilitate corruption, investigating empirical factors without following exclusively one of the logics. Crucially, in her view, the logic of appropriateness and the logic of consequences are not contradictory, but both might inform the actions of agents. For this reason, she proposes to examine both the formal institutional framework that shapes and constrains the behaviour of social actors, but also informal practices and social norms that orientate and limit their action. Such an approach allows consideration of behaviour as an actor's response to maximise their individual preferences and as the result of cultural and societal influence.

For the purpose of the present chapter, her contribution is particularly appropriate to examine the different elements that the existing literature on Spanish corruption has identified as causes for this phenomenon. We undertake an anatomy of the literature on Spanish corruption following the elements that her equation highlights: Corruption/control of corruption = Opportunities (Power discretion + Material resources) – Deterrents (Legal + Normative).

Anatomy of local urban corruption in Spain

Opportunities

The first set of factors highlighted by Mungiu-Pippidi is the structure of opportunities for actors, which concerns the elements that predispose actors towards malfeasance. With regards to local urban corruption, such factors include both the incentives and the facilities inviting local public representatives and officials to engage in criminal acts of corruption involving the management of the local lands. Mungiu-Pippidi further identifies two elements: discretionary power opportunities and material resources for corruption. We examine them in turns.

Discretionary power opportunities

Discretionary power opportunities regard the arrangements that facilitate privileged access to public power for some private interests. Elements such as collusive arrangements, purposely poor regulation encouraging administrative discretion and a lack of transparency that turns information into privileged capital for power-holders and their relations, might generate incentives towards corruption (Mungiu-Pippidi, 2013: 28).

To examine this element it is first necessary to outline the territorial power distribution in Spain in order to understand which tier of government has a function relating to local urban development. Three tiers of government exist in Spain: local authorities, about 8,117; regional governments, called Autonomous Communities, 17; and the national State. The relationship among them is not hierarchical, but each tier has certain attributed functions. Local authorities are in charge of providing all urban local services, which include, among others, the elaboration of the urban development plans. They need to be elaborated respecting the standards set by both the State and the regional governments with regards to environmental, public health, safety and security measures. The State is in charge of adopting basic legislation on all these matters (Art 149) without prejudice to the powers of the Autonomous Communities to establish additional protection rules and to elaborate from the common State requirements (Art 148).

Municipalities in Spain follow the strong mayor model, just as do those in France, Portugal and Italy. This means that municipalities are mostly of a small size and concentrate many powers in the head of the council – the mayor. Indeed, with the exception of large cities such as Madrid, with over three million inhabitants and Barcelona with over 1.5 million, 91% of the Spanish town councils have less than 10,000 inhabitants. As Table 13.1 shows, Spain has one of the smallest municipalities, in terms of average population size, of the OECD countries, second only to France. It also shows that the Spanish mayors operate with both significantly fewer elected representatives and members of staff than other OECD countries following other models, such as the council manager model, the committee leader model or the collective model. As it is typical of the strong mayor model, the mayors are ultimately responsible for both the management of the local administration and the direction of the priorities of the political agenda.

Table 13.1 Composition of local authorities in OECD countries

	Average number of council members (2002)	*Average population per municipality (2002)*	*Average number of employees per local government (2002)*
Denmark	17	18,800	610
Sweden	45	30,200	1,040
Finland	28	10,900	200
The Netherlands	19	24,200	90
Australia	10	19,100	80
Norway	29	9,000	190
Ireland	26	103,000	800
UK	42	120,000	730
USA	7	6,600	130
Belgium	22	17,000	90
France	14	1,600	220
Spain	**8**	**4,800**	**40**
Portugal	29	32,000	130
Italy	18	7,200	90

Source: adapted from Mouritzen and Svara (2002) and Fundación Alternativas (2009).

With regards to urban development policy, the mayor is responsible both for the adoption of the local urban plan and for ensuring that enforcement actions are taken against urban developments breaching it. The local plan typically includes details such as the quantity and type of building, green areas and local public facilities, and thus it defines what municipal land is fit for building. To adopt the local urban plan, the mayor is supported by the Council's General Secretary (the highest-ranking professional official in the local government), whose agreement is also required. De facto, however, the Spanish mayors have led the process of authorising and issuing building licences, and have acted discretionally and with little transparency. Indeed, the position of General Secretaries has been frequently filled only temporally by staff whose position depended directly on the mayor. In addition, the procedure for elaborating and ratifying local development agreements has been regulated only since 2007. During the period when the corruption cases came into being, mayors and landowners and/or urban developers negotiated the conditions for urban development bilaterally with minimum legal requirements to report to citizens or even to the municipal corporation on the content of the agreements. Such a degree of discretion provided great opportunities for mayors and private interests to malpractice. Measures to attempt to control the undesired effects of these large and concentrated powers have been taken – as we see further below in the deterrents section – but with limited impact.

Having identified this as one of the factors favouring corrupt exchanges, various measures have been adopted to open up the procedure to scrutiny. In 2007, the new Land Act introduced measures and controls to facilitate institutional transparency, such as the publication before their adoption of all the instruments for spatial and urban planning and the involvement of the municipal council in the adoption of planning decisions, land exchanges and certain asset disposals (Article 11). In February 2013, with the adoption of the Act 19/2013 on Transparency, Access to Public Information and Good Governance, Spain met the international commitments on transparency measures, by regulating the right of citizens to access public information, and by establishing measures for actively publicising information.

Material resources for corruption

Material resources for corruption refer to elements such as state assets, concessions and discretionary budget spending, foreign aid, "and any other resources which can be used and abused, turned into spoils or generate rents" (Mungiu-Pippidi, 2013: 28).

Local urban development in Spain generates large material resources that may act as incentives for corruption. The adoption of local urban plans has huge financial implications, for both landowners and local authorities. When the local authority designate plots of land as urban, it gives them a much higher value, which multiplies several times the owners' capital gains. Urban development has also large consequences for the council's economy, as building gives local authorities several sources of revenue. First, as a result of owning urban land, landowners pay from 10% to 15% of the land value to the municipality, either in the form of land or money. Other revenues resulting from urban development are the construction tax, paid for engaging in construction projects (new buildings or renovation works and fees for planning permission). In this sense, as urban areas grow in the municipality, the money generated by these revenue sources also increases. Both local governments and landowners are interested parties in urban land development.

During the decade from 1997 to 2006, known as the "prodigious decade" (Burriel 2008), a significant share of Spain's economic growth was based on the construction sector, fuelled by low interest rates, access to private debt and a new legislative framework that, from 1997, eased the requirements to make new land available for construction (Ferrán Aranaz, 2006; Naredo, 2010; Fernández Durán, 2006). Figure 13.2 shows the total number of houses built from 1991 to 2009 in the Mediterranean coast (in the darker colour) and in total in the country. During this period, more than 5.5 million houses were built, with 865,000 units started in 2006 alone. In certain years during that decade, more houses were built in Spain than in Germany, France and the UK put together.

This construction boom meant that Spain was building housing for 16 million people while population increased by only 5.5 million during the period (Burriel, 2008). The boom happened in the context of sky-rocketing housing prices and real estate speculation, which multiplied the material resources available for corruption. In this sense, as various researches attest, the construction boom and urban corruption in Spain have been closely linked (Jiménez, 2009; Rullán, 2011; González Perez, 2010; Jerez *et al.*, 2014). The connection has been such that the plummeting of the real estate market in 2008 meant a drop in the corruption cases.

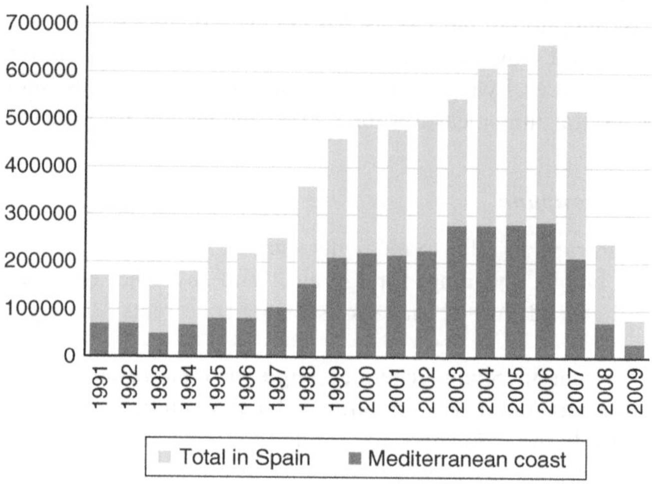

Figure 13.2 Houses initiated in Spain and in the Spanish Mediterranean coast (1991–2009).
Source: Adapted from Rullan (2011).

Deterrents

The second set of elements that Mungiu-Pippidi highlights are the existing deterrents or constraints. This includes measures that aim at restricting actors' behaviour, discouraging actors from engaging in corrupted practices. Significantly, Mungiu-Pippidi does not only consider legal deterrents, but also the societal deterrents, in the form of cultural norms, that might impose certain constraints onto actors.

Legal deterrents administered by the State

The legal deterrents administered by the State are "an autonomous, accountable and effective judiciary able to enforce legislation, as well as a body of effective and comprehensive laws covering conflict of interest and enforcing a clear public-private separation" (Mungiu-Pippidi, 2013: 28). In the case of local urban corruption, the definition includes all formal mechanisms existing to monitor and control the action of local representatives and local administrators.

The effects of legal deterrents have been widely examined in the literature on corruption. Indeed, much of our previous work has examined the institutional mechanisms designed to monitor and control the performance of policy-makers at the local level (Jiménez *et al.*, 2014; García Quesada *et al.*, 2013; García Quesada *et al.*, 2015; Villoria, 2007; Fernández, 2011, Urquiza, 2006). From such studies, we can identify four main types of deterrents:

(a) Legislation to control conflict of interests. Legal provisions exist to create a regime of incompatibilities to guarantee the independence of local representatives and administrators. They stop people that carry out professional activities related to those offered by the local authorities from standing for office (Article 177.2, Law on General Electoral Regime – LOREG). It also prohibits elected representatives from having other professions or activities that may hinder their ability to function independently (regulated by Law 53/1984 on Incompatibilities – LIPSAP). This legislation also seeks to avoid any risk of nepotism and favouritism (see Articles 28–29, Law 30/1992 on Administrative Procedures).

(b) Internal administrative controls. The highest-ranking Council civil servants – Secretaries, Comptrollers and Treasurers of the Council – are in charge of ensuring that all measures adopted by local representatives are legally and financially sound. The Secretaries certify the legality of all acts of the local council and provide legal advice and guidance to public representatives, ensuring that these acts are in agreement with all legal requirements and standards. The Comptrollers examine the expenditure and income of the local authorities, checking that the information is accurate and reliable, and verify that the accounts meet legal demands. The Treasurers organise all payments by the local council, direct local tax levying and issue reports, opinions and proposals on economic and financial issues as requested by local representatives and provide custody of funds (see Articles 2 to 5, Royal Decree 1174/1987 of Local Civil Servants).

(c) External administrative controls. The regional governments are responsible for land use and zoning within their region (Article 148.1.3, Spanish Constitution, and Sentence Constitutional Court 61/1997, 20 March). For this reason, once the local authorities adopt their urban plans, they need to submit them to the regional governments, which need to revise and approve them before they come into force at the local level. Regional governments check that urban plans fit with the general regional planning objectives and policies. If they identify an irregularity in a municipal plan, they can warn the local government about it, ask for a modification of the plan or refuse to ratify it in its current form (Article 60, LRBRL). Regional governments can discipline local authorities if they breach regional rules on land use and zoning.

(d) External judicial control. The appeal to judicial control is a crucial mechanism for controlling the performance of local public representatives and for penalising corrupt exchanges. Administrative Courts may hear about all sorts of circumstances concerning urban planning such as illegal administrative rules and urban plans, buildings and constructions that do not meet the requirements of the planning permit or local urban plans, breaches and delays, etc. Court sentences are always compulsory (Title III, chapter I) Law 29/1998 of the Administrative Courts). Criminal Courts hear about acts that the Penal Code defines as crimes "against the Administration": exerting unlawful influence, bribery, failure to act, embezzlement of funds, etc. Such crimes by local representatives are punishable directly with fines, prohibition from holding public office and imprisonment. Thus, the Courts function as the direct enforcement authorities and are crucial for deterring and for containing corruption exchanges.

Crucially, these studies present evidence that, while the formal mechanisms exist, their actual implementation has been weak and failing (Jiménez *et al.*, 2014; García Quesada *et al.*, 2013; García Quesada *et al.*, 2015; Villoria, 2007; Fernández, 2011, Urquiza, 2006). With regards to the application of the regime of incompatibilities, local authorities have frequently ignored its application and so local representatives have taken decisions on issues that directly concerned their personal interests. Secretaries, Comptrollers and Treasurers have depended on mayors for their appointment and the exercise of their daily functions. In practice, their control powers have been limited to warning local politicians of their culpability, without being able to stop the adoption of an unlawful decision. For their part, regional authorities have in practice merely exerted a control of legality of local administrative procedures for adopting urban plans, without examining the opportunity and substance of local entities' activities. Regional governments have been unwilling to initiate disciplinary measures against local authorities failing to comply with legal norms. Judicial controls are rarely promptly imposed: courts regularly investigate cases up to several years after the occurrence of the alleged crime, resulting frequently in the case failing because of the application of the statute of limitation. Furthermore, the ultimate disciplinary action that can follow an illegal building action – the demolition of the affected building – has hardly ever been exercised, thus diluting its deterrent effect[1] (see García Quesada *et al.*, 2013).

Normative deterrents

Finally, the last set of elements concerns the normative deterrents, which refer to societal norms endorsing "public integrity and government impartiality, and permanently and effectively monitoring deviations from that norm through public opinion, media, civil society, and a critical electorate" (Mungiu-Pippidi, 2013: 29). The importance of this element is that it highlights that corruption derives not only from an inadequate formal incentive structure, but also from the prevalence of certain expectations contrary to the common good. Rothstein and Uslaner (2005) have provided evidence that fighting corruption is harder when people mistrust government institutions, perceive that they operate with prejudices and believe that all political parties are the same. In this sense, it is important to examine societal norms and beliefs to see to what extent they provide an environment adequate for or against crime control.

Normative deterrents have received only partial attention in the existing literature on local urban corruption in Spain. Jiménez *et al.* (2014) have examined whether the extent and persistence of the urban corruption cases can be explained by local populations' acquiescence. They show that the degree of general trust (or trust to strangers) and trust in institutions in Spain is below the European countries' average. Indeed, as Table 13.2 shows, more people in Spain than in other countries believe that people outside their closest circle cannot be trusted, and they consider that the courts and the Treasury discriminate against those with less power and resources. In this sense, the data coincide with the expected results: a society where distrust abounds facilitates corrupt exchanges, as the well-being of

Table 13.2 Levels of generalised trust in European countries (1999–2007)

Turkey	10.2	Croatia	38.7	Lithuania	52,8	Ireland	72.1
Cyprus	21.2	Andorra	40.8	Luxemburg	53,9	Germany	75.8
Portugal	21.9	Poland	40.9	Greece	54,6	Iceland	830
Bosnia and Herzegovina	32.4	Spain	40.9	Russia	55,4	Belarus	85.2
Slovakia	33.4	Malta	42.2	Ukraine	60,0	The Netherlands	90.6
Latvia	35.9	Romania	43.6	Italy	60,8	Switzerland	107.4
Moldova	36.7	Hungary	44.8	Great Britain	61,7	Finland	117.5
France	37.9	Estona	48.4	Belgium	63,0	Denmark	131.9
Serbia	38.2	Czech Republic	48.8	Montenegro	68,2	Sweden	134.5
Slovenia	38.6	Bulgaria	50.9	Austria	70,2	Norway	148.0

Source: Diez Medrano (no year).

others is disregarded. At the local level, however, the results are not so clear-cut: the degree of trust is similar across the country, disregarding the degree of local corruption (Jiménez *et al.*, 2014).[2] Indeed, the trust score between the inhabitants of Lanzarote or Marbella, where well-known cases of local corruption have been discovered, and of Menorca, where anti-corruption pre-empting measures have been applied, was strikingly similar. Whether this means that people do not establish their convictions following direct or local experience, or whether other factors beyond trust – such as local economic incentives – are complementary or competitive in explaining local urban corruption, is unclear.

A major challenge for studies on normative deterrents has been to distinguish between rhetoric and actions – the difference between what people say and what they do. Jiménez *et al.* (2014) have shown that a large majority of voters have preferred a rhetorical praising of certain principles such as sustainable development and environmental protection while, in practice, they have abstained from selecting agents committed to delivering on such promises, and instead have voted for candidates favouring a loose application of rules and a weak enforcement for the sake of promised economic growth. Following Gambetta and Origgi's categories (2009) we find that Spanish voters have favoured low quality exchanges, in which the stated preferences and actions do not match. With their actual behaviour (voting) a majority of the electorate has rewarded representatives that have promised work opportunities and capital gains at the expense of the environment and illegal urban practices, even when they have failed to deliver on such promises. In this sense, the prevalent societal norms have not been conducive to the fight against corruption.

Indeed, research on corruption in Spain has highlighted the widespread feeling of impunity that has followed corrupt acts: political parties involved in corruption scandals have been hardly penalised in the elections held during the building boom (Jiménez 2008; Jiménez and Caínzos 2006). Researchers have examined the reasons. Anduiza *et al.* (2013) explore whether party supporters have been more tolerant toward corruption cases when they affected their own party, and confirm that this is the case: the same offence has been judged differently depending on whether the responsible politician is a member of the respondent's party, of unknown partisan affiliation or of a rival party. Riera *et al.* (2013) argue the need to consider certain sociological particularities of the voters to examine when corruption is penalised and when it is not. They present evidence that the electorate has not been completely immune to corruption, but its effect has been neither homogeneous nor constant across elections. Penalising corruption has been contingent upon several factors, including the characteristics of the voter, their ideology, their personal economic situation, political sophistication, etc. (Jiménez and Caínzos, 2006). In this sense, these studies have indicated the need to distinguish between types of social actors, as they hold different normative compasses at different moments in time. Future research on normative deterrents is likely to build on these particularities.

Conclusions

This chapter has examined local urban corruption in Spain, understood as criminal practices by which local authorities favour private interests. We have analysed the challenges faced and the strategies followed by scholars to examine this phenomenon and given evidence of its presence in Spain during the building boom from 1997 to 2007. An anatomy of the explanations for corruption has been proposed, following the analytical model by Mungiu-Pippidi (2013), which has helped to organise the different contributions. The explanations show that both incentives and deterrents, formal and informal, have featured as forces either favouring or resisting corruption during that period. Corruption happened in Spain with the interaction of various factors: local authorities, and particularly the mayors, were in charge of managing a resource – the land – capable of generating high financial gains, especially in the coastal areas. This power, together with de facto deficient mechanisms for monitoring and penalising illegal activities, created the conditions for corrupt activities to grow. Engaging in such illegal practices became both very profitable and involved little risk. Corruption cases have not been extraordinary incidents, but the result of systemic failures, a system incapable of ensuring that principles and legal standards prevail.

From this analysis, one question stands out: is the Spanish example extraordinary? As other chapters in the present volume show (Selfa, this volume; Scalia, this volume) illegal and illegitimate actions have taken place in urban areas in many other countries across the world. Nonetheless, the cases of urban corruption in Spain have been so numerous and so serious in character that they have provided significant evidence to identify and examine their main features in detail. Local urban corruption in Spain, unlike that occurring in other countries, has been subject of detailed examination, which we have presented here. This is particularly the case with local corruption, where the existing cross-local variation in the degree of corruption has been largely unreported by international organisations, which instead have paid more close attention to corruption at the national level.

From these contributions we find that scholars have frequently focused on particular reasons to explain corruption. Given its nature as a concealed and complex phenomenon, this approach has frequently been necessary. The explanations, however, are not necessarily independent and competitive but complementary. Researchers in corruption need to reflect on how best to employ multi-factorial, and not single-factor, explanations of corruption. In our view, attempts at bringing the different explanations together and at studying how different factors interrelate can help, as well as sharpening our analytical tools to examine corruption, to provide valuable insights about how to fight against it.

Notes

1 Relevant cases can be found all across the Spanish geography, but particularly renowned cases are the hotel "El Algarrobico" (Andalucia), the hotels "Son Bou", "Papagayo Arena" and "Princesa Yaiza" in Lanzarote, the Marina Isla de Valdecañas in Extremadura, etc.

2 This is, nonetheless, the topic of a research project we have just initiated in 2017 on the subject of corruption in Spain.

References

Andersson, S. 2008. *Exploring Corruption in Sweden. Types of Corruption, Danger Zones and Control Mechanisms*. Saarbrücken: VDM Verlag.

Anduiza, E., Gallego, A. and Muñoz, J. 2013. Turning a blind eye: Experimental evidence of partisan bias in attitudes toward corruption, *Comparative Political Studies*, 46(12): 1664–1692.

Burriel, E.L. 2008. La «década prodigiosa» del urbanismo español (1997–2006), *Scripta Nova. Revista Electrónica de Geografía y Ciencias Sociales*, 12 (270), available at http://www.ub.es/ geocrit/sn/sn-270/sn-270/sn-270-64.htm.

De Graaf, G. 2007. Causes of corruption: Towards a contextual theory of corruption, *Public Administration Quarterly*, 31(1/2): 39–86.

Diez Medrano, J. no year. Interpersonal trust, available at at http://www.jdsurvey.net/jds/jdsurveyMaps.jsp?Idioma=I&SeccionTexto=0404&NOID=104.

Erlingsson, G.Ó., Bergh, A. and Sjölin, M. 2008. Public corruption in Swedish municipalities: Trouble looming on the horizon?, *Local Government Studies*, 34(5), 595–608.

Fernández Durán, R. 2006. *El Tsunami Urbanizador Español y Mundial*. Barcelona: Virus.

Fernández, G.R. 2011. *Para Comprender el Urbanismo Español (de Una Vez por Todas)*. Iustel, Madrid.

Ferrán Aranaz, M. 2006. Tipo de interés y oferta de vivienda nueva, *Ciudad y Territorio, Estudios Territoriales*, 148: 475–490.

Fundación Alternativas. 2009. Problemas institucionales y corrupción, In: Estefanía, J. (ed.) Report on Democracy in Spain/2009. Madrid: Fundación Alternativas.

Gambetta, D. and Origgi, G. 2009. L-worlds: The curious preference for low quality and its norms, Sociology Working Papers, Paper Number 2009–08, Department of Sociology, University of Oxford.

García Quesada, M., Jiménez Sánchez, F. and Villoria, M. 2013. Building local integrity systems in southern Europe: The case of urban local corruption in Spain, *International Review of Administrative Sciences*, 79: 618–637.

García Quesada, M., Jiménez Sánchez, F. and Villoria, M. 2015. Can't control/won't control: Opportunities and deterrents for local urban corruption in Lanzarote, *Crime Law and Social Change*, 63(1): 1–20.

González López-Valcárcel, B., Jiménez González, J.L. and Perdiguero García, J. 2015. Danger: Local corruption is contagious, *Working Paper 1/2015, Catedra Pasqual Maragall d'economia i territori*, Available at http://www.ub.edu/catedramaragall/wp-content/uploads/2015/02/Working-Paper-01-2015.pdf.

González Pérez, J.M. 2010. The real estate and economic crisis: An opportunity for urban return and rehabilitation policies in Spain, *Sustainability*, 2(6): 1571–1601.

Hofstede, G. 2001. *Culture's Consequences: Comparing Values, Behaviors, Institutions and Organizations Across Nations*. 2nd Edition, Thousand Oaks, CA: Sage Publications.

Huberts, L., Anechiarico, F. and Six, F. 2008. *Local Integrity Systems*. The Hague: BJU Legal Publishers.

Jerez Darias, L.M., Martín Martín, V.O. and Pérez González, R. 2012. Aproximación a una geografía de la corrupción urbanística en España, *Ería*, 87: 5–18

Jiménez, F. 2008. A review of the fight against political corruption. In Estefanía J (ed.) Report on Democracy in Spain/2008. Madrid: Fundación Alternativas, 214–298.

Jiménez, F. 2009. Building boom and political corruption in Spain. *South European Society and Politics*, 14(3): 255–272.

Jiménez, F. and Caínzos, M 2006. How far and why do scandals cost votes? in Garrard, J. and Newell, J. (eds.) *Scandals in Past and Contemporary Politics*, Manchester: Manchester University Press.

Jiménez Sánchez, F., García Quesada, M. and Villoria, M. 2014. Integrity systems, values, and expectations: Explaining differences in the extent of corruption in three Spanish local governments, *International Journal of Public Administration*, 37(2): 67–82.

Jiménez, F. 2016. Los efectos de la corrupción sobre la desafección y el cambio político en España, in Villoria, M. y J.M. Gimeno (eds.), *La Corrupción en España: Ámbitos, Causas y Remedios Jurídicos*, Barcelona: Atelier.

Klitgaard, R. 1988. *Controlling Corruption*. Berkeley: University of California Press.

Leff, N.H. 1964. Economic development through bureaucratic corruption. *American Behavioral Scientist*, 8: 8–14.

León, C.J., de León, J. and Araña, J.E. 2014. Relación entre corrupción y satisfacción, *Revista de Economía Aplicada*, 64(22): 31–58.

Loughlin, J., Hendriks, F. and Lidström, A. (eds) 2010. *The Oxford Handbook of Local and Regional Democracy in Europe*. Oxford: Oxford University Press.

Mouritzen, P.E. and Svara, J.H. 2002. *Leadership at the Apex. Politicians and Administrators in Western Local Governments*, Pittsburgh: University of Pittsburgh Press.

Mungiu-Pippidi, A. 2013. The good, the bad and the ugly: Controlling corruption in the European Union. *Advanced Policy Paper for Discussion in the European Parliament*. Available at http://www.againstcorruption.eu/wp-content/uploads/2013/03/ANTICORRP-Policy-Paper-on-Lessons-Learnt-final.pdf.

Naredo, J.M. 2010. El modelo inmobiliario español y sus consecuencias, Available at http://habitat.aqupm.es/boletin/n44/ajnar.html (accessed 30 August 2010).

Riera, P., Barberá, P., Gómez, R., Mayoral, J.A. and Montero, J.R. 2013. The electoral consequences of corruption scandals in Spain, *Crime, Law and Social Change*, 60(5): 515–534.

Romero, J., Jiménez, F. and Villoria, M. 2012. (Un)sustainable territories. Causes of the speculative bubble in Spain (1996–2010) and its territorial, environmental and socio–political consequences. *Environment and Planning C. Government & Policy*. 30: 467–486.

Rose-Ackerman, R. 1999. Political corruption and democracy, Connecticut, *Journal of International Law*, 14(2): 363–378.

Rothstein, B. and Tegnhammar, M. 2006. The mechanisms of corruption: Interest vs. cognition, *QOG Working Paper Series*, 3. Available at www.qog.pol.gu.se.

Rothstein, B. and Uslaner, E. 2005. All for all: Equality, corruption and social trust. *World Politics*, 58(1):41–72.

Rullan, O. 2011. La regulación del crecimiento urbanístico en el litoral mediterráneo español, *Ciudad y Territorio, Estudios territoriales*, 168: 279–297.

Sandholtz, W. and William Koetzle 2000. Accounting for corruption: Economic structure, democracy, and trade, *International Studies Quarterly*, 44(1): 31–50.

Schulz-Dornburg, J. 2012. *Ruinas Modernas, Una Topografia de Lucro*, Ambit, Barcelona.

Schwartz, S. 1999. A theory of cultural values and some implications for work, *Applied Psychology: an International review*, 48(1): 23–47.

Tanzi, V. and Davoodi, H. 1997. Corruption, public investment, and growth. *IMF Working Paper*, No. 139. Washington: International Monetary Fund.

Torcal, M. 2014. The decline of political trust in Spain and Portugal: Economic performance or political responsiveness, *American Behavioral Scientist*, 1–26.

Urquiza, J.M. 2006. *Corrupción Municipal. Por Qué se Produce y Cómo Evitarla*, Almuzara, Córdoba.

Villoria, M. 2007. Las nuevas medidas al servicio de la transparencia, la participación y el control en el gobierno local en la Ley del Suelo. *Ciudad y Territorio. Estudios Territoriales*, 29 (152–153): 1–21.

Villoria, M. and Jiménez, F. 2012. ¿Cuánta corrupción hay en España? Los problemas metodológicos de la medición de corrupción (2004–2011). *Revista de Estudios Políticos*, 156: 13–47.

Villoria, M., Van Ryzin, G. and Lavena, C. 2013. Social consequences of government corruption: A study of institutional disaffection in Spain. *Public Administration Review*, 73(1), 85–94.

Wollmann, H. 2012. Local government reforms in (seven) European countries: between convergent and divergent, conflicting and complementary developments, *Local Government Studies*, 38(1): 41–70.

Young, H.P. 1998. *Individual Strategy and Social Structure: An Evolutionary Theory of Institutions*. Princeton: Princeton University Press.

14 Corruption, crisis and planning policies

The Free-Trade Zone project in the metropolitan area of Valencia, Spain

Jorge Ignacio Selfa Clemente

PhD candidate at the Universitat Autònoma de Barcelona

Introduction

> Economic recession, inefficiency, regional government debt, wastefulness, a building bubble, land consumption, stories of corruption, discredit of policy, lack of leadership and social cohesion, limited caution regarding the future, self-interest, a lack of relevance of civil society, a lack of criticism and participation by the public, street disturbances, and repression against high-school students. All the problems of Spanish democracy seem to have been concentrated in the Valencian Community during the last few years.
>
> (Boira 2012, pp. 11–12)

The above quotation reflects a widespread feeling about the causes and consequences of the economic crisis, including corruption, after the financial crash of 2008 in the Valencian Community, one of Spain's 17 autonomous regions, located on the Mediterranean coast, with a population of five million and a 9.4% share of the Spain's GDP in 2015 (INE 2016). In 2011 and 2012, the Valencian society suffered a kind of shock, an 'Untertag' or 'perfect storm', as J. V. Boira (2012) very graphically described it. After a decade of economic growth based on the construction industry, the hosting of high-profile events that projected the image of Valencia internationally and a broad consensus regarding a planning policy that promoted urban expansion as the foundation of economic development, the global recession which began in 2008 revealed the artificial foundations upon which regional development was based. Moreover, a large number of corruption cases, implying misuse of public funds for private gains, were being reported at different governmental levels, which clearly contrasted with the impoverishment of the population as a consequence of the crisis, increasing unemployment and cuts to social services. Not surprisingly, the Valencian Community gained prominence in national and international media as the region of Spain where the effects of the recession were most evident. At the same time, the work from which the above quote is taken is an example of the attempts that emerged during the recession, aimed at constructing a new and deeper understanding of the crisis, and engaging in new political projects. This chapter aims to examine the treatment of corruption in these attempts to construct new narratives around the crisis in the Valencian Community and its effects on planning policy.

This chapter describes the context and processes by which corruption was defined and introduced into the debate surrounding planning policy after the financial crash of 2008 in the Valencian Community. In this Spanish autonomous region, a huge number of corruption cases, most of them related to urban development, were reported to the legal authorities, especially after the 2008 crash. In a short period of time, corruption came to be considered as a major concern by a significant part of society, and, consequently, it became a recurrent theme in political debates challenging the policies of local and regional governments. The analysis of the practices and processes that generated new perceptions and public debates on corruption, especially those related to planning policies, are studied in this chapter considering a single urban development project. The object of study is the Zona Franca de la Comunitat Valenciana – Paterna Parque Logístico Internacional. This was a project to build a free-trade zone in the municipality of Paterna, one of the main towns in the Metropolitan Area of the city of Valencia. It was proposed in 2012 and cancelled in August 2015 after reports of corruption and following the success of left-wing parties in the local and regional elections. The Zona Franca was conceived as a response to the crisis, but at the same time it had to face new economic, social and political conditions. This case study allows the examination of the actions of multiple actors in their questioning of a specific project through reporting (alleged) corruption.

By analysing the process by which corruption was introduced in political debates around planning policies in the Valencian Community in the context of the economic crisis, this chapter demonstrates that the full social and political significance of corruption depends on temporal and spatial contexts as well as on actions and practices performed by a multiplicity of actors. To do this, it is based on a conceptualisation influenced by assemblage thinking that pays attention to the changing nature of the processes that define the urban sphere and urban policy as well as the concepts and categories used in their description and the controversies surrounding them. In this way, the city and urban policy is understood as the interrelations of heterogeneous elements: actors, discourses, descriptive categories, laws, techniques, among others that are continuously subject to change in the framework of power relationships, interrelations that are not constituted without debates and controversies (McGuirk 2012, McFarlane 2011; Farías 2011). So, and as noted by McFarlane (2012) when considering formality/informality, the understanding of corruption goes beyond the use of the term as a descriptor of illegal or illicit acts and is considered as 'a multifaceted resource for naming, managing, governing, producing, and even critiquing contemporary cities' (p. 89). Following McFarlane's arguments, it can be argued that the very significance of corruption becomes a political issue of debate in planning disputes and controversies, since it allows plans, policies, spaces or processes to be depicted or judged as legal/illegal or licit/illicit. In the analysed case, corruption refers to illegal acts committed by politicians and public servants in the development of their duties. In fact, these illegal acts, considered public corruption, are well defined within Spanish legislation, as it will be explained below. However, corruption complaints are also related to acts not strictly illegal, that are not considered acceptable by a part of society, and therefore they are considered as illicit (see editors' introduction, this volume). The debates generated in the Valencia Community around corruption dealt precisely with delimitation of these terms: when an act is firmly considered as illegal, and which acts, independently of their legality, are described as not acceptable and why.

The political and economic context that framed the debates on corruption and urban policy in the Valencian Community is analysed, but special attention is paid to practices of agents in relation to corruption complaints. Multiple traces and situations of relevance to the development of the Zona Franca de Paterna, are considered: planning and technical documents, press releases, news, websites, acts or official inquiry commissions that were the result of the work and undertakings of multiple actors – local government, politicians, journalists or civic opposition groups. The analysis of this evidence reveals the practices of multiple agents and the relationships that they tried to establish and maintain to generate the definition and the uses of concepts such as corruption and crisis that those involved employed to influence planning policies according to their political agenda.

This chapter is organised in three main parts and a concluding section. The first part briefly presents the main political debates and conceptualisation of corruption in the Valencian Community. The second part describes the main effects of the economic recession on the Valencian Community and changes in how corruption is perceived. The third part deals extensively with the Zona Franca de Paterna project as an example of the reporting of corruption and the generation of debates and controversies in urban and regional planning. Finally, consideration of the Valencian case permits some conclusions to be inferred that may contribute to the analysis of the nexus between corruption and urban planning.

Understanding corruption in the Valencian Community

Since the mid-1990s, the Valencian Community had been ruled by a right-wing party that governed the regional institutions and most of the local councils. In a context of rapid economic growth fuelled by the construction industry, this party obtained absolute majorities in the regional Parliament and in most towns and cities until 2011. After the economic crisis of 2008, corruption became one of the main political themes in Spain and especially in the Valencian Community. This was even reflected in the international media, which used the Valencian case to illustrate the extent and significance of corruption in Spain (for example Minder 2011). In the Valencian Community evidence of corruption appeared even before the economic crisis, especially in relation to urban planning. Even so, it was not until the disclosure of major cases, affecting the presidency of the Regional Government (the Gürtel case in 2009) and major local administrations (the Brugal case in 2010), that corruption became clearly inserted into political debate and became a public concern. Besides these high-profile cases, others affected many important political figures. A local journalist, Sergi Cartillo (2013, p. 24), showed that in 2013 alleged corruption cases had affected the regional president, four regional vice-presidents, nine ex-regional ministers, the presidency of the regional parliament, four ex-spokespersons of the governing party, 14 regional deputies, the mayors of the three main cities of the Valencian Community, the presidencies of two provincial governments and more than 100 political officials. In these circumstances, corruption became a recurrent theme in the political disputes between conservative regional and local governments, and the left-wing opposition. The debates on corruption centred on the political responsibilities for governmental corruption and included disagreement on the very definition of what corruption was and who the corrupt politicians were.

From a legal point of view, corruption is well defined in the case of Spain. Even so, when politicians, journalists or activists deal with corruption, they also question the legitimacy of acts that are not strictly defined as unlawful. The *Consejo Superior del Poder Judicial,* the body that governs all of the Judiciary of Spain, defines public corruption crimes such as perversions of law in the field of public administration and urban regulation, breach of confidence in safe-keeping of public documents and secrets, influence peddling, embezzlement, bribery, negotiations prohibited to civil servants, abuse of functions by civil servants and corruption in international exchanges (*Consejo Superior del Poder Judicial* 2017). In spite of this, there were debates on the exact extent of corruption and its legal, political and ethical implications. Academics that dealt with legal, ethical and political consequences of corruption, such as Manuel Alcaraz (2010), advocated that reporting of corruption should extend further than the consideration of the alleged illegality of actions committed by politicians. So, the corruption complaints also dealt with the ethical and political aspects of these alleged crimes and other actions such as close friendship with allegedly corrupt entrepreneurs, the acceptance of gifts that cannot be clearly defined as bribery, or administrative misconduct falling short of an actual criminal offence. Conversely, politicians affected by corruption called for respect of the presumption of innocence, rejected any ethical or political responsibility for their behaviour until definitive judgements were issued by the courts and accused the opposition groups of taking politics into the courts. In this way, the very definition of corruption and its political significance became an issue of debate and dispute in the Valencian Community. These two stances on corruption can be clearly seen in the speech of one of the opposition members of the Regional Parliament in November 2014:

> When we ask you to assume political responsibility, you say no, that we should respect the courts and the presumption of innocence. When we ask for inquiry commissions you say that everything should be judged in court. When we go to court, you say that we take politics into the courts.
>
> (Blanco 2015, p. 77)

At the same time as the definition of corruption, in addition to the political responsibilities derived from it, became a topic of debate, a whole series of discourses appeared to expose and explain the relationship between corruption and the urban policies implemented. This was especially the case with complaints about corruption related to urban planning which were reported by activist movements and the academic community, even before the disclosure of the most high-profile cases. Since the mid-1990s urban development had become one of the main economic sectors in the Valencian economy, and as a result an extraordinary expansion of urban space took place, in most cases in valued environmental or cultural heritage areas. This expansion was vigorously promoted not only by national and regional legislation, but also by administrative decisions at a local and regional government level that in most cases remained opaque to public scrutiny (see the following section for more details on this issue). In parallel with the urban transformation of large areas, grassroots movements opposed to development projects and existing land policy (Diaz Orueta 2010) succeeded in their aims in most cases, even bringing their concerns to the notice of the European Parliament. In fact, from 2003 onwards, the European Parliament compiled complaints regarding urban planning in Valencia and passed several resolutions on urban policy in the Valencian Community (Burriel 2009c) referring to environmental protection, propriety rights of small owners and extensive corruption. In one of the resolutions, the reporter stated that she:

> Believes, nevertheless, that the absence of clarity, precision and certainty with regard to individual property rights contained in existing legislation, and the lack of any proper and consistent application of environmental law, are the root cause of many problems related to urbanisation and that this, combined with a certain laxity in the judicial process, has not only compounded the problem but has also generated an endemic form of corruption of which, once again, the EU citizen is the primary victim, but which has also caused the Spanish State to suffer significant loss.
>
> (Auken 2009, p. 11)

Parallel to the activists' complaints, efforts from the academic community were devoted to exposing a deeper understanding of the causes and consequences of urban sprawl in the Valencian Community as well as the relationship between corruption and planning policy. These academic approaches tried to demonstrate the economic, social and environmental unsustainability of the urban model adopted in the Valencian Community at the time that corruption was exposed as an essential practice in planning policies (Romero 2009, Burriel 2009a, 2009b, Azagra and Romero 2007). The wave of urbanisation that took place was explained by the interrelation of elements such as a permissive legislation, a great demand for residential property, the prevalence of the construction industry in the regional economy and the lack of effective territorial management tools. It was, furthermore, considered that this situation implied several illegal and illicit practices focused on undermining planning recommendations or adapting them to private interests, as well as a clear permissiveness by the regional government in its duty of control, a process that was even classified as 'State capture' (Romero 2009, p. 238). These practices were legitimated by the prevalent social and cultural context, since there was no perception of environmental values, long term economic strategies were not considered, and there was a prevailing understanding of urban development as a guarantee of economic wealth. Although these processes were exposed mainly within specialised circles and publications, academics and experts also disseminated work on these issues in the popular press (Romero 2005; Gaja, 2007).[1]

When the crisis began, these discourses were clearly reinforced. Evidence of the consequences of the failure of the economic and urban model was clearly perceived (and suffered) by a significant part of society while cases of corruption grew in number and importance. Research was focused on describing and quantifying the effects of the crisis: the increase in unemployment, the weakness of the economic structure, public and private debt and austerity policies, the misuse of large areas of land and the sharp decline in government revenue (Romero *et al.* 2012, Gaja 2015). Moreover, academics produced an ensemble of non-specialised publications aimed at informing the general public about the causes and consequences of the construction crisis and the role played by corruption (Boira 2012, Miralles 2014, Sorribes 2015). Finally, all this work relating corruption to wider policies, contributed to discrediting and undermining the legitimacy of policies of urban expansion, since these policies in many cases contravened or subverted urbanistic regulations to benefit private interests closely related to politicians. This reinforced the existing political controversies and debates, as well as the negative perception of corruption by the public.

The building bubble, economic crisis and perception of corruption in the Valencian Community

Although the economic recession that has affected the Valencian Community and Spain since 2008 was the result of multiple factors, mostly derived from the international financial crisis, it is generally accepted that the excessive weight of construction activity and private real estate profits as the drivers of economic growth, leading to a building boom and extensive urban expansion, was significant. The vast amount of land transformed into urban spaces under the process of urban development between 1997 and 2007 has been called an 'Urbanising Tsunami' (Gaja 2008) or 'The Prodigious Decade of Spanish Urbanism' (Burriel 2008).[2] An idea of the magnitude of this Spanish building bubble can be given in figures. According to the National Statistics Institute (INE) more than 725,000 new homes were built in Spain in 2006. This figure can be compared to that of Italy (278,602 in 2005) or France (561,700 in 2006) (Miralles 2014, pp 14–16), so that Spain (with 46 million inhabitants) constructed as many new homes as Italy and France together (59 and 66 million inhabitants respectively). In the Valencian Community 99,275 new houses were built (13.99% of the national total, compared to 10.75% of the population). Consequently, a large part of the GDP of Spain and the Valencian Community depended on building activity in 2006 (10.75 % and 11.20% respectively), while in 1996 the share was below 7% in both cases (Miralles 2014, p 23). The priority given to building development in the economy was promoted at central, regional and local government levels. In the Valencian Community, the regional government supported urban development by using a legal structure that favoured the urbanisation of large tracts of land by private companies. This transformation was presented by both the government and private lobbies as being of public benefit, since it would guarantee economic wealth for the future in a society focused on services and tourism (Naredo and Montiel 2011, Burriel 2008, 2009a). Moreover, the construction industry was supported by 'Keynesian' (Alcaraz 2009, p. 68) policy based on hosting high-profile events (the America's Cup, Formula 1 racing) and infrastructure development, such as the city of Science and Arts, a complex of iconic white buildings designed by the architect Santiago Calatrava in the city of Valencia, aimed at boosting tourism and new urban developments.

Corruption was already evident at that time. Rivero-Rodríguez and Fernández (2011) reported 80 cases of corruption in local councils in the Valencian Community between 2003 and 2007 and Jerez *et al.* (2012) detected 94 cases based on information obtained in the media. The previously mentioned resolutions of the European Parliament, relating to Valencia's urban planning laws and the urban model they proposed, also referred to corruption in the Valencian Community. Although corruption related to urban development in the Valencian Community was reported before the recession, its effects on society and the economy were not perceived by the population as negative. In October 2008 only 0.4% of the population considered corruption a significant problem in the Valencian Community according to an opinion poll conducted by the Regional Government statistical services (Generalitat Valenciana 2008).

Building activity started to decline in 2007, triggering the economic recession in Spain. The Valencian Community was especially affected by this crisis. Some figures can help in understanding the magnitude of the crisis in Valencia. In 2011 the number of newly built homes went down to 7,400 from nearly 100,000 five years earlier. The decline in building activity in the early years of the recession, followed by a decline in industry and the service sector from 2010 onwards, resulted in a sharp increase in unemployment, from 5.7% in 2006 to 15% in 2011 (Salom and Pitarch 2014). Two other processes were related to the crisis. First, the substantial reduction in public expenditure from 2010 onwards, because of austerity policies imposed by the European Union and privatisation strategies. The Spanish Government forecast a reduction in public budgets, between 2010 and 2015, of 21% in health services, 20.4% in education and 4.7 % in social services (Mira-Perceval *et al.* 2013). As Romero *et al.* (2014) stated, these policies especially affected regional and local government administrations, since they were the main providers of social services in Spain. Second, the inability to solve the crisis coupled with the huge number of corruption cases provoked a crisis of confidence in political institutions that finally resulted in protest movements, including urban disturbances, during the so-called Valencian Spring in 2012 (Caballer 2012). At that time corruption was perceived by the population in a completely different way. In December 2012, 31.2% of the population considered corruption to be a problem according to an opinion poll by the Regional Government (Generalitat Valenciana 2012).

The social and economic context was completely different to that of 2008 due to recession, unemployment, austerity policies and social cuts. As has already been explained, critical discourses, mainly from the academic community, identified strategies based on expansive planning policies and high-profile events as local factors that triggered the effects of the recession in the Valencian Community. If corruption was not directly to blame for the recession, the great number of cases related to the development of urban planning and high-profile events made it possible to challenge the legitimacy of the planning policy, since this seemed to be more oriented towards hidden private benefits than to public wealth. The relationships between corruption, the economic crisis and urban development, which finally challenged the urban and territorial policy developed over the previous years, were identified and publicised by different means: parliamentary activity by left-wing political parties that publicly denounced corruption and resultant inquiries into the main cases (Bayarri 2013), work by journalists,[3] fictional productions such as the award winning novels of Rafael Chirbes (2007 and 2013), the TV adaptation of one of these in 2010 and activities by grassroots and civic movements. All of them contributed not only to the exposure of corruption, but also to explaining its effect on society. Notable among the protest actions performed by grassroots movements is the *Ruta del Despilfarro* (The Wastefulness Route), which received significant attention in national and international media and illustrated well the practices and discourses that were taking place in the Valencian Community during the economic crisis. This Route was organised as a visit to urban spaces related to, on the one hand, holding high-profile events, urban speculation or corruption and, on the other hand, to inequality, social spending cuts and the impoverishment of the population caused by the recession. In doing so, the relationship between high-profile events, corruption, debt and crisis, which can be summarised under the word *despilfarro*, was vigorously exposed by the performative activities of the *Ruta* (route). The impact of these practices gained their maximum visibility when they were seized upon as a basis for explaining the economic and social crisis in Spain and Valencia, and were given coverage by the international media (Gil 2013).[4]

The case of the development of the Paterna Free-Trade Zone. Controversies surrounding planning policy and corruption

After the crisis that affected the Valencian Community, new urban projects had to face a social and economic context that questioned most of the basis that had supported urban expansion in the previous years. The economic rationality of the projects was challenged as well as their legitimacy in a period of austerity policies and after the report of a huge number of corruption cases related to urban planning. This was the case with the project of Zona Franca in the municipality of Paterna, a city of the metropolitan area of the Valencia. Paterna, with nearly 70,000 inhabitants in 2014, is one of the main cities in the metropolitan area of Valencia, with a strong industrial sector developed in the second half of the twentieth century. Its economy is also based on a service sector that includes technological and university research zones. The large area covered by the municipality allowed the development of large residential areas that attracted inhabitants from the city of

Valencia and an influx of immigration. Traditionally governed by left-wing parties since the re-establishment of democratic local councils in 1979, control of the city council of Paterna passed to the Spanish conservative party in 2007. Due to the economic specialisation of Paterna, the city was especially affected by the crisis, since effects on the construction industry were passed on to the industrial and service sectors (Salom and Pitarch 2014). As part of the strategies to stimulate the recovery of economic activity, in June 2012, the mayor of Paterna first presented a project for the development of a free trade zone. In the opinion of its supporters, the project would bring about relatively immediate economic recovery and reindustrialisation of the municipality and, by extension, of the Valencian Community (Ajuntament de Paterna 2013d, 2014a). Henceforth, and for a period of more than two years, the municipality of Paterna undertook a series of actions aimed at making the project of the Zona Franca de Paterna a reality.

The Zona Franca was presented as the development of a space for logistics and industrial activity, based on Spanish and EU legislation that would allow special conditions on taxation and flows of foreign trade goods. It would be situated in the north of Paterna on an area of 50 hectares with especially good transport links within the metropolitan area of Valencia, and it was promoted in the local press as a magnet for companies, especially from China, taking advantage of good connections to the nearby port of Valencia (Costa 2012).

The implementation of the Zona Franca project involved a very broad set of actions. These were intended both to meet the administrative requirements, and the work of finding investors interested in the project. While part of this body of work, such as obtaining land availability or contracting technical studies, was carried out directly by the council, another significant part of these activities was delegated by the council to a municipally owned company. The public company, *Gestión y Proyectos de Paterna* (Paterna Project Management), hereafter GESPA, the activity of which focused on general provision of services within the municipality, assumed particular importance in the process of promoting the project. The marketing department of GESPA was entrusted with managing all the promotional aspects of the project, which included carrying out or outsourcing work as, among others, the translation of documents, purchasing of Internet domains or the organisation of 'commercial activities' in different countries to promote the project or find investors (GESPA 2015).

The creation of a free-trade zone would necessarily require the involvement of the Spanish Ministry of Finance and Public Administration (MHAP) of the General State Administration, based in Madrid, which was to authorise the creation of the Zona Franca and the management body necessary for its governance. The Ministry requirements focused on two themes. The first one was the need to certify the availability of the land on which the free-trade zone would be built. Second, the need for better technical information about the project, which involved the drafting of a Free-Trade Zone Management Plan by an international consulting firm.

The preparation of the Management Plan (Ajuntament de Paterna 2013c) was of special importance for the development of the project. Its content not only needed to fulfil the technical requirements of the MHAP, but also to encompass the strategies used by Paterna in seeking support for the construction of the Zona Franca as a financial product. This Management Plan was established as the main instrument intended to avoid the creation of controversy around the project. Thus, the economic impact model developed by the international consultants preparing the Management Plan established the different types of benefits that the project should generate. These were defined as 71,000 jobs and an increase of almost 3.56 billion euros in regional GDP. Similarly, the feasibility study included in this Plan determined a rate of return (IRR) of 15.7% on investment. An analysis of various forms of management of free-trade zones in several other countries led the Plan to recommend private participation in the project. For this purpose, the Management Plan suggested different procedures of materialisation and opted specifically for a public-private contractual partnership with an expanded time line.

Along with these administrative requirements, the project needed other actions that would ensure both the necessary private investment and the attraction of industrial and logistics companies. Finding investors was of special significance, since, according to the management model proposed for the Zona Franca, the 288 million euros that were deemed necessary for its construction would need to come from a private investor that would design, build and undertake long-term management of the infrastructure in exchange for a concession fee (Ajuntament de Paterna 2014b). The most prominent example of these efforts included up to eight trips of local council representatives, including the mayor, to commercial fairs and existing free-trade zones in China and Turkey, tagged as 'commercial activities' looking for potential investors or operators interested in the development of the project, between November 2012 and May 2014 (GESPA 2015), trips whose management was entrusted to GESPA.

In April 2014, the selection process for investors competing for the award of the Zona Franca concession began. Seven major international groups specialised in the management and operation of logistics and transport infrastructure and urban developments were invited. Having received no positive response to this invitation within the two months stipulated, the period was extended. On 3 June, the municipality sent documentation to MHAP for the application to grant the status of Free-Trade Zone to Paterna. The Mayor of Paterna resigned on 31 July 2014, the day before the opening of an inquiry into illegal financing related to the Gürtel case, one of the most high-profile cases of corruption in the Valencian Community and Spain, leaving the project virtually paralysed (García and Sena 2014).

Reporting corruption and questioning the Free-Trade Zone project

Parallel to the work of the city council focusing on the development of the Zona Franca, other actors were developing opposition to the project. The project was challenged by political opposition groups and grass-roots movements that questioned both the feasibility and the legitimacy of the project. The feasibility of the project was called into question by referring to cost in a period of crisis and budget cuts, and to the administrative and technical difficulties of carrying out the project, which did not seem to have been satisfactorily resolved by the city council. Besides, the project's legitimacy was questioned by drawing it into debates on corruption and planning policy that echoed those already existing elsewhere in the Valencian community, which referred to misuse or wastefulness of public funds during the crisis and the subversion of urban planning for private benefits.

It was the complaint by a local political group, taken to court in November 2013, which put corruption at the forefront of debates around the Paterna Free-Trade Zone (Coalició Compromís 2013b). This complaint dealt with possible illegal practices in promoting the project, including: recourses to unjustified emergency procedures, which prevented greater scrutiny of the actions of the City Council; the use of a public company (GESPA) for the outsourcing of services, which dodged the control groups of the municipal opposition and official inspectors; hiring companies whose managers were part of the municipal workforce, which would be expressly prohibited by legislation; and finally a set of non-justified expenses related to the international promotion of the project. This complaint led the court to investigate the mayor and other political representatives for embezzlement, one of the crimes considered as public corruption by the Spanish legislation. All of this questioned the legality and, consequently, legitimacy of actions and expenses related to the promotion of the Free-Trade Zone project.

This complaint added to other existing corruption allegations affecting Paterna's city council and the political party in power. In 2013 an investigation was opened into a contract irregularly allocated for the construction of the municipal concert hall, and another into the possible illegal financing of the election campaign of 2007. The latter involved a company, one of the managers of which was also responsible for marketing in the public company GESPA, which was handling the promotion of the Zona Franca (Nieto 2014). Therefore, the allegations of corruption in Paterna's planning policy were reaffirmed more vigorously. The website of the opposition party that reported the corruption to the courts pointed out:

> It will now be the Provincial Prosecutor's Office who decides to clarify the irregularities detected by the civil servants, and to decide where responsibilities lie for the approval of both the expenses related to the mayor's trips to China and the fraudulent selection of companies linked to municipal employees and with whom the mayor designed the election campaign in 2007.
>
> (Coalició Compromís 2013a)

Opponents of the project insisted on linking the development of the Zona Franca with corruption, non-transparent decisions or waste of public funds. Thus, political opposition parties explained the fact that the main immediate beneficiaries of the operation would be large real estate groups who were owners of a significant part of the land where the Zona Franca would be developed, and would be negotiating with the local government administration hidden from public scrutiny. Political opposition groups reported in local information websites that this land would be expropriated after undergoing a significant increase in value (Paterna al día 2014a):

> We are talking of land that has been devalued by the crisis, land belonging to companies that have always, from the shadows, been demanding initiatives such as the Zona Franca, to add value their investments.
>
> (Paterna al día 2014a)

Criticism focused also, from the outset, on the timing of the project in a period of crisis and severe restriction of social spending. In the case of Zona Franca, it was feasible to relate the charges referring to its promotion with the wider complaints of wastefulness. The so-called 'Ruta de la Mola' was organised by local environmental and social activist groups in the image of the Valencian Wastfulness Route. Through a tour of different areas of Paterna and the place where the Zona Franca would be located, the route explained the negative effects of the project, leading to a demand for an alternative use of the space as green areas (Paterna al día 2014c). On several occasions, at city council meetings on the project, political opposition groups noted the difficulty of justifying expenditure on promotion of the project when they could not implement important social services because of the social cuts, and they called for funds assigned to promotion of the Zona Franca to be transferred to social projects (Ajuntament de Paterna 2013b). On other occasions, the project was accused of promoting a type of urban development which emulated the mistakes that had produced the economic crisis (Ajuntament de Paterna 2013a).

The initiation of a judicial investigation into possible illicit acts committed in connection with the promotion of the Zona Franca joined other charges of open corruption in which the mayor of Paterna was implicated, which led him to resign in July 2014. This meant effectively abandoning the project and activities linked to its promotion (Ajuntament de Paterna 2015a).

In April 2015, just one month before regional and local elections, the court decided to close the inquiry on the alleged illegal practices relating to the promotion of the Zona Franca. Although the public prosecutor appealed against this resolution, the former mayor and other political representatives were momentarily exonerated of any legal responsibility. A press release was published on the local council website, which reflected the court's decision and presented a point of view regarding the apportioning of responsibility related to corruption that was opposed to that advanced by opposition groups. The new mayor of Paterna classifies the case as:

> An example of the misuse that a political party can make of the Judiciary [and] if something has been characterised as the opposition, to take everything to the courts, not to clarify the truth but to seek an indictment and to discredit our work with false accusations.
>
> (Ajuntament de Paterna 2015c)

But the definitive cancellation of the Zona Franca project came after the elections in May 2015 with the start of a new administration. The new city council launched an official inquiry between the months of July and August 2015 (Ajuntament de

Paterna 2015b), where the different political groups put questions to participants in the project. Finally, a document presenting conclusions was drafted, which compiled the arguments and discourses created during the previous years at a local and regional level, giving the city council the legitimacy to cancel the project. The questions asked to various participants involved in promoting the project of the Free-Trade Zone during the course of the inquiry and the conclusions of the process avoided explicit references to corruption. They did, however, highlight the apparent lack of legality of some of the procedures (such as payments for travel, hiring external companies, the role of the company GESPA), and therefore question the legitimacy of the project itself. In addition, the whole argument about the economic impact and the economic outlook presented in the Management Plan was challenged: the conclusions of the commission specifically defined the project as economic 'wastefulness'. The basis of the arguments of the new city council were reinforced when, in addition to the publication of the minutes and conclusion of the official inquiry on the official council website, the invoices relating to the promotion of the Zona Franca de Paterna were also published and certain expenses, such as a Chinese flag or hiring the services of a model, were presented as non-justified and examples of misspending. Finally, an addendum was included to the document setting out new actions required to clarify possible legal responsibilities in relation to expenses relating to the promotion of the Zona Franca de Paterna.

Conclusions

By revealing the processes through which corruption entered into the debates and disputes concerning planning policy in the Valencian Community, and specifically in the context of the project of the Zona Franca de Paterna, this chapter permits some conclusions to be drawn that may contribute to the understanding of the relations between the controversies generated around corruption, planning and urban policies. These conclusions refer to a reflection on the definition of corruption (and it can be extended to other categories such as illegal, illicit and informal) as a result and as a source of power relations in urban space, and therefore subject to continuous disputes. A second conclusion stresses the fact that the changing conceptualisation of corruption is achieved through practices that are spatially and temporally contingent, which finally permits the introduction of new elements into the explanation of the spatial variations related to debates and disputes on corruption and urban planning.

The analysed case shows how, in the midst of the economic crisis in the Valencian Community, corruption became a recurrent theme, the conceptualisations and uses of which are the object of political debates that transcend the existing legal conceptualisation of public corruption as defined in Spanish law. The disputes on corruption give rise to conflicting conceptualisations of the bounds of what is permitted to politicians, what constitutes corruption, and the consequences that the resulting acts have on urban spaces. A restricted definition of corruption, limited to those cases with condemnatory court judgements, contrasts with another one that widens the definition of corruption to practices that are not strictly illegal and that considers their effects on a society affected by the economic crisis. It is through the establishment of these arguments that the urban and planning policies designed in the Valencian Community and Paterna in the context of the crisis are judged, evaluated and eventually contested. Consequently, the multiple, changing and opposing conceptualisations of corruption are understood as part of power strategies deployed by multiple agents. So, the present chapter reinforces the idea that far from being a well-defined category, the concept of corruption is open to political dispute, independently of the legal certitude provided by state regulations or legal systems. Taking into consideration the political significance of the definition of categories such as corrupt, informal, illegal or illicit in urban and planning policies, the processes by which these categories are created, made visible or removed from controversies becomes a key issue in understanding the changing and conflicting relations of power in cities and their influence in the urban reality and its policies.

As is shown in the Valencian case, the definition of corruption and its inclusion in political debates occurs as a result of the actions of multiple agents. The creation of discourses on planning policies and corruption, its diffusion by different means, the translation of these discourses into local contexts, demonstrations, inquiry commissions, the reports of alleged crimes to the courts and parliamentary activity, among others, all contributed, to a greater or lesser degree, to creating an understanding of corruption, its effects and consequences and to make it a subject of political debate. The multiplicity of practices deployed permit, at specific moments and places, the configuration of explanations and judgements by merging processes, discourses, practices and experiences that occur in different spaces and on different scales: from the references to the concept of waste disseminated in Valencia and in the global media, to the daily effects of the crisis experienced by the population, and including specific actions of dubious legality, or parliamentary activity. The consideration of practices when dealing with the conceptualisation of corruption and its political evaluation opens up the opportunity to explain spatial differentiations related to acquiescence of alleged illegal or illicit acts, since the evaluation and judgement of these acts take place through practices whose result cannot be pre-defined by context and is subjected to continuous redefinition. The result of these practices would depend on the ability of agents to maintain in time and diffuse in space a new understanding of corruption by creating explanations and relations with other processes, as seems to be the case in the Valencian Community. A comparative analysis of the results of practices in different spaces, denouncing and reporting corruption, may contribute to explaining the different spatial incidence and acquiescence of corruption cases in the Spanish regions, which exist despite a common legal and political context (García and Jiménez, 2018).

However, a comprehensive analysis of the effects of these practices on the incidence and acquiescence of corruption in different spaces will require some of the limitations of the approach adopted in this chapter to be overcome. These limitations refer to a deeper understanding of the effects that the multiple practices have on the perception and evaluation of corruption across society, specifically in electoral behaviour, and the explicit consideration of the power relations and disparity of resources that frame, but also are framed and transformed by, the actions and practices of multiple actors.

Notes

1 For a detailed study of the contribution of experts in the popular press, and of academics dealing with urban planning and corruption before the economic crisis, see Baron-Yelles, (2010).
2 Gaja (2008) and Burriel (2008) offer a detailed explanation of causes and consequences of the Spanish building boom.
3 Palencia *et al.* (2012) analysed a sample of the political news of eight Spanish television channels in April 2010 and showed that 45.4% of political news made reference to corruption.
4 Gil (2013) discusses the international media coverage, especially that of the BBC, of the Wastefulness Route and the debates generated by the Valencian Regional Government that defended prestigious, high-profile projects as investments for the future of the region's tourism.

References

Ajuntament de Paterna, 2013a. *Acta de la sessió ordinaria celebrada per l'ajuntament en ple Dimecres 26 de juny del 2013.* Paterna: Ajuntament de Paterna.

Ajuntament de Paterna, 2013b. *Acta de la sessió ordinaria celebrada per l'ajuntament en ple Dimecres 27 de novembre del 2013.* Paterna: Ajuntament de Paterna.

Ajuntament de Paterna, 2013c. *Plan director de la Zona Franca de la ciudad de Paterna.* Paterna: Ajuntament de Paterna.

Ajuntament de Paterna, 2013d. *Zona Franca De La Comunidad Valenciana. Paterna Parque Logístico Internacional.* Paterna: Ajuntament de Paterna.

Ajuntament de Paterna, 2014a. *Documento número 1. Solicitud de constitución de la Zona Franca de Paterna.* Paterna: Ajuntament de Paterna.

Ajuntament de Paterna, 2014b. *Informe sobre justificación del proyecto "zona franca de La comunidad valenciana. Paterna Parque Logístico Internacional" como inversión financieramente Sostenible.* Paterna: Ajuntament de Paterna.

Ajuntament de Paterna, 2015a. *Acta de la comisión de trabajo del Ayuntamiento de Paterna sobre la Zona Franca. 27 de Julio.* Available from: http://www.paterna.es/es/noticias/8862-conclusiones-de-la-comisi%C3%B3n-de-investigaci%C3%B3n-de-la-zona-franca.html [Accessed 1 December 2016].

Ajuntament de Paterna, 2015b. Conclusión de la comisión de investigación sobre la Zona Franca 20 de agosto de 2015. Available from: http://www.paterna.es/es/noticias/8862-conclusiones-de-la-comisi%C3%B3n-de-investigaci%C3%B3n-de-la-zona-franca.html [Accessed 1 December 2016].

Ajuntament de Paterna, 2015c. *El juzgado archiva la denuncia de compromís contra la alcaldesa y cuatro concejales.* Available from: http://www.paterna.es/es/component/content/article/7-noticias/8041-el-juzgado-archiva-la-denuncia-de-comprom%C3%ADs-contra-la-alcaldesa-y-cuatro-concejales.html [Accessed 1 December 2016].

Alcaraz, M., 2009. *De l'èxit a la crisi. Pamflet sobre política valenciana.* Publicacions de la Universitat de València.

Alcaraz, M., 2010. Les cares de la corrupció. Dret, ètica i responsabilitat política. *L' Espill*, 36, 11–23.

Auken, M., 2009. *Report. On the impact of extensive urbanisation in Spain on individual rights of European citizens, on the environment and on the application of EU law, based upon petitions received.* (2008/2248(INI)). European Parliament.

Azagra, J. and Romero, J., 2007. *País Complejo. Cambio social y políticas públicas en la sociedad valenciana, 1977–2006*. Publicacions dela Universitat de València

Baron-Yelles, N. 2010. Les Espagnols face à la corruption urbaine. *Géographie et Cultures*, 74. Available from: http://gc.revues.org/1739 [Accessed 1 December 2016]

Bayarri, F., 2013. Si los medios hubieran prestado a la corrupción tanta atención antes como ahora, las cosas serían diferentes. Entrevista con Ángel Luna. *Pasajes. Revista de Pensamiento Contemporáneo*, 42, 22–31.

Blanco, I., 2015. *Botiflers!!*. Valencia: Balandra Edicions

Boira, J. V., 2012. *Valencia, la tormenta perfecta*. Barcelona: RBA.

Burriel, E., 2008. La "década prodigiosa" del urbanismo español (1997–2007). *Scripta Nova, Revista Electrónica de Geografía y Ciencias Sociales*. XII 270 (64). Available from: http://www.ub.es/geocrit/sn/sn-270/sn-270/sn-270-64.htm. [Accessed 1 December 2016].

Burriel, E., 2009a. Los límites del planeamiento urbanístico Municipal. El ejemplo Valenciano. *Document d'Anàlisi Geogràfica*, 54, 33–54.

Burriel, E., 2009b. La planificación territorial en la Comunidad Valenciana (1986–2009). *Scripta Nova. Revista Electrónica de Geografía y Ciencias Sociales*, XIII 306. Available from: http://www.ub.es/geocrit/sn/sn-306.htm [Accessed 1 December 2016].

Burriel, E., 2009c. La Unión Europea y el urbanismo Valenciano. ¿Conflicto jurídico o político? *Boletín de la AGE*, 49, 5–23.

Caballer, N., 2012. Así fue la #primaveravalenciana. *El País*, 25 February. Accessible from: http://politica.elpais.com/politica/2012/02/25/actualidad/1330209412_287179.html [Accessed 1 December 2016].

Castillo, S., 2013. *Tierra de Saqueo. La trama valenciana de Gürtel*. Barcelona: Cuadrilátero de libros.

Chirbes, R., 2007. *Crematorio*. Barcelona: Anagrama.

Chirbes, R., 2013. *En la orilla*. Barcelona: Anagrama.

Coalició Compromís, 2013a. *Compromís denuncia en fiscalia l'ús irregular de fons públics a través de l'empresa municipal GESPA*. Available from: http://compromisperpaterna.com/2013/11/21/compromis-denuncia-en-fiscalia-lus-irregular-de-fons-publics-a-traves-de-lempresa-municipal-gespa/ [Accessed 1 December 2016].

Coalició Compromís, 2013b. *Denúncia encomana màrqueting global*. Available from: http://www.laveupv.com/documents/escrit-compromis-paterna.pdf. [Accessed 1 December 2016].

Consejo Superior del poder Judicial, 2017. *El CGPJ reúne los principales indicadores de la actividad judicial contra la corrupción en un repositorio de acceso público*. Available from: http://www.poderjudicial.es/portal/site/cgpj/menuitem.65d2c4456b6ddb628e635fc1dc432ea0/?vgnextoid=ff545cdebb199510VgnVCM1000006f48ac0aRCRD&vgnextfmt=default&vgnextlocale=es_ES [Accessed 1 March 2017].

Costa, M., 2012. Paterna proyecta un parque logístico con zona franca para las inversiones chinas. *Las Provincias*, 2 June. Available from: http://www.lasprovincias.es/v/20120602/horta-morvedre/paterna-proyecta-parque-logistico-20120602.html [Accessed 1 December 2016].

Diaz Orueta, F., 2010. Regímenes urbanos y movimientos ciudadanos en Valencia. *Cuaderno Urbano. Espacio, Cultura y Sociedad*, 9 9, 275–294.

Farías, I. (2011) The politics of urban assemblages, *City* 15, 3 4, 365–374.
Gaja, F., 2007. ¿Corrupción urbanística o corrupción del Urbanismo?. *Levante*, 14 January Available from: http://www.levante-emv.com/opinion/3403/corrupcion-urbanistica-o-corrupcion-urbanismo/263378.html [Accessed 1 December 2016].
Gaja, F., 2008. El tsunami urbanizador en el litoral mediterráneo. El ciclo de hiperproducción inmobiliaria (1996–2006), *Scripta Nova. Revista Electrónica de Geografía y Ciencias Sociales*, XII 270 (66). Available from: http://www.ub.es/geocrit/sn/sn-270/sn-270-66.htm. [Accessed 1 December 2016].
Gaja, F., 2015. Reparar los impactos de la burburja constructora. *Scripta Nova. Revista Electrónica de Geografía y Ciencias Sociales*, XIX 517. Available from: http://www.ub.edu/geocrit/sn/sn-517.pdf [Accessed 1 December 2016].
García, C. and Sena, L., 2014. El alcalde de Paterna anuncia por sorpresa su dimisión. *Levante.* 31 July. Available from: http://www.levante-emv.com/comarcas/2014/07/30/alcalde-paterna-anuncia-sorpresa-dimision/1144205.html [Accessed 1 December 2016].
García, M. and Jiménez, F., 2018, Corrupt cities: The illicit in local urban development. The Spanish case. *In*: Chiodelli, F. Hall, T. and Hudson, R., eds. *The Illicit and Illegal in the Governance and Development of Cities and Regions: Corrupt Places*. London: Routledge
Generalitat Valenciana, 2008. *Barómetro de Octubre 2008. Resultados. Tablas Cruzadas por variables socioeconómicas*. Presidència de la Generalitat. Available from: http://www.argos.gva.es/fileadmin/argos/Documentos/Encuestas/200810B_cruce.pdf [Accessed 1 December 2016].
Generalitat Valenciana, 2012. *Barómetro de Diciembre 2012. Resultados. Tablas Cruzadas por variables socioeconómicas*. Presidència de la Generalitat. Available from: http://www.argos.gva.es/fileadmin/argos/Documentos/Encuestas/200810B_cruce.pdf [Accessed 1 December 2016].
GESPA, 2015. *Memoria anual 2014.* Paterna: Gestión y servicios de Paterna.
Gil, J., 2013. Splash out then watch the crash. *El País*, 7 January. Available from: http://elpais.com/elpais/2013/01/07/inenglish/1357588719_861289.html [Accessed 1 December 2016].
INE, 2016. *Anuario estadístico de España, 2016.* Madrid: Instituto Nacional de Estadística.
Jerez, L. M., Martín V. O. and Pérez, R., 2012. Aproximación a una geografía de la corrupción urbanística en España. *Ería*, 87, 5–18.
McFarlane, C., 2011. The city as assemblage: Dwelling and urban space. *Environment and Planning D*, 29, 649–671.
McFarlane, C., 2012, Rethinking informality: Politics, crisis, and the city. *Planning Theory & Practice*, 13 1, 89–108.
McGuirk, P., 2012. Geographies of urban politics: Pathways, intersections, interventions. *Geographical Research*, 50 (3), 256–268.
Minder, R., 2011. Spaniards take to streets before vote. *The New York Times*. 19 may. Available from: http://www.nytimes.com/2011/05/20/world/europe/20iht-spain20.html [Accessed 1 December 2016].
Mira-Perceval, Pérez, J. A. and Romero, J., 2013. Deslegitimación política y descrédito fiscal de las Comunidades Autónomas. *Pasajes. Revista de Pensamiento Contemporáneo*, 41, 96–113.
Miralles, J. L., 2014. *El darrer cicle immobiliari al País Valencià, o el progrés de la misèria*. Valencia: Fundació Nexe.
Naredo, J. and Montiel, A., 2011. *El modelo inmobiliario español y su culminación en el caso valenciano*. Barcelona: Icaria.

Nieto, J., 2014. Anticorrupción pide al TSJ que investigue al PP de Paterna en el caso Gürtel. *El Mundo*. 1 August. Available from: http://www.elmundo.es/comunidad-valenciana/2014/08/01/53da9e2de2704ef0708b4594.html [Accessed 1 December 2016].

Palencia-Lefler, M., Pont-Sorribes, C. and Guerrero-Solé, F., 2012. La corrupción en la construcción de la imagen de la política en los noticieros de televisión. *Estudios Sobre el Mensaje Periodístico*, 19 2, 841–853.

Paterna al día, 2014a. Compromís denuncia que grandes constructoras serían las primeras beneficidas con la zona franca, in *Paterna al día*. 10 February, Available from: http://paternaaldia.com/compromis-denuncia-que-grandes-constructoras-seria-las-primera-beneficidas-con-la-zona-franca [Accessed 1 December 2016].

Paterna al día, 2014b. EU Paterna traslada la lucha contra Puerto Mediterráneo y Zona Franca a otras localidades afectadas *Paterna al día*. Available from: http://paternaaldia.com/eu-paterna-traslada-la-lucha-contra-puerto-mediterraneo-y-zona-franca-otras-localidades-afectadas/ [Accessed 1 December 2016].

Paterna al día, 2014c. Más de un centenar de vecinos se dan cita en el entorno de La Mola con el fin de paralizar Puerto Mediterráneo y la Zona Franca, *Paterna al día*. 24 November. Available from: http://paternaaldia.com/mas-de-un-centenar-de-vecinos-se-dan-cita-en-el-entorno-de-la-mola-con-el-fin-de-paralizar-puerto-mediterraneo-y-la-zona-franca/ [Accessed 1 December 2016].

Rivero-Rodríguez, G. and Fernández Vázquez, P., 2011. Las consecuencias electorales de los escándalos de corrupción municipal 2003–2007. *Estudios de Progreso*. Madrid: Fundación Alternativas.

Romero, J., 2005. Capitalismo de casino. *El País*. 22 December. Available from: http://elpais.com/diario/2005/12/22/opinion/1135206005_850215.html [Accessed 1 December 2016].

Romero, J., 2009. *Geopolítica y gobierno del territorio en España*. Valencia: Tirant lo Blanch.

Romero, J., Collado, V. J. and Rodríguez, M. T., 2014. La economía política de la desigualdad. Los recortes en el sector público y sus repercusiones para el estado del bienestar en España. In: Albertos, J. M. and Sánchez J. L., *Geografía de la crisis económica en España*. Publicacions de la Universitat de València.

Romero, J., Jiménez F., and Villoria M., 2012. (Un)sustainable territories: Causes of the speculative bubble in Spain (1996–2010) and its territorial, environmental, and sociopolitical consequences, *Environment and Planning C: Government and Policy*, 30 (3), 467–486.

Salom, J. and Pitarch, M. D., 2014. El Área Metropolitana de Valencia en la crisis. In: Albertos, J. M. and Sánchez J. L., *Geografía de la crisis económica en España*. Publicacions de la Universitat de València.

Sorribes, J., 2015. *Valencia 1940–2014: Construcción y destrucción de la ciudad*. Publicacions de la Universitat de València.

15 Who is corrupt and where lies corruption? Thinking with land use planning violations in Bangalore

Jayaraj Sundaresan

Introduction

In mid-2011, led by an ideologically diverse group of civil society leaders, India witnessed one of the most significant nation-wide public demonstrations (perhaps paralleled only by the social movement against the national emergency four decades ago and the Independence movement more than six decades ago). Organized by a loose collective named India Against Corruption, millions rallied against the long-standing experience of rampant political and bureaucratic corruption in their everyday life. Incidentally, this was also triggered by a series of scams that was exposed, then related to large scale embezzlement of public funds, bribe exchanges, collusion and nepotism on a wide range of government transactions – ranging from spectrum auctions to public housing allocation for the families of war heroes and martyrs. The collective called for a citizen-involved promulgation of a national ombudsman (called Jan Lokpal), a high-powered committee of supposedly incorrigible members to be appointed by the government and which would have unbridled *suo moto* powers to investigate anyone within the country across the hierarchies of government.

An authority of all authorities constituted of incorrigible and wise men was the way, the leaders and followers thought, to address the experience of rampant corruption, even though, ironically, it was around the same time that the Chief Vigilance Commissioner was removed on the grounds of corruption by the Supreme Court of India (BBC 2011). This collective anger against the experience of corruption was triggered by longstanding and extremely widespread practices of bribery, embezzlement, fraud, collusion, extortion, patronage and so on in public-public, public-private and public-business transactions that continue to mark social, political and economic life in India. From defense procurement to political party funding, public service examinations to public appointments, mining and infrastructure projects to environment and development and welfare programs, all are rife with practices that violate the code of public office conduct and the rule of law. The ubiquity of such practices has made it part of the deep social psyche that a triumphant, honest public official appears to be more of a heroic movie character than a real life figure. Hardly a daily edition of any newspaper goes by without an item on corruption.

While corruption is a powerful moral currency around which public mobilizations have been organized in recent decades, it remains a mode through which everyday governance is organized in India (see, for instance, Bardan 1997: CMS 2005; Gupta 1995; Wade 1985). Political and civil society activists, government officials, international organizations and scholars have all been discussing the various extents of, forms and causes of and remedies for corruption for a very long time. Even though the dominant scholarship in development and public policy focuses on the developmental trajectory, institutional imperatives, incentives and remedies (Bardan 1997; Guhan and Paul 1997; Sukhtankar and Vaishnav 2015), most scholarship has concentrated on bureaucratic corruption in implementing development and welfare programs, and on political corruption and its connection with election expenditure (Sridharan 2014). A few anthropologists and human geographers have examined the social meanings of corruption (Gupta 1995 and 2012), as well as its concomitant transformation, locating it in the wider socio-economic context (see for example Weinstein, 2008 on the involvement of mafia in land development). While India is rapidly urbanizing, scholarship that examines how corruption is linked to urbanization and urban planning is rare.[1] This gap is partially due to the influence of international scholarship that focused on the informality of the urban poor as the dominant conceptual and theoretical perspective through which to view the Indian city (and also partially due to the difficulties of conducting research on corruption). This chapter contributes to this scholarship.

Conceptually, I adopt an interactive framework in which corruption, illegal and illicit mutually co-produce one another (see also Chiodelli *et al.*, this volume). Further, moving beyond the exceptional gaze on the urban poor, I focus on the relationship between corruption and urban planning, using case studies about land use planning violations from the non-poor neighbourhoods of Bangalore.

I examine the connections between land use planning violations and corruption to demonstrate how the practice of bribes, favours and collusions dominate and transform the ideal-typical urban planning apparatus to suit the demands of individual landowners and social groups, rather than abling regulation in response to any abstract notion of public interest. I theorize the extent of everyday corruption as a consequence of the assumptions behind the design of formal planning institutions, instruments and protocols, and suggest that any analysis and re-imaginations of the 'state and public order' should be conceived as programs embedded within the social and political practices. I argue that a functional analysis that isolates the institutional domain of rule from the social domain of everyday transactions becomes less helpful in thinking with corruption. Therefore, instead of methodologically circumscribing the domain of analysis to the public sphere (mainly governmental – executive, legislative and constitutional), this analysis considers the public and private as co-produced and socially embedded.

This research draws primarily from material generated from ethnographic research of planning and violation networks conducted in Bangalore for 14 months during 2008–2010 as part of my PhD research.[2] I also draw from about 20 years of engagement with urban planning in India as an architect and planning consultant to public, private and civil society clients, training government officials, planning curriculum development and more recently as a participant in collective action domains in Bangalore. Specific findings from the ethnography were triangulated not only using the material obtained during the specific time-bound field work but were also corroborated with observations from my continuing embedded experiences across a number of urban regions in India, particularly Bangalore. This enabled me to overcome many of the methodological difficulties inherent in researching corrupt, illicit and illegal practices.

Corruption and urban planning – the conceptual terrain

In the past few decades, there has been a consensus among scholars that urban planning practices are a rampant and fecund site of corruption (Chiodelli and Moroni 2015; Deysine 1980; Dodson *et al.* 2009; Gardiner 1985; Gardiner and Lyman 1978; Nientied 1998; Server 1996). Even though scholars differ on the definition, typology, methods and content of analysis, causal explanations, impacts and on how to address corruption, there are two broad conceptual approaches based on 1) motives and, 2) framing.

Regarding motives, scholarship on corruption is divided between those who believe in restoring a formal institutional system of the state as the main sphere of democratic governance and those who understand democratic governance as continuing negotiatory domains emergent from political praxis, where formal state institutions act as one (though significant) among many actors. The first group therefore identifies corruption as a major problem to be solved; to them corruption is not oil but sand in the governmental machine, preventing efficient and fair processes, and creating unequal rules of the game (Ades and Di Tella 1997, Chiodelli and Moroni 2015). The second group argues that the very problem in the analysis of corruption is this ideology and that corruption indeed performs certain beneficial societal functions as through corrupt practices individuals and groups contribute to the making of their common good and, 'as such the existence of corruption per se indicates only that these [corrupt] groups participate in the decision making process than would otherwise be the case' (Leff 1964, p. 8).

This ideology has undoubtedly influenced the framing as well as the domain and content of analysis – i.e, what corruption is; how to define it; what is its typology; where, how and why it exists; and how to address it. The believers of formal institutionalism adopt a narrow definition for corruption, usually expressed as 'trading the privilege of public office for private or pecuniary benefit'. They argue that corruption results from the opportunities that exist in any land use planning and development system, where the officials and politicians have incentives (lower costs and higher benefits) to exercize their discretionary power to capitalize on those opportunities (Chiodelli and Moroni 2015; Gardiner 1985). For them, this is a matter of formal institutional design and its ability to address issues of human behaviour (human weakness). Discussing Western planning practice, Chiodelli and Moroni (2015) argue: 'in order to combat corruption, it is vital to devise reformed institutions that can perform as correctly and fairly as possible notwithstanding the presence of imperfect human beings'. They continue, 'landowners and developers are not in themselves more prone to corrupt [behavior], it is a certain planning system in itself that incentivizes certain behavior' (p. 451). Therefore, they propose the institutional mantra of a radical reform of traditional Euclidean planning, based on the implementation of a limited set of land use rules which must be abstract, general, end-independent and prevalently negative; the aim is to reduce discretionality and differentiation in planning, which are viewed as the main institutional incentives of corruption within a planning system. Gardiner (1985), however, goes beyond this to argue that 'Opportunities for corruption will be increased by any legal or administrative requirement which is a pre-condition to private sector activity' (p. 127).

Many think-tanks and activist/lobby/campaign groups in India that are active in this debate adopt this framework that public interest is best achieved through tweaking the operations of formal institutional processes, and that the dishonest public official is the key impediment in that process (Bhatnagar *et al.*, no date; Janagraha, no date; Paul 2002 and 2011; Transparency International 2015). Analysis of corruption from this framework examines the relationship between a norm and its deviation; in particular, the breach of a contract embedded within a 'public' institutional framework for private benefit, by the very parties that are responsible for instituting, implementing or enforcing it. Practices that constitute political, bureaucratic or corporate corruption are identified as illegitimate based on an ideal or existing contract that has a public code of conduct (Williams 1999, p. 505; Heidenheimer 2002, p. 10). The main components of this analysis involve the identification of a deviation (from norm – public order, rule of law, job contract) by embedded actors (public actors or principal agent), with a specific intention (of private gain). Building on this framework, it is argued that certain states, regions, political and economic cultures are more corrupt than others. Transparency International, for example, ranks India as 76 out of 168 countries.[3] In these portrayals, it is the public official who is evil or weak. Many scholars recognize that poor people in cities of the Global South manage to live through multiple pro-active negotiations that involve political patronage, collusions as well as bribe exchanges, but even in some of this literature, corrupt government officials and the state are seen as villains who exploit the conditions of the urban poor.[4] When a public official deviates from the official code of conduct and accepts bribes, for example, it is termed corruption; when a citizen deviates from the public code of conduct or regulation and offers bribes for example, it is termed violation. Very seldom have the connections between violations and corruptions been examined closely, i.e., how the individual citizen's or various social groups' deep interest in maximizing their interest by violating governmental norms creates a demand in the everyday social world, promoting and sometimes coercing a culture of corrupt behaviour(s) from public officials, or in the longer-term building a broad network of coalitional actors that transforms the very foundations of institutional governance.

Anne Desyine (1980) notes how from the early theories that focused on the 'evil motives of dishonest individuals' (p. 451), scholarship on corruption in the United States has moved on to understanding the political system as one in which corruption is the norm and that deviants are the honest officials in public departments. Through election financing, business in politics, campaign funding and so on, corrupt practices create a mutual benefit society and obligatory associationalism. This self-propelling machine builds itself on the consequent disbelief in formal democratic institutional forms. Contrary to the former scholarship, there is a recognition that an 'outside the system' is rarely available to 'monitor the monitors' and that the possibility of an 'ultimate enforcer' is elusive. In such political systems approaches, political, bureaucratic and corporate corruption conjoin as interconnected practices; corruption, illicit and illegal become indistinguishable and get reconstituted as mutually co-creating practices.[5] Consequently, from narrow definitions and ambitions to fix the governmental machine, analysis of corruption has come to recognize it as the inherent characteristic of the modern governmental machine embedded in a social world of political democracy and that it is integrally connected to values in the social world (Banfield 1975; Desyine 1980). Thus, any analysis of corruption should engage with wider social and political values that have been recognised – stated as 'dishonesty in society' (Desyine 1980) – or a 'society that protects and fosters corrupt values' (Banfield 1975, p. 459). Similarly, outlining the various 'facilitators' between socio-cultural logic and corrupt daily practices that lie behind the production of the 'corruption complex' in Africa, De Sardan (1999) argues that the administrative apparatus is rather schizophrenic – split between the official and practice norm of the everyday social world. De Sardan (ibid.) goes on to hypothesize that any anti-corruption effort that aims to address the helplessness caused by 'the infernal mechanism' of corruption, 'the development of movements of "puritanical" tendency intended to bring about a reform of the public morals may be among the ultimate means' (p. 48). In the understanding and analysis of corruption, therefore, the 'social' is back.

These diverse motives and framings have also influenced definitions; for example, is illegality a prerequisite? Is the purpose personal or political gain or should others be included too? (Desyine 1980). For example, Nathaniel Leff (1964, p. 8) defines corruption, 'as an extra-legal institution used by individuals or groups to gain access over the bureaucracy', because it allows them avenues for participation. In this chapter, through discussing the case studies, I adopt a wider definition in which corrupt, illicit and illegal practices interact and shape each other – as an institutionalized method of producing urban space. Adopting such a relational analysis and thinking with such practices in the case of land use violations in Bangalore, I demonstrate how diverse actors shape such practices which are embedded in one another. Consequently, I propose that analysis of corruption should examine such practices, connecting it to and not isolated from violations. Connecting violations with corruption helps to extend the frontiers of the study of corruption and examines the actual governance regime, rather than conducting a normative evaluation based on an ideal typology of the state. Further it enables a focus on the 'social', rather than conducting an isolated analysis of the so-called official (public) domain. It helps to ask what are the moral implications of such a regime, as well as locating the specific history of the form of the norm – in this case the planning history in its context. It also offers an opportunity to think about explaining the very origins of specific forms and notions of public order and their inclusions, exclusions, subscriptions and conscriptions.

Land use planning, corruption and violations in Bangalore

Bangalore is the fifth largest urban agglomeration in India, with roughly 8.5 million people in about 750 sq .km and a consistent population growth of between 3.5 and 5.5 per cent for more than five decades (Census of India, 2011).[6] Bangalore is the largest urban agglomeration among those that have emerged post-independence, and is at the forefront of defining India's urban millennium. Formal urban planning institutions (planning acts, organizational structure, process and protocols, actors and instruments) have been in operation there for more than five decades. The Directorate of Town Planning acts as chief technical advisor to the regional state government, called Karnataka. The Karnataka government appoints the principal planning and infrastructure development authority called the Bangalore Development Authority; in a comprehensive planning ideology the Structure Plan, Outline Development Plans and Master Plans are updated frequently. Implementation and enforcement of the plan are shared between the development authority, the local metropolitan government and numerous public institutions that operate to manage and regulate wetlands, water supply and sewerage, for instance. At Ministry level, very high-ranking bureaucrats manage and oversee the functions of all these departments, and hierarchically there are cascading levels of authorities, personnel and instruments legally instituted to ensure that urban space is planned, serviced and governed effectively. To monitor this, there is a state vigilance department, as well as a local government ombudsman to check corruption and illegal transactions. However, hardly any component of urban Bangalore can be studied without confronting experiences and narratives of corruption in urban planning practice.

It is well known that, in Bangalore as well as more broadly in India, for example, planning and urban governance officials (from a Commissioner to a Local Engineer) have frequently had to pay money to ministers or political brokers to get specific appointments that are considered lucrative (from bribes and favours);[7] consultants have to pay bribes or organize favours at many levels to obtain master planning, infrastructure or development consulting contracts; most large and small infrastructure project contractors have to pay a significant proportion of the total project cost (up to 40 per cent) at many levels of the hierarchy to obtain contracts as well as to receive fees due to them for already completed works; 'greasing money' needs to be paid to enable files to move inside the planning authority to obtain planning permission even for entirely legal project proposals; services (water, electricity, sewerage), connections and licenses (commercial or industrial) are almost impossible to obtain without paying extra money to engineers; monies need to be paid to local engineers and councilors during the construction stage of most projects to avoid the project being delayed using stage-wise permission processes (Transparency International 2015). Such rent-seeking practices are restrictive, frustrating and costly for the people at large, and the sense of powerlessness over their own democratic state is very significant; which is why hundreds of thousands of people could be mobilized collectively during the Jan Lok Pal movement to demand for a National Ombudsman as an authority of all authorities.

However, understanding these practices only based on their restrictive nature gives an insufficient understanding at best and an erroneous one at worst; these practices in fact enable a large part of the urbanization and urban life of India – in the sense that one can and most people do get innumerable things that are enabled as well as prohibited by the planning act or rule of law done through such practices. For example, the so-called informal economy and housing that constitute more than half of urban India, as well much of the housing and building stock in which the other half (rich, middle and the working class) live and work, are implicated with many practices of bribes, collusion and favours. Both poor people as well as the well-off squat, or encroach on public and private lands through tampering entries in the book of land records, violating land use zones or influencing the implementation and enforcement and litigation procedures through paying bribes and favours, facilitated by networks of government officials, ministers and politicians, estate agents, middle men, developers and so on. Such practices ensure street vending; property tax avoidance; construction without planning permission; violation of planning and building bylaws including reclamation of wetlands; building extra floors or with legally insufficient building offsets; obtaining trade licenses; violating zonal restrictions; allowing untreated waste water or dumping of solid waste into public waterways; obtaining service connections without adequate planning permission; encroaching on and converting sidewalks into front gardens; violating labour law in order to evade housing for construction workers and so on.

In the case of land use regulations, violations of the land use plan dominate the urban landscape of Bangalore. Even though there is no official comprehensive documentation, from my own documentation and interviews anything between 60–80 per cent of the entire built landscape of Bangalore could be some sort of violation of planning and building norms (see Pizzo and Altavilla in this volume for a similar situation in the case of Rome). As one high-ranking bureaucrat put it, “in Bangalore, everyone goes for violation” (interview 2008). Different from the popular perception that planning violations in Indian cities are the creation of a highly corrupt state and planning authority, in what follows I show how popular demand to maximize private benefits is deeply implicated in the phenomena.

Land use violations: Manjunath and his neighbours

In 2010 during my fieldwork, I came across the house of Mr Manjunath[8] in a very wealthy neighbourhood of Bangalore. Manjunath’s house was located at a corner where two quiet internal streets in the neighbourhood met. The house is a two-storied detached bungalow with a spacious front garden, protected by a boundary wall. Majunath rented his ground floor to a tenant and he lived on the first floor. A children’s play area with swings, a see-saw and a small pool marked the garden corner, where the two streets met.

The agenda of my walk in the neighbourhood that day was to study the drainage ecology and engineering of a water tank[9] adjacent to Manjunath's house. The tank was visibly defunct and mostly dry, with patches of stagnant wastewater pools, wild growth and disused land, partly encroached by individuals from the adjacent village as well as the wealthy neighbourhood.

This particular tank was part of the network of more than 500 large and small tanks that defined the wetland ecological landscape of Bangalore for at least a few centuries, shaping the region's drainage, microclimate, ground water and vegetation pattern. These tanks were interconnected through drainage canals that cascaded water across them during monsoons, and together they form the large wetlands network that harvested rainwater as well as mitigated floods across the region. Originally these tanks and canals were constructed for irrigating the agricultural fields and as drinking water reservoirs for the adjacent villages or as temple tanks.

Urbanization of the region during the second half of the last century witnessed the reclamation of more than half of the tanks and drainage canals for public infrastructure works (roads, bus stands or housing, for example) or private encroachment by individuals as well as institutions (housing and commercial establishments for instance). It is in the context of studying the transforming wetlands ecology that I came across the children's play area at the corner of Manjunath's garden, because I noticed that it was constructed by reclaiming the main drainage canal that brought water to the adjacent tank, the damage to which was of interest to my research at the time.

Manjunath had constructed his garden by encroaching on the public land to which the drainage canal belonged. During my survey, I noticed that the drainage canal disappeared before Manjunath's house. I could recognize that Manjunath's garden – especially the children's play area – was constructed on top of the canal, because his building was adjacent to the tank; therefore the canal reappeared and opened onto the tank after his garden on the opposite side of the adjacent road.

Assuming that Manjunath encroached and reclaimed the drainage canal, with some effort I managed to meet and ask him where was the rest of the drainage canal. Manjunath confirmed that he indeed did build the children's play area reclaiming (filling) the drainage canal, and also pointed out that all the neighboring houses along the street are built on top of the canal. Further, Manjunath told me that initially he did not build his house on top of the canal, and that he had built his boundary wall and his garden on his own property, leaving the canal and public land intact. This, however, made the encroachment and violations by his neighbors very conspicuous, because the canal emerged after the neighboring houses outside Manjunath's boundary wall before it went under the perpendicular road and drained into the tank. Therefore, the neighbors pressurized Manjunath to cover up the visible portion of the canal. After a few years, Manjunath agreed to build his garden on top of the canal. This made the canal disappear entirely, thereby also making the neighbors violations and encroachments invisible. Manjunath said that he was uncomfortable with this arrangement and had submitted a letter to the local authority that he would be more than happy to retract his garden if the authority so desired. However, the authority seemingly had no interest in this. The pressure to extend his garden also came from the local councilor and the local ward engineer, both of whom, it seems, were present during the reconstruction of the boundary wall to make the children's play area. These local officials were the mutual associational network that initially enabled these violations and encroachments through accepting favours and bribes from the residents on that street. Therefore, understandably, it was in their interest to make it invisible, to avoid any potential future action. Many of these drainage canal networks, as well as wetlands systems, have been encroached in this way by thousands of landowners over a very long time in Bangalore to such as extent that they are beyond easy detection in the many official mapping exercizes that have taken place in recent decades. Reflecting this, a recent high court judgment resorted to a 1908 map to identify encroachments where frequent floods seriously damage property in the wider neighbourhood (*The Hindu* 2016). Many of these violations also get regularized over the course of time, sometimes during the master planning process or with special regularization acts.[10]

In other words, Manjunath's violation is the consequence of the widespread interest in maximizing private benefits by appropriating public infrastructure. Landowners, contractors and developers pay local authority officials and politicians in order for them not to take any action. It is extremely hard for honest officials to take action in such cases, because they will be accused of partisan behaviour, pointing to other violations in the neighbourhood. If an officer persists and takes any action, then most of the time, s/he will be transferred from their post. Consequently, an honest politician or official will turn a blind eye, or negotiate not to violate excessively (multiple interviews 2008–2010). In 2005, when a local neighbourhood collective challenged in the High Court the large-scale illegal conversion of residential land use for commercial purposes (enabled through multiple opportunities offered by corruption), it resulted in an ugly litigation process.[11] With the active involvement of officials and politicians, the local neighbourhood was divided into two camps with a very few residents demanding implementation of the rule of law and the majority, which also included local politicians, real estate agents, land owners and developers, rallying against the litigants, demanding they withdraw the petition. Eventually, rather than take action against any properties that violated or any officials that promoted violation by taking bribes, the litigation resulted in the demolition of some of the petitioner's own houses, shaming them in newspaper reports and forcing them to withdraw from the petition[12] (multiple interviews 2008–2010).

A large part of the planning programme is also made as a consequence of these illegal transactions. For example, politicians and officials (usually, a network of property developers, middle men, politicians, officials, land owners and even bank officials) routinely gain immensely from officially (in the plan or later) re-categorizing or de-notifying land owned by their network from restrictive development zones to developable land (or developable at higher density). During my fieldwork, I interviewed a real estate agent and two planners, part of a large network of actors that helped a developer to successfully encroach, reclaim, convert and develop parts of a very large wetland for commercial land use. In this case the moncy paid to planning officials alone was more than 100,000 USD for changing the color of land use in the Master Plan draft. Given the scale of this project, for it to be eventually possible on the ground (it is a successful office district now), monies would have been paid to a very large number of officials, bureaucrats and politicians across all levels (from Ministry to local levels) for clearing the relevant files and not raising objections (multiple interviews 2008–2010). Through such practices, publicly owned lands are routinely converted to private land through manipulation of land records, land use plans, housing projects, long lease or encroachments. According to a 2006 legislative committee report on encroachment of public lands in Bangalore urban district, 13,614.37 acres (approximately 55 sq. kms) of public land has been encroached by various private parties (Ramaswamy, 2006). The report notes that, in most cases, the encroachers have been able to obtain a legal property identity number from the government as a result of bribes and favours. Many of my interviewees from the local government confessed that there are innumerable cases where encroached public land has been allotted individual property identity numbers as private property (multiple interviews 2008–2010).

Similarly, zoning is routinely deployed to legalize illegal land uses, reclaim wetlands and public land and increase the value of land banks in the urban periphery; new large infrastructure projects are planned where land is already purchased by the political (and bureaucratic) benamies[13] and their allied network to gain from government acquisition and the escalation of value. Landowners and property developers use bribes and favours routinely to influence the planning process and ensure that the zonal and density regulations of their land parcel are beneficial to them rather than restrictive. For example, through the help of government officials many networks managed to access the Master Plan 2005–2015 preparation process inside a French consulting company office in Bangalore, and ensured that their land parcels were zoned in beneficial land use categories rather than restrictive ones while the plan document was being prepared (multiple interviews 2010). Further, this Master Plan draft developed for a further two years changing its land use colors (for those who manage to have access to it) after the consultants handed over the draft to the government, until it was adopted and released officially in 2007 (multiple interviews 2010). Innumerable projects (small as well as large) in cities are routinely developed and implemented only for the kickbacks that result; in addition, many already approved, paid for and completed project files are sometimes never implemented. I interviewed many Right To Information (RTI) activists[14] who, after obtaining information on unimplemented projects, have been approached by officials and politicians with requests to refrain from publicizing the information in return for implementing the project. Some RTI activists frequently comply with such requests (multiple interviews 2008–2010), because RTI activism is a very dangerous terrain; an ideological rather than pragmatic approach to the process could even be life-threaterning (ACHR 2011). In a context where officials and activists generally struggle unsuccessfully for decades to get Higher Court's orders implemented,[15] such a cautious approach is understandable. Government lawyers are brought over many times so that a weak case is presented in the court during litigations against the government.

I now consider another instance when an official decided to take an important action against these practices that went into litigation.

Violations and valley zones: Saving the wetlands

During the Comprehensive Development Plan (of 2005–2015) preparation process, the French consultants deploying their advanced GIS technologies identified the connection between settlement topography and drainage ecology in Bangalore. Their Draft Final Plan submitted to the government proposed a restricted development zone within specifically earmarked areas (called valley zones) to protect the city's ecological security (BDA 2006). This news that the draft master plan had proposed a new restricted development zone on areas related to the wetlands network spread very rapidly in Bangalore. The number of planning applications (for developments) by owners of private land parcels within the earmarked valley zone areas increased rapidly and dramatically; with the hope of obtaining a planning permission before the new draft plan was officially adopted. The planners came under immense political pressure to approve planning applications based on the previous master plan document that did not have any valley zone category based reservations (multiple interviews with planners 2010).

Sensing the danger in this and the impact that it could have on the ecological foundations of Bangalore, the then Chief Planner of Bangalore restricted issuing permission for planning applications for properties within the valley zone areas. The Chief Planner wanted to develop planning mechanisms (instruments such as transfer of development rights, for example) to protect the wetlands and identify appropriate compensation for the loss of development rights. A consortium of developers and individuals, however, challenged this decision at the High Court and an ex-Attorney General of India represented them in the court (Padmaraj and Jagannathan 2006). After a complex hearing process, the High Court supported the Chief Planner's decision, i.e., a temporary freeze of planning permissions to properties on wetlands and valley zones. In fact, the honorable Justice agreed that the Chief Town Planner had the responsibility as well as the powers to think about the long-term future of the city through the process of land use and development control (interviews with senior government planners 2010; Padmaraj and Jagannathan 2006). However, in the process that followed this judgment, the petitioners appealed to the Supreme Court of India in Delhi; meanwhile the Chief Planner was transferred from his post and a more compliant planner appointed. The government (planning authority) law department did not represent itself adequately at the Supreme Court and needless to say the petitioners (developers consortium) won their appeal there (multiple interviews 2010).

What I would like to draw attention to in this case is that the attempt of the chief planner to save the public commons of the city by exercising his authority (as a public interest ideologue) was subverted by concerted efforts by the private interest-maximizing network of developers, landowners, politicians, ministers, public officials, middlemen, lawyers and so on. While some planners and bureaucrats were punished for adhering to the public interest, other planners and public officials were rewarded for enabling selected private interests to gain. This was enabled through the presence of a system of corrupt transactions that creates mutual obligatory networks of association that can be invoked every time a systemic change requires the installation of compliant actors and networks. The legal master plan is thereby created through illicit networks formed through a wide range of practices of corruption.

Violated geographies produced through these transactions dominate the built form and landscape of the city. Therefore, to address the many complex juridical situations that emerge during specific litigation and to maximize political popularity, a regularization scheme known as Akrama-Sakrama was introduced in 2007 (GoK 2007). The act enabled the regularization of most forms of unauthorized constructions and violations. When I asked a senior civil servant, known to have been central to helping with this legislation, why was it introduced, the reply was: 'what else can one do with such large scale of violations'? (interview 2008). Before the promulgation and adoption of this act, the 2005–2015 Master Plan adopted in 2007 reclassified and regularized many areas that deviated from the previous land use plan using a new category of 'mixed land use'. The planners who had worked on the Master Plan confessed that these were already mixed land use areas due to violations and there was no option other than to reclassify them, irrespective of any other planning logic (multiple interviews 2010).

The relationship between planning and violations in Bangalore should be understood as a circular relationship between plan violation and planning for violation. Rather than planning followed by enforcement, violation followed by regularization dominates the planning methodology. This form of production of urban space is enabled through many forms of social, political and economic transactions that seamlessly move between corrupt, illicit and illegal transactions. As many government planners noted, in Bangalore 'everyone is a planner' (interview, 2008), meaning that a large number of people get proactively involved at various stage of planning (decision making, implementation, enforcement) to produce the kind of geographies that they desire, inhabit and that generate revenues for them. This not only includes the city's slums and squatters, but also the rest of the built fabric – commercial high streets, public housing cooperatives, rich and middle class gated enclaves, office buildings, tech parks and so on. The public official is only one among the many actors forming these large networks of complex institutional and interactive governing practice. These networks span political parties, businesses and local community associations and are formed of actors from inside and outside government. Monies or favours need to flow across the hierarchy (top to bottom as well as bottom to top) on most transactions. Such an interlinked process has evolved over a very long time into deeply established practices of governing.

Vernacular networks and planning governance in Bangalore

In the above section I have shown how the demand to violate planning norms is closely connected to the networks of governance whose actions move easily between corruption, illicit and the illegal practices. Corruption should be understood as a consequence of such collective demand. Public officials on the supply side of governance, eventually through multiple iterations of transfers and appointments or by choice, end up being acquiescent or active participants in this demand-supply network. It is hard to be a so-called honest and clean public official faced with this incessant demand in India. A few perceptible and grounded scholars have documented such parallel governance systems that mark Indian democracy (Harris-White 2003; Kishore 2015; Wade 1982 and 1985).

Although deeply instantiated, these processes occasionally get challenged and disrupted by various factors including political or social enmities, changes in the paradigm of the governing collective, or a new so-called honest public official in some position of power. However, like the many-headed hydra, broken pathways usually get replaced with newer ones very quickly – creative innovation of this kind is usually termed as *jugaad* in Hindi. Once, the head of a large business conglomerate told one of my friends during her field work in 2010 that India is not just a free market, but the freest of all the markets, in the sense that one can get almost anything done if one knows how to move through the right networks and can pay the right cost. This attitude was substantiated during one of my interviews when I asked a developer in Bangalore, who specializes in the reclamation of restricted wetlands if the planning law poses any problem for his practice. I was told that, usually, they are able to change most restrictions to suit their practice (interview 2010).

The nature of these vernacular transactions is so extremely intricate that it challenges the utility of the ideal typical state apparatus, the rule of law and the bureaucratic process and protocols as key to enable desired public interest outcomes. Therefore, officials sometimes adopt complex *jugaad* processes, that are not necessarily considered legal or official, to enable outcomes that they think are in the public interest. For example, a public official, the head of one of the Bangalore's planning and governance institutions, called an environmentalist friend and asked her to file a public interest litigation in order to save a wetland from being appropriated for real estate, because he realized that it could not be saved using the public official's own powers. In the long drawn out process that followed, this public official had to devise many methods that were not entirely legal and within proper official protocol to support the litigation (multiple interviews 2008–2010). Suppose, instead of an environmentalist friend, the public official had called up a real estate friend to move quickly to stake a claim over the land. In this case, the public official would have been labelled corrupt, even if he did not benefit privately from such a deal. The normative foundation of the conventional analysis of corruption is dependent also on moral imperatives of intent.

Conclusions

I demonstrated that urban planning in Bangalore is rife with practices that can be deemed illicit as well as illegal, i.e., practices that cannot be considered right or morally acceptable based on specific frames of reference, or that deviate from the spirit and the letter of the law respectively. A relational approach in which the internal and external boundaries of these categories are allowed to move and shift to accommodate political cultures in diverse geographies, reveals that in Bangalore urban planning is a site of willful as well as coerced exchanges of bribes, favours, collusion, embezzlement, fraud and so on, that co-produces robust mutual associational networks and fundamentally reshapes the planning apparatus. This network, as well as the corrupt, illicit and illegal geographies, is shaped by demands present in the everyday social world, that aim to maximize private and political interests – individual landowners as well as specific social groups like the urban poor, middle class or neighbourhood groups and political parties. Public officials are only one among the many actors who enable the successful operation of these networks. These practices can be called corruption as long as we adopt a wider definition, such as that of Nathaniel Leff (1964): 'as an extra legal institution' (p. 8), that allows people access to participate in avenues and modes of governing from which they were excluded in the first place. Such vernacular governance (Sundaresan 2014) transactions are co-produced by the public official and the rest of the population at intersectional domains of state and society; the ideal-typical public order, the rule of law and the bureaucratic state is usually in its shadow state – at best as an active participant, or at worst as an absentee. When very large numbers of the population demand processes and outcomes that violate the norm of public order for either individual or collective benefits, then in many senses the argument that the existing public order or the rule of law is not really conducive to the interest of many publics becomes an important challenge to take into account. As Williams (1999, p. 516) argues, corruption then becomes politics by those who do not agree with the particular idea of public order manifested in the rules, laws, processes and protocols of the formal institutions of governing of 'the state'. Defending the 'occupancy urbanism' of the poor, Benjamin (2005 and 2008) for example defends such political patronage, through which the urban poor find themselves tenure security in the city, thus challenging the black and white legality created by the Master Plan. I would go further to argue that the notion of the public of the planning regime of Bangalore is based on the mutually producing public-private ontology – i.e., the mutually re-producing liberal democratic welfare state and the liberal individual as its subject as well as performer of rule and provision. The public in this epistemology is an abstract collective of private liberal individuals. In a political culture of governance, in which people do not relate to each other as liberated individuals – either as public officials wedded to the Weberian idea of –the role-fulfilling, disinterested professional (Gupta 2012, p. 81), or as a private citizen committed to the particular ideology of the state as a space of liberation, empowerment and solidarity – corruption analysis should focus beyond the public domain. Further, a public that is a negotiatory domain of the different publics or communities of interest is yet to be institutionalized in the system of urban planning and governing in India.

This is because the urban planning system in India is based on a continuation of quasi-colonial practices, in which spatial planning regimes are deployed to make the cantonments as well as to control the population (Legg 2007; Robinson 1995), whose members are considered subjects rather than the citizens of rule. In its geographies of origin, modern urban planning practice emerged and was continually transformed as a result of municipal movements and collective, grounded and sustained negotiations, campaigns and experimentation by social reformers, activists, industrial elites, property owners and politicians who endeavored to tame the ills of the industrial city (Hall 2002; Sanyal 2005; Sutcliffe 1980 and 1981). However, modern urban planning arrived in India first through colonial rule and, after independence (1947), through the international development agencies and planning consultants who were invited to India by the political elites. The first prime minister of India, Pandit Jawaharlal Nehru, said during the inauguration of the modern city of Chandigarh that it is an experiment 'that hits you on the head and makes you think' (Kalia 1999, p. 29). This exemplifies the post-independence urban planning regime as an apparatus of the modern state of social reform. In other words, the modern urban planning discourse (and the consequent public interest) became established in the government supported by its enthusiasts and believers – mostly elites – without much popular movement involvement or legitimacy as a method to reform the existing social spatial, cultural and political world of the Indian city. Therefore, the institutional design of the planning process adopted in post- independence India emulated colonial governmental practices. For example, urban local government in Bangalore is subject to the rule of the regional state government, Karnataka; instead of preparing their own plan, they receive a Master Plan – prepared by a consultant with little involvement from the citizens or communities – from the Karnataka government to be implemented and enforced. There is neither popular involvement nor legitimacy; therefore, disobedience and deviant practices, though they appear corrupt from the perspective of conventional definitions, strive to be understood as politics.

Adopting a relational and interactional approach to studying domains and experiences of corruption and violations can help to understand how agents, institutions, processes, moralities and domains of the state and society, public and private get constituted differently in different places (Haller and Shore 2005). This is particularly true in post-colonial geographies of the Global South, where there has been limited historical opportunity to establish non-hegemonic forms of institutions of modern rule based on the public-private epistemology. Reflecting on this is an opportunity to build the skeleton of a public order beyond the canonical models of rule by examining moral, ethical and logistical implications of these vernacular practices of governing in the everyday social sphere. Such an approach could help to reformulate the form and content of public order in diverse political cultures. Many of the fundamental questions that emerge from this discussion on the origins of public order are outside the scope of this chapter, but are nevertheless useful to destabilize the categories with which theories, policies and institutional forms continue to get judged as weak or failed, especially in the post-colonial geographies of thc Global South. It is certainly important to ask if one should keep making plans and policies that are far removed and aimed to change the political culture of millions of citizens, or should one imaginatively redesign the institutional processes that are in conversation with specific political cultures. Unless this happens, people will crack open the bureaucratic machine through deploying the power of political democracy to make habitable spaces for themselves.

Notes

1 Benjamin (2005), Parekh (2015), Sundaran (2010) and Weinstein (2008) are notable exceptions. However, these authors' intention was not to examine corruption per se; rather, it occurs as a background in their theorization of the politics of urban and land transformations, local economy and subversions of modernity.
2 Submitted to the London School of Economics and Political Science in 2014. http://etheses.lse.ac.uk/979.
3 See Transparency International's series of Global Corruption Reports, https://www.transparency.org/research/gcr/.
4 Even a well put together discussion on the ingress of mafia on land development in Mumbai by Weinstein (2008) somehow gets located in this global narrative on the Global South. However, the scholarship that views these transactions as claiming of political space portrays the government officials (politicians and bureaucrats) as beneficial agents enabling a porous bureaucracy or part of 'political society' (Benjamin 2008; Chatterjee 2005).
5 See also Wade (1985) for a detailed discussion on this based on studies from South India.
6 www.census.gov.in
7 See Wade (1985) for a detailed discussion on South India.
8 All names are changed in this chapter to protect the privacy of the individuals concerned.
9 The word 'tank' here refers to the large man-made water retention and harvesting structures that form a network of regional drainage ecology.
10 A discussion on the latest regularization drive follows in the article.
11 W.P 13336 of 2005, in High Court of Karnataka between Vijayan Menon and others against State of Karnataka and others.
12 For a detailed discussion on this, see 6.3, page 229 in Sundaresan (2014).
13 Proxies- http://zeenews.india.com/home/i-will-not-walk-away-from-bmic-but-will-complete-it-kheny_336416.html, Nov 18, 2006, http://www.thehindu.com/news/cities/bangalore/Kheny-says-Gowda-made-him-an-offer/article16531237.ece, March 7, 2010.
14 A RTI activist is a person who uses the right to information act as a method of activism to expose graft.
15 Obtaining favorable ruling through prolonged and arduous litigation is sometimes easier compared to getting them implemented.

References

ACHR – Asian Center for Human Rights. 2011. RTI activists: Sitting ducks of India. New Dehli, Asian Centre for Human Rights. Retrieved from: www.achrweb.org/ihrrq/issue3-4/India-Sitting-Ducks-2011.pdf.

Ades, A. and Di Tella, R. 1997. The new economics of corruption: A survey and some new results, *Political Studies*, 45, 496–515.

Banfield, E. C. 1975. Corruption as a feature of governmental organization, *Journal of Law and Economics*, 18(3), 587–605.

Bardan, P. 1997. Corruption and development: A review of issues, *Journal of Economic Review*, 35(3), 1320–1346.

BBC 2011, March 3. India anti-corruption chief PJ Thomas forced to resign. BBC News. Retrieved from: www.bbc.com/news/world-south-asia-12631887.

BDA. 2006. *Draft Comprehensive Development Plan, Bangalore*. Government of Karnataka.

Benjamin, S. 2005. Touts, pirates and ghosts, in *Bare Acts*. New Delhi: Sarai Reader, Centre for Study of Developing Societies.

Benjamin, S. 2008. Occupancy urbanism: Radicalizing politics and economy beyond policy and programs, *International Journal of Urban and Regional Research*, 32(3), 719–29.

Bhatnagar, D., Deewan, A., Torres, M. M. and Kanungo, P. no date. *Citizens Report Card on Public Services*, Bangalore, India, World Bank, available from: http://siteresources.worldbank.org/INTEMPOWERMENT/Resources/14832_Bangalore-web.pdf, (Last accessed, 17/03/2017).

Census of India. 2011. Population Tables, Census of India, www.census.gov.in, Government of India.

Chatterjee, P. 2005. *The Politics of the Governed*. New York: Columbia University Press.

Chiodelli, F. and Moroni, S. 2015. Corruption in land-use issues: A crucial challenge for planning theory and practice, *Town Planning Review*, 86(4), 437–455.

CMS. 2005. *India Corruption Study to Improve Governance*. New Delhi: Transparency International.

Deysine, A. 1980. Political corruption: A review of the literature, *European Journal of Political Research*, 8, (4), 447–462.

Dodson, J., Coiacetto, E. and Ellway, C. 2009. Corruption in the Australian land development process: Identifying a research agenda, *Governance*, 9, 1–25.

Gardiner, J. A. 1985. Corruption and reform in land-use and building regulation, in M. Wachs (ed). *Ethics in Plannning*, New Brunswick: Transaction Publishers, pp. 121–142.

Gardiner, J. A. and Lyman, T. R. 1978. *Decisions for Sale: Corruption and Reform in Land-Use and Building Regulation*. New York: Prager Publisher.

Government of Karnataka. 2007. *Karnataka Town and Country Planning Act*, 2007 Amendment, Government of Karnataka.

Guhan, S. and Paul, S. 1997. *Corruption in India: Agenda for Action*. New Delhi: Vision Books.

Gupta, A. 1995. Blurred boundaries: The discourse of corruption, the culture of politics, and the imagined state, *American Ethnologist*, 22(2), 375–402.

Gupta, A. 2012. *Red Tape: Bureaucracy, Structural Violence, and Poverty in India*. Durham, NC: Duke University Press.

Hall, P. 2002. *Cities of Tomorrow: An Intellectual History of Urban Planning and Design in the 20th Century*. Massachusetts: Blackwell.

Haller, D and Shore, C. (eds) 2005. *Corruption: Anthropological Perspectives*. London: Pluto.

Harris-White, B. 2003. *India Working: Essays on Society and Economy*. Cambridge, UK: Cambridge University Press.

Heidenheimer, J. 2002. *Political Corruption: A Handbook*. New Jersey: Transaction Publishers.

The Hindu. 2016, September 21. Encroachments on active drains will be demolished: T.B. Jayachandra. *The Hindu*. Retrieved from: www.thehindu.com/news/cities/

bangalore/Encroachments-on-active-drains-will-be-demolished-T.B.-Jayachandra/article14599960.ece#.

Janagraha. no date. I paid a bribe. Web portal, available from http://www.ipaidabribe.com/about-us#gsc.tab=0 (last accessed 18/03/2017).

Kalia, R. 1999. *Chandigarh: The Making of an Indian City*. Delhi: Oxford University Press.

Kishore, R., 2015. Urban 'failures': Municipal governance, planning and power in colonial Delhi, 1863–1910, *Indian Economic & Social History Review*, 52(4), 439–461.

Leff, N. 1964. Economic development through bureaucratic corruption, *The American Behavioural Scientist*, 8(3), 8–15.

Legg, S. 2007. *Spaces of Colonialism: Delhi's Urban Governmentalities*. Chichester: Wiley-Blackwell.

Nientied, P. 1998. The question of town and regional planning in Albania, *Habitat International*, 22(1), 41–47.

Olivier De Sardan, J. P. 1999. A moral economy of corruption in Africa? *The Journal of Modern African Studies*, 37(1), 25–52.

Padmaraj and Jagannathan. 2006. Judgement delivered in 2006 for the W.P. no.3301/2005 and 3616/2005 Between Town Planner Member, BDA and BDA versus T. Vijayalakshi and Others, High Court of Karnataka at Bangalore.

Parekh, A. 2015. *The Private City: Planning, Property, and Protest in the Making of Lavasa New Town, India*. PhD Thesis submitted to the London School of Economics, http://etheses.lse.ac.uk/3203/, last accessed 18/03/2017.

Paul, S. 2002. *Holding the State to Account: Citizen Monitoring in Action, Bangalore*. Bangalore: Books for Change.

Paul, S. 2011. Fighting Corruption, *Economic & Political Weekly*, 46(35): 17–19.

Ramaswamy, A. T. 2006. *Karnataka Legislature Joint House Committee on "Encroachment of Government Lands in Bangalore CityUrban District*. Interim Report Part 1 and 2, Bangalore.

Robinson, J. 1995. *The Power of Apartheid: State, Power and Space in South African Cities*. Oxford: Butterworth-Heinemann.

Sanyal, B. 2005. *Comparative Planning Cultures*. London: Routledge.

Server, O. B. 1996. Corruption: A major problem for urban management some evidence from Indonesia, *Habitat International*, 20(1), 23–41.

Sridharan, E. 2014. *India: Democracy and Corruption*. Working paper presented at the Democracy Works Project seminar at Centre for Development and Enterprise, Johannesburg.

Sukhtankar, S. and Vaishnav, M. 2015. *Corruption in India: Bridging Research Evidence and Policy Options*. India Policy Forum 11, 193–261. Available at SSRN: https://ssrn.com/abstract=2685819.

Sundaram, R. 2010. *Pirate Modernity: Delhi's Media Urbanism*. London: Routledge.

Sundaresan, J. 2014. *Urban Planning in Vernacular Governance Land Use Planning and Violations in Bangalore*. The London School of Economics and Political Science, PhD Thesis, available from http://etheses.lse.ac.uk/979/.

Sutcliffe, A. 1980. *The Rise of Modern Urban Planning, 1800–1914*. London: Mansel.

Sutcliffe, A. 1981. *Towards the Planned City: Germany, Britain, the United States and France, 1780–1914*, Oxford: Basil Blackwell.

Transparency International. 2015. *Corruption in State Town and Country Planning Departments in India*. New Delhi: Transparency International.

Wade, R. 1982. The system of administrative and political corruption: Canal irrigation in South India, *Journal of Development Studies*, 18(3), 287–328.

Wade, R., 1985. The market for public office: Why the Indian state is not better at development, *World Development*, 13(4), 467–497.

Weinstein, L. 2008. Mumbai's development mafias: Globalization, organized crime and land development, *International Journal of Urban and Regional Research*, 32(1), 22–39.

Williams, R. 1999. New concepts for old?. *Third World Quarterly*, 20(3), 503–513.

Index

For Product Safety Concerns and Information please contact our EU representative GPSR@taylorandfrancis.com Taylor & Francis Verlag GmbH, Kaufingerstraße 24, 80331 München, Germany